In Search of the Good Life

In Search of the
GOOD LIFE

A Pedagogy for Troubled Times

FRED DALLMAYR

THE UNIVERSITY PRESS OF KENTUCKY

Publication of this volume was made possible in part by a grant
from the National Endowment for the Humanities.

Scholarly publisher for the Commonwealth,
serving Bellarmine University, Berea College, Centre College of Kentucky, Eastern
Kentucky University, The Filson Historical Society, Georgetown College, Kentucky
Historical Society, Kentucky State University, Morehead State University, Murray
State University, Northern Kentucky University, Transylvania University, University
of Kentucky, University of Louisville, and Western Kentucky University.

Editorial and Sales Offices: The University Press of Kentucky
663 South Limestone Street, Lexington, Kentucky 40508–4008
www.kentuckypress.com

11 10 09 08 07   5 4 3 2 1

Library of Congress Cataloging-in-Publication Data

Dallmayr, Fred R. (Fred Reinhard), 1928-
  In search of the good life : a pedagogy for troubled times / Fred Dallmayr.
      p. cm.
  Includes bibliographical references and index.
  ISBN 978-0-8131-2457-5 (hardcover : alk. paper)
1. Political sociology. 2. Political science—Philosophy. 3. Democracy.
4. Ethics. 5. Civics. 6. Theological virtues. I. Title.
  JA76.D234 2007
  306.2—dc22   2007012692

This book is printed on acid-free recycled paper meeting the requirements of the
American National Standard for Permanence in Paper for Printed Library Materials.

Manufactured in the United States of America.

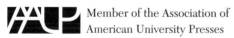 Member of the Association of
American University Presses

To my wife and children

Your word is a lamp unto my feet, and a light to my path.
—Psalms 119:105

He has shown you what is good; and what does the Lord
require of you but to do justice, and to love kindness, and to
walk humbly with your God.
—Micah 6:8

Democracy is a form of government only because it is a form
of moral and spiritual association.
—John Dewey,
The Ethics of Democracy

Contents

Appendixes

Preface

Caminante, so tus huellas
el camino, y nada más;
caminante, no hay camino,
se hace camino al andar.
　　　　—Antonio Machado

This book was written in dark times, in an attempt to stave off despair.
It was begun when war had once again been launched—an unprovoked and illicit war that by now has cost the lives of several hundred
thousand people (mostly civilian). The rhetoric surrounding the war
was deceptive, full of "double-speak" and disinformation. In large
measure, the public media—those institutions designed to provide
genuine information and to stimulate critical debate—had fallen in
line with official governmental pronouncements, thus abdicating their
educational role. To make matters worse, the intellectual community
in large numbers had followed the lead of the media, thereby en-
hancing the dominant mood of conformism and silencing the voice
of conscience and public dissent. In this somber surrounding, I remembered (almost by happenstance) an ancient teaching that has
reverberated through the centuries, an adage that I had learned as
a schoolboy: the point of politics is to promote the well-being of the
people and to cultivate the "good life" *(eu zen)*. It seems to me that
most of the forces in contemporary life have conspired to erase this
adage from memory or to render it unintelligible.

　　Born out of anguish, this book is addressed to people who, like
me, are troubled by the agonies of our time. It is not intended principally for academic philosophers or political theorists untouched by
such agonies. As it happens, much of political theorizing or philoso-
phizing today is a "professional" enterprise, that is, confined strictly to

a discourse among professionals or "experts." Although participants often display remarkable erudition and sophistication, the concern fueling this discourse is primarily one of academic prestige and professional advancement, which is not the concern of ordinary people in the lifeworld. Given the degree of academic self-enclosure, the gulf separating political theory and public life today tends to be profound, with dismal effects on both philosophy and politics.

One of the main aims of the book is to correct or narrow this gulf. For this reason, the book is written largely in ordinary or commonsense language, with only minimal resort to academic terminology (where it seemed unavoidable). Basically, the chief addressees of the text are ordinary laypeople—what in the Middle Ages were called *homines idiotae.* Several chapters in the book deal explicitly with the role of *idiotae,* the streetwise people in the marketplace. In order to reach such people, many portions of the book address not only their minds, or reason, but also their hearts, or emotion. As Mahatma Gandhi once remarked, if one wishes to affect or transform human conduct, one needs "to appeal not only to the head but to the heart of people." This saying is quite correct, since it is the heart that provides the wellspring of motivations for human conduct. I realize, of course, that this dimension has been almost totally smothered or buried under an avalanche of "objective" data and technological gadgets; my hope lies in the word *almost.*

Seeking to cultivate and transform human conduct is the province of pedagogy, of pedagogical prodding or inducement. In our troubled times, much of this pedagogical effort has to be directed toward memory work, that is, the retrieval of buried or suppressed memories regarding well-being and the good life. One of the chief obstacles or stumbling blocks for this book is the widespread resistance to, or outright rejection of, pedagogy as such. Under liberal or libertarian auspices—dominant in Western societies—concern with well-being and the good life is considered a purely private matter that must be kept out of the public domain. In accord with the liberal disaggregation of social life, individuals are said to be sovereign masters of their conduct and ethical maxims, while every attempt at public pedagogy is viewed as a "road to serfdom" (or worse). To be sure, in their better moments, even radical advocates of this view realize that, based on such premises, social and political life is impossible. If ethical conduct is entirely a matter of arbitrary individual choice, then it seems that the same freedom (or license) must be granted to murderers, rapists, and torturers.

The usual rejoinder here is that the enforcement of penal laws is sufficient to maintain order. However, can laws and penal sanctions really do the job in the absence of a widespread sociability or willingness to be sociable without legal coercion? Can social life be maintained by police and military power alone? I am quite willing to meet liberals halfway—or perhaps more than halfway. I fully agree that well-being and the good life cannot be part of governmental ordinances or public policies. To this extent, the outlook of this book is far removed from "moral majoritarianism" or any ethics promulgated by governmental decree. This book seeks to steer a course between a privatized ethics extolled by liberals and a "publicized" ethics promoted by devotees of state power. Basically, the contextual locus of the argument here is civil society, the arena of schools, churches, and civil associations. And the language of the argument is not one of command or injunction but one of gentle counseling and exhortation.

In one other aspect, I go a considerable distance toward the liberal position, and this is manifest in the title of the book. *In Search of the Good Life* implies that the topic is a quest or query, not a final resting place. It denies any claims that I have found the good life or that I am in possession of a finished doctrine or dogma about it. My aim is not to cajole but simply to invite others to join me in my search. The title also militates against a complacent relativism that, safely ensconced in its agnosticism, refuses to venture forward or join in the search. (To this extent, the title resonates with one of my earliest texts called *Beyond Dogma and Despair.*)

In pursuing this middle path, I take my bearings from that streetwise Athenian Socrates, who claimed to have a peculiar kind of "unknowledge"—namely, to know that he knows nothing. This kind of knowing is precisely what is needed in any genuine search or quest, for if we completely knew what we were looking for, there would be no need for a search; and if we were completely in the dark about the target, we would not even know where or how to look for it. This is the issue Socrates addresses in the dialogue *Meno*, when questioned about the possibility of searching for truth or goodness. "You look on this as a piece of trick-logic," Socrates responds to the questioner, "as if a man cannot try to find either what he knows or what he does not know. Of course, he would never try to find what he knows, because he knows it and in that case has no need of trying to find; or what he does not know, because he does not know what he will try to find." In the same dialogue Socrates uses strong language in castigating complacent agnostics who use their ignorance as an alibi for not searching: "One thing I would fight for to the end, both in word and deed if I were able: that if we believed that we must try to find out what is not known, we should be better and braver and less idle than if we believed that what we do not know is impossible to find and that we need not even try" (*Meno*, 80E, 86B–C).

My book follows this path, searchingly and without pretense of having arrived. The book does not try to articulate a full-fledged "moral theory"—where, all too often, "theory" is far removed from "praxis." I take my departure from an assumption well known to ethicists: the so-called primacy of ethics over morality, of practical ethical life over moral axioms or imperatives. This does not mean that moral axioms or principles can or should be entirely ignored; it means that such principles are merely abstracted, distilled or "cribbed" from practical life—a life that is multiple and unwieldy and can never be fully reduced to, or domesticated by, rules. Instead of invoking abstract principles, ethics (in the sense used here) respects the thick fabric of human life located in space and time. As a corollary, ethical pedagogy relies not so much on general rules as on example: on the conduct of some exemplary figures in concrete circumstances. Basically, exemplarity here means that, in some respects, particular figures have managed to illustrate or exemplify what one might mean by goodness or, rather, the search for the good life. To be sure, exemplary conduct can never be transferred or translated directly from one setting to another. Every effort of translation—and of comparative inquiry—requires attention to both the similarities and the differences of human conditions.

The first part of the book discusses a number of exemplary figures or "searchers" taken from different historical periods, from the Middle Ages to modernity and the heyday of Enlightenment. The assumption underlying the chosen figures is not one of progressive historical decay or of steady civilizational progress or advance; rather, the emphasis is on how, under different historical and geographical conditions, different thinkers have struggled with the agonies and confusions of their own time while remaining faithful to the task of searching. In light of the ecumenical spirit demanded by our age of globalization, the exemplary figures in part I have been chosen from the West as well as from South and East Asia. (I must apologize that I do not include figures from the Islamic world or from Africa. However, in other contexts, I have paid tribute to a number of such thinkers, from Ibn Rushd and Hafiz to Amilcar Cabral. The examples chosen certainly do not mean to privilege some regions over others.) In part II of the book, the discussion turns to lessons that might be drawn from historical examples for an ethical pedagogy in our time. Starting from the question "Why the Classics Today?" I turn attention to such issues as the proper and improper ways of spreading democracy globally, the possibility of "transnational" citizenship, the problem of politicized "evil" (in the so-called axis of evil), and the role of religious faith in our predominantly secular—or perhaps postsecular—age.

Searching for the good life means to be journeying, to be under way, to be on the road. That is why I began this preface with some lines by Antonio Machado, which might be rendered in English as follows: "Walking, under your feet the road or path, and nothing else; traveling you do not have a way, one finds the way by going." Being under way in life means to take a journey that is full of unexpected turns and surprises; but it is not simply a cul-de-sac. Students of East Asian thought and culture will find a similarity between Machado's *camino* and the *tao*, or uncharted path. Students of recent European philosophy may find a further resemblance between this *tao* and Martin Heidegger's *Wege* (as expressed in his formula *Wege nicht Werke*).

I would like to express my gratitude to a number of fellow travelers on my path—or along parallel paths. First, I want to mention my friends and colleagues Calvin Schrag, Hwa Yol Jung, William Connolly, Krzysztof Ziarek, Bhikhu Parekh, Roxanne Euben, and Anthony Parel. A special thanks is due to my recently deceased friends Paul Ricoeur and Iris Marion Young. Among a broader circle of acquaintances I owe a considerable intellectual debt to such colleagues as Charles Taylor, Bernhard Waldenfels, John Caputo, and (more recently) Richard Kearney. For a number of years, the present director of the University Press of Kentucky, Stephen Wrinn, has been a strong supporter of my endeavors; this is a good occasion to express my gratitude and friendship to him. My deepest debt of gratitude, of course, goes to my wife, Ilse, and our children, Dominique and Philip—without whom there is nothing.

Introduction

Some seventy years ago, in the midst of darkening global horizons, a prominent American intellectual formulated a stunning vision that combined good government or public ethics with a general "regime of peace." The name of the intellectual was Walter Lippmann, and the book announcing his vision was titled *The Good Society*. The book was first published in 1936, at a time when fascism was deeply entrenched in Germany and Italy, a totalitarian ideology was ruling Russia, and Japan was preparing for war—dark horizons indeed. But the situation was even more ominous and foreboding because nearly all the "advanced" countries were under the spell of a shared belief: that social well-being could be assured through political power and ideological management, and that peace and security were the fruits of quasi-military governmental controls. In Lippmann's words: "Although the partisans who are now fighting for the mastery of the modern world wear shirts of different colors, their weapons are drawn from the same armory, their doctrines are variations of the same theme." Their weapons, he continues, "are the coercive direction of life and labor of mankind; their doctrine is that disorder and misery can be overcome only by more and more compulsory organization; their promise is that through the power of the state men can be made happy." Against this battery of shared assumptions, Lippmann pits an entirely different outlook—one predicated on the centrality of ethical "goodness" and the cultivation of public virtues as the gateway to general peace.[1]

In taking this opposing stand, *The Good Society* could draw on a long tradition of teachings, a tradition nurtured by two strands deriving, respectively, from Athens and Jerusalem. From Jerusalem comes the idea that human beings are not ultimately under the control of worldly rulers but are placed in the care of God, who has put a divine imprint on their hearts. Lippmann appeals to that legacy when he

1

writes that, in light of biblical teachings, "the pretensions of despots became heretical," and "the prerogatives of (sovereign) supremacy were radically undermined." In light of the same legacy, the "inviolability of the human person" was declared, a notion that served as the rock on which "the rude foundations of the Good Society" could be built.[2] The other strand can be traced back especially to Aristotle, who, in his *Nicomachean Ethics,* presented the ethically "good life" as the very meaning and telos of human existence. At the beginning of his *Ethics,* Aristotle reflects on what is "good" and even the "highest good" in human life and concludes that this highest good consists in "happiness" (*eudaimonia*); such happiness is a corollary of "living well" (*eu zen*) and "acting well" (*eu prattein*), that is, leading ethical or virtuous lives both alone and in a public community. Relying on common opinion, he states that "both the many and the cultivated" identify goodness with happiness and assume "that living well and doing well are the same as being happy."[3]

Here, I want to explore this alternative conception traceable to Athens and Jerusalem—a conception that, in my view, stands in stark opposition to the modern glorification of sovereign power, totalizing ideologies, and abstract procedures. I do this in three steps. First, I pursue Lippmann's argument in greater detail to see precisely how he wanted to obviate modern (or late modern) ills. Next, I turn to a more recent reformulation of the idea of a "good society" and an ethically grounded public philosophy offered by political theorist Michael Sandel. Finally, I explore the implications of these initiatives in our era and their possible contributions to an ethically informed global civil society and a global "regime of peace."

Lippmann's Good Society

Despite Lippmann's career as a newspaper columnist, his *Good Society* is not an ordinary piece of journalism. What testifies to this career is the book's lucidity and literary eloquence; what distinguishes it is its weighty substance transgressing concerns of the moment. Basically, the book takes issue with a long-standing preference or addiction in Western intellectual and political life: the addiction to will or willpower and, indeed, to sovereign will, in preference over the observance of ethical standards and shared rules of conduct. The addiction can be traced from Machiavelli's *Prince* to Thomas Hobbes's *Leviathan* all the way down to the totalitarian movements of the twentieth century. In a telling fashion, *The Good Society* launches a frontal attack on the idea of absolute sovereign power of rulers—an idea historically defended by both the Stuart kings and Hobbes. It sides instead with the great defenders of the "common law," understood as the historically grown storehouse of rights and obligations defining the meaning of a shared ethical life. As Lippmann writes: "It is no coincidence that the very conception of equal rights under a common law to which all men, including rulers and sovereign states as well, are subject should have been formulated by men like [John] Selden, [Sir Edward] Coke, [John] Locke, and [Hugo] Grotius, who were members of a society where men lived by large [multilateral] transactions," rather than under the monological edicts of a ruler. It was this civil (or civilized) habit of life that proved to be the undoing of the Stuart monarchy, for it was during that period that "the English developed the conviction that the essential principle of a free government was to impose fundamental limitations upon the state and its rulers, that, as Chief Justice Coke told James I during their historic conference in 1612, the king is 'under God and the law.'"[4]

Lippmann returns to the same topic in a later section of his book titled "The Struggle for Law," where *law* means not just a piece of legislation or sovereign edict but a shared bond or mode of bonding. Referring again to the historical encounter between Coke and James I, the section is quite clear about the character of the law to which the king was subject. "We must note particularly," Lippmann states, "that the law which Coke said was above the king was not an abstract formula, but the common law of England interpreted in English courts. This law was not a series of commandments promulgated by the sovereign"; rather, it was "the product of the gradual judicial development of immemorial usage through the decisions of specific controversies under an established procedure." Without denying the intervention of human will or decision at particular junctures of the historical development, Coke's point was that the broad fabric of the common law in its complexity could not be traced to human fiat or the will of a lawgiver. Put differently: "Because no man or set of men made the whole law, the law was felt to be transpersonal, to override the ordinary human will, even of the king, and to establish rights and duties for all men founded upon something besides the will of any man." The struggle between king and common law continued under Charles I and surfaced with vehemence in 1627 when Sir Thomas Darnel was imprisoned for refusing to supply money for foreign wars. In court, Darnel's case was argued—in Lippmann's words—"by one of the greatest English lawyers, John Selden." According to the historical record: "The main question to which [Selden] addressed himself was whether an English freeman could be lawfully imprisoned by the special command of the King or his Council *without any other cause than the will of the King being stated*." Although Selden lost this case, his plea was later vindicated in 1679 when Parliament passed the Habeas Corpus Act.[5]

A central argument of Lippman's study is that the "struggle for law"—so valiantly carried forward by Coke, Selden, and others—is being lost (or has already been lost) in our time. Referring to the "nemesis" of a lawless politics, the text recounts the ill effects of the cult of power. "The generation to which we belong," we read, "is now learning from experience what happens when men retreat into a coercive organization of their affairs." Basically, the idea of controlling social life through willpower or willed organization—in the absence of wisdom and ethical cultivation—is a chimera, because power merely produces counterpower, and forced order produces chaotic disorder. "For more than two generations," the text continues, "an increasingly coercive organization of society has coincided with an increasing disorder." In this situation, it is time to inquire "why, with so much more authority, there is so much less stability; why, with such promises of greater abundance, there is retardation in the improvement, in many lands a notable lowering, of the standard of life." In the ongoing struggle for power—a poor substitute for the "struggle for law"—what is completely missed or ignored is the effect of human finitude and lived experience, an experience that, being open-ended, can never be completely managed or controlled. The dilemmas of power, in fact, are "insoluble" as long as people believe that the only way to "solve" social problems is "through command from a sovereign." Despite the incongruence of this belief, the dominant pedagogy of the age is a pedagogy of power, insisting "that there are no limits to man's capacity to govern others and that, therefore, no limitations ought to be imposed on government."[6]

The cult of power is reinforced, and actually reaches is apogee, in state-sponsored militarism and the hankering for war. It is in wartime or in preparation for war that sovereign power sheds all restraints and imposes "total" control in the name of national security. In Lippmann's words: "It is the war spirit that most readily imposes unanimity for collective action among masses of men," while sidelining or disparaging all "lesser purposes." At this point, the text cites a statement by Mussolini to the effect that "war alone brings up to its highest tension all human energy and puts the stamp of nobility upon the people who have the courage to meet it"; a similar statement ascribed to Hitler notes that "in everlasting battles mankind has achieved greatness," while prolonged peace would doom it to destruction. The danger of the warmongering spirit is particularly great when political and military power coincide, such as when a president is also the commander in chief and stands to gain glory through warfare: "When an army takes to itself . . . to declare war, to determine national policy, to make its own laws and enforce them as it sees fit [for example, through military tribunals], the condition known as militarism prevails. It means that the military have ceased . . . to be under God and the law." When such conditions prevail, the military-political "leader" is prone to wage war not only against external "enemies" but also against the domestic population (or segments of it) by transforming citizens, presumably endowed with civil rights, into mere subjects. To quote Lippmann again: "The dissenter, the conscientious objector, the indifferent and the discontented, have no rights which anyone is bound to respect. . . . In the degree of their interference with the prosecution of the war [or the reigning war spirit], they have no more standing against military authority than has been enjoyed by the victims of Lenin, Trotsky, Stalin, Mussolini, and Hitler."[7]

As an antidote to sovereign power (patterned on military power), Lippmann's study champions liberalism or a regime of genuine human freedom—but a regime that does not coincide with laissez-faire liberalism wedded to unrestrained economic competition guided solely by the profit motive. According to defenders of the laissez-faire doctrine, economic enterprise and the market exist outside social bonds and regulations, operating in a kind of presocial "state of nature" where private initiative is completely untrammeled. For Lippmann, the doctrine is an utter "fallacy," ignoring the social-political character of human beings (as Aristotle had taught). As he points out, liberalism started as a rebellion against absolutism and mercantilism—systems in which all human activity was centrally controlled. Against this centralized control, liberals legitimately wished to open a space for free initiatives (a space variously called "civil society" or the "market"), but surely not a space outside civil and legal bonds. The problem is that, after being successful in the struggle against absolutism, liberals became sterile and dogmatic; in other words, an initially "liberating" kind of liberalism became increasingly stifling and "absolutist" (by ignoring the social contextuality of action). In Lippmann's account, after mercantilism was destroyed, the question arose: "what laws were to govern the new economy?" And it was here that liberals became stranded:

> As so often happens among old and triumphant revolutionists, the dynamic ideas which had brought the liberals to power were transformed into an obscurantist and pedantic dogma. The liberals turned to writing metaphysical treatises on the assumption that laissez-faire is a principle of public policy. They sought to determine by abstruse and a priori reasoning what realms of human activity should and what realms should not be regulated by law.[8]

For Lippmann, the fallacy of laissez-faire is grounded in a still deeper and more troubling mistake: the assumption of a rigid dichotomy between a "civil" and a "natural" condition, between public and purely private realms, between law and no law. "The whole effort," he writes, "to determine what should be governed by law and what should not be, was based on so obvious an error that it seems grotesque"—the error of assuming that the economy is presocial and that there are two radically separated fields of human activity, "one of anarchy and one of law." A Robinson Crusoe may live outside social bonds, but his first human contact shatters that isolation. In any case, in a human community, "there is no such thing" as splendid isolation. "All freedom, all rights, all property, are sustained by some kind of law. So the question can never arise whether there should be law here and no law there, but only what law shall prevail everywhere." Lippmann quotes with approval Ernest Barker on this issue: "It is not the natural ego which enters a court of law. It is a right-and-duty-bearing person, created by the law, which appears before the law." Barker's statement applies even to so-called rugged individualists who roamed the American West at one time. "Without the implied willingness of the state to intervene with all its power, the rugged individualist who preached laissez-faire would have been utterly helpless: he would not have obtained or given valid title to any property; he could not have made a contract, however free." In Lippmann's account, then, the assumption of an economic state of nature—a realm without civic bonds and where "the big fish can eat the little fish" with impunity—was both a philosophical and a practical error whose consequences were "catastrophic." *The Good Society* is eloquent in castigating both this error and its social implications. The "unanalyzed assumption" of latter-day liberals, we read at one point, that the exchange economy is "free" in the sense of being "outside the jurisdiction" of civil laws, brought them up "against a blank wall." "It became impossible for latter-day liberals to ask the question, much less to find the answer, whether the existing law was good and how it could be reformed"—that is, whether and how the new market could be reconciled with the demands of a "good society."[9]

The worst-case scenario resulting from the cited error is one in which laissez-faire economics is combined with sovereign, militarized state power (or one in which the state is colonized by laissez-faire interests), because in that case, the harsh inequalities engendered in the economy are reinforced and sanctioned by governmental fiat. Faced with both political and economic coercion, liberalism (to be true to its name) can only be a philosophy of resistance; only in this way can it regain its original "liberating" élan. An outlook that from the outset has been opposed to arbitrary will and sovereign power, Lippmann writes, "must mean the determination to resist arbitrariness, to check it, to cut it down, to crush it, wherever and whenever it appears." For the liberal ethos, all arbitrary power is wrong. Hence, liberalism is "*not* the doctrine of laissez-faire, let her rip, and the devil take the hindmost"; rather, it is an outlook fostering the fair treatment of all. It is important to note that Lippmann's text is not antiliberal, but it seeks to salvage the promise of liberalism—the promise of a society free from arbitrary controls—on a new, ethical level. As an astute student of history, he is well aware that modernity has unleashed enormous energies of freedom (in civil society) and that a return to the social unity and homogeneity of earlier times is impossible (without severe compulsion). As he writes, the point of the liberal agenda is "to accommodate the social order to the new economy" of the market. However, this goal cannot be achieved by abandoning the market to the whims of predatory "captains of industry"; rather, it can be achieved only "by continual and far-reaching reform of the social order" in the direction of equity. Only in this manner is it possible to foster the growth of a "good society," one in which individual freedom and social responsibility are reconciled.[10]

The struggle to restore the promise of liberalism is, for Lippmann, equivalent to the "struggle for law," for a social life animated by shared standards. To repeat an earlier point, *law* here does not mean a legislative edict or fiat but rather something like a lived social ethics, akin to what Montesquieu calls the "spirit of the laws." As Lippmann writes eloquently: "The laws depend upon moral commitments which could never possibly be expressly stated in the laws themselves: upon a level of truthfulness in giving testimony, of reasonableness in argument, of trust, confidence, and good faith in transactions." From this perspective, it is "not enough" that people should be "as truthful as the laws against perjury require" or "as reasonable as the rules of evidence compel a lawyer to be." Rather, to maintain a "good" order, people must be "much more truthful, reasonable, just, and honorable than the letter of the laws." In good Aristotelian fashion, the text continues: "There must be an habitual, confirmed, and well-nigh intuitive dislike of arbitrariness; a quick sensitivity to its manifestations and a spontaneous disapproval and resistance." Again, borrowing a leaf from Aristotle (though without citing his name), the emphasis on good habits is linked with the cultivation and practice of "virtues": "There must be a strong desire to be just. There must be a growing capacity to be just. There must be discernment and sympathy in estimating the particular claims of divergent interests; there must be moral standards which discourage the quest for privilege and the exercise of arbitrary power." The capstone of Lippmann's study is the linkage of a virtuous regime, or a regime devoted to the good life, with a regime of peace. "The regime of peace," he writes, "is coterminous with the organized communities in which governments and individuals live under equal [and equitable] laws. The region of common law is the pacified region of the globe. Within it, big states and little ones, creditor and debtor nations, 'haves' and 'have-nots,' exist together in peace and are drawn together for the defense of their peace."[11]

Reformulating the Good Society

Lippmann's study was not just an academic exercise, a theory devoid of practice. In many ways, it reflected his own ethical-political conduct. In this context, it is appropriate to recall his public engagement at the end of World War I when, together with Edward House, he drafted the Fourteen Points Peace Program; served as delegate to the Paris Peace Conference in 1919; and helped draw up the Covenant of the League of Nations, a testimonial to his commitment to shared moral bonds extending beyond the nation-state. His public engagement never abated and actually grew stronger later in life. After World War II, he gave his support to the creation of the United Nations and the European Marshall Plan, hailing these initiatives as antidotes to militarism and the rampant "war spirit" in the world. His opposition to this war spirit was put to the test repeatedly during subsequent decades. Thus, to the dismay of partisan leaders, Lippmann vigorously opposed the launching of quasi-imperialist warfare in distant lands (epitomized by the war in Vietnam); he also challenged the proclivity of nationalistic regimes to wage war against domestic populations in the form of "witch hunts," illegal seizures, and extensive surveillance (as happened during the McCarthy era). In 1955, at the height of the cold war—when the meaning of *war* was extended to become virtually synonymous with *politics*—Lippmann published a text that restated his vision of a good society: *The Public Philosophy.* There, quoting Montesquieu, he reaffirmed his attachment to an ethically responsible liberalism, to a freedom that "can consist only in the power of doing what we ought to will, and in not being constrained to do what we ought not to will."[12]

Lippmann did not live to see the new millennium, a time when the war spirit leaped beyond the older (cold war) rhetoric to signify the global human condition (under the aegis of a potentially permanent "war on terrorism"). Actually, developments in the United States since the Second World War have been moving in a direction radically contrary to Lippmann's vision: toward a steady expansion of laissez-faire liberalism to the point of its elevation as a virtually uncontested, totalizing ideology. Partly in response to the danger of communism, defenders of laissez-faire extended the doctrine from the economy to the political domain, and as a result, the government itself became an arena for the pursuit of private agendas and ambitions. Unconstrained by civic bonds, exiled from civil society, state policy was steadily tailored to the whims of power lust, profiteering, and self-aggrandizement. In this manner, Lippmann's worst-case scenario (mentioned earlier) was in danger of being realized: the combination of a predatory economy and a predatory politics. To be sure, as in Lippmann's time, the assumption of an economic and political "state of nature" granting untrammeled freedom remains a complete fallacy and chimera, contradicted by real-life constraints yet liable to yield catastrophic consequences. In fairness, one must note that "resistance" (Lippmann style) to the reigning ideology has not been entirely lacking. Recent decades have seen the upsurge of a moral perspective termed "virtue ethics" that can trace its roots back to Aristotle. However, largely confined to the academy, advocates of this perspective have tended to focus on "private" (family-related) issues while steering clear of the public domain.[13] Animated by more political concerns, a network of intellectuals has simultaneously emerged whose members are called (or call themselves) "communitarians." However, the arguments they advance are often nostalgic in character and insufficiently attentive to the demands of modern freedom.[14] There are exceptions to this latter limitation, however, and prominent among them is Michael Sandel, who recently published a book titled (echoing Lippmann) *Public Philosophy: Essays on Morality in Politics*.

By comparison with its predecessor, Sandel's book is both more nuanced and more specific in some of its recommendations. What links the study with Lippmann's vision is the shared commitment to a civic, ethically responsible liberalism and to a conception of freedom oriented not toward narrow self-interest but toward the "good life" in a "good society." Like Lippmann, Sandel sees the malaise of contemporary public life in the upsurge and predominance of laissez-faire liberalism; going somewhat beyond the earlier formulation, he traces the same malaise to versions of utilitarianism (wedded to the maximization of pleasure) and proceduralism (placing its trust entirely in the abstract rules of a "procedural republic"). What connects these doctrines in an overarching ideology is the sidelining of civic conduct and of the ethical motivations needed for the viability of procedures. In Sandel's words: "The central idea of the public philosophy by which we live [today] is that freedom consists in our capacity to choose our ends for ourselves," untrammeled by social rules (as if we still lived in a "state of nature"). As a corollary, our politics in recent decades has given way to "a procedural republic, concerned less with cultivating virtue than with enabling persons to choose their own values." In the manner of Lippmann (though less decisively), Sandel's book links the laissez-faire ideology with the cult of willpower and sovereign mastery. "The voluntarist conception of freedom," we read, "promises to lay to rest, once and for all, all the risks of republican politics"; under the auspices of that conception, "the difficult task of forming civic virtue can finally be dispensed with." Somewhat later, the text speaks of the chimera of "sovereign selves."[15]

As an antidote to the laissez-faire doctrine, Sandel champions a renewed public philosophy patterned on the tradition of "civic republicanism"; as a counterpoint to an abstract proceduralism, he pleads for a "formative politics," that is, a politics concerned with the formation or cultivation (*Bildung*) of ethical civic dispositions. As he points out, the voluntarist conception of freedom, with its stress on independent selves "unencumbered by moral or civic ties antecedent to choice," suffers from a basic defect: the lack of a civic pedagogy. Above all, the conception "cannot account for a wide range of moral and political obligations that we commonly recognize, such as obligations of loyalty or solidarity." By insisting on absolute individual freedom, the conception "denies that we can ever be claimed by ends we have not chosen—ends given by nature or God, for example, or by our identities as members of families, peoples, cultures, or traditions." To remedy this defect, a renewed public philosophy must pay attention to civic education and democratic character formation. Here is a passage that ably pinpoints the pedagogical requisites of the "good society."

> To deliberate well about the common good requires more than the capacity to choose one's ends and to respect others' rights to do the same. It requires a knowledge of public affairs and also a sense of belonging, a concern for the whole, a moral bond with the community whose fate is at stake. To share

> in self-rule therefore requires that citizens possess, or come
> to acquire, certain civic virtues. . . . The republican concep-
> tion of freedom, unlike the [laissez-faire] liberal conception,
> requires a formative politics.[16]

A chief roadblock faced by a renewed civic-republican perspective is
the presumed "neutrality" of the state, that is, the aloofness of the government and official power holders from ethical (and religious) standards or beliefs. As previously indicated, this doctrine of aloofness is a
corollary of the extension of laissez-faire economics into governmental politics; the result is that, like private entrepreneurs, public power
holders are free to do as they please—and what pleases power holders
most is more power and self-aggrandizement. Sandel wants no part of
this. A revitalized civic-republican politics, he writes, "cannot be neutral toward the values and ends its citizens espouse"—mainly because
such neutrality will boomerang on citizens via the ethical indifference
of governments. All actions, whether public or private, are ethically
charged and cannot be artificially "neutralized" without severe social
costs. One of the distinct merits of Sandel's study is that it points out
the costs of neutrality. Such aloofness, he states with some urgency, is
liable to create "a moral void that opens the way for intolerance and
other misguided moralisms." Our time certainly has its share of such
misguided or untutored moralisms, often with obnoxious and democratically untenable consequences. "Where political discourse lacks
moral resonance," Sandel comments sagely, "the yearning for a public
life of larger meaning finds undesirable expression. The Christian Co-
alition and similar groups seek to clothe the naked public square with
narrow, intolerant moralisms; fundamentalists rush in where liberals
fear to tread." Elaborating on the same theme, he points to the rhetoric and activities of the "Moral Majority" as evidence that "a politics
whose moral resources are diminished with disuse lies vulnerable" to
narrowly dogmatic "solutions." Basically, a main reason that liberalism
has faltered in recent years is "its failure to argue for a vision of the
common good." This has left the field open to reactionaries yearning
for political and economic power, but not for the good life.[17]
    More forthrightly than in Lippmann's case, Sandel's study con-
fronts the main objections usually raised against the vision of a good
society, especially the objections regarding its possibility and its desir-

ability. The first objection typically stresses the obsoleteness of civic-republican ideas, pointing to the disappearance of agrarian lifestyles and independent townships under the impact of industrialization and corporate capitalism. In the absence of traditional communities, where should civic loyalties take hold? Sandel does not flinch but zeros in on an aspect frequently sidestepped by social theorists: laissez-faire economics itself. In addition to the strengthening of community life wherever possible, his study pleads for reform in "the structure of the modern economy," for public policies that would deal with "the unprecedented mobility of capital" and "the unaccountable power of large corporations." Such policies, he states, should address economic issues "not only from the standpoint of maximizing GNP" but also from that of "building communities capable of self-government on a manageable scale." This is certainly a formidable challenge, but one cannot talk about possibility or impossibility until one has put one's shoulder to the wheel.[18]

The second objection, no less weighty, has to do with the danger of politicized morality (or moral majoritarianism) and with the "risk of coercion" in attempts to "instill" civic virtue. Again, Sandel confronts the issue, acknowledging the possibly "coercive face" of what he calls "soulcraft" (as a supplement to "statecraft"). As he notes, however (I think rightly), the risk is not unavoidable: like genuine education (or *Bildung*), the vision of a good society does not need to rely on coercion or manipulation. In this context, Sandel points to the "gentler kind of tutelage" present in nineteenth-century America, when civic spirit was maintained "not by coercion but by a complex mixture of persuasion and habituation"—by what Alexis de Tocqueville calls "the slow and quiet action of society upon itself." Sandel could (and should) have mentioned at this point the educative role of good example, especially the example of public leaders. When public leaders' conduct instantiates the good life (*eu zen*), the contours of the good society can emerge almost by osmosis.[19]

Another important factor operating as a restraint on moral coercion is the pronounced pluralism of ethical and religious beliefs in contemporary society—a pluralism that is by no means equivalent to relativism. When different beliefs exist side by side, the outcome is not necessarily the imposition of one creed on all others or the dismissal of all creeds as equally spurious. Rather (and this is the challenge and opportunity of multiculturalism), there is also the chance for all groups to learn from one another about conceptions of goodness and truth—a learning that presupposes mutual recognition, which in turn is predicated on shared civic engagement (which is by no means ethically indifferent). Sandel fully endorses ethical and religious pluralism, provided such pluralism does not decay into an atomistic "identity politics" (restoring the voluntaristic paradigm). The "civic strand of freedom," he writes, is not necessarily coercive or monological, and in fact, it is vitiated when it operates monologically; hence, the good life can find "pluralistic expression" in the form of dialogue and mutual learning.[20] In support of this pluralistic outlook, Sandel refers to Jewish philosopher David Hartman, whose publications have underscored two modes of pluralism: one interpretive, the other ethical. For Hartman, interpretive pluralism emerges from his "covenantal theology" and reflects the "open-ended character of Talmudic argument" (at the heart of halachic Judaism). Going beyond the Jewish context, ethical pluralism takes seriously the ethical beliefs of both other religious faiths and secular morality as expressions of a common search for goodness or the good life.[21]

Another distinctive feature of Sandel's study is his attention to the process of globalization—a process that has gained considerable momentum since Lippmann's time. Sandel is equally suspicious of an old-style nationalism that is oblivious of global pressures and a bland cosmopolitanism that leaps briskly beyond communal loyalties. In an age in which "capital and goods, information and people flow across national boundaries with unprecedented ease," he writes, "politics must assume transnational, even global forms, if only to keep up." If this is not done, economic power will go unchecked by any democratically sanctioned politics. And if cosmopolitanism and global governance are disconnected from concrete, historically grown allegiances, all the ill effects of Leviathan-style sovereignty are bound to surface (now on a larger scale). In the apt words of the text, cosmopolitanism is "wrong to suggest that we can restore self-government simply by pushing sovereignty and citizenship upward. The hope for self-government today lies not in relocating sovereignty but in dispersing it." What democratically inclined people today should aim for, in Sandel's view, is not a "world state" or a global community patterned on the nation-state but rather a "multiplicity of communities and political bodies—some more extensive than nations and some less—among which sovereignty is diffused." In our present situation, everything depends on the development of a multidimensional global civil society and the fostering of a broad civic culture marked by intersecting global and local (what some people call "glocal") loyalties. From this perspective, the proper basis for a democratic politics in our age, for Sandel, resides in "a revitalized civic life nourished in the more particular communities we inhabit."[22]

Perhaps the most inspiring and forward-looking part of Sandel's study is a section titled "Beyond Sovereign States and Sovereign Selves." There, Sandel clearly rejoins Lippmann's attack on political voluntarism, his preference for Coke and Selden over the Hobbesian Leviathan, and his invocation of Aristotle's stress on civic virtues. However, the last invocation comes with a twist—a multicultural, vaguely "postmodern" twist. "Since the days of Aristotle's *polis*," he writes, "the republican tradition has viewed self-government as an activity rooted in a particular place, carried out by citizens loyal to that place and the way of life it embodies." This kind of "localism" is no longer possible in a society that has moved through the successive emancipatory thrusts of modernity and on to the self-questioning of a narrowly self-enclosed freedom. Today, the text continues, democratic self-government requires "a politics that plays itself out in a multiplicity of settings, from neighborhoods to nations to the world as a whole." In turn, such a politics "requires citizens who can abide the ambiguity associated with divided sovereignty, who can think and act as multiply situated selves." This reconceptualization of self-governing freedom entails, as its corollary, a rethinking of the meaning of civic virtue—and of ethical virtue itself—beyond a narrowly conceived self-cultivation in the direction of a multilateral learning process and political praxis. In Sandel's words: "The civic culture distinctive to our time is the capacity to negotiate our way among the sometimes overlapping and sometimes conflicting obligations that claim us, and to live with the tension to which multiple loyalties give rise."[23]

Toward a Global Good Society

About two decades ago, at the end of the cold war and the onset of new, more amorphous wars, an American social theorist wrote a book about what is most needed in the emerging global context. The author's name: Elise Boulding; the title of her book: *Building a Global Civic Culture: Education for an Interdependent World.* For Boulding, the term *civic culture* signifies a mode of human being-in-the-world: "the patterning of how we share a common space, common resources, and common opportunities, and manage interdependence in that 'company of strangers' which constitutes [loosely] the 'public.'" (She might have added common stories, common memories, and common beliefs.) The important point for Boulding is what happened to the term in the age of globalization. "When we think about civic culture," she writes, "we are usually thinking about our own society. Yet there is also a larger company of strangers—the five [now six] billion residents of the planet." In the face of this large global context, her study is troubled by the same question raised by Sandel in his discussion of dispersed loyalties. "How are we going to approach this complex confrontation about our future world?" she queries. "How will we go about extending the concept of civic culture to the planet itself and developing a sense of a world public interest" (or a global good society)? As she realizes, the path ahead is difficult and fraught with the perils of local chauvinism and bland globalism because it challenges us to navigate our way on the cusp of local and global commitments: "Can we stay rooted in our own communities, retain the best of our own national ways, and still develop cooperative strategies for meeting human needs everywhere, in a linked system of mutual aid that respects the integrity of other ways of life?"[24]

For Boulding, global education and multicultural pedagogy are crucial. Required is a pedagogy that is far removed from indoctrination and manipulation because it cannot be monological or monolingual but has to be dialogical and even multilogical. As she notes, "the learning task is a large one," but it is not out of reach. "As it happens, we are all learners and all teachers, all of our lives." In fact, "learning sites are everywhere—at home, in our neighborhood, in the places where we work and play and talk and act." In addition to traditional learning sites, however, there is a vaster arena looming; we need to develop a "world civic culture," a worldwide "learning community" involving people from different backgrounds and traditions. Learning is always demanding and taxing, but when it involves exposure to unfamiliar lifeworlds or alien ethical or religious beliefs, learning is bound to be wrenching, involving existential transformation. Boulding cites John Dewey's questions about democratic education: "What kind of person is one to become, what sort of self is in the making, what kind of world is in the making?" Education involves not just the "self" but also the "world," or better yet, it has to include ethical self-cultivation as well as public world-cultivation. In Sandel's (somewhat awkward) formulation, "soulcraft" has to be joined with "statecraft"; in Boulding's (more apt) phrasing, the fostering of "good intentions" has to be assisted by the formation of "enabling institutions, customs," and perhaps even "some shared ritual." Above all, education cannot just mean *Bildung* for an elite; in Paulo Freire's memorable expression, it must reach out to the many, offering a "pedagogy of the oppressed." In a similar vein, education cannot address the brain alone—encouraging a "brain trust" or "expertocracy"—but must address the whole human being, offering, in Freire's terms, a general "pedagogy of the heart."[25]

An important aspect of Boulding's study—linking it with Lippmann's vision formulated half a century earlier—is the connection of civic culture or virtue with a "regime of peace." A crucial chapter is entitled "Peace Praxis: The Craft and Skills of Doing Peace." What this title indicates is that peace is not just a static condition to be passively contemplated but the fruit of a strenuous "struggle for law" (Lippmann's term), or, perhaps better, it is an engaged struggle for justice and the good life. Boulding uses *peace* as an active and quasi-transitive term (almost like a verb) and prefers to speak of "doing peace in the midst of conflict." In line with her pedagogical outlook, she insists that "peace doing" is something that needs to be learned and strenuously cultivated; it does not just happen by itself (although, from another angle, it is something like a "gift," transgressing our willpower). Above all, peace doing (or peacemaking) is situational or contextual, requiring good judgment or discernment (*phronesis*). Such doing, she writes, "happens in settings and follows patterns," and three types of settings are particularly significant for peace praxis: negotiation tables, "sword-into-plowshares demonstrations" at symbolic public sites, and "declared zones of peace." The establishment of peace zones reflects popular demands but must be sanctioned by public authorities in towns, countries, or groups of countries; most frequently, such zones are declared "nuclear-free zones," where nuclear weapons are specifically outlawed. Boulding's discussion of this topic bears some resemblance to recent attempts to establish "cities of refuge" or places of hospitality where civilian populations are protected from the ravages of warfare.[26]

In our globalizing era, education for civic culture has to draw on resources that are available all around the world; such resources include religious and ethical traditions, the accumulated treasures of literature and the arts, and ordinary life practices and experiences garnered from communal relations. In formulating his vision, Lippmann invokes a number of these resources in an effort to chart a pedagogy for humanity leading from savage barbarism to the civilized conditions of the good society. "The passage from barbarism into civilization," he writes, "is long, halting, and unsure; it is a hard climb from the practice of devouring one's enemies to the injunction to love them." Apart from noting culturally differentiated teachings and legacies, Lippmann focuses on a maxim or standard—perhaps a minimal standard—that has been acknowledged as wise and workable by cultures around the globe: the Golden Rule. He refers to a number of versions of this rule, including the Upanishadic saying, "Let no man do to another that which would be repugnant to himself," and the *Analects* of Confucius counseling, "What you do not want done to yourself, do not do unto others." For Lippmann, the rule is a maxim that arises when human beings "recognize each other as ethical persons" (rather than mere objects), when they acknowledge in others an inalienable dignity and perhaps even a divine imprint. He offers examples from history showing the cutting edge of the rule, and these examples resonate fully with experiences in our own time: "If we asked why the Venetian Senators of the eighteenth century were wrong when they employed assassins for the 'public good,' we can reply that they were wrong because they violated the essential dignity of other men. . . . And we can say that France was governed badly when Richelieu said it could not be governed without the right of arbitrary arrest and exile."[27]

Likewise, *In Search of the Good Life* draws on religious, philosophical, and cultural resources as helpmates in the quest. The first part of the volume invokes a number of exemplary historical teachers or "searchers," and the second part explores recent and contemporary contributions to a pedagogy cultivating a global civic culture. The first part guides readers from the Middle Ages to the zenith of Western modernity, with a chapter devoted to each of the following topics: Saint Bonaventure's spiritual journey to the divine; the attempt of Indian poet-saint Jñanadev and his friends to "walk humbly with their god"; Nicolaus of Cusa's search for "truth" in the midst of ignorance and diversity; Leibniz's encounter with the religious and ethical teachings of Confucius; Montesquieu's "struggle for (the spirit of) law" and civic culture, as recorded in his *Persian Letters;* and Friedrich Schiller's plea for an "aesthetic education of humanity" issued at the height of the European Enlightenment. The gaps in this account are obvious to any reader (they are painfully evident to me). The most glaring omissions are names such as al-Farabi, Mencius, Erasmus, and Johann Gottfried Herder. Memorable is al-Farabi's teaching, stated in *The Virtuous City* and *Aphorisms of the Statesman,* to the effect that good rulership involves the continuous cultivation and practice of civic virtues, with the aim of fostering the well-being or happiness (the good life) of all inhabitants. Also memorable is the teaching of Mencius, China's "second master," that rulers are required to practice justice and virtue and that people are entitled to resist, and possibly oust, bad and unjust rulers. The work of Erasmus is particularly memorable for his *Education of a Christian Prince* and his combination of the practice of virtues and the "regime of peace." In turn, Herder is memorable for opening up the horizons of a global multiculturalism without chauvinistic self-enclosure and for defending an ethical pluralism without relativism. To these figures I might add the name of the neo-Confucian Chen Te-hsui, who lived in the time between al-Farabi and Erasmus. Following in the footsteps of Confucius, Chen stressed the importance of combining knowing and loving (or "mind and heart") and of placing both in the service of equity and the good life.[28]

The second part of this book deals with recent and contemporary issues relating to global pedagogy. The first chapter raises the question of the meaning and contemporary significance of the "classics" (from both the West and the East) and, relying on the teachings of Hans-Georg Gadamer and Theodore de Bary, provides the answer by pointing to the transformative quality of classical works and their role as resources of resistance against political oppression. The next chapter probes the present-day agenda of global democratization and queries whether this agenda should be pursued by military or peda-

gogical means (cannons or canons). Following is a chapter devoted
to the closely related problem of "radical evil," a stark issue that cannot be ignored in our time. Again, the main options available appear
to be military "eradication" or ethical pedagogy and transformation.
The next topic addressed is the possibility of "transnational citizenship." Drawing inspiration from both the classics and Saint Augustine,
I highlight multiple citizenships and "citizen pilgrims" as possible
"paths beyond the nation-state." The next chapter discusses religious
faith in our time, emphasizing that its proper role resides not in clerical or theocratic domination but in "preserving the salt of the earth,"
that is, practicing faith in ordinary life. The final chapter, a memorial tribute to Paul Ricoeur, examines his manner of balancing the
competing claims of love and justice—a balance that maintains just
retribution but grants ultimate primacy to love's redeeming quality (as
exemplified in contemporary "truth and reconciliation" commissions).
Again, the discussion in the second part is highly selective. For me,
the most glaring gap is the omission of Mahatma Gandhi, whose nonviolent struggle for the good life has served as a political guidepost to
me for many years. I will conclude by invoking Chen Te-hsiu, who has
admirably captured the gist of public pedagogy in these couplets:

> Discipline the self by incorruptibility;
> Pacify the people by humaneness;
> Preserve the mind by balanced equity;
> Perform your duties with diligence.[29]

Part I

Prominent Searchers in the Past

1. A Pedagogy of the Heart
Saint Bonaventure's Spiritual Itinerary

Some eight hundred years ago, a young man in Italy received a summons to rejuvenate religious practices through a life of poverty and humble devotion. The young man's name was Giovanni Francesco Bernardone, and he lived in the town of Assisi in Umbria. Following this summons, he divested himself of all worldly possessions and founded a religious order that spread rapidly throughout Europe.[1] Two years after his death (in 1226), he was canonized and became revered as Saint Francis. However, in his own lifetime, he was known simply as the *poverello,* a poor, humble mendicant following in the footsteps of his Lord. Eight centuries have passed since the *poverello*'s time, and his legacy is nearly extinguished. Societies and peoples everywhere have grown by leaps and bounds. During the past four centuries in particular, Western modernity has relentlessly embarked on a quest for "progress," which basically means growth in all domains: scientific knowledge, economic wealth, and military-industrial power. Although beneficial in some respects, "progress" has also exacted a heavy toll—in particular, human addiction and subservience to growth. Poverty and the simple life—I mean the voluntary poverty of Francis, not the involuntary type still suffered by millions—have become nearly unintelligible to people swept up by the tide of consumerism and possessivism.[2]

Although he authored a series of beautifully stirring canticles and sermons, Saint Francis did not elaborate in writing many of his basic theological, philosophical, and pedagogical views, leaving that task to some of his devoted followers. Among the latter, the most prominent was Saint Bonaventure (1217–1274), who is also known as the "second founder" of the Franciscan order (he served as its Minister General for seventeen years) and as the "Seraphic Doctor" (in remembrance of the winged seraphim that appeared to Saint Francis on Mount La Verna in 1224).[3] Compared with the *poverello*, the younger disciple was more scholarly and erudite in an academic sense. Educated at the University of Paris by some of the best teachers of the time, Bonaventure lectured at that university and finally received his *magister* of theology there, in the same year as Thomas Aquinas. Yet, despite his more academic leanings, he never moved far away from his spiritual mentor: no matter how philosophically and theologically refined, all his writings exude the gentle spirit and humble devotion of the saintly *poverello*.[4] In this chapter I discuss some of Bonaventure's writings in an effort to highlight his admirable blending of learning and devotion (or what Erasmus called the twinning of *eruditio et pietas*). I concentrate chiefly on two texts: "The Life of Saint Francis" (*Legenda Maior*) and "The Soul's [or Heart's] Journey into God" (*Itinerarium Mentis in Deum*). Following a discussion of these texts, I draw some parallels between Bonaventure's itinerary and the pedagogical teachings of other religious traditions, and finally, I reflect on the contemporary relevance of his work, drawing attention especially to Paulo Freire's *Pedagogy of the Heart*.

Life of Saint Francis

Francis of Assisi died when Bonaventure was still a young boy, making it highly unlikely that the two saints ever met.[5] Notwithstanding this distance, the younger man remained fervently devoted to the legacy of his spiritual guide, a fact evident in all his writings, but especially in his detailed and lovingly narrated story of Francis's life. The story was commissioned by the General Chapter of the Franciscan Order and, in due course, emerged as the official biography of Saint Francis, sidelining some earlier accounts. In preparing his biography, Bonaventure conducted extensive research using available sources and also met and interrogated some of Francis's early companions who were still alive at the time. In his own words, his chief aim was to "gather together the accounts of [the saint's] virtues, his actions and his words—like so many fragments, partly forgotten and scattered—so that they may not be lost when those who lived with him pass away."[6] As this statement indicates, his aim was not simply to offer a factual account or a story of external events, but rather to illuminate through these events the saint's spiritual motives and "virtues." Ewert Cousins, in his introduction to the biography, finds in the text two main layers: one strictly chronological, the other thematic and spiritual. While the first recounts successive events in the saint's life, the second illustrates his commitment to the "practice of virtues" and is thematically arranged under three main headings: self-overcoming (or purgation), illumination, and perfection.[7]

Proceeding in chronological order, the first several chapters of "The Life of Saint Francis" recount the time from his birth to the founding of the Franciscan order. In Bonaventure's words, the young Francis "lived among worldly sons of men and was brought up in worldly ways" and, in due course, was assigned "to work in a lucrative merchant's business." Yet, "with God's protection," he did not abandon himself entirely to worldly attractions and "even among greedy merchants" did not "place his hope in money and treasures." Still, he tended to be distracted by the external affairs of business, which drew him down to "earthly things." A prolonged illness and a number of spiritual experiences slowly awakened him from these worldly distractions and prompted him to embark on an inner search. He began to withdraw "from the bustle of public business" and to seek out "solitary places" suited for prolonged prayer and meditation. Gradually his character came to exhibit the distinctive "Franciscan" features, especially a sense of humility and the love of poverty and the poor—a love manifest by his visits to the houses of lepers, whom he embraced while distributing alms. A decisive turning point, according to the biography, was the summons Francis received while praying in the church of San Damiano near Assisi. The summons called on Francis to "repair" the church, which he first interpreted to mean repairing the actual building; later, however, he realized that it also meant restoring the church's inner spirit. Begging for funds and investing his own physical labor, he set out to repair not only San Damiano but also another nearby church and eventually a third church called Saint Mary of the Angels, or "Portiuncula," where he subsequently took up residence and which became his favorite place. In Bonaventure's words: "The holy man loved this spot more than any other in the world; for here he began humbly, here he progressed steadily, and here he ended happily."[8]

Having repaired the physical structure of the churches, Francis proceeded to honor the deeper meaning of the summons by gathering a group of followers who could serve as the "salt," or leaven, to rejuvenate the church. The guiding motto of the new fellowship was taken from the Gospel of Matthew (10:9), which says that followers "should not keep gold or silver or money in their belts, nor have a wallet for their journey, nor two tunics, nor shoes, nor staff." As the number of followers grew, Francis decided to call the fellowship the Order of the Brothers of Penance, a religious community bound together by a set of monastic "rules" prescribing, above all, poverty and service. Armed with these rules, the *poverello* went to Rome to seek the approval of Pope Innocent III, who was skeptical initially. As Bonaventure records: "He hesitated to do what Christ's little poor man asked because it seemed to some of the cardinals to be something novel and difficult beyond human powers." Eventually, however, the pope relented and gave the new order permission to preach and spread the gospel in its own way. Encouraged by this permission and inspired by the religious zeal exhibited by Francis and his followers, a great number of people—both clerical and lay, men and women—began to flock to Assisi to share in the exemplary way of life exhibited by the *poverello* and his community. These people clearly were not attracted by the prospect of fame or worldly goods. In the words of Bonaventure, it was poverty and the example of a simple lifestyle that "made them prompt for obedience, robust for work and free for travel. Because they possessed nothing that belonged to the world, they were attached to nothing and feared to lose nothing." Thus, this devout surrender and willingness to serve became the basis of a marvelous freedom: "They were safe everywhere, not held back by fear, nor distracted by worldly care; they lived with untroubled minds and, without anxiety, looked forward to the morrow."[9]

This praise of the gifts of faith leads Bonaventure quite naturally to a discussion of the various ethical and spiritual virtues exemplified in Francis's life. First among these virtues is self-overcoming or austerity, that is, the taming and redirection of the selfish desires and appetites of the ego. This taming is a first and necessary step on the path toward any kind of ethical life. As Francis used to say, "it would be difficult to satisfy the needs of the body without giving in to the earth-bound inclinations of the senses" and thus becoming attached to worldly goods in a slavish way. Hence, he was alert and carefully "watched over himself" so as not to lose the freedom required for the pursuit of his calling. Still, practicing austerity did not cause him to lose a sense of balance or moderation. "He was not pleased," Bonaventure writes, "by an over-strict severity that did not put on a heart of compassion and was not seasoned with the salt of discretion." Among all the virtues, none are as closely associated with Saint Francis as humility and love of poverty. For the *poverello*, humility was "the guardian and the ornament of all the virtues," and he strove "to build himself up on this virtue like an architect laying the foundations." Attachment to this virtue prompted Francis to shun clerical offices and monastic rank orders. He preferred "to obey rather than command," Bonaventure states. "Therefore he relinquished his office of General [of his order] and looked for a guardian whose will he would obey in all things." Humility and love of poverty went hand in hand. Seeing that poverty was the "close companion" of Jesus but widely rejected by the world, Francis was eager to embrace it and to encourage others to follow his example. In Bonaventure's stirring words: "No one was so greedy for gold as he was for poverty; nor was anyone so anxious to guard his treasure as he was in guarding this pearl of the gospel." When speaking about poverty, Francis himself was fond of quoting from Luke (9:58): "The foxes have their holes and the birds of the air their nests, but the Son of Man has nowhere to lay his head."[10]

Bonaventure turns next to what Cousins calls the domain of inner "illumination," which includes the virtues of piety, charity, and zeal for prayer. *Piety*, in Francis's case, had a broader scope than the English term suggests; like the Latin *pietas*, it denoted not only devotion and reverence but also kindness, affection, fidelity, and compassion. Thus, the *poverello*'s piety "drew him up to God through devotion," but it also attracted him to his neighbors and fellow human beings with kind affection and compassion and even prompted him to turn to nature and the animal kingdom in a mode of "universal reconciliation with each and every thing." Regarding his fellow human beings, the biography tells us that Francis "responded with a remarkably tender compassion to those suffering from any bodily affliction" and that "his soul melted at the sight of the poor and infirm." Regarding nature and the animal kingdom, Francis was filled with the most "abundant piety, calling creatures, no matter how small, by the name of brother or sister, because he knew they had the same source as himself." As with piety, *charity* in Francis's life had a broad meaning, embracing not only almsgiving but also love and loving surrender (*caritas, agape*). In Bonaventure's words: "The ecstatic devotion to his (kind of) charity so bore him aloft into the divine that his loving kindness was enlarged and extended to all who shared with him in nature and grace." *Praying*, likewise, carried extensive connotations; instead of being an occasional or intermittent activity, prayer pervaded all aspects of the saint's life. "Whether walking or sitting, whether inside or outside, working or resting," the biography states, "he was so intent on prayer that he seemed to have dedicated to it not only his heart and body but also all his effort and time." Instead of being a chore, praying was a "delight" to the *poverello*, who had already become "a fellow citizen of the angels."[11]

Moving along the path of self-overcoming and inner illumination, Francis steadily climbed to the summit of spiritual virtues, which are scriptural understanding, power of preaching, and union with the divine. As Bonaventure notes, Francis was not a learned man in the sense of academic or scholastic training; however, the fervor of his devotion allowed him to penetrate more deeply into scriptural meanings than did most theologians. Thus, he managed to probe the "hidden depths" of scriptures, and "where the scholarship of the [academic] teacher stands outside, the affection of the lover briskly entered within." Not a gifted preacher, and actually "unskilled in speech" (2 Corinthians 11:6), Francis succeeded in overcoming this defect through his spiritual devotion, becoming an effective and widely acclaimed spreader of the gospel. His words, Bonaventure comments, were "like a burning fire" filling the minds and hearts of listeners "with admiration." The reason was not rhetorical finesse but the soundness of the proclaimed message: "It made no pretense at the elegance of human composition, but exuded the perfume of divine revelation." The ultimate pinnacle of Francis's spiritual ascent was the union or communion with the divine, manifest by the imprinting of the Lord's stigmata on his body. This transformation happened on Mount La Verna, where he had retreated to pray and fast for forty days. In the words of his biographer: "By the Seraphic ardor of his desires, he was being borne aloft into God; and by his sweet compassion he was being transformed into him who chose to be crucified because of the excess of his love." The transmutation was accompanied by the vision of a seraph with six wings descending from heaven and covering the saint's body; as subsequent events proved, healing powers resulted from the angel's touch. According to Bonaventure, "Thus it was established that these sacred marks were imprinted on him by the power of the One who purifies, illumines and inflames through the action of the Seraphim."[12]

Following the event on Mount La Verna, Francis had only two more years to spend on earth. Despite mounting infirmities, he devoted these years to prayer and service. "He was ablaze with a great desire, "Bonaventure writes, "to return to the humility he practiced at the beginning, and to nurse the lepers as he did at the outset." When his final days approached, he asked his friars to bring him to his favorite church, Saint Mary of the Portiuncula. There he stripped himself of his monk's habit, allowing himself to be clothed only in a beggar's tunic; having lived his life "out of zeal for poverty," he did not wish to wear a garment in his final hours "unless it were lent to him by another." In this manner, the *poverello* "fell asleep in the Lord" on October 3, 1226. Learning of Francis's passing, Pope Gregory IX quickly proceeded to gather evidence of the friar's saintly life and submit that evidence to his cardinals, even those "who seemed less favorable to this cause." Having received unanimous endorsement, the church completed Francis's canonization in 1228, two years after his death. The healing powers deriving from the seraph's embrace continued to show their effects in subsequent decades and even centuries. Bonaventure concludes his biography with these words: "So, from the day of his passing to the present, in different parts of the world, he radiated forth with remarkable miracles through the divine power that glorified him. For the blind and the deaf, the mute and the crippled, paralytics and those suffering from epilepsy, lepers and those possessed by evil spirits, the shipwrecked and the captives—all these were given relief through his merits."[13]

The Soul's Journey

For Bonaventure, the life of Saint Francis was in many ways the perfect example of what constituted the core of spiritual learning and ascent. All the virtues of the *poverello*—from self-overcoming (purgation) to illumination and perfection—illustrated the kind of ethical-spiritual pedagogy that, in the biographer's view, was capable of guiding human beings steadily on the path of salvation. In philosophical and theological terms, this kind of pedagogy antedated Saint Francis of Assisi, although he managed to embody it in the most admirable way. In Cousins's words, with a genius for speculative synthesis, Bonaventure "produced a type of spiritual *summa* that integrates psychology, philosophy, and theology." Grounding himself in Augustine and Anselm of Canterbury, he "brought together the cosmic vision of the Pseudo-Dionysius with the psychological acumen of Bernard of Clairvaux and Richard of St. Victor." Proceeding in this fashion, Bonaventure "achieved for spirituality what Thomas Aquinas did for [scholastic] theology and Dante for medieval culture as a whole."[14] Nowhere is this spiritual summa more fully expressed than in the work for which Bonaventure is perhaps most well known: "The Soul's Journey into God" (*Itinerarium Mentis in Deum*). Lawrence Cunningham supports the notion of a grand synthesis when he writes that the "Journey" has been "rightly judged to be an excellent example and a fine summary of a theological and mystical tradition that stretches back into the Patristic period" and finds major expression in the wisdom of the Christian Neoplatonists, Augustine, and Anselm. By focusing on the "Journey," he adds, "the interested student of our Western Christian heritage can see in a relatively few pages the sources of a spirituality that was at one time normative for the West and which still has an influence on contemporary spirituality albeit in hidden or implicit ways."[15]

The "Journey" was written by Bonaventure in 1259 during a retreat at Mount La Verna in Tuscany, the same site where Francis had reached the summit of his transformation. In the prologue to his text, the author expresses his deep indebtedness to Francis and his hope to find at La Verna the same spiritual vision and peace granted to his mentor: "Following the example of our most blessed father Francis, I was seeking this peace with eager spirit—I a sinner and utterly unworthy who after our father's death had become the seventh Minister General of the [Franciscan] friars." The apparition of the six-winged seraph on La Verna provides Bonaventure with the structure of his treatise, in the sense that the six wings symbolize the six stages in the transformative ascent guiding the soul from the world to God. Actually, as Cousins points out, the six stages can be condensed into three main phases of a journey: the path leading from (1) the experience of external nature to (2) the depth of spiritual inwardness and finally to (3) the contemplation of God as the source and matrix of both outer and inner domains. The three stages, he adds, are in turn reflections of a trinitarian vision or, more precisely, of a conception of the trinity (largely derived from Pseudo-Dionysius) as "the mystery of the self-diffusion of the Good" and the return of this self-diffusion to its source.[16] In an intriguing fashion, this self-diffusion is linked by Cunningham to the notion of *kenosis,* or the "self-emptying" of God in Christ—a self-emptying recaptured in the Franciscan commitment to poverty. As he writes, the understanding of poverty in Francis "must be linked to his *kenotic* Christology." Hence, mystical ascent for Bonaventure is not simply an exercise in "traditional ascesis" but rather "a working out of the implications of the Franciscan emphasis on *kenosis*—the emptying out of oneself in the imitation of Christ."[17]

Following the prologue, with its recollection of the seraphic vision, the opening chapter begins the soul's journey with an examination of God's "traces in the world." Bonaventure initially reminds the reader of the basically tripartite structure of the journey: the movement from the experience of the external world to the exploration of inner spirituality to the soul's final communion with God. Corresponding to the three steps on the ladder of ascent (body, spirit, and divinity), he observes that human beings are endowed with three main "perceptual orientations": "The first is oriented toward the external world and is called animal or sensual power; the second is directed inwardly and is called spiritual sense, while the third goes beyond itself and may be called soul or heart" (seen as a divine resonance chamber). As previously indicated, the three stages can be subdivided into half-steps, an operation that yields a sixfold journey corresponding to God's creation of the world in six days, as well as to the six wings of the seraph. The bottom rung of the ladder for Bonaventure is the simple experience of the external world without analysis or rational judgment. In the open-minded soul, this experience is bound to lead to wonder, delight, and praise. "Whoever is not enlightened by the splendor of creation," he writes, "is blind. Whoever is not aroused by its voice is deaf; whoever is not compelled to give praise is mute; whoever fails to recognize first beginnings in the face of such evidence is a fool." For Bonaventure, the entire sensible world enters the human soul through the five senses, a perception that yields first delight and then the task of rational inquiry and judgment. Rational inquiry (the second rung on the ladder) leads to deeper understanding of the sensible world, an understanding disclosing its inner workings and proportions, its similarities and differences, as well as its operating laws (of cause and effect). Clearly reflecting Neoplatonic influences, the text at this point links the design of the sensible world with mathematical correlations, noting that Augustine himself claimed that "numbers are in bodies" and that the world reflects "numerical harmony."[18]

While the external world of nature manifests only divine "traces," the inner spirit of human beings discloses more clearly the "divine image" or the image of God "stamped upon" the inner human faculties. With this turn to inwardness, the text states, "we leave the outer court and enter into the sanctuary, that is, the threshold of the tabernacle." According to Bonaventure, the inner human mind is endowed with three main faculties: memory, rational intelligence, and judgment or deliberation (oriented toward the highest good). Memory here is taken in a broad sense as encompassing all temporal modes of understanding, for it is by memory that we "retain the past by recall, the present by perception, and the future by anticipation." Rational intelligence involves the grasp of definitions, propositions, and inferences. This grasp is sometimes apodictic and sometimes only contingent or probable; the understanding is apodictic when we know "with certainty that propositions are true" or that "a conclusion necessarily follows from its premises." Judgment involves deliberation about, or inquiry into, "whether this or that thing is better"—a deliberation that is inevitably related to a conception of "that which is best" and hence is guided by a desire for that which is intrinsically good. These three faculties, in Bonaventure's view, are nurtured, illuminated, and further perfected by divine grace, seen as the complement of human reason. At this point, reason allows itself to be lifted up by scriptural teachings, meditation, and the practice of the "theological virtues." Thus, while the third step in the soul's journey revels in the "powers of the rational mind in its operations, functions, and scientific modes of thinking," the fourth step advances to a reflection on these same powers "elevated by the theological virtues, the spiritual sense, and mystical encounter."[19]

All the preceding steps must be seen as preparatory to the final ascent, that is, to the soul's entry into the "tabernacle." As Bonaventure notes, God can be contemplated not only in his "traces" in the external world or in his "image" implanted in human beings but also (and most preeminently) by turning to the "higher light" that shines on our life and soul. This higher light is able to illuminate—or render at least partially transparent—two main features: the basic nature of God seen as "divine unity," and the basic attributes of the "divine persons" correlated in the trinity. For Bonaventure (following Aristotle), the basic nature of God is "being" as such, mysteriously expressed in the biblical formula "I am who I am" or "I am the one who is (or shall be)." Being as such is seen here as encompassing and embracing even nonbeing; since the latter is only a "privation of being," it can be grasped by the intellect "only through being." Considered as pure being, the godhead is not merely potential but wholly actual; since it exhibits no defect or gap, it is perfect, and since it lacks diversification, it is unitary or "one." To be sure, fixated on empirical things or "beings," the human mind has difficulty perceiving the "being" of all things. Just as being is the core of the godhead, the correlation of the three divine persons in the trinity is marked by essential "goodness," indeed, by perfect goodness of a kind that "nothing better can be conceived." For Bonaventure, perfect goodness here means the highest degree of communication or communion, that is, a mutual sharing in openness and love. From this full communication, he writes, there derives the highest "consubstantiality" of the divine persons, and from this derives their supreme likeness, which in turn demands their "coequality and co-eternity." All these features together account for a supreme "intimacy with each dwelling in the other through circuminsession" (that is, through interpenetration and complementarity). At this level, complete union is joined with individuality, consubstantiality with plurality, and intimacy with a "sending or going forth" in distance.[20]

With these six steps, the journey of the soul into God is nearly complete—except for the fact that the six days of the week are followed by the Sabbath, when the human soul is meant to rest in "mystical ecstasy" while experiencing union with the divine. Accordingly, the seventh and final chapter of Bonaventure's text is the most exhilarating and uplifting part of the entire work. The soul's final ascent here is portrayed as a complete "passing over" (or Passover) from ordinary experience to mystical rapture and communion. Saint Francis serves again as the perfect model of this completion. The final union, we read, was "shown to blessed Francis on top of the mountain" when, "in rapturous contemplation," he saw the seraph and when, "propelled out of himself and carried off to God," he became the "supreme exemplar of contemplation," just as he had previously been the model of action. Through the example of Francis, the chapter continues, "all spiritual men are invited by God, rather than by any word, to the same passing over and the same ecstasy of the soul." At this juncture, mere book learning and verbal elegance are of no avail, for "words and books are unimportant where the gift of God is everything." Carried away by ecstasy, the book appropriately concludes by invoking a passage from *De Mystica Theologia* (attributed to Pseudo-Dionysius), which speaks of "a highest summit where the final, absolute, and totally limpid mysteries of theology are hidden in the dazzling obscurity of a silence pregnant with hidden teaching; an obscurity in which everything is made manifest and which fills to overflowing invisible intellects with the radiance of all hidden and ineffable good things."[21]

A Pedagogy of the Heart

Despite a hiatus of eight hundred years—and despite certain metaphysical accents somewhat alien to contemporary sensibilities—Bonaventure's writings still speak to us with remarkable freshness, conveying across the centuries a plethora of both timeless and timely lessons. A prominent feature of the discussed texts is the centrality assigned to Saint Francis as a practitioner of poverty and dispossession—a dispossession that made him an ideal messenger of peace. Both the "Life" and the "Journey" pay ample tribute to the peaceable and peacebuilding qualities of the saint. The prologue to "The Life of St. Francis" speaks of Francis as a "lover of holy poverty" sent by the "most high" as a herald so that "he might prepare for the Lord a way of light and peace in the hearts of the faithful." He preached to men, the prologue continues, "the gospel of peace and salvation, being himself the angel of true peace." In turn, the prologue to the "Journey" opens with a prayer asking God to illuminate the author and direct his path "on the way of peace." The message of peace preached by Jesus, Bonaventure states, was "proclaimed anew by our father Saint Francis," who "began and ended every sermon with an invocation of peace" and who "in every greeting offered the salutation of peace." In every moment of contemplation, he adds, Francis "breathed out peace as a citizen of that heavenly Jerusalem about which the man of peace who was peaceful with those who hated peace said: 'Pray for the peace of Jerusalem.'" This attitude was by no means whimsical or fortuitous: "For Saint Francis knew that the throne of Solomon was founded on nothing else but peace, as it is written: 'His place is in peace and his abode is in Sion.'"[22]

Following in the footsteps of Francis, Bonaventure displayed a peaceable disposition throughout his life, devoting himself to the fostering and preservation of peace. An occasion to demonstrate this disposition arose soon after he was appointed Minister General of the Franciscan order. During this time, the order was rent by a deep factional split between those with rigidly austere and even millenarian leanings (the so-called Spirituals) and a more moderate faction that wanted the Franciscan spirit to unfold in manifold ways (the so-called Conventionals). Though personally favoring the second group, Bonaventure was unceasing in his efforts to restore harmony among the different wings of the Franciscan family—efforts that were at least partially successful. In Cousins's words: "Through his personal holiness, the respect he commanded and his gifts of reconciliation, he was able to give form and direction to the moderate position, thus meriting to be called the 'Second Founder' of the Order."[23] Another occasion presented itself toward the end of his life when Pope Gregory X requested Bonaventure's assistance in preparing for the Ecumenical Council to be held in Lyons in 1274. The aim of the council was ambitious and far-reaching: to achieve the reconciliation and reunion of the Church of Rome with Greek Orthodoxy. Again, Bonaventure eagerly rose to the challenge, resigning his position as Minister General in order to devote himself fully to the task of reconciliation. He was present at the opening ceremonies and served as principal preacher at the liturgy that closed the council and proclaimed the "Union of Greeks and Romans" in June 1274. As Cunningham writes, however: "The labors of the Council and his other responsibilities proved too much for his constitution and, a month after the close of the Council, he died in Lyons and was buried there in the Franciscan convent."[24]

Bonaventure's efforts in Lyons anticipated by a few centuries the labors of two other peace builders: Nicolaus of Cusa, who sought to reconcile once again Western and Eastern Christianity, and Erasmus of Rotterdam, who devoted his life to restoring peace and communion among Catholics and Protestants. There is another parallel between Bonaventure and his successors that deserves mention: their ability to combine and reconcile reason and faith, knowledge and belief, or (in Erasmus's favorite expression) *eruditio et pietas*. As previously noted, Bonaventure had been educated by the best teachers of the time at the University of Paris, and he had lectured at the same university for several years. Although he appreciated and continuously nurtured the taste for learning and erudition, he was simultaneously attracted to simple piety and humble devotion—the dominant features of the Franciscan way of life. To quote Cousins again: "An intellectual himself and a trained theologian of the University of Paris, he saw no radical conflict between learning and Franciscan simplicity; hence he encouraged learning and cultivated centers of study."[25] Bonaventure himself was quite aware of and explicit about his dual commitment to inquiry and pious devotion. As he wrote in one of his letters: "I acknowledge before God that what made me love the life of blessed Francis so much was the fact that it resembled the beginning and growth of the Church. For, as the Church began with simple fishermen and afterwards developed to include renowned and skilled doctors, so you will see it to be the case in the Order of blessed Francis."[26] When canonizing him in 1482, Pope Sixtus IV stated in his bull: "Bonaventure was great in learning, but no less great in humility and holiness. His innocence and dove-like simplicity were such that Alexander of Hales, the renowned doctor whose disciple Bonaventure became, used to say of him that it seemed as though Adam had never sinned in him."[27]

A further dimension of bridge building in the lives of both Francis and Bonaventure merits attention: the relation between faith and engagement, between piety and social practice. This issue is too often sidestepped both by self-styled "spiritual" people and by social activists, with the former construing piety as an alibi from social engagement and the latter celebrating action for its own sake (that is, as not being needful of purification and prayer). This sidestepping exacts a heavy price on the side of believers and activists alike. Failing to heed the call for social justice, faith becomes privatized and ultimately a mode of self-indulgence. In the absence of prayer and "self-emptying" meditation, activists are too readily exposed to the temptations of self-aggrandizement and lust for power (as history amply teaches). A central endeavor of both Francis and Bonaventure was to keep prayer and action correlated and in balance—an endeavor shared in recent times by spiritually sensitive leaders such as Mahatma Gandhi and the Dalai Lama. In his "Life of St. Francis," Bonaventure articulates the dual commitments and their correlation in a memorable passage:

> For he [Francis] had wisely learned so to divide the time available to him that he expended part of it in working for his neighbors' benefit, and devoted the other part to the peaceful ecstasy of contemplation. Therefore, when in his compassion he had worked for the salvation of others, he would then leave behind the restlessness of the crowds and seek out hidden places of quiet solitude where he could spend his time more freely with the Lord and cleanse himself of any dust that might have adhered to him from his involvement in social matters.[28]

This passage is ably seconded by the Tibetan Buddhist leader when he remarks (in a recorded interview): "In general, if one can do both, it is best. For the greatest part of the year we have to live in society, we have to lead a good [social] life. . . . But for a few weeks, for two or three months, to go on retreat, to forget worldly business and to concentrate solely on one's [spiritual] practice, this I think is the best way."[29]

There remains yet another—perhaps the most crucial—feature characterizing the lives of both Francis and Bonaventure: the endeavor to preserve the relation between nature and spirit, between humans and the divine (along trinitarian lines). Saint Francis, of course, is well known for his sermons to animals and his marvelous canticle addressed to "Brother Sun and Sister Moon." In turn, Bonaventure begins his "Journey" with the contemplation of nature's wonders, seen as "traces" or vestiges of God's spirit, and culminating in a paean to nature (cited earlier).[30] In stressing the correlation of nature and the divine, Bonaventure's "Journey" comes close to the "cosmotheandric" vision articulated in our time by Raimon Panikkar, a philosopher of religion. Deviating from both a radical transcendentalism (centered on divine heteronomy) and a radical immanentism (centered on humans or nature or both), Panikkar emphasizes a kind of "mutual in-dwelling" (*perichoresis*) of the three dimensions of the divine, the human, and nature. In his words: "The cosmotheandric principle could be stated by saying that the divine, the human, and the earthly—however we may prefer to call them—are the three irreducible dimensions which constitute the real, that is, any reality inasmuch as it is real."[31] No great labor of exegesis is required to perceive the relevance of this vision for contemporary ecological efforts, in particular, the endeavor to rescue nature from the onslaught of both technological mastery and meta-physical-theological vilification. As Enrique Dussel writes, commenting on Panikkar: "We are made aware by the ecological movements of the deadly risk for the human race entailed by the destruction of Mother Earth. It is simply a matter of suicide: nature's death is our death."[32]

At least equally important as their ecological relevance is the *kenotic* zeal of the Franciscan saints: their self-emptying openness toward nature, spirit, and the divine, and their corresponding turning away from possessions in favor of (voluntary) poverty and simplicity. In an age dominated by materialistic accumulation and unlimited consumerism, the humility and simple lifestyle practiced by the Franciscans may yet constitute the greatest challenge to the reigning "idols of the market" (*idola fori*). Cousins, the renowned expert on Bonaventure and Cusanus, eloquently articulates the contemporary significance of the Franciscan saints along both ecological and practical-economic lines. "In an age when the environment is being threatened by pollution," he writes, "modern man can learn much from Francis's respect and love for creation. At a time when our natural resources are being depleted and when the Third World is demanding in justice its equal share of available goods, Franciscan poverty may have a new prophetic message for our age." This message deserves a hearing for the sake of both justice and peace. Cousins also perceives Franciscan spirituality as providing an important resource for nurturing an inter-faith dialogue in our globalizing world. "Bonaventure's Franciscan joy in the fecundity of God and creation," he states, "may be extended into the sphere of religious experience and provide a theoretical context for opening to ecumenism and the convergence of world spiritualities."[33]

In our time, many people share a sense of looming ecological di-
saster and the immense gulf yawning between affluence and poverty,
between First World societies and people living in Third or Fourth
World countries. By itself, however, such awareness often remains
passive and fatalistic. To resist the temptations of apathy, transformative education is needed, an education that, in addition to spreading knowledge, strengthens the commitment to social justice. Here,
Franciscan spirituality offers crucial guideposts. Following the example of the Franciscan saints, transformative education needs to combine action or practice with meditative prayer, and it must address
not only the intellect but also the heart (or soul). Shortly before his
death, Brazilian educator Paulo Freire (famous for his book *Pedagogy
of the Oppressed*) completed a study titled *Pedagogy of the Heart.* In
that text, Freire placed himself squarely in the legacy of Franciscan
humility and faithfulness. "It is not easy to have faith," he writes, and
the difficulty arises "because of the demands which faith places on believers"—specifically the demands of justice, humility, and tolerance.
The proper practice of transformative faith, he adds, requires *kenosis,* a kind of self-emptying that gets rid of the obsession with power
and status: "While genuine faith can emerge among the abused and
marginalized, it is less likely to blossom among the arrogant. In order
for the latter to be touched by faith, they first need to be emptied of
the power that makes them all-powerful." In the spirit of Francis and
Bonaventure, Freire concludes that it is possible and imperative to
be humble and unassuming without accepting humiliation, and to be
strong in the practice of justice without being hostile or aggressive.
This possibility, however, depends on a "pedagogy of the heart" or an
itinerarium mentis in Deum.[34]

2. Walking Humbly with Your God

Jñanadev and the Warkari Movement

From afar (O so far) I begin to see the city of Pandharpur.
—Vasant Sawant

Coming from the West, the contemporary traveler to India often has the sense of visiting another planet. Many customs and practices seem alien or remote, as do the underlying beliefs and motives. If this is true of contemporary India, how much greater would this sense of distance be if visiting medieval India? That place, with its philosophy, literature, and religion, would seem like a lost city, surrounded by nearly impenetrable underbrush. How would one approach such a place, from our modern angle, without disrupting or violating its intrinsic order? Clearly, if such a visit were attempted, one would have to approach not as a conquistador but rather as a student, eager not to impart instruction but to receive it. These considerations guide my steps as I seek to encounter and interrogate one of the great and justly revered figures of medieval India: the Marathi poet-saint and thinker Jñanadev (1275–1296). (His name is often rendered Dnyanadev or Dnyaneshwar, and he was a near contemporary of Saint Bonaventure.) Accordingly, the tenor of my comments throughout is that of a commemorative search—a search for whatever Jñanadev may have to teach a visitor coming from my time and place.

Even at first glance, Jñanadev's lifework is enticing and impressive. In his short life, he managed to compose a major philosophical treatise (the *Amritanubhava*), a large number of religious poems

40

(so-called *abhangas*), an extensive poetic commentary on the Bhaga-vad Gita (titled, after his name, *Jñaneshwari* or *Dnyaneshwari*), and a number of shorter works. Appreciation and admiration are bound to deepen by a closer reading of these texts. Despite a diversity of genres, Jñanadev's writings are held together or animated by a common theme. This theme—which may well be Jñanadev's chief legacy to modern visitors like us—is the centrality of love, or *bhakti*. Here, *bhakti* does not mean an emotive sentimentalism but rather a genuine turning-about of the whole being (including mind, heart, and senses). In this respect, his outlook stands in sharp contrast to that of Western modernity, which in large measure has been wedded to a "cognitive" project conducted chiefly under scientific auspices: the project of rendering everything "known" and hence amenable to (technical) control.

Without spurning knowledge, Jñanadev's voice reaches us on a different level. Faithful to the teachings of the Bhagavad Gita, he gives pride of place to *bhakti marga,* without dismissing the other paths, or *margas.* Although of a subtle mind (and despite his given name), Jñanadev is not primarily a devotee of *jñana,* if by that term we mean an abstract reasoning seeking to gain universal knowledge of things. Similarly, he is not simply a doer or a political activist, if (for the moment) we translate *karma yoga* in that sense. Still, over the centuries, his life and work have inspired a large group of followers in his homeland, with concrete practical consequences. For present purposes, I focus my discussion on three main topics: the lifeworld of Jñanadev as the nourishing soil of his writings; the central direction of his philosophical thought, as revealed chiefly in the *Amritanubhava;* and the so-called Warkari Panth, a popular movement largely inspired by his work and centered around periodic pilgrimages to the sacred city of Pandharpur.

An Outcaste Brahmin

Although distant in time and place, Jñanadev's work is not entirely inaccessible to us because, by his own admission, his poetry has always been anchored in the concrete life experience of an ordinary human being who was not given to exotic flights of fancy. Hence, no visit to this medieval saint could be fruitful without some acquaintance with the fortunes and misfortunes of his life. Although surrounded by legend, much of his actual life story—including his genealogy—has been transmitted over the centuries more or less intact, with only minor variations. My point here is not to recount the details of his life story or his ancestry—something that has been done repeatedly by experts on medieval India. Instead, I want to recall, in the spirit of this commemorative search, some particularly striking or revealing aspects of his story that may also harbor a lesson for us and our time.

As we know, Jñanadev's life was marked by much agony and suffering. In large measure, this suffering had to do with his family's situation and its disjointed place in society. James Edwards calls him an "out-caste Brahmin," which in many ways seems an apt description. This status as an outcaste derived from certain actions of his father, a Brahmin named Vithalpant from the Deccan village of Alandi. These actions came to overshadow the entire family, including his four children (of which Jñanadev was the second), and although they may have been unconventional, they were neither criminal nor (in the main) morally reprehensible; in fact, they remain religiously and existentially memorable. As the story goes, Vithalpant got married at a young age to a woman named Rukmini (or Rakhumabai) who loved him dearly and in due course bore him three sons and one daughter. Of a somewhat melancholy disposition, and uncomfortable with ordinary family duties—the life of a householder—Vithalpant left his family and traveled north to Banaras, where he joined an ashram of ascetic *sannyasins*. This is where the lesson begins.

As it happened, the chief pandit of that ashram, a wise man called Ramananda (or Ramashrama), soon went on a pilgrimage through the south of India, which brought him to Alandi. There, by chance, he met a tearful and desolate Rukmini, who told him of the departure of her husband. Quickly discerning the identity of that husband, Ramananda returned to Banaras and ordered Vithalpant to rejoin his family in Alandi. Obedient to his guru, Vithalpant did as he was told and resumed the householder's life, fully aware of the dire consequences of this move. Once back in Alandi, he and his wife were outcast by the ruling Brahmin elite, who denounced Vithalpant for mixing up the life stages and for contaminating *sannyasa* (renunciation) with worldly family concerns. What was most painful was that the ostracism extended from the parents to their offspring, who were now literally the children of nobody (because a *sannyasin* could not have children). As reported by Edwards, the whole family spent the rest of their lives "amid persecution, ridicule, and poverty." Despairing of any earthly remedy for their ills, Vithalpant and his wife committed suicide by jumping into the river Ganges—in Edwards's account, they "sought penance and oblivion by drowning"—when Jñanadev was just eight years of age.[1]

What I want to focus on here is neither the beginning of the story (Vithalpant's departure from home) nor the ending (the joint suicide)—aspects that may engender mixed reactions. Instead, what I want to commemorate is the central drama of the story: Rukmini's unwavering love, the wisdom of the guru Ramananda, and Vithalpant's return to his family. It seems to me that the story illustrates two radically different and conflicting conceptions of religion and the path to salvation. On the one side, religion denotes surrender to a distant and forbidding overlord who demands complete denial of earthly bonds; on the other side, it means the practice—indeed, the loving practice—of concrete human relations, including family obligations. The contrast also involves conflicting images of the divine: on the one side, God is an external overseer forever uncontaminated by human concerns and agonies; on the other side, the divine is intimately involved and actively present in worldly affairs—a presence that can be discerned with the help of a loving heart. To this extent, Vithalpant's story illustrates a central point of *bhakti* religiosity: that the path to God leads *through* the world, in an ascent of love.[2] This bifurcation of religious views also implies a social bifurcation or stratification. Whereas a remote or shrouded God is held to be accessible only to a small elite of pandits, or the privileged priestly caste, *bhakti* religiosity is available to everyone in all walks of life. Whereas the Alandi priests, in their arrogance, claimed to "possess" God by virtue of their Vedic knowledge (*jñana*) and rituals, Vithalpant learned that the divine can never be possessed but can only be pursued or intimated by giving service.[3]

The lesson of Vithalpant's experience is underscored and corroborated by another story dear to *bhakti* religiosity. This story has to do with the origin and religious significance of the city of Pandharpur. Although not directly part of Jñanadev's biography, the story is more than incidentally related to the saint's life, given that Pandharpur was visited in pilgrimage by both Vithalpant and his son and serves as a permanent destination for all Warkari pilgrims. The central figure of the story is a *muni* (sage) named Pundalik who lived in Pandharpur with his family. According to the story, the young Pundalik led a dissolute and self-indulgent life, and he showed little concern, and in fact great disrespect, for his parents and other relatives. Later, however, his heart was turned around and he became a caring son who was eager to help his aging and ailing parents. At this point, a great deity, the god Vithoba, paid a visit to Pandharpur and to Pundalik's home. As it happened, Pundalik was busy caring for his father, massaging his feet, when he noticed the approach of the deity; he interrupted his ministrations only long enough to throw a brick over his shoulder for Vithoba to stand on to protect his feet from the mud (it was the rainy season). Far from being outraged or offended, Vithoba was deeply touched by Pundalik's devotion and decided to make that spot his dwelling place. Thus, since that time, Vithoba has remained standing upright on the same brick (now the heart of the main temple in Pandharpur), teaching us that love of God is not separate from love of family, friends, and fellow beings. In fact, to love God means precisely to love our fellow beings (beginning with those close to us).[4]

Returning to Jñanadev, I want to recount a few instructive episodes from his life. One such episode is the story of the "Veda-reciting buffalo." Following the suicide of their parents, the children were reduced to begging and a condition of abject poverty. To remove the stain of the outcaste, the children decided to approach the highest-ranking priests in the Deccan and plead for mercy. Thus, Jñanadev and his older brother journeyed from Alandi to the priests in Paithan (according to the historian Mahipati, Jñanadev was then about twelve years of age). Instead of showing sympathy and mercy, however, the Brahmins only heaped insult and ridicule on the orphaned boys, calling them ignorant beggars and illegitimate offspring of a *sannyasin*. Meanwhile (according to Mahipati), on a nearby road, a man was leading an old, worn-out buffalo with packs strapped to its back. The animal was barely able to move, but its master urged it forward with violent lashings, which caused it to nearly collapse in a flood of tears. Jñanadev, filled with pity and in tears himself, pleaded with the man to desist. Far from sharing his pity, the Brahmins only intensified their ridicule, chiding Jñanadev for showing concern for a dumb beast while being unconcerned about higher learning, especially the teachings of the Vedas. The young boy, however, rose to the occasion by posing a question to the priests. Was it not the teaching of the Vedas, he asked, that the sacredness of all life is a manifestation of *brahman* or the divine? Dumbfounded and outraged, the priests retorted that, by Jñanadev's logic, Vedic learning should be accessible not only to Brahmins but also to brute beasts. Undismayed, Jñanadev placed his hand on the animal's forehead, and "there was a deep utterance of a Vedic song coming from its mouth."[5] I am concerned here not with historical accuracy but rather with symbolic significance. What the story teaches, I believe, is (again) that the divine is not the property of a learned elite; rather, it is spread out as a gift, a largesse, over all creation. (Christians may recall that Jesus reportedly told the priests in Jerusalem that God is able "from these very stones to raise up children to Abraham" [Matthew 3:9]).[6]

Another episode involves Jñanadev's encounter with a mighty yogi named Changdev (or Changadeva), a man reportedly endowed with uncanny magical powers and intensely proud of those powers. As the story goes, Changdev—whose magic enabled him to ride on a tiger and use a snake for a whip—was prodded by Jñanadev's fiercest enemy in Alandi, a fellow named Visoba Chati, to square off against Jñanadev to squash the young man's spreading reputation of saintliness. Spurred by his numerous disciples, Changdev decided to challenge Jñanadev to a contest of yogic powers. In response, Jñanadev sent Changdev a sixty-five verse poem known as the *Changdev Pasashthi*. This poem, instead of dazzling the reader with exotic insights or magical tricks, simply celebrated God's infinite love for his creatures, a love that humans should reciprocate with a gentle heart and in generous fellowship. On reading this poem, Changdev felt ashamed of his conceit and self-importance. Descending from his tiger, he bowed before Jñanadev and placed his head on his feet, indicating the surrender of magic to *bhakti*. Again, my concern here is not with historical detail but with the story's lesson. As we know, there are many conceited yogis in the Western world today, people who have parlayed their yogic powers into huge financial empires. Here, Jñanadev cautions us to be on guard. As he writes eloquently in his *Jñaneshwari:*

Like a foolish farmer giving up his old business and beginning something new every day, the man overpowered by ignorance installs new images of gods often and again, and worships them with the same intensity. He becomes the disciple of a guru who is surrounded by worldly pomp, gets himself initiated by him and is unwilling to see any other person who has got real spiritual dignity. He is cruel to every being, worships various stone images and has no consistency of heart.

For a reader from the West, these lines from *Jñaneshwari* as well as the Changdev story may evoke the memory of Micah's pithy and timeless standard of true religiosity: "to do justice, love kindness, and walk humbly with your God" (Micah 6:8).[7]

A final aspect of Jñanadev's biography that deserves to be mentioned is his own relation with his fellow beings. Throughout his life, Jñanadev's attitude was exemplary in its display of gentleness and forbearance, especially toward his sworn enemies. There were, however, some special relationships that testify to the quality of his heart. According to some accounts, Jñanadev was linked in affection and perhaps in love with the daughter of his archenemy Visoba Chati. But the story is too apocryphal, and patterned too much on well-known romantic models, to deserve much credence. Another linkage, however, is amply attested to by historical records: Jñanadev's friendship with the poet-saint Namadev, who was five years his senior. According to these accounts, the two saints first met in Pandharpur and immediately struck up a close companionship. While in Pandharpur, Jñanadev became a devotee of the god Vithoba (the deity Pundalik had induced to stay in that city) and also commended Namadev to the god's care. Subsequently, the two saints went on a prolonged pilgrimage together, visiting most of the holy places in northern India, including Banaras and Delhi. When they returned to Pandharpur (in 1296), a great festival was held in their honor, and according to Bahirat, many contemporary saints participated, including "Goroba the potter, Sanvata the gardener, Chokhoba the untouchable, Parisa Bhagawat the Brahmin, and others."

It was at the end of this festival that Jñanadev expressed the wish to return to Alandi and enter *sanjivan samadhi* (final release). On hearing this, Namadev was desolate, but he honored his friend's wish. Back in Alandi, the sons of Namadev first swept clean the place of burial. Then, Bahirat reports: "Namadev besmeared the body of

Jñanadeva with the sandal-paste, marked his forehead with the pigment of musk, waved sacred lights and paid homage to the dearest of his heart." At the completion of the *samadhi,* according to Mahipati's account, all the bystanders were gripped by deep sorrow remembering the "sweet company" of the saint. Namadev himself was inconsolable and asked Vithoba to allow Jñanadev to return to life for another meeting. And "tradition says that Namadev and Jñanadev again met in loving conversation," testifying to the immortality of genuine friendship and the companionship of noble and loving hearts.[8]

A Nectar of Wisdom

In light of his life story, and especially its ending—complete absorption into the divine—it is clear why Jñanadev is celebrated chiefly as a saint, a person whose devotion offered inspiration both to his contemporaries and to those living in the centuries to come. Still, an appreciation of his life's impact would be truncated without attention to his written works and the intellectual or philosophical outlook displayed therein. As previously indicated, Jñanadev's writings are not esoteric treatises addressed to a small elite of pandits (they are composed not in Sanskrit but in vernacular Marathi). Rather, they were nurtured by, and continually hark back to, his concrete life experience, thus giving evidence of a life reflectively lived.[9] An exemplar of humble devotion, Jñanadev was also a *thinking* saint and, moreover, an imaginatively poetic thinker, as illustrated by his *Jñaneshwari* and *Amritanubhava,* works that are justly famous for both their searching insights and their poetic style (thus confounding the rigid compartmentalization of philosophy, poetry, and theology). For present purposes, I center my attention on the *Amritanubhava,* a philosophical poem written at the behest of his older brother and guru Nivrittinath, at a time when Jñanadev was probably in his late teens.

In the philosophical literature, Jñanadev is sometimes compared with the great intellectual *acharyas* (teachers) of medieval India. Thus, according to some interpreters, Jñanadev's outlook is akin to that of the philosopher-saint Shankaracharya, with some believing that Jñanadev provides nothing but a poetic embellishment of Shankara's views. Stressing the devotional or *bhakti* element, other interpreters have likened his thought to the modified nondualism (*vishisht-advaita*) of Ramanuja or, less frequently, to the strict dualism of Madhva or the pure monism of Vallabha. Although suggestive, all these interpretations need to be taken with a grain of salt. On the positive side, such comparisons evince a willingness to treat Jñanadev on a par with India's great philosophical thinkers and teachers. On the downside, these readings also tend to shortchange the originality of Jñanadev's views, thus depriving modern readers of a distinct learning experience. For these and other reasons, I am inclined to agree with Bahirat when he writes that prevalent interpretations have, on the whole, "underestimated the distinct individuality of Jñanadeva" and that there is a need to reexamine "his philosophy independently and to set in clear relief his views on the ultimate problems of life." I also concur with his statement that Jñanadev's opus is a living philosophy and not "a matter of mere antiquity or a dry skeleton of speculative games."[10] His writings not only provided inspiration for *bhakti* movements in his native Maharashtra; they also offer food for thought for contemporary philosophy in general.

As its title indicates, the *Amritanubhava* is meant to be a "nectar of wisdom" that offers readers a glimpse into the nature of "ultimate experience." In the language of the Upanishads and also of much of Western philosophy, the text is meant to serve as a guide to the understanding of *brahman,* or "being" (although Jñanadev refrains from using the term *brahman*). Here, the first crucial distinctiveness of his thought emerges: *being* for Jñanadev is not an object of thought; it is what allows thought to happen in the first place. Differently phrased, *being* precedes and enables acts of cognition; in a way, it always operates "behind our backs" before and even during our attempts to approach and formulate its nature. To this extent, *being* is not a concept; it is preconceptual. Nor is it just a category of reason (in the sense of a Kantian "condition of possibility"); rather, it is a presupposition of thinking and living as such. In a similar vein, *being* antedates method and epistemology rather than being grounded in them; in Gadamerian language, Jñanadev foregrounds the "truth" of *being* over the "method" or methodology of its philosophical analysis. His text, in fact, is somewhat cavalier about the traditional methods or epistemologies (*pramanas*) sanctioned by classical Indian philosophy. Without dismissing them completely, he finds their validity limited and experientially limiting. Thus, sense (or sensory) experience "makes sense" only in light of another, deeper understanding; likewise, reason is "rational" only through excess or by exceeding itself. Jñanadev is cautious about exclusive reliance on classical scriptural authority—a *pramana* strongly accentuated by the school of Vedanta and also by adherents of Mimamsa and Purvamimamsa (scriptural interpretation). For Jñanadev, the truth of experience is not so much validated or authenticated by scriptures; rather, scriptures gain their authoritative standing through their congruence with experiential truth. As he states: "The absolute does not prove or disprove itself with the help of any norms or methods of knowledge. . . . The lamp lit up at midday neither dispels darkness nor spreads light."[11]

Operating behind our backs, ultimate experience antedates the division between subject and object and also the dualities of existence and nonexistence and of knowledge and nonknowledge (or ignorance). For Jñanadev, the division between knower and known is not so much a warrant of correctness or objective truth; rather, it is the derivative outgrowth of an experience that ultimately confounds and contaminates both. In the fifth chapter of *Amritanubhava,* Jñanadev comments on the classical designation of *being* as *sat-chit-ananda,* that is, as the confluence of existence (or reality), consciousness (or knowledge), and bliss. According to Jñanadev, these terms offer guideposts or clues, at best; they cannot be used (either singly or in combination) as objective descriptions of *being* without becoming intrinsically incoherent. None of the terms is properly self-contained, since each points beyond itself (toward its other). In Jñanadev's words: "The poisonousness of the poison is no poison to itself." In a similar way, the terms *existence* and *consciousness* (or *knowledge*) gain meaning and contours only by reference to their counterterms *nonexistence* and *nonconsciousness* (or *nonknowledge*). Hence, the expression *sat-chit-ananda* should be seen not as offering an objective or exhaustive definition of *being* but rather as a stand-in or placeholder for reflection to ward off affirmation of its opposites. For Jñanadev, the terms *existence, consciousness,* and *bliss*—as used in classical scriptures—were not meant descriptively but rather as vehicles to shield *being* from its identification with nonexistence, unconscious materiality, and pain (*dukkha*). To cite the *Amritanubhava* again: "Being by itself, the absolute is beyond the ordinary conceptions of existence and non-existence." Such terms as *nonexistence, nonconsciousness,* and *nonbliss* are counterterms or "countercorrelations" of the scriptural terms and are needed to profile the latter. Properly construed, the expression *sat-chit-ananda* does not "denote the nature (of being), but differentiates it from its opposites." Looked at from this angle, the scriptural words appear as "the residues of our thought"; in the light of *being* itself, "they vanish like the clouds that shower rain, or like the streams that flow into the sea or the paths that reach their goal."[12]

In these lines, Jñanadev clearly distances himself from an essentialist metaphysics, but without lapsing into antiessentialism or a bland negativism. Influenced perhaps by Buddhist teachings, his text steers clear of positive affirmation but remains equally on guard against an extreme form of *shunyavada*, whereby *shunya* (emptiness) is reduced to a sheer vacuum or radical negativity. As is well known, a turn to emptiness in this sense is sometimes (though probably incorrectly) ascribed to Madhyamika Buddhism as formulated by the philosopher Nagarjuna. More recently, in the context of Western thought, the critique of "foundational" (or essential) metaphysics has encouraged in some quarters a flirtation with a radical "antifoundationalism," a term meant to signal the triumph of absence over presence, of contingency over necessity, and of artifact over (stable) nature. For Jñanadev, the exchange of foundation for nonfoundation is a bad and unwarranted bargain. In his view, the absolute cannot be definitely grasped by either affirmation or negation, nor by a bland synthesis of the two. The fourth chapter of *Amritanubhava* offers a strong and persuasive indictment of the retreat into negativism, or a purely negative antifoundationalism. If one asserts that the absolute "neither exists nor non-exists," he writes, one seems to allow the possibility of its nonexistence. But, he adds, "if the situation is such that nothing at all exists, who then knows [and can say] that there is nothing?" Hence, the theory of emptiness (as nothingness) appears as an "unjust imputation" to *being*, for "if the extinguisher of a light is extinguished along with the light, who knows that there is no light?"[13]

Shying away from epistemic description, Jñanadev (rightly) prefers the use of poetic-religious language. Regarding the relation between *being* and *world*—a relation sometimes termed "ontic-ontological difference"—his text avoids both duality and coincidence, invoking instead the image of parenting. The opening chapter of the *Amritanubhava* pays tribute to the loving union of Shiva and Shakti, seen as "the limitless primal parents of the universe." The two deities are mutually lover and beloved, in an unending sport of love. In their loving embrace, the two are "neither completely identical nor completely different"; while trying to maintain duality for the sake of allowing embrace, their difference is "abashed to see their intimacy merging itself in sweet union." Thus, Jñanadev says, "it is through God [Shiva] that the other is Goddess [Shakti], and without her the Lord is nowhere." Just as "two lips utter but one word and two eyes give one vision," in the same way, "the two [Shiva and Shakti] engender one world."[14] Here (I believe) it is important to pay attention to the image of parenting or engendering, as distinct from the images of emanation, on the one hand, and instrumental creation or fabrication, on the other. As presented by Jñanadev, parenting involves a creative act whereby the union of parents gives birth to their offspring in a manner that allows the latter to *be* (on their own). Seen as parents, Shiva and Shakti are not abstract transcendental principles from which the world could emanate or be derived through a process of "transcendental deduction"—a process in which the derivative is already fully contained in its premises and thus is deprived of autonomous being or life. Likewise, in the case of fabrication, the product is already preshaped in the mind of the producer, like the shoe in the head of the shoemaker (which denies life to the shoe). Parenting, however, implies the joining of partners, male and female, in a life-giving and life-sustaining union.

Jñanadev's portrayal of divine parenting differs not only from general cosmological theories but also from more specific doctrines indigenous to the Indian tradition. One such view is the conception of *purusha* and *prakriti,* as formulated by versions of the Samkhya school of philosophy. In this view, *purusha* denotes something like "spirit" or "transcendental spectator," while *prakriti* means "matter" or "material energy." Carried to its logical conclusion, this doctrine implies the thesis of two ultimate principles constantly at odds with each other. In his account of divine parenting and the loving embrace of Shiva and Shakti, Jñanadev completely rejects this Manichean view, with its bent toward schizophrenia as a universal pathology. A modified version of the Samkhya outlook can be found in Advaita Vedanta, provided the latter is interpreted as an essentialist metaphysics along quasi-Platonic lines. In the eyes of some interpreters, Shankara's thought can be reduced (perhaps rashly) to a stark "two-world" formula, that is, to an outlook separating a realm of essences from one of appearances, a true world (*brahman*) from a merely illusory world (*maya*), and genuine knowledge from a spurious claim to knowledge arising from ignorance (*mayavada, ajñanavada, avidya*).

In this reading of Vedanta, the ordinary world of human experience is merely a figment of the imagination that must be discarded in order to break through to true epistemic insight. Leaving aside the correctness of this construal, it is clear that Jñanadev's experiential approach to thinking clashes sharply with any two-world formula. In fact, the seventh (and longest) chapter of *Amritanubhava* is entirely devoted to a refutation of *ajñanavada* or *mayavada*, though without any mention of Shankara (which may be telling). As Jñanadev shows persuasively, the bifurcation between essence and appearance, knowledge and illusion, is deeply incoherent and contradictory. If the "true" world is the only valid and comprehensive one, how can an "apparent" world even arise, without disrupting the former's truth and comprehensiveness? Moreover, banished from knowledge, how can ignorance be "known" to be illusory? In Jñanadev's words: "How can ignorance that pales before inquiring thought, get eye-sight and see itself in the form of the visible world in front of it?"[15]

In rejecting the two-world formula, Jñanadev restores dignity and integrity to ordinary life experience, but without allowing it to drift into pure contingency and *avidya*. Faithful to his image of parenting, his text presents the ordinary world (or lifeworld) as the living offspring of divine union, and as such, it is neither completely subsumed under nor cut adrift from that union. In this portrayal, what links offspring and parents is neither logical derivation nor empirical causation but rather mutual love and devotion (*bhakti*). Loving care is not simply a subjective feeling but the very core of being itself. In the ninth chapter of his *Amritanubhava*, Jñanadev describes the relation between offspring and parents in terms of "natural devotion," which is said to be a "wonderful secret," without demanding esoteric knowledge. Commentators have linked this devotion with the doctrine of *sphurtivada*, meaning devotional or mystical insight, or the theory of *childivas*, which regards the world as the "sport" of *being* or as the sporting delight of divine union. What these concepts suggest is some kind of pantheism (or, better "pan-en-theism"), but its character needs to be carefully pondered. Jñanadev does not claim that the world, or everything in the world, is divine as such (which would be a form of immanentism), but only that it is divine "secretly" or "wondrously," in the sense that the secret is manifest to loving eyes (which can release in things the divine power, or *shekinah*). Without *bhakti*, the world may seem to tumble into darkness and despair, but in fact, the eyes of love are never really shut because knower and known, seer and seen, are always already held in caring embrace. In Jñanadev's words: "The non-dual enters of its own accord the courtyard of duality; and the unity deepens along with the growth of difference."[16]

For Jñanadev, natural devotion is an ordinary experience available to every being in the world, but it is also a "wondrous secret" that deserves to be tended by a caring and loving heart. In its continually sustaining power, devotional care is not so much a distant goal that needs to be deliberately pursued or implemented; rather, it is always there, lying in wait for humans, inviting them to settle down in its comfort. Viewed in terms of the traditional *purusharthas* (goals of life), *bhakti* is a peculiar kind of nongoal, without being negligible or marginal to human life. Compared with the supreme goal of *moksha* (salvation), *bhakti* offers a unique mode of emancipation—a liberation not *from* but *in* the world, allowing humans to live freely and caringly. Here is how Jñanadev expresses it: For the *bhakta*, "the enjoyment of sense objects becomes sweeter than the bliss of emancipation (*moksha*), and in the home of loving devotion, the devotee and god experience their sweet union." At this juncture, the glory of emancipation simply serves as "a sitting carpet for the *bhakta's* condition." Seated on this carpet, every human being can enjoy *amritanubhava*, that is, "the festival of this nectar of spiritual experience."[17]

Walking Humbly with Your God

Jñanadev's thought, as reflected in his writings, has not been consigned to library archives. His work still provides living inspiration to *bhakti* religiosity in his native Maharashtra and throughout the Indian subcontinent. The closest linkage, however, is with a particular *bhakti* movement, the so-called Warkaris, whose devotion centers around periodic pilgrimages to Pandharpur. This linkage goes back to Jñanadev's own pilgrimage to that city with his friend Namadev, at which time Jñanadev became a devotee of Vithoba and was introduced to the practices of Warkari pilgrims. Following his *samadhi*, both his life and his writings developed into primary exemplars of genuine religiosity for the Warkari movement, as well as crucial sources and focal points of *bhakti* devotion. Throughout the ensuing centuries, and down to the present, Jñanadev's poems continued to be remembered and chanted by pilgrims in the form of popular *bhajans* (songs), just as his teachings are transmitted in *kirtans*, which combine song and dance with exegetic commentary and instruction.

Given its deep ties to the poet-saint, the character and distinctive practices of the Warkari movement closely emulate his legacy. Throughout his short life, Jñanadev was always at the mercy of the arrogance and vindictiveness of the ruling priestly elite, which relegated his family to outcaste status. Jñanadev never reciprocated harshly or in kind; clearly, he was animated by a completely different standard of religiosity: the standard of castelessness, nonhierarchy, and caring human fellowship. Congruent with *bhakti* devotion, this standard became a model for the Warkari movement. According to the account by Eleanor Zelliot, three main features of Jñanadev's life carried over into the Warkari movement: "implicit criticism of Brahmanical narrowness, egalitarianism in spiritual matters, and family-centered life." These features were thoroughly embraced by his friend Namadev, who in many ways was instrumental in shaping the outlook and living ethos of the movement. Under Namadev's guidance, the movement gathered an extraordinary company of saints and poets, a company that reflected "almost the complete range of the populace of Maharashtra" at the time. Among others, the group included Parisa Bhagavata, a Vaishnava Brahmin; Changdeva, the yogi turned saint; Visoba Khechara, a Shaivite and guru of Namadev; Gora the potter, who used to evaluate saints as "baked" or "half-baked"; Savata the gardener; Sena the barber; Jagamitra Naga, the banker turned beggar; Janabai, the serving maid of Namadev; and, above all, Chokhamela the untouchable Mahar, whose wife, son, and sister all wrote *abhangas* to Vithoba. Later, according to Zelliot, the movement even included a number of Muslims, most importantly, Sheikh Muhammad, the Muslim *bhakta* and *sant*. Among later followers were Eknath, the householder Brahmin and editor of *Jñaneshwari*, and the Shudra poet-saint Tukaram, a contemporary of Shivaji.[18]

The cross-caste and socially nonexclusive character of the movement also carries over into a kind of religious nonsectarianism. Although organized in local or neighborhood sections, or *dindis*, the Warkaris freely welcome nonmembers and fellow travelers of diverse sectarian and religious backgrounds into their processions to Pandharpur (as illustrated in Mokashi's *Palkhi*). This open attitude—not to be confused with syncretism—seems at least indirectly connected with the non- or multisectarian character of Pandharpur as a place of worship. Etymologically, the name of the city derives from Pandurang, a name of Shiva—the deity originally worshipped there. Arriving in the city at a later date, the god Vithoba never completely erased the earlier tradition. Theologically, Vithoba (or Vitthal) is viewed not just as an avatar but also as a *swarup* (or original form) of Vishnu-Krishna. In *bhakti* literature, following the god's arrival, Vithoba was also given the epithet "Pandurang." However, as Zelliot notes, the usage is perplexing, because "Panduranga means the White One—a strange epithet for a black god." The perplexity persists in present-day Pandharpur, where "the temple of god Vithoba, a *swarup* or original Vishnu, is surrounded by temples of Shaivite gods."[19]

The situation is even more complex, however, because the manifest images of deities—Shiva and Vishnu-Krishna—appear to be overshadowed by an awareness of the formless or hidden "otherness" of the divine. In Zelliot's words, Vithoba is "an almost quality-less god," curiously distanced from the luxuriant mythological narratives that usually surround Hindu gods. To this extent, the reigning deity in Pandharpur, and the sacredness of the city itself, seems intriguingly placed at a crossroads between the manifest and nonmanifest, between revealment and concealment, familiarity and nonfamiliarity—or, in Indian terminology, between *saguna* and *nirguna*—which is a fitting reflection of Jñanadev's legacy. To quote Charlotte Vaudeville on this point: "The spiritual attitude [of the poet-saints, or *sants*] tends to blur not only the distinction between *nirguna* and *saguna,* but also the traditional distinction between Shaivism and Vaishnavism. In Maharashtra—as well as Gujarat and later on in Karnataka—it is possible to follow step by step the gradual merging of the Shaiva faith into the nonsectarian Vaishnava *bhakti* of the *sants.*"[20]

The unusual character of Warkari religiosity is also reflected in the movement's relation to pilgrimage. As mentioned, periodic pilgrimages to Pandharpur are central to the Warkaris' life, but not in the same way as pilgrimages to other holy places such as Banaras or Dwarka. In the general Hindu tradition, the focus is typically on the destination of the pilgrimage, the sacred center of worship. But in the case of the Warkaris, the accent is not so much on the destination as on the journey itself. Differently phrased, sacredness is not an extrinsic end but rather the very heart of the pilgrimage; Pandharpur "inhabits" the journey from beginning to end. In the words of Philip Engblom, the Warkaris' journey is "more than just a means to attain the goal of *darshan* of Vitthal in Pandharpur"; it carries it own significance "as a spiritual discipline." As Engblom comments, the term *Warkari* comes from the root *wari*, which means "journeying" or "coming and going." Hence, a Warkari is basically (and not just occasionally) a wayfarer or pilgrim. However, the character of this wayfaring must be carefully noted, especially in the age of jet travel and restless migration in the "global village." Obviously, Warkaris are not tourists or vacationers traveling to distant places for fun and exotic thrills. Nor are they simply vagabonds or aimless nomads, moving about for no particular reason except for the purpose of being "on the road." Although not governed by an external goal or destination—and, in that sense, going "nowhere"—the Warkaris' journeying is not just a pointless drifting. Instead, it displays a kind of "discipline" because it is undertaken as an act of devotion (or *bhakti*). To this extent, the Warkari is a *homo viator* (in the sense of Gabriel Marcel), a wayfarer whose main concern is the search for the proper "way" and the proper manner of being "on the way."[21]

This kind of search is manifest in the general conduct of the Warkaris, who go about their ordinary lives with an ear for the more than ordinary or divine. Throughout the centuries, from the time of Jñanadev, one of the main attractions of the Warkari Panth has been its nonesoteric and nonelitist quality and its openness to those from all walks of life. Emulating Vithalpant, most of the great poet-saints of the movement have not been *sannyasins* but rather family people or householders. As Engblom says, "they advocated the practice of the path of devotion (*bhakti marga*) even while living within the entanglements and responsibilities of life in the family and in society (*samsara*)." Or, to rephrase this statement, precisely by leading their ordinary lives, they followed the path of devotion. Being worldly—

though in a peculiarly nonworldly way—the Warkaris' conduct in ethical terms cannot be reduced to either transcendental or empirical (or naturalist) formulas. Journeying along the path of *bhakti* cannot be captured in transcendental imperatives (along Kantian lines) from which individual steps can be deductively derived. Nor is the pursuit of the path governed purely by instinct or subliminal drives. As formulated by Jñanadev, "natural devotion" implies a certain trust in human inclinations, as opposed to their stark suppression (under the auspices of duty or *sannyasa*). However, instead of being geared toward consumerism or vain self-gratification, inclinations here have a transformative quality, serving as vehicles on the ascending path of love. In the words of S. V. Dandekar, a leading figure in the Warkari movement in recent times (specifically its Jñanadev section): "Instead of killing the passions—lust, anger, etc.—one simply turns them over to Hari [God]."[22]

In our secularist age, with its aversion to absolute principles or vistas, the distinctive worldliness of Jñanadev and the Warkaris still deserves to be commemorated and emulated. Especially to Western readers floundering in the wasteland of possessiveness and abstract knowledge, the journeying of the Warkaris may teach us how it is possible to "walk humbly with our God." Jñanadev's short life was, in its entirety, just such a humble walk with God. The legacy of his example has radiated through the centuries down to our day, as only a message of love can. It is fitting to conclude this chapter with lines from the closing prayer that he attached to his *Jñaneshwari:*

And now may God, the soul of the universe,
Be pleased with this my offering of words.
And being pleased may he give me
This favor in return:

That the crookedness of evil-doers may cease,
And that the love of goodness may grow in them.
May all beings experience from each other
the friendship of the heart.[23]

3. Wise Ignorance
Nicolaus of Cusa's Search for Truth

In his approach to the problem of knowledge, Nicolaus of Cusa (1401–1464) can rightly be considered, as Ernst Cassirer observes, "the first modern thinker." The title belongs to him because he first grasped a principle that modern Western philosophy has erected into an unimpeachable doctrine: the principle that rational or scientific knowledge, properly construed, has to be anchored in measurement and empirical comparison—methods that completely sideline traditional metaphysics (with its claim to deliver speculative knowledge). In his long string of writings, Nicolaus of Cusa never ceased to stress this need for measurement, but with a dramatic twist. Had he limited himself to this emphasis, he would have been a modern thinker just like a host of others. What distinguishes him is that he allowed his modern rationality to be touched by a sensibility for the unconditional, the absolute, or the divine—and again, he did so with a dramatic twist. Contrary to the conventional modern opposition between reason and faith, knowledge and belief, Cusanus saw rationality itself inhabited by self-transgression, by a yearning for something that cannot be strictly known but can only be intimated in a mode of "knowing unknowledge" or "learned ignorance." To this extent, although he was modern, Cusanus was also a more than modern thinker, someone who might be able to speak to us today. In the words of Cassirer, yearning for the good or divine "must spur on and give wings" to our thought, "even though the 'what,' the substantive essence of the good, remains inaccessible to knowledge. Here, knowing and not knowing coincide."[1]

The movement from rationality to knowing unknowledge involves not merely a cognitive growth but also an existential transformation or pedagogy—a practical as well as intellectual journey animated by love (traditionally expressed as *amor Dei intellectualis*). In many ways, Cusanus's entire life story can be seen as a restless journey propelled by an intense love of learning and goodness. It will suffice here to recall a few way stations on this remarkable thinker's path. Cusanus was in his early teens when he left his father's house to receive instruction from the Brotherhood of the Common Life, a pedagogical community devoted to personal-experiential piety (the so-called *devotio moderna*) and inspired by German mysticism, especially the teachings of Meister Eckhart. From there, the young man moved to Heidelberg to learn about the emerging and highly innovative construal of medieval philosophy and theology (the *via moderna*). The most decisive influence on his intellectual development, however, came during his Italian period in Padua, where he encountered the rising trend of Renaissance humanism, with its combined accent on both classical (especially Greek) studies and undogmatic, personalized modes of inquiry.

After these youthful peregrinations, Cusanus's mature period was spent mainly in the service of the church: as secretary to the archbishop of Trier, as bishop of Brixen and cardinal in Rome, as emissary of the Vatican to Germany (1450–1452), and finally as personal counselor of Pope Pius II. Although deeply immersed during his later years in church business and practical and political matters, he left behind an incredible wealth of philosophical texts, letters, and other literary documents—a wealth that has staggered great contemporary thinkers (such as Cassirer and Karl Jaspers). For present purposes, rather than attempting a bland overview, I want to join Cusanus in some of his intellectual journeys, focusing on three major aspects: his emphasis on experiential learning and piety; his key notion of the "coincidence of opposites" (linked in "learned ignorance"); and his concern with interreligious harmony and peace.

A Layman's Pedagogy

In many of his writings, Cusanus privileges the outlook of the ordinary layman, the man of the street or the marketplace (*idiota*). No fewer than three of his important texts include the term *layman* in their titles: *The Layman on Wisdom* (*Idiota de Sapientia*), *The Layman on* the *Mind/Spirit* (*Idiota de Mente*), and *The Layman on Experiments* (*Idiota de Staticis Experimentis*). This emphasis is always philosophically significant, but it is especially so in our modern and contemporary era. In large measure, modern Western philosophy has been professionalized, or transformed into an academic discipline; what is called analytical philosophy is, above all, a discourse confined almost entirely to academic logicians and epistemologists. Concerns voiced by ordinary people on the street, by contrast, tend to be sidelined as ignorant chatter unworthy of serious attention. It is on this score that recent trends in European (or Continental) philosophy have initiated a break with the dominant modern mold. The movement of phenomenology, in particular, has called thinkers back into the domain of ordinary experience, into the context of the "lived world" (or lifeworld) antedating or undergirding rational analysis. Under the influence of this and related initiatives, philosophers have come to appreciate again the role of implicit or tacit knowledge (or unknowledge) as a precursor to possible knowledge, of prereflective understandings (or prejudgments) as a preamble to reflective insight. Seen in this light, Cusanus's work resonates in many ways with European existentialism, with its accent on lived experience and human "being-in-the-world."[2]

The privilege accorded to the layman is beautifully articulated in the dialogue titled *The Layman on Wisdom*. Cusanus first sets the stage: "A poor untutored layman (*pauper quidam idiota*) met in the Roman Forum a very wealthy orator whom he smilingly though courteously addressed in the following manner" (a manner clearly reminiscent of Socrates in the marketplace). The layman says, "I am quite amazed at your pride, for even though you have worn yourself out with continual study of innumerable books, yet you have not been moved to humility. The reason is that the 'knowledge of this world,' in which you believe to excel, is actually foolishness in the sight of God; it puffs men up, whereas true knowledge humbles them. I wish you would realize this because it is the treasure of all happiness." To which the orator retorts: "What presumption you display—you an ignorant and untutored layman—in disparaging book learning without which no advance is possible!" Without being irritated in the slightest, the layman responds with great gentleness: "It is not presumption but rather charity or love which keeps me from being silent. For I perceive that you pursue wisdom with much wasted effort, and it is from this futility that I would like to rescue you, if possible." In elaborating on an alternative path to wisdom, the layman does not dismiss book learning per se, but only the extent to which books are treated as the final authority in lieu of actual experience. He adds, reprimanding the orator (and academic philosophy in general): By relying on books, "you trust in [external] authority and in this way you are deceived; because someone has written a text, you are ready to believe. But"—and here comes the layman's (and Nicolaus of Cusa's own) cri de coeur—"I want to tell you that wisdom cries out in the streets, and her very cry indicates how she dwells 'in the highest'" (habitat in altissimis).[3]

The last comment reveals the uncanny quality of the layman's streetwise approach to wisdom, its peculiar mundane-transmundane character (if one wishes, its ontic-ontological status). The continuing dialogue steadily draws the layman and orator into the depths of this street wisdom, announced a few pages later with these words: "The highest wisdom consists in knowing how, in similes, the unattainable may be reached or attained unattainably" (attingitur inattingibile inattingibiliter). Suddenly, we are no longer simply on the street but on a road filled with ordinary-extraordinary surprises. It is Cusanus's very own road, although one charted by many earlier travelers. In her bilingual (Latin-German) edition of The Layman on Wisdom, Renate Steiger draws attention to a host of intellectual and religious precursors. As she points out, ever since the time of Saint Augustine, the term laypeople (homines idiotae) had been applied to individuals speaking and writing in a simple, vernacular idiom. The term was taken over by some of the large mendicant orders of the Middle Ages; thus, Francis of Assisi described himself and his followers as laypeople (idiotae). The orientation reached its pinnacle in the nonmonastic lay movements of the late Middle Ages connected with the devotio moderna, and especially in the Brothers of the Common Life at Deventer (where both Cusanus and later Erasmus received formative instruction). These movements, in turn, were inspired by some of the great mystical thinkers of the past, stretching from Dionysius the Aeropagite, Johannes Gerson, and Meister Eckhart to Bernard of Clairvaux and the Imitatio Christi. According to Steiger, what distinguished the entire lay tradition was, above all, "a pathos of immediacy: the immediacy of concrete experience as contrasted with mere book learning and a purely scholastic treatment of real life." It was also such a pathos because "wisdom was no longer the exclusive province of clerics and doctors."[4]

Though deriving rich sources of inspiration from the past, it is well known that Cusanus's emphasis on laymen and lived experience resonated profoundly with important strands in Renaissance thought. Here again, Cassirer can be consulted with benefit. As he observes, innovative thinkers of the Renaissance period could no longer rely on prevailing academic teachings, which remained "bound to forms of scholastic thought and scholastic erudition." This tradition-bound outlook was hostile both to genuine philosophy and to art. Thus, the poet Petrarch vigorously rejected the "pretensions" of current academic training, proudly professing "his ignorance" (perhaps his learned ignorance) in such matters. The most prominent figure influenced by Cusanus's approach, however, was undoubtedly Leonardo da Vinci, an artist and intellectual who was always at odds with ossified habits of thought. Drawing on Pierre Duhem's famous investigation of Leonardo's background, Cassirer insists that the painter received "a great number of problems immediately from the hands of Cusanus" and developed them further in his own way. In Cassirer's view, what linked the painter with the German cardinal was above all their shared approach toward learning and inquiry: "For Leonardo, Cusanus represents not so much a specific philosophical system but, what is more important, a new kind and a new orientation of research." In his own iconoclastic way, Leonardo divided thinkers and artists into two opposed groups: the original discoverers, and the imitators or commentators. "The first type—the 'primitives,' to use his term—recognize only one pattern and one model for their work: experience; and for this they deserve the name of discoverers. Their followers, on the other hand, abandon nature and reality and lose themselves in a world of merely conceptual distinctions (*discorsi*)."[5]

Where Cassirer goes astray is in his emphasis on Renaissance science and logic (coupled with mathematics), to the detriment of the transgressive qualities of Cusanus's and Leonardo's thought.[6] As a thoroughly modern thinker himself, his tendency is to treat medieval inspirations as somewhat backward legacies—a treatment that shortchanges the innovative spirituality of Cusanus, his experiential linkage of the mundane and transmundane, the sensible and the supersensible. Returning to Cusanus's text *The Layman on Wisdom*, this linkage is forcefully underscored in the layman's claim that wisdom cries in the street but simultaneously dwells "in the highest" (in altissimis). The sensible-supersensible nexus is subsequently reaffirmed and endorsed by both interlocutors in the dialogue. As the layman observes, the "highest" is actually nothing else but "infinity"—but an infinity that is not divorced from all finite phenomena and experiences, but somehow intimated or anticipated in them. The text at this point unleashes a veritable torrent of seeming paradoxes that center around this uncanny intimation: the supersensibility of the sensible, the infiniteness of the finite. Rooted in this intimation, genuine wisdom is "unimaginable in all imagination, insensible in all sensation, untastable in all taste, inaudible in all hearing, invisible in all sight, unaffirmable in all affirmation, undeniable in all negation, indubitable in all doubt." What is involved here is not a simple contradiction nor an esoteric paradox, but rather the insight that all phenomena and experiences presuppose, as their condition of possibility, a kind of groundless ground that serves as their inexhaustible horizon. Since this ground is inexpressible in all formulations or propositions, "there can never be an end to attempts at expressing it, because in all thought *that* remains unthought whereby and by virtue of which everything is."[7]

It is important to note that, in Cusanus's presentation, the sensible is never simply expendable in favor of the supersensible, the finite in favor of the infinite—something that would transform his thought into abstract speculation. Rather, sensation remains the preamble or gateway to learned ignorance or unknowing knowledge, just as, in hermeneutics, preunderstanding is always the condition of understanding, and prejudgment is a condition of judgment. "Wisdom," the layman asserts boldly, "is a matter of tasting (sapientia est quae sapit), and nothing tastes better to the human intellect." In fact, "one should never consider anybody wise whose words are based only on hear-say rather than actual tasting." Rather than being a purely deductive exercise, wisdom is predicated on this kind of "internal relish and taste," which does not mean that it is reducible to taste experience. Cusanus, through the words of the layman, at this point develops the important notion of "foretaste" or pregustation (akin to hermeneutical preunderstanding). Because it dwells in the highest, he notes, wisdom "is not [fully] tastable in any relish or taste. Therefore, it is tasted untastably," which does not remove it from all tasting. "To taste in an untastable manner," he adds, "is, as it were, to savor something from afar as, for example, we could say by the aroma of something that we get a fore-taste (*Vorgeschmack, praegustatio*) of it." To be sure, this foretaste does not amount to a full grasp, but only to an intimation or cue; yet it is an indispensable cue in the pursuit of ignorant wisdom, because without this cue, we would not know what to look for or where to look. If the sweetness of wisdom could not be "tasted with an inner relish, it would not be able to attract us so powerfully." Thus, as finite crea-tures, human beings need to follow the cue provided by taste. Just as the aroma of something sweet smelling or the odor of a precious oint-ment draws us nearer, so "the eternal and infinite wisdom resplendent in all things invites us, through a certain fore-taste of its effects, to hurry toward it with a wonderful desire (*mirabili desiderio*)."[8]

Following the desire for wisdom, the human intellect steadily draws closer to and eventually finds what it is looking for, and much more, because divine wisdom is not just an increase in cognitive knowl-edge but a leap into something vaster and inexhaustible—namely, un-knowing knowledge or wise ignorance, which is a synonym for infinite life. Human intellect or spirit, the layman observes, "moves toward wisdom as toward its own proper life. And it is sweet-tasting to the spirit continuously to ascend to the font of life, even though the latter is inaccessible [in its infinity]. For, to live steadily in a more happy way means: to ascend to life (*ad vitam ascendere*)." At this point, Cusanus (through the layman) draws an explicit parallel between the desire for wisdom and the lover's desire for the beloved object or person—a love that is inexhaustible and continuously beckons the lover on: "If someone loves something because it is lovable, he is delighted to find that the beloved object or person contains infinite and inexpressible motives of love. And this is the lover's most joyful experience when he comprehends the incomprehensible loveliness of the beloved." As Cusanus adds, navigating briskly along the chasm of the sensible and supersensible: "The lover would never delight so much in his love if the beloved were something simply comprehensible or manageable—as compared with the situation where the lovability of the beloved is ut-terly immeasurable, indeterminable, and incomprehensible," for "this is the most joyful comprehension of incomprehensibility." What the text here adumbrates is the notion of a nourishment that sustains not only finite or mortal but also immortal life, a notion familiar from many biblical passages as well as from Christian liturgy: "Wisdom is the infinite and inexhaustible food of life from which our spirit lives eternally, because it is unable to love anything other than wisdom and truth."[9]

What must be remembered here again is that the movement toward wisdom and immortal life is not merely an abstract intellectual exercise but a complete existential engagement involving body, soul, and mind. To this extent, the movement also has a practical, ethical significance, disclosing a profound layman's pedagogy. The gist of this pedagogy is that the divine or immortal life cannot be possessed, appropriated, or controlled; instead, loving the divine involves a self-surrender or self-abandonment of the lover in favor of the beloved. In the layman's words: "Hence it is necessary to surrender and let go of one's belongings. For eternal wisdom does not allow itself to be obtained unless the human being relinquishes his possessions for the sake of wisdom alone." Together with a long line of ethical teachings stretching back to the ancients, Cusanus (speaking as the layman) perceives self-surrender or abnegation of selfishness as the key to ethical life. Whereas selfishness or self-centeredness is the source of vice and moral corruption, turning lovingly or caringly to what lies beyond oneself is the seedbed of virtue and righteous conduct. "That which we have from our own" (or from our selfish selves), layman-Cusanus affirms, "are our vices, whereas the fruits of eternal wisdom are none but good things" (non nisi bona). Accordingly, the spirit of wisdom does not inhabit a selfish person who is a "slave to sin" nor a soul inclined toward evil; rather, it dwells in a "purified field" (purged of selfishness) and in its own cleansed image as in its "sacred temple" (in templo sancto suo). The layman's pedagogy at this point joins classical as well as biblical instructions in extolling an ethics of transformation geared toward a steadily improved practice of virtues: "The field that wisdom tills is a plantation of virtues. From this field spring forth the fruits of the spirit: which are justice, peace, courage, temperance, patience, and the like."[10]

Belief, Knowledge, and Wise Ignorance

In the manner of the streetwise Socrates, the layman's arguments start from concrete sense experience and never leave that experience completely behind. In its multifaceted richness, sense experience antedates and preshapes rational analysis; even under the aegis of rational analysis, it remains potent as an anticipation or foretaste of a more than rational—that is, an unknowing or ignorant—wisdom. In summarizing his discussion of Cusanus's philosophical approach, Cassirer comments: "The mind can come to know itself and to measure its own powers only by devoting itself completely and unconditionally to the world." This means that "sensible nature and sense-knowledge are no longer merely base things, because in fact they provide the first impulse for all intellectual activity." Thus, although the movement of understanding may proceed to rational insight, it always departs from preunderstanding and hence passes "through the world of the senses." Cassirer quotes at this point a passage from Cusanus's text *The Layman on Mind/Spirit,* which reads in his translation: "The human mind/spirit is a divine seed that comprehends in its simple essence the totality of everything knowable; but in order for the seed to blossom and bear fruit, it must be planted in the proper soil, which is the soil of the sensible world." Elaborating on this passage and deriving a broad lesson from it, Cassirer states that the basic character of the "copulative theology" sought by Cusanus lies in the "reconciliation of mind and nature, of intellect and sense."[11]

The understanding offered by sense experience can also be called a sensory "belief." Such a belief needs to be tested, but it can never be fully uprooted or replaced by rational cognition. In his posthumously published book *The Visible and the Invisible,* Maurice Merleau-Ponty opens his investigation by giving center stage to the notion of "perceptual faith" and its complex relation to rational reflection. In its resonance with Cusanus's thought, Merleau-Ponty's formulation is sufficiently intriguing to be cited here:

> We see the things themselves, the world is what we see: formulae of this kind express a faith common to the layman and the philosopher, the moment he opens his eyes; they refer to a deep-seated set of mute "opinions" implicated in our lives. But what is strange about this faith is that, if we seek to articulate it into theses or statements, if we ask ourselves what is this *we,* what *seeing* is, and what *thing* or *world* is, we enter into a labyrinth of difficulties and contradictions.

For Merleau-Ponty, perceptual faith is a belief that is not simply mistaken; it is a prejudice or prejudgment that can be clarified but never erased by rational analysis (or what he calls philosophical "reflection"). In other words, perception of the world does not deliver cognitive truths, but it does provide cues that cannot simply be discarded. The task of analytical reflection is to translate experiences into propositional statements, sense belief into "warranted belief" or knowledge—a task that is incumbent on philosophers, but ultimately elusive. "The movement of reflection," Merleau-Ponty writes, "will always at first sight be convincing: in a sense it is imperative, it is truth itself, and one does not see how philosophy could dispense with it." The question is "whether this movement has brought philosophy to the harbor, whether the universe of thought to which it leads is really an order that suffices to itself and puts an end to every question." Together with Cusanus, the French thinker does not believe that rational reflection is the end of the story. Such reflection, he adds, "thinks it can comprehend our natal bond with the world only by *undoing* it in order to remake it, only by constituting it, by fabricating it. It thinks it finds clarity through analysis."[12]

It is commonly agreed that Cusanus's quest for knowledge proceeds through three stages that are variously labeled "sense-experience, reason (*Verstand*), [and] intellect (*Geist, Vernunft*)," or "sense, intelligence, and learned ignorance." Cusanus himself acknowledges this tripartition in several of his writings; thus, his *De Beryllo* states explicitly: "There are three modes of knowing: sense experience, reason, and higher intellect (*intelligentsia*)."[13] In a study devoted to Cusanus, Karl Jaspers makes this tripartite sequence a cornerstone of his discussion. The stages in his (somewhat simplified) treatment are "*Sinn, Verstand, Vernunft (sensus, ratio, intellectus)*." Sense experience, he writes, aims with all sensory organs at "real" phenomena; reason, in turn, supplies "categories (forms, types)" for the comprehension of phenomena, while intellect draws "through the shipwreck of reason" closer to the divine. By itself, sense experience is amorphous and ambivalent; by contrast, reason introduces clarity by relying on "distinctions, oppositions, and the exclusion of contradictions." Higher intellect, finally, opens the path—through the "coincidence of opposites"—to the realm of "learned ignorance." Using a different formulation, Jaspers observes that sense experience is wholly positive and affirmative, whereas reason "affirms and negates" (in accord with rational criteria); intellect finally moves "beyond affirmation and negation" in the direction of coincidence. An important aspect of Cusanus's teaching, he adds, is that each of the stages of knowing has its own integrity and significance in the ascent toward truth. By the same token, none of the stages is complete or exhaustive by itself; rather, truth can be found only in the interrelation and interpenetration of stages—a relation that is less a linear sequence and more a circular movement (akin to the hermeneutical circle). This point is underscored in a passage from *De Coniecturis* (On Conjectures) that states that reason and intellect need to be nourished by sense experience, which generates "wonder": "Thus intellect in a circular motion returns to itself."[14]

The passage cited by Jaspers is taken from a chapter that deals with "human nature" or, more specifically, with the nature of the "human soul" or psyche. In line with Platonic and Neoplatonic teachings, Cusanus distinguishes among three psychic levels, corresponding to the three modes of knowing mentioned before. At the same time, in line with traditional speculations, the chapter invokes the distinction between "possibility" and "actuality" (*potentia* and *actualitas*), linking that distinction with the levels of the soul. Proceeding in this manner, the text clarifies the relation between belief and knowledge by stipulating, in a nutshell, that precognitive, sensory belief constitutes the condition of the possibility of higher knowledge, yet at the same time, such belief is drawn or catapulted—through the medium of foretaste (*praegustatio*)—toward truth, which constitutes its telos, fulfillment, or actualization. In Cusanus's words, the sensible region of the soul is intelligible truth "only as a possibility" (*in potentia*). This possibility is rendered possible or empowered by the "light of the intellect," which descends into "the shadows of sense experience," just as sense experience gradually ascends to the light of truth. Thus, in relation to the intelligible realm, human understanding remains in the mode of possibility, whereas in relation to the lower, sensory experience, it has "the status of actuality" (*in actu*). By means of sensation, human understanding is aroused from its slumber and moved to the perception of the possible and probable (*verisimile*). In this manner, higher intelligence is prompted to intervene; propelled beyond a merely "dormant possibility," it is awakened to its proper task: the search for genuine knowledge, which is the search for the "actuality of knowing" or the actual knowledge of truth.[15]

In its ascent toward truth, human understanding moves through the stage of reason, which Cusanus associates mainly with calculation and measurement and which he regards as a step (but *only* a step) toward knowledge in the mode of learned ignorance. This ascent is discussed in several of his writings, but with particular eloquence in *De Docta Ignorantia,* which explores the relation between knowing and not knowing (or unknowledge). "Every inquiry," the opening chapter states, "relies on comparison and utilizes the method of comparative relation or proportion." Employing the rules of reason and logic, inquiry seeks to establish comparative values and relationships, whether in simple or difficult matters. Since comparative method reveals "identity in some respect and difference (or alterity) in another respect," such inquiry cannot proceed without quantification. Harking back to Pythagorean and Platonic teachings, Cusanus finds a close connection between comparative logic and mathematics. "Number," he emphasizes, "encompasses all things which are related comparatively." This includes all things that can be compared in terms of bigger-smaller, higher-lower, longer-shorter, stronger-weaker, and the like. Hence, being a necessary condition of comparative-logical method, number is present "not only in mathematics but also in all things which in any manner whatsoever can be the same or different either substantially or accidentally." The text at this point pays explicit tribute to the Greek roots of this conception by stating: "Perhaps it was for this reason that Pythagoras deemed all things to be constituted and understood by the power of number."[16]

Although important in its own domain, comparative rationality cannot yield full knowledge of truth and, when claiming to be final, may actually obstruct further inquiry. This is so because, beyond all comparative measurement, there is an unmeasurable dimension that escapes the categories of more or less. This dimension cannot be plumbed by calculating reason as such; yet, despite this barrier—which is the barrier between finitude and infinity—it constantly calls on human understanding to transgress itself in the direction of ultimate truth. In this dimension, we find the notion of greatest or maximal bigness, but outside of any measurement, relationship, or comparison. This bigness, or maximum, comprises all possible beings; but, not being subject to comparison, it actually coincides with the minimum, which likewise inhabits all things. This coincidence, in turn, points to an absolute realization where possibility and actuality converge—a domain that is not fully accessible but also not fully inaccessible, provided we approach it in the manner of Socrates, who confessed knowledge of his ignorance (*se nihil scire nisi quod ignoraret*). In the words of Cusanus, since the desire for understanding cannot be baseless or in vain, "we assuredly desire to know what we do not know (or to know our un-knowledge). If we pursue and achieve to fulfill this desire, we will attain to learned ignorance (*docta ignorantia*)." This kind of learned ignorance or knowing unknowledge is the highest mode of truth that human beings can attain. "It is evident," the text adds, "that, regarding ultimate truth, we cannot know anything but this: that we know it as incomprehensible in its fullness." This means that the essence of things, or the truth of beings, cannot be fully understood—a circumstance that is not the end but rather the beginning of genuine understanding. Basically, the more deeply we understand our ignorance (or nonunderstanding), "the closer we approach the truth." Put differently, "The more a person knows his or her un-knowing, the more learned he/she will be."[17]

As can be seen, truth for Cusanus is not simply an abyss of unknowledge—a pure negativity that can be dismissed or discarded by understanding—but rather an intelligent or knowing abyss that ceaselessly calls on human understanding to explore its depths.[18] His writings are replete with, and famous for, their explorations of these depths. One of his last texts, titled *De Venatione Sapientiae* (On Hunting for Wisdom), mentions, among others, three main fields where wisdom might profitably be pursued: learned ignorance, actualized possibility, and "non-otherness." Regarding the first field, the text basically reiterates insights that are familiar from earlier works, especially the point that ultimate truth is neither completely unknowable—that is, inaccessible even to intimation or foretaste—nor completely accessible to human reason. As Cusanus states, using theological vocabulary: "In their very being all things testify to God's being, or differently put: everything derives its being from the divine ground." This ground, however, is also an unground (echoes of Meister Eckhart), exceeding human cognitive competence. Hence, just as God's being cannot be fully plumbed in its depth, so too "the essence of all things in their depths remains shielded from our cognition," leaving us in a state of inquiring ignorance. For this reason, Aristotle described the essence of things as something "always looked or searched for" (*semper quaesitam*), or as an unending horizon. Human wisdom or learnedness can in fact be gauged by this standard of knowing ignorance: "The more someone realizes that the ultimate cannot be known, the more learned or wiser he/she is."[19]

The second field explored in the text is that of actualized possibility, or fulfilled being (*possest*). Cusanus distinguishes here between all things that have become or are in the process of becoming, on the one hand, and the ground (or unground) of all becoming, on the other. "None of the things which can become," he writes, "is ever free of the further possibility to become other than it is. Only God is actualized possibility or full being (*possest*) because God is in actuality what can be (*actu quod esse potest*)." The domain of becoming is marked by distinctions, differentiations, and "alterations," in the sense that things can become other than what they were before. In the field of actualized possibility, by contrast, all distinctions drop away, even (echoes of Meister Eckhart again) the distinction between being and nonbeing. As Cusanus writes, in a bold formulation: "God is prior to all differentiation: He is prior to the distinction between actuality and possibility, prior to the distinction between possible becoming and possible making, prior to the difference between light and darkness, even prior to the difference between being and non-being, between something and nothing, between difference and indifference, and so on." This field clearly lies beyond traditional, especially Aristotelian, logic, with its emphasis on the law of noncontradiction. Philosophers clinging to this logic, the text states, have not been able to "enter this hunting ground" and hence have failed to "taste the fruit of highly delectable hunts (*delectabilissimis venationibus*)." Supposing that their search must obey the principles of noncontradiction and of the mutual exclusion of being and nonbeing, such philosophers have "failed to look for God—who antedates and transcends this principle—in the field of actualized possibility (*possest*) where the difference between possibility and actuality vanishes."[20]

The third field, or "hunting ground," mentioned by Cusanus is that of the "not-other" (*non aliud*). This field is particularly intriguing in light of recent speculations insisting on the "radical otherness" of God or the divine—speculations that obviously prompt the question how a God who transcends the dichotomy between sameness and otherness can still be "radically other."[21] Grappling with this question, Cusanus prefers to use the term *not-other* precisely for what some recent thinkers call *otherness*. "In searching for what precedes possible becoming," he writes, "our intellect must be attentive to the fact that the target of the search precedes also the 'other' (*aliud*). For, what precedes possible becoming cannot possibly become 'other,' given that otherness comes later." For Cusanus, the term *not-other* designates both itself and everything else: "If I ask 'What is the not-other?,' one may appropriately respond 'The not-other is none other than the not-other.' And if I ask: 'What then is the other?,' one will answer again rightly that the other is none other than the other. Hence, the world is none other than the world." To avoid misunderstanding, the text adds a passage that some contemporary philosophers, especially those familiar with "deconstruction," will no doubt appreciate: "You should note, however, that not-other does not simply mean identical or same. For whereas the same is none other than the same, the not-other precedes the same and everything that can be designated." Hence, if one wishes to call God the Not-Other (because he is not other regarding any other), "nonetheless he is not identical with anything." For example, being not-other regarding heaven, "He is yet not identical with heaven." Wedded to traditional logic, most philosophers have again failed to enter this unique hunting ground, "where negation does not contradict affirmation, since the not-other does not stand opposed to any other." As Cusanus concludes, stunningly: "Even nothingness is none other than nothing. In the exquisite words of blessed Dionysius (the Areopagite): God is 'all in all and nothing in nothingness.'"[22]

Toward Concord among Beliefs

Nicolaus of Cusa's writings are a treasure trove of startling insights—a trove too vast to be fully canvassed in these pages. One thing, however, that emerges clearly in all his writings, including those cited above, is the animating spirit pervading them—a spirit of goodwill, friendliness, and reconciliation. The same nonopposition, or "coincidence of opposites," that he discovered in his favorite "hunting grounds" was also a guiding theme in both his intellectual and practical endeavors. Some aspects of this theme surfaced in the preceding discussion and deserve to be highlighted, such as the balanced reconciliation (without identity or separation) between belief and knowledge, reason and affectivity, and learning and ignorance. As indicated earlier, some of these distinguishing features can be recuperated in facets of contemporary thought, particularly Cusanus's emphasis on ordinary experience and vernacular or "lay" wisdom. This has been recaptured in recent phenomenology and existentialism and is designed to serve as an antidote to spurious forms of professionalization and the sway of "expert" knowledge. Equally important for contemporary thought is the emphasis on knowing unknowledge or learned ignorance—a perspective capable of making headway in some current philosophical conundrums, especially those relating to "foundationalism" and "nonfoundationalism." By placing ultimate reality beyond rational knowledge, Cusanus takes a stand against a dogmatic foundationalism that claims to have an authoritative grasp of truth. At the same time, however, by not abandoning the yearning for and foretaste of ultimate truth, his work provides a bulwark against an equally dogmatic relativism (often coupled with skeptical self-indulgence).

There is a further dimension where the cardinal's work speaks to us today with particular eloquence: the domain of interfaith harmony and cross-cultural understanding. In this age of globalization, when different faiths and cultures are more closely pushed together, cultivation of mutual understanding and respect is urgently required to counteract the danger of civilizational (and sometimes religiously inspired) violence. Cultivation of such harmony was one of Cusanus's central, lifelong commitments, and it was fueled by the multiple tensions and antagonisms festering during his own time. The basic motivation undergirding this commitment was his philosophical and theological "relationism" (not relativism): the conviction that truth or true knowledge cannot be seized or monopolized by a dogmatic authority but is best promoted through the interrelation of distinct perspectives (with each sincerely searching for the truth). In the words of Norbert Winkler's thoughtful introduction to the cardinal's work: "The notion of 'relation' which scholasticism had reduced to an accidental property, is elevated by Cusanus to the rank of a substantive and constitutive category." The upshot of this change is an unorthodox and innovative conception of the relation between the "one" and the "many," where the "one" serves only as a common lodestar but not as the domineering master of the "many." "The starting point here is no longer a compact substance to which the quality of a relation needs to be added as an accident; rather, the very being of an entity resides in its infinite relationality (which can never be exhaustively mapped)." Hence, Winkler notes, the universe envisaged by Cusanus is one "in which all parts are indeed gathered together but in such a way that no part can be the sum or the universe itself."[23]

The first occasion for Cusanus to test the viability of this outlook came in 1431–1432, at the church council in Basel. At the opening of the council, partly in response to corruption scandals in Rome, the so-called conciliar movement was at the height of its influence and popularity. Called as a legal adviser to the council, Cusanus immediately proceeded to formulate an ambitious new vision of church governance that would grant considerable power to the bishops, while accepting the pope as the presiding officer, or *primus inter pares.* This vision was the gist of his first major treatise, *De Concordantia Catholica* (On the Concord of the Church), and it instantly gained him broad recognition. Reacting to the divisions tearing Christianity apart, the treatise boldly defended the idea of a universal church council, viewed as the publicly "assembled body of Christ," in which bishops and the pope together would guide the affairs of the church on the basis of a collegial and amicable consensus. As Cusanus observed in the preface: "In trying to promote a general concord, I need to take into account the entire assembly of faithful people which we call the Catholic Church as well as the various related parts of that Church." This task required that proper attention be given to "the distinctive character and structure [of the Church] and existing relations between its members so that finally we can envisage a loving and harmonious concord among all, which alone can secure the well-being and eternal salvation of that assembly." Although recognizing the special status of the pope as the successor of Peter, the text admonished the Roman bishop not to place himself outside or entirely above the assembled church, thereby creating friction and ill will: "What the Roman bishop should consider is that the living unity of the Church is maintained through divine and canonical rules, and that all parts [of the Church] have a common sense in the abundance of divine spirit and natural right."[24]

In the end, Cusanus's conciliatory intervention came to nothing.

As debates in Basel turned increasingly polemical and divisive, Cusanus left the conciliar fold and joined the papal party—a shift of allegiance that many observers (with some justice) have deplored as a surrender to pragmatic politics.[25] Irrespective of questions surrounding his conciliar engagement, there can be no doubt about the cardinal's continued commitment to religious harmony during the rest of his life. The next major demonstration of his irenic outlook came two decades later, in the immediate aftermath of the Turkish conquest of Constantinople in 1453. In that same year, Cusanus published a text that is rightly viewed as a crucial stepping-stone toward religious ecumenism: *De Pace Fidei* (On Interreligious Peace). The book is not a doctrinal tract; it takes the form of a wide-ranging conversation among religious and philosophical leaders representing no fewer than seventeen major religions and cultures around the world. The goal of the conversation is not the imposition of a dogmatic unity but rather the achievement of peace among religions and cultures, despite their outward differences. Referring explicitly to the violence surrounding the fall of Constantinople, the introduction of the book appeals fervently to God, as the creator of all things, to "rein in the persecution, raging now more than ever because of different religious rites." The antidote to the raging violence can be found only in the true spirit of faith, which alone can transcend interreligious animosities. Hence, Cusanus pleads: "Lord, come to our aid. For this rivalry (among religions) exists for the sake of you whom all revere in everything they seem to worship. . . . If you would deign to do this, the sword and the bilious spite of hatred and all sufferings will cease; and all will know that there is only one religion in the variety of rites (*religio una in varietate rituum*)."[26]

The conversation recorded in the book covers many important religious themes, and their complexity exceeds the scope of these pages. Among the themes discussed are the relation between strict monotheism and Christian trinitarian beliefs, the difference between Abrahamic faiths and forms of polytheism (with or without idolatry), and the role of religious sacraments and rituals. The common tenor pervading the discussions is the primacy of sincere faith over rituals, of the need to love and search for the hidden God over the comfort of habitual practices. As the concluding section observes, speaking through Saint Paul: to seek "exact uniformity" in rites means "to disturb the peace";

in fact, "a certain diversity [of rites] may even increase devotion when each nation strives to make its own rites more splendid through zeal and diligence, thereby surpassing others and obtaining greater merit with God as well as praise in the world." It is clear that the perspective adopted in *De Pace Fidei* is not far removed from, and actually quite consonant with, Cusanus's arguments about learned ignorance and the divine "hunting grounds" for truth. In each case, the sincere yearning for ultimate horizons is accorded preference over dogmatic claims to possess and monopolize truth. This point is recognized by the book's translators when they write that the crucial issue for Cusanus, in both philosophy and theology, is the loving and faithful surrender to God's grace seen as a precondition of peace. The concord pursued in *De Pace Fidei,* they state, is "a peace not only *of* faith but worked out *by* faith, a peace available, indeed, only *through* faith," emanating from the "experience of faith." Seen in this light, Nicolaus of Cusa presented "the *religio una in rituum varietate* as a remedy from the very heart of things, out of the structure of divine reality, as 'coincidence,' the enfolding and unfolding process of God's work in the world."[27]

A major religion dealt with in the book—and in many ways its catalyst—is Islam. As it happens, Cusanus had been interested in Islamic theology and practices for quite some time. By the time of the council of Basel, he had obtained for his own study a twelfth-century translation of the Qur'an, together with other texts relating to Muslim doctrine. Following his departure from Basel, he traveled on a papal mission to Constantinople to guide the Byzantine emperor and Orthodox Church leaders back to Italy for interfaith deliberations; on that occasion, he also encountered numerous Muslims.[28] In light of this background, the fall of Constantinople in 1453 held for Cusanus not only a geopolitical but also an intense personal significance. Tellingly, he did not join in the clamor for revenge and violent retribution that was unleashed throughout Europe; nor did he support the ongoing demonization of Muslims in general and Turks in particular—an attitude that was surely unpopular with many of his contemporaries. Pope Nicholas V called on European rulers to launch a large-scale crusade against the Turks and promised indulgences to those who supported the war effort. By contrast, Cusanus counseled restraint and a peaceful settlement of disputes. Together with some of his friends, especially John of Segovia, he even advocated the convening of a top-level Muslim-Christian conference where grievances could be aired. Despairing of the prospect of such a conference, he decided to put down on paper his vision for interreligious harmony: *De Pace Fidei*.

Despite the completion of this text, the issue for Cusanus was not laid to rest. Less than a decade later (in 1460), he began an intensive scholarly exploration of the teachings of Islam; the result was a three-volume study titled *Cibratio Alkorani* (Sifting the Qur'an). In opposition to polemical texts virulently denouncing Islam as ungodly, Cusanus's study aimed to offer a more balanced explication of the Qur'an, although polemical and apologetic accents are not lacking. As he states in the study's preface: "It is our aim, by relying on the gospel of Christ, to 'sift' (*cibrare*) the book of Muhammad and to demonstrate that his book in many respects supports and corroborates the gospel (if such corroboration were needed) and that, where there is divergence, this proceeds from ignorance or ill will."[29] In its entirety, the work is much too complex to permit a detailed review here. In the present context, it must suffice to draw attention to the guiding spirit animating the text: the spirit of "devout interpretation" (*pia interpretatio*), that is, an interpretation guided by faith that seeks glimpses of a shared yearning for the divine in the texts of an alien faith. Cusanus himself highlights this approach when he writes: "Suppose we admit . . . that the goal and intent of the Qur'an is not to detract from God the Creator nor from Christ or God's prophets and envoys . . . , then reading the Qur'an in this light can yield distinct benefit." Listing a number of exegetical rules operative in *Cibratio Alkorani*, Jasper Hopkins properly emphasizes the faith dimension of reading. *Pia interpretatio,* he writes, is not simply a neutral analysis; nor is it the same as "charitable construal, though it involves such construal in the sense of interpreting the Qur'an's teachings in such a way that through them God is glorified." Centrally, in Cusanus's sense, devoutness of reading means "an interpretation that gives glory to God and bears witness to Christ."[30]

Cusanus's practice of devout (or at least friendly) interpretation was not restricted to Islam or Abrahamic religions; it occasionally extended farther east into Asia. As indicated earlier, his *De Pace Fidei* presents a nearly global ecumenical conversation, including participants from such distant cultures as the Persian, Chaldean, and Indian.

It is known that the cardinal was familiar with Marco Polo's reports about Asian and particularly Chinese customs, which at the time attracted considerable attention in Europe.[31] Above and beyond these direct references, however, one can detect an affinity between some of Cusanus's views and various Asian philosophical perspectives. Thus, the assumption of a deeper layer of experience antedating and preshaping human cognition bears some resemblance to the Indian notion of *brahman*, especially as this notion has been developed in so-called Vedantic philosophy. In fact, the key concept of "nondualism," emphasized by the school of Advaita Vedanta, might be fruitfully compared with the cardinal's accent on "not-other" (*non aliud*). Still, to prevent the equation of nondualism with simple fusion or identity, Cusanus always insisted on the need to approach the divine humbly and with a loving spirit—an outlook approximating that of the Indian school of "modified nondualism" (*Vishisht-Advaita*), associated with Ramanuja. Regarding the cardinal's favorite "hunting grounds" of learned ignorance and noncontradiction (or coincidence of opposites), one can readily find affinities with Buddhist teachings, especially those of the Mahayana philosopher Nagarjuna and his delineation of a "middle way" (*madhyamika*) between opposites. As Nagarjuna stresses: "The speakable (what can be affirmed) is the deniable (what can be denied), for it is determinate. The ultimate truth which is indeterminate is the unutterable *dharma*."[32]

In *De Venatione Sapientiae*, composed a year before Cusanus's death, we find a statement that might have been penned by the Asian philosopher but is actually ascribed to a Neoplatonic thinker. "As Dionysius (the Areopagite) correctly stated," we read, "with regard to God it is imperative both to affirm and to deny opposing propositions," which may allow us to come to know the truth "unknowingly" or attain the divine "unattainably." The transgression of opposite propositions also applies to the conundrum of immanence and transcendence—where Cusanus denies both the coincidence of creator and creatures and their radical otherness, citing the statement of Saint Paul that although God is not available in human "shrines," he is "not far from each one of us, . . . for we are indeed his offspring" (Acts 17:24–28).[33]

Another of Cusanus's later writings, titled *De Visione Dei* (On the Vision of God), offers a nondualist or perhaps modified nondualist formulation of the relation between humans and the divine. As the text

points out, we are able to "see" or have a vision of the divine only because we are first of all seen or "envisaged" by the divine. "You, Lord,"
we read, "are where speech, hearing, taste, touch, reason, knowledge
and understanding are the same and where seeing is one with being
seen, and hearing with being heard, tasting with being tasted, and
touching with being touched." This relation between seeing and being seen is equivalent to the bond of love, which is a proper point
at which to conclude this chapter, because Nicolaus of Cusa's entire
work is ultimately nothing but a sustained paean to the love of God:
"You have shown yourself to me, Lord, as in the highest degree lovable, for you are indeed infinitely beloved. But . . . unless there were
an infinite lover, you would not be infinitely beloved, for your being
infinitely loved corresponds to the power of loving infinitely. Hence,
you my Lord, are love: a love that loves and a love that is beloved, and
also the love that is the bond between the two."[34]

4. The Natural Theology of the Chinese

Leibniz and Confucianism

> Is goodness indeed so far away? If we really wanted it, we
> would find that it was at our very side.
>
> —Confucius

In introducing their translations of Leibniz's writings on China, David
Cook and Henry Rosemont Jr. observe:

> The vision of Leibniz for a close understanding and com-
> munication between China and the West has not yet come
> to realization. The growth of knowledge of Chinese culture
> in the United States and Europe has not been matched by
> a similar growth in its dissemination, especially at the pub-
> lic level; and the respectability of narrow specialization in
> the academic disciplines provides a ready-made excuse for
> all but China scholars to professionally ignore the world's
> oldest continuous culture, inherited by one quarter of the
> human race.[1]

These comments, penned more than a decade ago, are even more
pertinent today. Let me start with a brief anecdote. Not long ago, at
the annual meeting of one of the largest American social science associations, I attended a panel featuring distinguished experts in the
field of international relations and politics. One of these experts, after alerting listeners to the deep frictions troubling our world, began

to hold forth on the United States' need to prepare for a coming war with China, spelling out in detail the steps required to meet this challenge. Listening to the speaker, I grew increasingly alarmed and dismayed; looking around, I expected to find a similar dismay among the rest of the audience. To my consternation, this was not the case: most people were listening passively or complacently, with some occasionally nodding their heads in approval. Seeking solace in my distress, I left the room and went to another panel dealing with political theory, where, to my chagrin, I found the panelists completely aloof from contemporary problems, entertaining them-selves instead with postmodern wordplays and recondite paradoxes. It was at this point that I remembered the lines written by Cook and Rosemont, and I recalled discussions I had had with Rosemont some time back, when he had deplored the enormous distance—or naïveté—separating much of American academia from the world in which we live.

It seems to me that this distance is likely to lead to two equally unpalatable outcomes: unreflective hegemonic ventures seeking to eradicate difference, or modes of parochial retreat that are unable to cope with global challenges. In my view, Henry Rosemont is one of those rare individuals who is willing to swim against the tide both as a professional specializing in Chinese thought, and thus able to cor-relate Western and Chinese traditions of philosophy, and as a public intellectual committed to building bridges between East and West and fostering a more peaceful and harmonious global order. As I have come to realize, it was this oppositional stance, and especially the commitment to global peace, that led Rosemont, early in his career, to the writings of Gottfried Wilhelm Leibniz, that rare philosopher of the Enlightenment who was keenly devoted to improving relations between Europe and China as a gateway to more peaceful relations among societies and cultures around the globe. In this chapter, I first sketch Rosemont's approach to Leibniz and his perception of the latter's philosophical and political role in his period. Next, I briefly recapitulate some main arguments in Leibniz's writings on China and especially his famous "Discourse on the Natural Theology of the Chi-nese." Finally, I offer some afterthoughts on the prospects of a global ecumenism as envisaged by Leibniz and Rosemont (as well as other contemporary thinkers).

Rosemont and Leibniz

"If Erasmus of Rotterdam was the 'Universal Man' of the late fif-teenth and early sixteenth centuries, Gottfried Wilhelm Leibniz was a major candidate for the title two hundred years later." With these words, Cook and Rosemont open their study on Leibniz's writings on China.[2] These words are entirely apt. Like Erasmus before him, Leib-niz was a Renaissance man, combining an incredible range of talents and competences: philosopher, scientist, mathematician, diplomat, public official, and indefatigable writer of letters. No one approach-ing his oeuvre can avoid being awestruck by both the amplitude of his interests and the depth of his insights. Yet, something more is needed to explain Rosemont's particular fascination. Surely, as a student of Chinese thought, he could have confined himself to the translation, reediting, and explication of ancient Chinese texts or to the explora-tion of the changes introduced by neo-Confucianism and later by the influx of Western liberal and revolutionary ideas. Although not averse to any of these enterprises, Rosemont chose a different path, one that distinguishes him (in my view) from many other China scholars.

Basically, his fascination with Leibniz seems traceable to a num-ber of affinities. For one thing, like the German thinker before him, Rosemont is steeped in the tradition of Western philosophy and brings this tradition to bear on his study and interrogation of Chinese texts. In this manner, he is able to negotiate between different intellectual frameworks—something that academic Sinologists and other area specialists are rarely able to do. More important, there are both intel-lectual and political parallels between our time and that of the Ger-man thinker. Intellectually or philosophically, our time is largely prey to an overbearing scientism and instrumental-technological rational-ism that seems bent on sidelining if not erasing humanistic and ethical concerns. To this extent, our time is heir to the Cartesian worldview, with its dualism of subject and object, spirit and matter, and its predi-lection for treating the entire world (outside the internalized subject) as a causal mechanism amenable to technological control. It was this worldview, inspired by Descartes, Bacon, and others, that eventu-ally became the backbone of much of Enlightenment philosophy and later the harbinger of nineteenth- and twentieth-century scientism and empiricism. It was also this outlook against which Leibniz remon-strated in many of his writings, after having been attracted to it in his youth because of its promised escape from the blinders of medieval scholasticism.

Leibniz's opposition to Descartes is well known and a matter of historical record. As he wrote pointedly to his contemporary, the French philosopher Malebranche: "In my view, one can impossibly assume that a substance marked by pure extension without thought [matter, or *res extensa*] could relate to and act upon a substance construed as pure thought without extension [mind, or *res cogitans*]." In this letter, Leibniz asks his French colleague to dispel his doubts about the following (Cartesian) propositions: "that matter and spatial extension are one and the same; and that mind/spirit can subsist without any connection with a body." In view of the incongruence of these propositions, the conclusion for Leibniz was clear and demonstrable: that "matter is more than mere extension"—specifically, that it is both mass and "living force" or "*Kraft*" (a conception that in many ways recaptures the Aristotelian notion of entelechy).[3] Though critical of Cartesian dualism, this counterposition does not simply embrace a unitary substance without differentiation (a view often attributed to Spinoza). Cook and Rosemont perceptively pinpoint the gist of this metaphysical or ontological perspective. "Rejecting the dualism of Descartes and the monism of Spinoza," they write, "Leibniz instead stressed plurality, diversity, harmony, and higher-order unity that could be grasped by reason" (where *reason* is not synonymous with the Cartesian *cogito*). Whereas Spinoza, in opposing Descartes, concluded that "there could therefore be only a single substance," Leibniz argued for an "indefinitely large number" of substances called "monads," which, though basically self-contained, could "all dance to the same tune played in a pre-established harmony composed by God." As Cook and Rosemont add, this perspective was "original with Leibniz" (although parts of it can in fact be traced to Giordano Bruno and Nicolaus of Cusa) and, in many ways, "bears a close resemblance to the Chinese metaphysical view of the world."[4]

The indefinite multiplicity of individual substances, in Leibniz's opinion, was not equivalent to fragmentation or chaotic dispersal. Such dispersal is prevented by the fact that all monads are connected to and embroiled with one another in a shared world; in other words, they all interact with one another not in a cause-and-effect nexus but in the manner of a mirror cabinet, where each part mirrors all others and the world. Given this basic correlation, monads for Leibniz do not require "windows." In the lucid account of Hans Heinz Holz: "The individual element is always already a manifestation of the whole. Therefore, no windows are needed to relate one monad to others; each *is* itself the others—though only in a mirroring sense." Every mirror, he adds, "carries the mirrored in itself," without the need for special openings: "its whole being is mirrored."[5]

Friends and students of Rosemont know how much of his own work is concerned with mirroring. One of his most probing and revealing publications is titled *A Chinese Mirror: Moral Reflections on Political Economy and Society*. As he writes there: "The more openly and deeply we look into another culture the more it becomes a mirror of our own, and my reflections of and on China are given here in the hope that the American Dream will one day be replaced by a more universal dream, one that can be shared by all peoples, holding their humanity in common."[6] In large measure, *A Chinese Mirror* constitutes an endorsement of Leibniz's interactionist or relational view of the world; by the same token, it is also a critical rebuke of the Cartesian mind-body, spirit-nature bifurcation. In the latter respect, the book inserts itself into a broader post-Cartesian or anti-Cartesian philosophical trend stretching from Friedrich Nietzsche to Martin Heidegger and beyond. In another context, in his book *Rationality and Religious Experience,* Rosemont addresses the issue frontally, stating: "The ancient Chinese did not have Cartesian bodies; they did not have Cartesian minds either. Unlike the numerous Chinese graphs that may be translated as 'body' on occasion, there is only one rendered as 'mind': *xin.*" But there is a catch, because "*xin* equally reasons, reflects, hopes, fears, and desires," thus bypassing a "sharp cognitive/affective split" (a corollary of the mind-body ontology).[7]

Apart from philosophical affinities and convergences, there are notable political parallels connecting our time with the age of the German thinker, especially those having to do with warfare and violence. Leibniz was born in 1646, two years before the Peace of Westphalia concluded the Thirty Years' War, which had devastated Europe and nearly decimated its population. Far from pacifying the situation, the Westphalian settlement ominously set the stage for new conflicts. Its governing principle of *cuius regio eius religio* unified religion and politics in a perilous fashion, thus preparing the way for new and intensified religious and nationalist rivalries. In addition, some dynastic regimes—especially Spain and the Hapsburgs—had not yet abandoned broader imperial ambitions, and those designs were viewed with intense suspicion by their neighbors. We hardly need to be reminded of the continual violence tarnishing our own age, marked by two world wars, a cold war, and the onset of an indefinite period of global "terror wars" carried forward under the aegis of a global superpower. In this situation, the example of Leibniz can provide helpful inspiration, given that his intellectual and political efforts were always directed toward peacemaking and mutual reconciliation. In the words of Cook and Rosemont: "He wished to reconcile Catholics and Protestants, and to halt the internecine strife plaguing the European states of his day" by concentrating on the common bond between confessions. Moreover, he believed that China could become part of a global mutuality through a further differentiation between basic beliefs and dogmatic or doctrinaire accretions. From the vantage of basic beliefs, the doctrines in dispute between Catholics and Protestants, as well as between Christians and Chinese, could be seen "as relatively unimportant in the larger scheme of things" and could be "adjudicated to the satisfaction of all on the basis of [non-Cartesian] reason"—the result being "international peace and harmony among and between all of the world's peoples."[8]

With regard to China, these hopes were complicated, and ultimately frustrated, by a number of prominent doctrinal or ideological disputes in which religious-theological and power-political motives were curiously (or perhaps predictably) linked. Theologically, the chief bone of contention was how Christian religion could best be disseminated among the Chinese people. Two issues demanded primary attention in this respect—one terminological, the other more practical. The first issue was whether the Chinese language provided a suitable equivalent to the Christian notion of "God." The second issue was whether some quasi-religious rituals performed by the Chinese were compatible or incompatible with the practice of the Christian faith. On both questions, Matteo Ricci, the Jesuit founder of Christian missions in China, adopted a conciliatory or accommodationist position. As someone deeply conversant with the Chinese language, Ricci held that it did indeed offer equivalents or at least reasonable analogues to the concept of God. Regarding customs and rituals, he found them to be mostly civic or social in character and hence not in conflict with Christian practices. Although Ricci's views were adopted by many Jesuits who followed him to China, his accommodationist stance was fiercely opposed by Franciscan and Dominican missionaries, as well as by religious and political authorities back in Europe. To the anti-Ricci faction, the Chinese were basically heathens and atheists who were attached to a gross materialism devoid of spiritual qualities. Given this lack of spirituality, their language made no room for the divine, and their rituals and customs were simply idolatrous and an affront to Christian doctrine. The sternest and most uncompromising assault on accommodationism was mounted by theologians at the University of Paris. Radically Augustinian (or else Jansenist) in outlook, these theologians insisted on the utter "fallenness" of human nature (especially Chinese nature), a condition that could be remedied only through the redemptive intervention of divine grace—in China, through the intervention of Christian missionaries from Europe.

The last point indicates the conflation (perhaps inevitable) of theological and political considerations. The linkage was further underscored by the collusion between religious motivations and intra-European dynastic rivalries. Cook and Rosemont mention the "curious" fact that accommodationist missionaries hailed mainly from lesser European countries, while the anti-Ricci forces received powerful support from the Spanish crown, which was still hankering for a "universal" Catholic empire. As they point out, Jesuit missionaries tended to come from a "variety of ethnic backgrounds" and worked in China "under the general jurisdiction of the Portuguese." In contrast, more hard-line missionaries tended to be "under the patronage of the Spanish crown" and entered the country mostly from the Philippines. "China," they conclude, "thus became contested territory for evangelical efforts, because where missionaries go, merchants will follow, and colonies can be established, all of which can enlarge the coffers of the imperial court."[9] Perhaps one should add—and Rosemont would probably agree—that where missionaries and merchants go, soldiers and armies are likely to follow. This fact is amply demonstrated by the Spanish conquest of the Americas, where missionary endeavors (to spread the "good news" among the Indians) were accompanied by military subjugation (often pursued with incredible brutality and resulting in what we would now call genocide).

On the Natural Theology of the Chinese

In the conflict between Ricci and the anti-Riccians, Leibniz on the whole favored the accommodationist position—for religious reasons, but probably for political reasons as well. Rosemont, in turn, follows both Ricci and Leibniz—again, for both reasons. The conciliatory attitude is prevalent in all of Leibniz's writings on China, which Cook and Rosemont have collected and translated and on which they comment with erudition and sympathy. The collected writings are four: an early piece written as a preface to a journal of Chinese studies (*Novissima Sinica*), another short piece dating from roughly the same time (1700) on the civil cult of Confucius, a somewhat later paper on Chinese rites and religion, and a longer treatise composed shortly before Leibniz's death (1716) on the natural theology of the Chinese. All four writings aim to defend certain good and valuable qualities in Chinese culture that Europeans (including missionaries) should not rashly dismiss but might even embrace, to their benefit; chief among these qualities are a basic moral goodness and decency, an ingrained civility, and a loyalty toward fellow beings and ancestors—all of which might be summed up under the label "natural religion." In the struggle against the anti-Riccians, this emphasis on natural religion or goodness is a central point. On the one hand, if (following the Jansenists) one assumes that Chinese nature is basically corrupt and devoid of all religious sentiment, it follows that Christian faith can be imposed on them only from the outside (by force, if necessary). On the other hand, if one assumes an indigenous potential for goodness among the Chinese, Christian faith can be readily accommodated with Chinese natural religion or added as a supplement.

With regard to the positive qualities of Chinese culture, the comments in Leibniz's preface are most outspoken and probably grated on the sentiments of Eurocentric Christians at the time (just as they are likely to grate on some Western sentiments today). The preface offers a comparison of the respective merits of European and Chinese culture, a comparison that is not very flattering to the Europeans. To be sure, as a renowned scientist, Leibniz does not ignore European accomplishments in that area. Basically, for him, Europeans are superior in the domains of logic, mathematics, and other "theoretical" disciplines: "We excel by far in the understanding of concepts which are abstracted by the mind from the material, that is, in things mathematical." In addition, Europeans excel in "military science," owing not to Chinese ignorance but rather to deliberate choice: "For they despise everything which creates or nourishes ferocity in men." Once the focus shifts from logic and mathematics to praxis and civility, a very different picture emerges. In Leibniz's words: "Certainly they surpass us (though it is almost shameful to confess this) in practical philosophy, that is, in the precepts of ethics and politics adapted to the present life and use of mortals." In these domains, the Chinese certainly have "attained a higher standard" and "in a vast multitude of people" have virtually "accomplished more than the founders of religious orders among us have achieved within their own narrow ranks."[10]

The preface is replete with praise for Chinese virtuous behavior: the reverence shown to elders, the almost "religious" conduct of children toward their parents—such that "for children to contrive anything violent against their parents, even by word, is almost unheard of"—the willing performance of duties, and the respect and civility shown among equals. Leibniz does not hesitate to rub the difference in, saying that the Chinese "rarely show evidence of hatred, wrath, or excitement," whereas "with us," respect and courtesy last only for a short while, "quickly to be followed by contempt, backbiting, anger, and enmity."[11]

If such was the relation between European and Chinese cultures, one might legitimately ask what benefit European missionary activities could produce. Undaunted, Leibniz boldly (even provocatively) remolds the missionary project into one of reciprocal learning. Given Chinese excellence in civil matters, he writes, "it is desirable that they in turn teach us those things which are especially in our interest: the greatest use of practical philosophy and a more perfect manner of living, to say nothing now of their other arts." Such reciprocity was urgently needed for Europe's own benefit and improvement. According to Leibniz, given "the condition of our affairs, slipping as we are into ever greater corruption," it is obvious that "we need missionaries from the Chinese who might teach us the use and practice of natural religion, just as we have sent them teachers of revealed theology."[12] For their part, Europeans must take great care so that evangelization becomes neither predatory or domineering nor too reticent or self-effacing.

Similar points are made in "The Religious Cult of Confucius" and

"Remarks on Chinese Rites and Religion." Regarding Chinese rituals, Leibniz urges the need for caution and prudent judgment, for
after all, "worship depends not so much on rites as on feelings" and
sincere dispositions; hence it is necessary to weigh carefully "in what
spirit the Chinese worshipped their ancestors or those of great merit."
The general rule to be followed with respect to customs or rituals is
to ponder their deeper meaning, often revealed in older teachings,
rather than cling to outward and perhaps corrupted forms. Adopting the legal rule *in dubio pro reo,* Leibniz offers this maxim: "Nothing prevents us from thinking well of the ancient doctrines until we
are compelled to proceed otherwise. At least their most venerable
precepts of life hold out strong hope of actually being doctrines of a
religion of salvation" (or at least of a natural religion preparatory to a
religion of salvation).[13]

The longest of the collected writings is Leibniz's "Discourse on
the Natural Theology of the Chinese." Based on extensive studies and
steadily deepened reflections, the discourse presents the opinions of
the aged philosopher on a number of topics, ranging from Chinese
conceptions of God to their views on spiritual substances, the nature
of the soul, its immortality, and similar issues. In the present context,
the briefest glimpse must suffice. Cook and Rosemont single out four
main parts of the text: a first section dealing with Chinese analogues
to the Christian notion of God and spiritual substances; a second part
affirming a parallel between the Chinese view of "material" or embodied spirits and the Christian conception of angels; a third part asserting the compatibility of Chinese and Christian concepts of the
human soul and its immortality; and a fourth section, or appendix,
exploring the correspondence between Leibniz's own binary arithme-
tic and ancient Chinese teachings, as set forth especially in the *Yi Jing*
(Book of Changes).[14]

The accommodationist approach coupled with admiration is evident throughout. Regarding Chinese culture in general, we read early
in the text: "There is in China a public morality admirable in certain
regards, conjoined to a philosophical doctrine, or rather a natural theology, venerable by its antiquity, established and authorized for about
3,000 years, long before the philosophy of the Greeks." Given this
ancient pedigree, the text adds, it would be "highly foolish and pre-
sumptuous on our part, having newly arrived compared with them,

and scarcely out of barbarism," to dismiss or condemn their teachings simply because of an initial impression of strangeness. On a philosophical level, Leibniz discovers in Chinese thought a highest principle called *Li*, which in his view is comparable to Aristotle's "prime mover" or entelechy and, moreover, combines "summary unity" with "perfect multiplicity" (*unum omnia*).[15] On a religious or theological level, Leibniz joins Ricci in detecting an analogue to "God" in the Chinese term *Xangti* (lord of heaven), who is said to govern heaven and earth. "For me," he concludes, "I find all this quite excellent and quite in accord with natural theory. . . . It is pure Christianity, insofar as it renews the natural law inscribed in our hearts—except for what revelation and grace add to it to improve our nature."[16]

Toward a Global Ecumenism?

In his writings on China, Leibniz treads a difficult and precarious path, both philosophically and theologically, and manages to bridge perspectives that many people (in the West) try to keep apart. Perhaps the most difficult, vertiginous path is the one he tries to steer between natural theology and revealed theology, between a creator God and a world principle, or between immanence and transcendence. The complexities of this in-between path are clearly manifest in "Discourse on the Natural Theology of the Chinese," but they pervade and overshadow Leibniz's entire oeuvre. Rosemont at one point captures this issue when he writes: "Leibniz wrote the *Natural Theology of the Chinese* and the *Theodicy*, as well as the *Monadology*; but he wrote the latter for very different reasons than he wrote the former, both of which metaphysically require a Christian transcendental realm in a way the *Monadology* does not." As he elaborates: "While God is decidedly important for the *Monadology*, He is not necessary." Conversely, "no atheist could write the *Theodicy*, and the *Discourse* was written largely in defense of the Riccian 'accommodationist' view of how Chinese conversion to the One True Faith could best be effected."[17] As has been shown here, however, even the "Discourse" does not opt decisively for one perspective but displays in its arguments the same complexity and ambivalence.

One factor that helped Leibniz pursue his precarious path was pragmatic (although I believe that there are also philosophical reasons for undecidability): his tendency to prioritize practical philosophy over Cartesian abstractions, or what we now call "orthopraxis" over "orthodoxy." In his *Rationality and Religious Experience,* Rosemont fully joins himself to Leibniz in this respect. After discussing some theological quandaries, he observes: "But I want to go further in de-emphasizing the importance of the specific metaphysical and theological underpinnings of each of the world's religions when studying their sacred texts and narratives." In this context, Rosemont turns attention particularly to the bifurcation between transcendence and immanence—a bifurcation that in large measure coincides with the distinction between revealed and natural theology and, even more broadly, with the difference between Western and Asian religiosity. "Consider again," he writes, "the transcendental realm, central to the Abrahamic heritage." By focusing on this realm "as a reality wholly other than the reality we experience in our daily lives," we empha-size and celebrate "the radical otherness of God, and the divinity of Christ" on whose grace alone redemption depends. Although hon-oring God's incomparable majesty, the focus on the transcendental realm simultaneously devalues our world and worldly engagement as "merely" mundane or immanent. From the angle of such a meta-physics, the text continues, it is difficult to appreciate certain kinds of worldly religious experiences, such as "the experience of belonging, of at-one-ment or attunement, in and with the world of our everyday lives." Equally important: "A preoccupation with the transcendental realm makes it extremely difficult to appreciate what the Incarnation and the Passion of Christ actually signifies: God is *in,* and not of, the world He created."[18]

From a philosophical (or epistemological) angle, focusing on the "transcendental realm" also means looking at the world from a transcendental or radically "universal" perspective—from which all worldly phenomena are dwarfed into mere "particularities." As it hap-pens, such a universalism has been the preferred option of much of Western metaphysics and social-political theory—an option that has tended to abet (though not to justify) the expansion of self-styled "uni-versal" regimes over merely particular populations. In the case of the conquest of the Americas, the Spanish monarchy presented itself as the embodiment of a "universal" mission: the mission to evangelize the entire world in the name of Catholic Christianity. In our time, the objective and content of the mission have changed, but not the global trajectory: the place of the Christian "good news" is now largely taken over by neoliberal principles of the market. The problem of every universalism—no matter how purely or transcendentally conceived—is that every attempt to "universalize" embroils it in the historical and social particularities of the world and thus contaminates its purity with "immanent" concerns. This contamination was obvious in the case of the Spanish empire, where gold and plunder played a central role (eclipsing the "good news"). It was also manifest when French revolutionary ideas were disseminated by Napoleon's armies. This means that—without opposing pure principles as such—friends of humanity or of a global ecumenism need to be wary of political agendas advertised as universal or universalizing programs.[19]

Rosemont has a healthy distrust of such programs promulgated today, especially the panacea of a new "world order" based on the market, the Internet, and consumerism. Commenting on global ecumenism, he remarks: "It would be foolish to believe that a capitalist economic system and communications advances could make it a reality. Not only is wealth distributed grossly inequitably today, the gap between rich and poor is widening, not narrowing." In the same spirit, he stresses the value of religious and humanist legacies in our time because they "can guide us back from the abyss of meaninglessness that is becoming increasingly characteristic of contemporary life, an altogether material life in which many of us are obliged to take jobs we do not like or find satisfying in order to buy things we do not need and that do not satisfy us either, all the while destroying our natural and social environment as we do so."[20]

Without completely dismissing transcendentalism (despite well-grounded apprehensions), Rosemont—together with Leibniz—reminds us of the importance of natural theology or an immanent religiosity, reflected in the Abrahamic context in the Incarnation and passion of Christ. Commenting on the Chinese "rites controversy," Cook and Rosemont characterize the accommodationist and anti-Jansenist position in these words (borrowed from David Mungello): "The Jesuits interpreted the Bible as a spiritual guide to completing God's work in the world rather than as a book which told a story of salvation whose geographical and cultural limits had already been reached."[21] More pointedly, *Rationality and Religious Experience* cites, with at least partial approval, these words of Alexander Pope: "Know then thyself, presume not God to scan; / The proper study of mankind [humankind] is man." However, the closest approximation of Rosemont's own kind of "religious experience" can be found in Confucianism, especially among the early Confucians, who—in Herbert Fingarette's marvelous phrase—were able to treat "the secular as sacred." Turning to the "spiritual discipline" of the early Confucians, Rosemont describes it as "a path that integrates the aesthetic, the moral, and the socio-political with the religious"—a path that is worthy of our emulation:

> As we follow that path, we will be led to see ourselves less as free/autonomous, unchanging selves/souls, less as altogether distinct from the physical world, and more as co-members of a multiplicity of communities, who, through sustained efforts, are increasingly integrated into an ever-larger community, something larger than ourselves. We must come to see and feel ourselves as fundamentally, not accidentally, intergenerationally bound to our ancestors, contemporaries, and descendants.[22]

To be sure, Rosemont's sensibilities are not limited to early Confucian texts or to Asian teachings in general. His entire opus, as it stands presently, is a testimonial of his commitment to global harmony and global ecumenism. At the end of *Rationality and Religious Experience* (which was initially presented as the first Master Hsüan Hua Memorial Lecture at Berkeley), this commitment is eloquently expressed in these terms: "I commend the sacred texts and narratives of the world's religions to your careful attention and study. Reread, and read in conjunction with the texts of other traditions, each tradition can be renewed, and come to be seen as collaborative rather than competitive with the others, and thereby, as conducive to lessening the distance between 'us' and 'them.'"[23] These lines, in my view, also capture admirably the irenic and conciliatory outlook of Leibniz, especially his key notion of the "compossibility" of differences.

In 1946, at the time of the 300th anniversary of his birth, several German philosophers paid tribute to the German thinker as a peacemaker (*Friedensstifter*) who was devoted to the overcoming of religious, ethnic, and economic class differences in a "compossible" ecumenism. Among others, Hans-Georg Gadamer praised Leibniz as an intellectual mentor who, at the end of the Thirty Years' War, devoted the energies of his entire life to the reduction and possible elimination of warfare and destruction. Fifty years later, in 1996, at another anniversary celebration, Gadamer linked Leibniz with contemporary European philosophy, especially the strand of hermeneutics, stating: "There is really no more hermeneutic exemplar in the history of philosophy than Leibniz, who himself maintained the inherent connection and reciprocal relatedness of alternative viewpoints and alternating perspectives ultimately for the structure of truth itself."[24] These words, as well as Rosemont's comments, resonate well with the concluding passage in Leibniz's preface written three hundred years ago: "May God provide that our joys be solid and lasting, undisturbed by imprudent zeal, by internecine conflicts among the men traveling on apostolic duties, or by our own unworthy example."[25]

5. Montesquieu's *Persian Letters*
A *Timely Classic*

> If I knew something useful to my nation but ruinous
> to another nation, I would not propose it to my ruler
> because I am a human being before I am a Frenchman.
> —Montesquieu

The age of Enlightenment is often portrayed as the upsurge of an abstractly rational universalism completely oblivious of, and even hostile to, historical tradition and especially the rich welter of regional and local ways of life. In its home country, the age of *lumières* eventually led to a complete break with and attempted eradication of the past—a rupture that stood in sharp contrast to developments in the English-speaking world. Latter-day devotees of the Enlightenment often propagate a bland universalism on the Jacobin model, but that outlook ignores the fact that the rays of *lumières* are necessarily refracted in the diversity of concrete practices and experiences on the ground. Quite apart from its general disdain for history, the Jacobin model also shortchanges the refracted character of enlightened thought in eighteenth-century France, where intellectual life was by no means monopolized by a handful of *philosophes* in Paris. A prominent exemplar of nonconformist thought is the Baron de Montesquieu, who maintained somewhat strained relations with both ruling orthodoxies and the Parisian salons. Precisely by virtue of his nonconformism, his work reemerges today as an important guidepost pointing (however vaguely) in the direction of "alternative modernities."[1]

Montesquieu's concern with cultural alternatives is demonstrated in his attention to non-Western societies and cultures, especially his reflections on Persia, assembled in his famous *Persian Letters* (*Lettres Persanes*), first published in 1721. In this chapter I discuss some of the distinctive features of Montesquieu's general oeuvre, limiting myself to a few salient points. Next, I pinpoint some particularly instructive passages of his *Persian Letters* that illustrate his talent as a thoughtful and critical comparativist. Finally, I highlight aspects that, in my view, demonstrate Montesquieu's continuing relevance, and especially the importance of the *Persian Letters* as a timely classic in the contemporary context.

Montesquieu as a Practical Philosopher

Montesquieu's work is complex and multifaceted, but it is by no means devoid of an overall philosophical coherence. Although it is a relatively youthful and experimental text, the *Persian Letters* fits into this overall coherence, whose design has often been either dismissed or badly misconstrued. Born and raised in a country deeply imbued with Cartesian teachings, Montesquieu was sufficiently a Frenchman and a modernist to stand opposed to oppressive prejudices of the past and to political despotism (especially that of Louis XIV's later reign); at the same time, however—partly under the influence of British empiricism—he was sufficiently endowed with common sense to appreciate the role of history and culture and hence to resist an abstract rationalism operating deductively from first principles. This middle position makes Montesquieu an odd figure located outside the usual battle lines of his period, and certainly outside the Cartesian bifurcations of mind and matter, reason and sense experience. Several modern philosophers, including Hobbes and Spinoza, placed history outside the pale of philosophy proper, which was seen as deductive argumentation; in retaliation, empirical historians sometimes expelled philosophy from real-life history, which was seen as a jumble of contingent data. Neither the *Persian Letters* nor *The Spirit of Laws* fits into these schemes. If Hannah Arendt is correct in saying that genuine thinking means reflecting on "what we are doing" or what is going on in concrete praxis, then Montesquieu is, in Arendt's sense, an eminently practical thinker or philosopher.[2]

Montesquieu's unconventional position—unconventional in terms of the paradigm of Western modernity—has given his interpreters endless headaches and led them to strange conclusions. His contemporary and kingpin *philosophe* Voltaire once remarked that Montesquieu was "Michel Montaigne turned legislator," a comment meant as a jesting critique of the baron's oddity (with "Montaigne" standing for skeptical empiricism and "legislator" for the chief ambition of progressive *philosophes*).[3] The bafflement persists today. Although some *philosophes*, such as d'Alembert, attempted to read him in their own light, many nineteenth-century interpreters, such as Auguste Comte, construed him as an empirical sociologist and positivist, which is only a short step from his reputation as a radical historicist and perhaps even a relativist and materialist.

During the twentieth century, Montesquieu came into a juggernaut of neo-Kantian antinomies, especially the antinomies of universalism and particularism and of moral absolutism and relativism—with the relativist verdict usually prevailing. A case in point is George Healy, the able translator of the *Persian Letters*, whose introduction begins by stressing a judicious balance but ends with a dismissive verdict. Although, like most *philosophes*, Montesquieu was weary of "traditional 'absolutes,'" he could not accept the contrary position "that there are no values in human relationships except those imposed by force or agreed upon in selfish and expedient conventions." Hence, like many of his contemporaries, he upheld the notion of "natural law" or the laws of nature, although he quickly insisted that in human society, "natural laws will vary in their explicit content as the material and historical conditions of societies vary." In this manner, his work sought to "unify radically opposed directions" and to balance the notion of natural law with its concrete application. Despite this noted effort, however, Healy in the end allows relativism to triumph. "On careful reading," he observes, many of Montesquieu's arguments "turn out to be full of unresolved problems," and he was often led "toward a position of complete moral relativism." His mature thought, above all, "increasingly turned from 'nature' to 'utility' as the basic test of the worth of an idea or institution."[4]

My point here is not to deny certain "unresolved problems" in Montesquieu's work but to remonstrate against the lopsided final verdict. What the verdict tacitly assumes is the binding character of the neo-Kantian bifurcation of norms and facts, of universal rules and contingent data—an assumption that is by no means warranted. Clearly, if norms are to be binding or even relevant, they must relate to the human condition in the world, which is inevitably concrete and varied from time to time and place to place. Even the most lofty maxims lose their traction unless they are practiced by people in their ordinary lives; moreover, unless they are linked with ordinary lives, maxims easily become punitive or despotic. Recognition of this connection was the hallmark of the Aristotelian legacy, which was completely shunted aside at the dawn of Western modernity. As Hans-Georg Gadamer notes, the concept of *ethos*, central to Aristotelian ethics, makes the following explicit: that " 'virtue' does not consist merely in knowledge [of norms], for the possibility of knowing depends, to the contrary, on what a person is like, and the being of each person is formed beforehand through his or her education and way of life." Hence, the crux of Aristotelian ethics resides in the "mediation between *logos* and *ethos*," between knowing and being.[5] Seen in this light, Montesquieu may be viewed as a budding Aristotelian "out of season"—a fact that is recognized by Kingsley Martin when he presents him as a philosophical Montaigne. Montesquieu, Martin writes, "did indeed share Montaigne's eager interest in the diversity of things; he enjoyed collecting and relating the various customs of people." However, bitten by the rational "virus" of his generation, he could not remain "an essayist or a skeptic: he was forced to attempt for the modern world the task which Aristotle had performed for the ancients."[6]

The Aristotelian legacy is evident in the opening books of *The Spirit of Laws*, where Montesquieu discusses the nature of law, the different types of political regimes, and their animating "spirit." The first sentence of the text establishes the tonality pervading the rest of the work: "Laws in their most general signification are the necessary relations derived from the nature of things." With this sentence, a basic insight is affirmed: laws are not simply commands or arbitrary conventions but rather "relations" or the outgrowth of complex relationships. For Montesquieu, as for Leibniz before him, everything is relational—not atomistic or individualistic. Hence, the first sentence is immediately followed by the observation that God has his relational laws (often called covenants), the natural universe has its relational laws, and so does the animal kingdom and the human community—testifying to the "sociable" character of human beings (an insight derived from Aristotle).[7] Somewhat later in the text, Montesquieu elaborates on the complex character of the relational "nature of things." Human beings, he writes, "are influenced by various causes, by the climate, religion, the laws, the maxims of government; by precedents, morals and customs, from whence is formed a general spirit that takes its rise from these." In this passage, the crucial idea of a "general spirit" animating laws and political regimes is put forward—an idea that served as a leitmotif throughout the author's life. More than a decade earlier, in his essay on the "greatness and decline" of Rome, he had stated the idea in these terms: "There is in each nation a general spirit upon which power itself is founded; when this power shocks this spirit, it suffocates itself, and it necessarily comes to a halt." What is advanced in these passages is a conception entirely outside the pale of an arid, analytical rationalism: that is, to be workable and beneficial, norms, power, and rationality itself need to be undergirded by a living spirit or ethos oriented toward some form of the (Aristotelian) good life.[8]

With some modifications, the Aristotelian legacy persists in the discussion of types of governmental regimes and their animating principles. The text distinguishes only three types of government (collapsing somewhat the traditional classification of regimes): monarchical, despotic, and republican or democratic governments. Each of these types is undergirded—for good or ill—by an animating ethos or motivating principle. In monarchies, the principle is said to be honor, predicated on the prevailing hierarchy of ranks and estates. In despotic regimes, people are basically motivated by fear (a reference to the later years of Louis XIV and probably to the theories of Thomas Hobbes). Only in republics or democracies does Montesquieu single out virtue as the wellspring of public life, where *virtue* means equal respect or mutual recognition coupled with affection. As Book 5 of his text makes clear, virtue here is not merely a theory but a practice, not merely a form of knowledge but a mode of feeling and sensation. "Virtue in a republic," he states, in a prominent anti-Cartesian passage, "is a most simple thing: it is a love for the republic; it is a sensation and not merely a consequence of acquired knowledge—a sensation that may be felt by the meanest as well as by the highest person in the state." Needless to say, love is a relational bond, and hence virtue in a republic is a deeply mutual or relational commitment: "Love of the republic in a democracy is love of the democracy, and love of the democracy is that of equality." Montesquieu does not tire of stressing the affective and relational character of democratic bonding. "Love of equality in a democracy," he states in another famous passage, "limits individual ambition to the sole desire, the sole happiness of doing greater services to the country than the rest of our fellow citizens. They cannot all render her equal services, but they ought all to serve her with equal alacrity." From this affective bonding, a basic pedagogical principle can be derived: "Everything depends on fostering this love in a republic, and to inspire it ought to be the principal business of education; but the surest way of instilling it into children, is for parents to set them an example."[9]

There is no need here to discuss in detail the various constitutional and institutional arrangements examined or recommended in Montesquieu's work. The need is made less pressing by the fact that many of his recommendations have become nearly common sense, with their adoption by many modern governments in Europe, America, and beyond. Prominent among these recommended arrangements are the separation or at least the differentiation of governmental powers, the distinction between religious and political authority, and the importance of liberty in a well-constituted republic or democracy—with *liberty* meaning "the power of doing what we ought to will [in accordance with democratic virtue] and not being constrained to do what we ought not to will."[10] Montesquieu's constitutional observations found a particularly receptive audience in America, both during the colonial period and at the time of the founding of the new republic. In the words of Norman Torrey: "The founders of the American commonwealth, especially Franklin, Jefferson, and Madison, were imbued with the principles of *The Spirit of Laws.*" Above all, the idea of the balance and separation of powers found "ready soil" in America and became a guiding principle of the constitution of 1789. Even before that, Torrey notes, the Frenchman's influence was felt in colonial charters and state constitutions, such as in Franklin's Pennsylvania and Jefferson's Virginia, especially in the fields of civil liberties and criminal justice—an influence culminating in the Bill of Rights.[11]

Quite apart from his legal and institutional contributions, Montesquieu's work also found genuine resonance among later philosophers both at home and abroad. A prominent case in point is Hegel, whose *Philosophy of Right* pays tribute to the French thinker in numerous ways, while bending the latter's views in the direction of his own absolute idealism. In his introduction, Hegel is already focused on the character of "law" and its relation to the "nature of things." "Natural law or law from the philosophical point of view," he writes (honoring but also undercutting Kantian bifurcations), "is distinct from positive law; but to pervert their difference into an opposition and contradiction would be a gross misunderstanding." Turning to the opening pages of *The Spirit of Laws,* Hegel adds that, on this point, "Montesquieu proclaimed the true historical view and the genuinely philosophical position, namely, that legislation [or law] both in general and in its particular provisions is to be treated not as something isolated and abstract but rather as a subordinate moment in a whole, interconnected with all the other features which make up the character of a nation and an epoch." Only when seen in terms of this interconnectedness do laws acquire "their true meaning and hence their justification." At a later point, in the section on constitutional law, Hegel repeats the tribute by stating that it was "Montesquieu above all" who kept in sight both the "connectedness of laws" and the "philosophical principle of always treating the part in its relation to the whole." With minor reservations, the praise also extends to the notion of a "general spirit" or ethical wellspring animating political regimes. "We must recognize," the section on the constitution (*Verfassung*) affirms, "the depth of Montesquieu's insight in his now famous treatment of the animating principles of forms of government." This insight is particularly evident in the discussion of democracy, where virtue is extolled as the governing principle, "and rightly so because that constitution rests in point of fact on moral sentiment (*Gesinnung*) seen as the purely substantial form in which the rationality of absolute will appears in democracy."[12]

The Persian Letters

Although presented as a series of written exchanges, the *Persian Letters* is by no means a random assortment of stray observations; rather, it reflects the overall coherence of Montesquieu's general position. Perhaps more clearly than *The Spirit of Laws,* the *Persian Letters* reveals Montesquieu's cosmopolitan (or non-Eurocentric) outlook, his taste for cross-cultural comparison, and his keen eye for societal differences and their roots. In this respect, the baron was definitely ahead of most of his French contemporaries. As Healy pointedly observes: "The French Enlightenment was densely populated with men who spoke of the world, yet remained, essentially, incorrigible little-Europeans." By contrast, "notwithstanding the Cartesian side of his mind," Montesquieu was "sincerely committed to the empirical and comparative method that most *philosophes* extolled but comparatively few really understood and fewer really practiced." His taste for cross-cultural comparison was nurtured by his own frequent travels abroad to Austria, Hungary, Italy, Germany, Holland, and England. In addition, he was an avid reader of travelogues, which at the time were flooding bookstores in France. With regard to Persia, historians of ideas have noted the influence of a number of books that were popular during the baron's youth. Needless to say, Montesquieu's acquaintance with Persia was entirely secondhand, which explains many of the shortcomings of his text. Nevertheless, to quote Healy again, "his failure to depict an authentic Persia was due more to inadequacies in his sources than to his motives or energies."[13]

The topics of the exchanges in the *Persian Letters* are varied and do not follow a single story line. Some of the letters deal with provocative or exotic topics that probably titillated eighteenth-century readers but are no longer of great interest today. On this issue, I agree with the translator's comment that the value of the *Letters* is not found in the "irreverent observations on popes and kings, or in the tangled story of Usbek's frustrated wives and eunuchs." Putting these topics aside and proceeding selectively, I want to highlight passages that, in my view, illustrate the broad coherence of Montesquieu's outlook. Regarding the relation between law and ethos or practical life, no story is more instructive than that of the ancient Troglodytes, a tribe of people inhabiting the southern edge of Arabia. Usbek, the Persian traveler who tells the story, first notes that the tribe once existed in a Hobbesian kind of condition, with everyone living in fear of others and trying to subdue or kill everyone else. Eventually, the tribe was nearly exterminated, with just two families surviving. Those two families then embarked on a completely new path: they were "humane, just, and lovers of virtue," and they "labored together for their mutual benefit." Each family was united by bonds of love, and the attention of the parents was directed solely toward "educating their children in ways of virtue." The children were taught "that individual interest is always bound to the common interest" and "that justice for others is a blessing for ourselves." Guided by this common ethos, the tribe lived a joyful and happy life, and in this condition, the people "could not fail to gain the gods' favor." Their relation to the gods was likewise free of selfishness, for they "knew only how to request good for their fellows." Greed and cupidity were alien to this happy land, and when giving presents to others, "he who presented the gift always believed himself the favored one."

So far, the story teaches the benefits or blessings accruing from living a good ethical life in opposition to a selfish and violent one. Unfortunately, the story does not end there. As the Troglodyte nation grew larger, the people thought it appropriate that they should have a king and formal laws and structures of government. They decided to choose as their king an old man respected for both his age and his virtue, but he was deeply distressed by the proposition. He said: "You offer me a crown, and if you absolutely insist, I must of course accept it; but rest assured that I will die of grief to see the Troglodytes, free since my birth, submit now to a master." Growing still more distressed and agitated, the old man exclaimed: "I see . . . your virtue is beginning to burden you. For in your present leaderless state you must be virtuous on your own; for if you were not you could not survive." This condition, however, now seemed too onerous to the people: "You prefer to submit yourselves to a prince and his laws, which would be less exacting than your own morality. You know that, under such laws, you will be able to indulge your ambition, acquire riches, and languish in mean pleasures; you know that, so long as you avoid actual crime, you will no longer need virtue." At this point, the deeper lesson of Usbek's story emerges into plain view: people should not abandon the practice of an ethical life in favor of formal legal structures and procedures, behind whose screen they might sink into lethargy or selfish greed. To this extent, the story concurs with the opening of *The Spirit of Laws:* law must be seen as embedded in concrete ways of life—a point that does not necessary militate against laws or lawmaking as such but certainly militates against granting them priority status. Laws can be "known" without being followed, but ethics requires self-motivated practice. Usbek's story actually begins with a maxim that anticipates its ending, and it is one that ethicists might fruitfully ponder: "There are certain truths which one must not only cognitively accept but must feel; such are the truths of morality."[14]

The benefits of ethically good regimes—or regimes grounded in an ethical way of life—are extolled in several letters. Writing to his Persian friend Rhedi in Venice, Usbek praises the enlightened conditions in some European countries, especially in republican regimes. "Benign government," he observes, "contributes marvelously to the propagation of the species. All the republics are constant proof of this, and especially Switzerland and Holland, which are the two worst countries in Europe with respect to terrain and yet are the most heavily populated." The reason for the latter is the attractiveness of the two countries, which is based on their cultivation of equality and their commitment to individual liberty, qualities that are characteristic of democracies: "The very equality of the citizens, which normally also results in an equality of wealth, brings abundance and life into all parts of the body politic and spreads them everywhere." This stands in stark contrast to countries under arbitrary or despotic rule, "where the prince, the courtiers, and a few other individuals possess all the wealth, while all the rest groan under a crushing poverty." This comparison leads Usbek to make some general reflections on the relation between nature and nurture, between innate dispositions and external conditions. In opposition to a kind of "essentialism" assuming a fixed human nature that persists under any and all conditions, Usbek admits the role of factors that either foster or obstruct human dispositions—an admission that stops far short of an external determinism. "Men," he states, "are like plants and never flourish unless well cultivated. Among poverty-stricken people the species falters and sometimes even degenerates." This passage may be compared with a statement in *The Spirit of Laws* that treats human nature not as a fixed entity but more like a potentiality for good or evil, with good or bad outcomes being traceable to the manner of cultivation. "Before there were intelligent beings," we read there, "they were possible; they had therefore possible relations, and consequently possible laws. Before laws were made, there were relations of possible justice."[15]

As a central attribute of good regimes, justice is a topic frequently mentioned in the *Letters*. As Usbek remarks in another message to his friend: "If there is a God, my dear Rhedi, he must necessarily be just," because otherwise, he would be "the worst and most imperfect of all beings." Quite in accord with the later *Spirit of Laws*, justice is found to reside not in the command of a superior or in arbitrary convention but in a relationship: "Justice is the proper relationship actually existing between two things; this relationship is the same whoever contemplates it, whether God, or an angel or, finally, man." Under the impulse of self-interest, greed, or ambition, human beings can lose their way and turn away from justice, whose voice "can hardly make itself heard in the tumult of the passions." This does not mean that human beings are "naturally" wicked or evil, but only that their better inclinations can be derailed by adverse influences: "No one is gratuitously wicked; there must be a determining cause, and that cause is always narrow self-interest." In a bold passage, Montesquieu (through the voice of Usbek) places justice on a par with religious faith, or even above it. "Even if there were no God," he asserts, "we ought to love justice always—which is to say, to try to resemble that being of whom we have such a beautiful idea and who, if he existed, would necessarily be just." Thus, even though we might exit from "the yoke of religion," we would still be "bound by that of justice." Growing even bolder, Montesquieu as Usbek attacks a certain brand of extreme fideism that, in elevating God beyond all worldly relationships, transforms him into a despotic monster: "All these thoughts lead me to oppose those metaphysicians who represent God as a being who exercises his power tyrannically, who make him act in a way we would not wish to act ourselves for fear of offending him." In opposition to this distant tyrant-God, it is comforting to turn one's glance toward human beings in whom justice is present, at least as a possibility: "How satisfying it is when a man examines himself and finds a just heart!"[16]

For Montesquieu, justice is a virtue applicable not only to domestic society but also to the relations between societies and countries. In this respect, the *Persian Letters* strongly opposes the Hobbesian conception equating interstate relations with a natural state of war. "Magistrates," Usbek affirms, "ought to administer justice between citizen and citizen; and each nation ought to do the same between itself and other nations. In this second administration of justice, only maxims applicable to the first can be used." This affirmation leads Usbek into the issue of war and peace between nations. Replicating almost verbatim the teachings of Vitoria and Hugo Grotius, he draws very tight limits around the notion of "just" warfare. "There are only two kinds of just war," he states, "those undertaken in self-defense and those which aid an attacked ally." Hence, there is no justice in an offensive or aggressive war, nor in making war "for the private quarrels of a prince" because someone has refused an honor due to the ruler or has treated his ambassadors without proper respect or for any similar motive. The reason for these restrictions, Usbek adds, is that "a declaration of war ought to be a just act in which the punishment is always in proportion to the crime"; hence, a prior determination has to be made that the infliction of death is warranted, "for to make war against someone is to will a death penalty." Given its gravity and finality, the death penalty must always be a last resort, because both virtue and religion impel us to seek life and its preservation in peace. Seen from this angle, conquest by itself "does not establish any right." As long as the subdued people persist, conquest contains "a pledge of peace and reparation for wrongs committed," but if the people are destroyed, it is simply "a monument of tyranny." "This, my dear Rhedi," Usbek concludes, "is what I call international law, the law of nations, or rather, the law of reason."[17]

At the time of the writing of the *Persian Letters,* European nations were involved in frantic efforts to expand colonial or imperial domination in the non-Western world. Montesquieu shows as little sympathy for these colonizing ventures as for unjust warfare. The reason for his distaste is both ethical and practical: ethically, the imposition of dominion on foreign populations shows a lack of the equality demanded in republics; practically, colonialism usually backfires. In Usbek's words: "The usual effect of colonization is to weaken the home country without populating [or advancing] the colony." His letter to his friend on this topic draws attention to the conquest of the Americas by the Spanish colonizers, an event coming on the heels of the discovery of the New World. The verdict is stern and uncompromising; in fact, it is difficult to find in the literature of the eighteenth century a condemnation of the conquest as forceful as this passage penned by Montesquieu:

The Spanish, despairing of keeping these vanquished nations subservient to themselves, decided to exterminate them and to send out loyal people from Spain to take their place. Never was a horrible plan more punctually executed.

A people, as numerous as the entire population of Europe, was seen to disappear from the earth at the approach of these barbarians who, in discovering the Indies, seemed only to have thought of disclosing to mankind the final degree of cruelty. By such barbarism they retained the land under their dominion.

In the long run, however, the Spanish venture in the Americas was bound to fail, because the homeland was incapable of filling the huge gap left by the destruction of indigenous peoples. Even when pursued with less cruelty, as in the case of the Portuguese, far-flung colonizing efforts were liable to run into similar dilemmas. Drawing on a large number of ancient and modern examples, Usbek concludes that rulers should shy away from colonization, especially if it requires military subjugation: "What prince would envy the lot of these conquerors? . . . It is the fate of colonizing heroes to ruin themselves either by conquering lands they soon lose or by subduing nations they are then obliged to destroy."[18]

Apart from the critique of colonialism and unjust wars, the *Persian Letters* is eloquent in its denunciation of religious fanaticism and its defense of religious toleration. Repeatedly, Usbek cites historical examples demonstrating both the inequity and the social costs of religious intolerance. One example is that of Shah Suleiman in the late seventeenth century, who had contemplated either expelling all Armenians from Persia or forcing them to become Muslims, in the belief that the country "would remain polluted so long as it kept these infidels in its bosom." If this policy had been carried out (which, in this case, did not happen), "this would have been the end of Persian greatness," for by exiling the Armenians, nearly "all the merchants and most of the artisans would have been eliminated in a single day." Another example (in which the policy was actually implemented) was the persecution of the Parsees (the followers of Zoroaster) by Muslim rulers, leading to their exodus in large numbers to India. As a result of this religious zealotry, Persia was deprived of "a hardworking people who, by their labor alone, were close to victory over the sterility of the soil." These and similar examples persuade Usbek of the moral as well as the practical superiority of religious toleration and, in fact, of the desirability of having several religions in a country side by side. He states, "members of tolerated religions usually render more service to their country than do those of the dominant religion," because, cut off from "customary honors," they can distinguish themselves only by their hard work. Moreover, the coexistence of several religions in a country encourages a healthy competition among them, with each religious group being eager to prove its worth and the purity of its beliefs. Thus, it has often been noted that the introduction of a new faith or sect in a country is "the surest way to correct abuses in the old." To the argument that the diversity of faiths leads inevitably to conflict and warfare, Usbek has a quick rejoinder: "It is not the multiplicity of religions which has produced wars, but the spirit of intolerance stirring those who believe themselves to be in a dominant position"—a spirit that, like "a kind of madness," testifies to a "total eclipse of human reason."[19]

Preference for religious toleration does not exclude criticism of perceived blemishes or possible abuses, especially since such blemishes rarely touch the core of a religious faith. Usbek's letters frequently single out dubious or harmful practices in both Christianity and Islam. Thus, in the example of the Spanish conquest, Catholic faith was involved at least as a pretext for invasion and plunder—a fact that tarnished the faith because of its complicity; a similar stain on the Catholic faith was the expulsion of Muslims and Jews from Spain prior to the conquest. A somewhat less grievous flaw of Catholicism is the practice of celibacy among priests and monks, whom Usbek calls Christian "eunuchs." This practice is hard to understand, he writes, "since I do not see how something which produces nothing can be a virtue." Obviously, Catholic theologians are involved in a contradiction when they say "that marriage is sacred and that its opposite, celibacy, is even more so." In the case of Islam, objections to certain policies of Persian rulers were mentioned earlier. Some other objections are more lighthearted. On a par with the issue of Catholic celibacy is the Muslim practice of polygamy. "I find nothing more contradictory," Usbek confides to his friend, "than the plurality of wives permitted by the holy Koran and the order, given in that book, to satisfy them all." This order, he continues, makes a good Muslim look like "an athlete, destined to compete without letup," but who, overburdened and weakened by his efforts, "languishes even on the field of victory." More seriously damaging is a pervasive religious arrogance that treats Muslims as invariably destined for paradise while consigning Christians to eternal hellfire. "Do you really think," Usbek asks a Muslim dervish in Tauris, "that they will be condemned to eternal punishment because they have been so unfortunate as not to have mosques in their country? Will God punish them for not practicing a religion which he has not made known to them?"[20]

The critique of flaws and abuses does not interfere with respect for religions in their diversity, especially when a distinction is made between core and periphery, between the basic meaning of faith and its accidental or ephemeral dross. In one of his letters to Rhedi, Usbek seeks precisely to disentangle the basic core of faith as a lived practice from marginal accretions. Commenting on Christian people in Europe, he detects an overabundance of rhetoric and a dearth of practice: "I see here people who dispute endlessly about religion, but at the same time apparently compete to see who can least observe [or practice] it." In all religions, however, irrespective of doctrinal differences, it is practice that ultimately counts: "Whatever religion one professes, its principal parts consist always in obedience to divine ordinance [that is, law as relationship], love of fellow men, and reverence for one's parents." With growing maturity, that insight was slowly spreading among people in Europe, and hopefully elsewhere. There was a growing awareness, Usbek states, that it was "a mistake to chase the Jews from Spain" and to persecute the Huguenots in France. More and more people had come to realize that "zeal for the expansion of one's religion is different from dutiful devotion to it," and that "love and observance of a religion need not involve hatred and persecution of people who do not so believe." If such awareness were to take hold everywhere, the day would dawn when the inner bond between religions would become manifest and people everywhere would worship the divine in truth and spirit. That day was already at hand between Christians and Muslims, for as Usbek writes to the dervish: "Everywhere [in all religions] I find Islam, although I cannot find Muhammad everywhere." The reason, he adds, is that "truth cannot be contained, and always breaks through the clouds surrounding it. Hence, a day will come when the divine will behold only true believers on earth—for time, which consumes everything, eventually also destroys error."[21]

A Classic for All Time

Read in conjunction with portions of *The Spirit of Laws,* Montesquieu's *Persian Letters* is not merely an entertaining period piece but also a storehouse of insights and important lessons for his period and for our time as well. For this reason, the *Persian Letters* can be considered a timely classic. Foremost among Montesquieu's lessons is the primacy assigned to ethics or ethical conduct over formal laws and procedures, that is, to lived practice over abstract knowledge. In both texts, "law" is treated as a relationship, as one element embedded in a web of related factors that ultimately constitute a way of life. With this accent on practical conduct, Montesquieu's work stands in sharp contrast to recent and contemporary moral theory, which almost uniformly tends to privilege formal procedures and maxims over practice. The outcome of this privilege is a hypertrophy (or overabundance) of theoretical formulas coupled with the widespread, and widely noted, atrophy of ethical behavior in most Western societies. The likelihood of this decay—of the replacement of virtue by abstract rules—is bemoaned with dramatic intensity in the final episode of the story of the Troglodytes (a story that present-day philosophers would do well to remember). To be sure (and to avoid misunderstanding), emphasizing lived practice does not make Montesquieu an anarchist or an antiinstitutionalist, a reading that would render unintelligible his concern with the separation of public powers and with the role of intermediary bodies on the regional and local levels.

An equally timely and crucial lesson to be derived from Montesquieu's work is the need for cross-cultural understanding and interfaith toleration. Together with Leibniz, Herder, and Goethe, the French baron ranks (at least incipiently) among the great cosmopolitan and ecumenical thinkers of the modern age. Particularly noteworthy here is that, in Montesquieu's case, cosmopolitanism and interfaith tolerance are linked with a deep appreciation of cultural and religious traditions; thus, they are not predicated on an abstract rationalism or universalism that stands aloof from the past and tends to reduce tolerance to mere neutral indifference. As in the case of Herder, cosmopolitan and interreligious engagement is, for Montesquieu, a matter of pedagogy working from the ground up, and hence cannot be imposed from the top down by abstract rules. Only by taking one's own cultural background seriously can one see why tradition matters to other people, and only by probing one's own faith (beyond its ephemeral dross) does one penetrate to the inner wellspring of all faiths, which, for Montesquieu, resides in piety and good conduct rather than theoretical knowledge. In the language of contemporary theologians, one might say that the French thinker prefers *orthopraxis* to *orthodoxy* in interfaith relations. In a similar manner, cosmopolitan or cross-cultural relations involve a balanced progression from local to regional to global attachments, that is, from family and town to country and finally to the world. In no case, however, are primary attachments allowed to thwart broader humanitarian loyalties. As Montesquieu writes forcefully at one point: "If I knew something useful to my country but prejudicial to Europe, or useful to Europe but prejudicial to humankind, I would consider it a crime."[22]

Closely connected with his cosmopolitanism is Montesquieu's celebration of international law and his condemnation of unjust warfare—issues that have crucial significance today. As noted earlier, following the great founders of the modern law of nations, Usbek's letter to Rhedi states unequivocally: "There are only two kinds of just wars: those undertaken in self-defense and those which aid an attacked ally." This statement renders unlawful and hence criminal all kinds of offensive wars, and especially "preemptive" wars. On this issue, too many contemporaries are willing to sacrifice their loyalty to humanity to an ill-conceived patriotism or, rather, chauvinism—as if licensing offensive warfare could not easily boomerang against one's home country. In this regard, Montesquieu's stress on the relational character of law remains compelling because, in terms of the law of nations, it means that the rules must be equally binding on strong and weak nations, on hegemonic and nonhegemonic powers in our shared world. A corollary of this championing of international bonds is the warning against foreign adventures and conquests, and especially colonization. In our time, colonialism is no longer openly practiced or defended, but it persists in many covert and subtle forms. A prominent contemporary variant is the quasi-missionary spreading of ideologies, often packaged under such labels as "modernization" or "development." Wherever resistance is encountered, the older methods of military force and subjugation are held in reserve and, if needed, deployed. In his *Persian Letters* and elsewhere, Montesquieu is no partisan of empires. As Usbek complains to Rhedi: "Empires may be compared to a tree in which the overly extended branches deprive the trunk of all its sap and are useful only to provide shade."[23]

Usbek's comments are not a marginal gloss, for they reflect one of Montesquieu's lifelong preoccupations: his concern about democracies' or republics' frequent slide into tyranny or despotic imperialism. The classical illustration of this decay was the transformation of the Roman Republic into a far-flung empire, a topic to which he devoted one of his longer historical studies: *Considerations on the Causes of the Grandeur of the Romans and of Their Decline* (1734). Even prior to the completion of this study, the concern surfaced eloquently in the *Persian Letters*. As we read in one of Rhedi's letters: "The astounding expansion of the Roman Republic would have been a great blessing to the world, if it had not involved the unjust distinction between Roman citizens and the conquered peoples" and if the republic had been able to preserve its "virtue" (of democratic equality). This preservation, however, was impossible: "Caesar crushed the Roman Republic and subjected it to an absolute power. Hence, for a long time Europe groaned under a violent military government, and Roman benevolence was changed into cruel oppression." Rhedi's comments strike a theme that Montesquieu reiterated in many variations. In Kingsley Martin's judicious words:

> From the history of Rome, Montesquieu developed one of his most famous generalizations. Beginning with a small territory, Rome attained strength as a Republic founded upon the virtue of its citizens. When its territory had been everywhere extended, the old methods of government were no longer adequate, the spirit of the Republic was corrupted, and new vices accompanied the growth of Imperialism. Constitutional monarchy soon degenerated into despotism, relying no longer on virtue but on force and fear.[24]

Martin's statement, summarizing Montesquieu's deep apprehensions, should give contemporary readers pause. If it is true, as some observers claim, that the New World is replicating the example of ancient Rome, there is ample reason to share the French thinker's worries.

Moreover, the retreat of republicanism is cause for alarm for citizens and noncitizens alike, because the rise of unchecked power threatens the liberties of both. In this respect, recent developments in Western societies are by no means reassuring. Almost everywhere, the "virtue" of democracy—which, as Montesquieu says, is love of equality—is increasingly shunted aside in favor of the unleashing of egotism, individual greed, and lust for power. Under the aegis of privatization (so called), civic republican bonds give way to the upsurge of a renewed Hobbesian state of nature, a condition in which "the big fish eat the little fish" and the socially and economically advantaged lord it over the poor and dispossessed. No democracy or republic can survive long in such a climate. Here is a passage from *The Spirit of Laws* that seems to have been written for all times, and especially for our time:

> When virtue is banished, ambition invades the hearts of those who are capable of receiving it, and avarice dominates the whole community. Desires of people then change their objects: what they were fond of before, now becomes indifferent. They were free with laws, now they want to be free without them. Every citizen is like a slave who has escaped from his master's house. What was an accepted maxim now is called harsh rigor. Rules are given the name of constraints, and loyalty the name of fear.[25]

This decay of civic virtue and equality is one of the greatest calamities that can befall a democracy, because there is virtually no remedy in sight. With the growing despotism and unaccountability of ruling elites, voices willing and able to remonstrate are increasingly silenced; hence, there is little or no room left for citizens to "speak truth to power" and to urge a change of course, particularly a return to democratic virtue. Those daring to speak up increasingly face the risk of persecution—a fact vividly illustrated by experiences recounted in the *Persian Letters*. As Usbek confides to a friend in Isfahan: "From my earliest youth I have been a courtier—yet, I can say that I was not in the slightest corrupted by it. Indeed, I formed the great plan of daring to be virtuous even at court." In his effort to implement this plan, Usbek "carried truth even to the foot of the throne and spoke a language previously unknown there," thereby disturbing flatterers and confounding "idolaters and their idol." Eventually, however, the plan could no longer be maintained because of growing intimidation and threats of reprisals. "When I saw that my sincerity made enemies," the letter continues, "that I provoked the jealousy of the ministers but not the favor of the prince, . . . I resolved to withdraw" by going into "self-exile from my country"—an experience paralleling that of innumerable self-exiles and expatriates in our own time. Given its likely severe consequences, truth-telling in front of rulers must not be done lightly or frivolously, but out of moral responsibility and following the voice of conscience. "Truth is a heavy burden, my dear Usbek," his Persian friend Rica reminds him, "when it must be carried even to princes! Therefore, it ought to be remembered that those who do so are constrained to it, and that they would never have decided to take a step so unfortunate for themselves in its consequences, were they not compelled by their sense of duty, their respect, and even their love."[26]

What Rica beautifully expresses in these lines is that dissidents and truth-tellers love their country not less than others but more; they want their country to return to the path of civic virtue and to abandon its errancy in the wasteland of despotism and imperial power. Moral dissidents are sometimes described as people offering "prophetic witness," and rightly so, because they confront rulers not on the plane of power but on the plane of justice. The *Persian Letters* contains a marvelous phrase testifying to the importance of such witnessing: "I would have men speak to kings as the angels spoke to our holy Prophet." The words are Rica's, but they reflect not only the sentiments of one particular Muslim; they reflect the sentiments of believers of different faiths and of citizens of different countries around the world. To be sure, prophetic witnessing seems to be a solitary activity, reserved for only a few individuals, but this is not necessarily so. Particularly among people who can still remember the benefits of democracy, witnessing may take the form of a broader social engagement. Everything depends on proper education or pedagogy, on the ability to arouse among people the memory of and the renewed desire for civic virtue and equality. The real difficulty lies in the task of educating rulers and privileged elites. All efforts toward improvement must concentrate on curbing the excesses of these elites, for their bad example is prone to corrupt everything. As Usbek writes in his final letter to Rhedi: "What crime can be greater than that committed by a minister [or ruler] when he corrupts the morals of an entire nation, degrades the hearts of the most upright, . . . and obliterates virtue itself? What will posterity say when it blushes over this shame of its forbears?"[27]

6. Beautiful Freedom
Schiller on the Aesthetic Education of Humanity

During his dark period, the Spanish painter Goya depicted the horrors and monsters that are lying in wait behind the facade of reason. In doing so, he anticipated some of the most troubling questions of our time: How is it possible that one of the most developed and scientifically advanced civilizations on earth could spawn a string of atrocities ranging from Auschwitz to Hiroshima to Abu Ghraib? How is it that such a vast expansion of knowledge and information could be accompanied by such a derailment of conduct and such an atrophy of ethical sensibilities? These questions have occupied major social thinkers in the West. In his "Protestant Ethic and the Spirit of Capitalism," Max Weber presents modern society as populated chiefly by two character types: "specialists without spirit" and "sensualists without heart." In turn, Alasdair MacIntyre, in his *After Virtue,* portrays contemporary Western society as dominated by a limited number of "stock characters," but chiefly by two: the "manager" wedded to the efficient functioning of anonymous rule systems, and the "aesthete" devoted to privatized consumption and gratification. In light of these stock features, he notes, contemporary society reveals a curious coexistence of two strands: the "realm of the organizational," governed by objective rules, and the "realm of the personal," governed by private whim.[1]

As it happens, these features are not a discovery of recent theorists. More than two hundred years ago, the German poet Friedrich Schiller penned these lines: "The Enlightenment (*Aufklärung*)—not unjustly praised by the educated elites of our time—is in the end a merely *theoretical* culture, a culture which, on the whole, is not only incapable of cultivating ethical sensibilities (*Gesinnung*), but in fact aids and abets the spreading corruption in society, rendering the latter incurable."[2] The lines are found in draft manuscripts preceding the 1795 publication of Schiller's famous "Letters on the Aesthetic Education of Humanity" (*Briefe über die ästhetische Erziehung des Menschen*). As one notices right away, the term *aesthetic* here does not coincide with "subjective whim," as in MacIntyre's usage, but rather refers to the entire range of human sensibilities that need to be cultivated for the moral and political benefit of humanity at large. In 1955, on the occasion of the 150th anniversary of Schiller's death, Thomas Mann praised the cosmopolitan humanism of Schiller, extolling it as the "demand of our time," provided humanism (*Humanität*) ceases to be a merely abstract axiom and embraces our hearts and sensibilities as well. This "comprehensive feeling," he said, is what is "needed" (*nottut*) above all.[3] Mann's words, I believe, have lost none of their urgency today.

This chapter is meant as a contribution to the 200th anniversary of Schiller's death. I realize that Schiller's argument in the "Letters"—and indeed, the entire worldview of the classical age of German literature—is quite removed from contemporary frameworks of understanding. For this reason, I first provide some historical background in an attempt to profile Schiller's work against prominent intellectual currents of modernity. Next, I offer a condensed discussion of the main points made by Schiller, paying special attention to his relations to the philosophers Immanuel Kant and Johann Gottlieb Fichte. In conclusion, I sketch the chief lines of subsequent historical responses (*Wirkungsgeschichte*) and present some final comments on the present-day significance of Schiller's work.

Diremptions of Modernity

The stock characters mentioned by MacIntyre have not always dominated social life in the manner they do today. For a long time—stretching from antiquity through much of the Middle Ages—the domains of thinking and doing, of rational knowing and feeling or sensibility, were more closely correlated (without being entirely fused). The same linkage prevailed between public and private spheres and hence among politics, ethics, and the arts. The philosopher who most clearly epitomized this relatedness was Aristotle, whose work served as a model and benchmark for many centuries. In the words of Hans-Georg Gadamer: "Aristotle gave expression to what was basically already implicit in the Socratic and Platonic doctrine about the knowledge of virtue—namely, that we do not just wish to *know* what virtue is, but to know it in order to become good." Accentuating the connection and correcting a potential "intellectualism" in Socrates and Plato, the Aristotelian notion of *ethos* highlighted primarily one point: namely, that "virtue does not consist merely in [theoretical] knowledge," since the very possibility of knowing depends on "what a person is like," and what a person is like is "formed beforehand through his or her education and way of life." Reflecting on the basic tenor of Aristotle's philosophy, and especially on the key feature of situated judgment (or *phronesis*), Gadamer reaches this conclusion: "The crux of Aristotle's philosophical ethics, then, lies in the mediation between *logos* and *ethos*, between the cognitive faculty of knowing and the substance of being."[4]

As is well known, the symbiosis depicted in these lines was dissolved in the late Middle Ages and with the onset of modernity. In a sense, the whole worldview of modernity can be seen as an assault on Aristotelian linkages and mediations. The rise of nominalism and voluntarism during late medieval times drove a wedge between knowing and willing (or doing) and also between public (or "universal") categories and private particularity. The decisive break with the past, however, was triggered by modern rationalism, and especially by René Descartes' equation of reason with an inner mental faculty. What emerged with Descartes' philosophy was the demise of classical holism in favor of a systematic dualism, or bifurcation, between mind and matter, inside and outside, subject and object, and reasoning and acting (as well as creating). In the political and social domain, the Cartesian split was supplemented and reinforced by modern political philosophy, especially by the writings of Thomas Hobbes and John Locke, with their insistence on the distinction between nature and artifact, between a presocial (and possibly antisocial) private individualism and a public rule governance based on contractual agreement. Taken together, all these modes of bifurcation created a profound tension in individual and social life; during the classical age of German philosophy and literature, they tended to be seen as diremptions

(*Entzweiungen*), calling for both theoretical and practical remedies. To be sure, modern initiatives were not only corrosive of the past but also effective in opening up new vistas for human freedom and new opportunities for innovative experiences and social interactions. Yet, rigidly pursued, these same accomplishments also carried the seeds of the traumatic crisis highlighted by Weber and MacIntyre in terms of the collision between rational management and private whim—a collision particularly damaging to ethical life and creative art.

Without doubt, the chief glory of Western modernity resides in the steady advancement of science and technology, coupled with the unleashing of market forces propelled by individual enterprise; in large measure, Western civilization tends to be identified today with these traits. Both advances, however, share a common drawback: the neglect of ethical and aesthetic praxis (that is, the older Aristotelian *ethos*). Whereas modern science aims at the cognitive grasp of the world in terms of lawlike propositions, modern market economies rely on the dictates of private desires and preferences (only precariously coordinated by anonymous rules). Faced with these dominant trademarks of Western modernity, modern ethics and aesthetics have suffered a common fate: to remain viable or even intelligible, they had to adjust to the dominant paradigms of the age—that is, cognitive rationality and subjective feeling. The history of ethics and aesthetics during the pre-Enlightenment and Enlightenment period gives ample evidence of this kind of adjustment (to which I allude here only briefly). On the one side, we have the emphasis on private feeling or sensation, as articulated by the "moral sense" school—a school loosely associated by MacIntyre with the rise of moral "emotivism." On the other side, we have strenuous efforts to subsume ethical and aesthetic praxis under the norms of cognitive rationality and to derive the former deductively from the latter—the hallmark of rational, modern "natural law." Most prominent among the advocates of the second approach were the pre-Kantian proponents of rationalist metaphysics such as Christian Wolff.[5]

Rationalist schemes of this kind were challenged by English and Scottish empiricism, with its emphasis on concrete sense experience. In large measure, English empiricists traced their intellectual ancestry back to Locke, for whom all knowledge was ultimately derived from sense impressions. In the field of ethics and aesthetics, however, the real starting point was the Earl of Shaftesbury's "moral sense" approach, according to which both ethical virtue and aesthetic beauty are predicated on individual psychological dispositions. Countering the extreme self-centeredness of the Hobbesian account, Shaftesbury argued that human conduct is molded not only by fear but also by pleasure and that, accordingly, human sentiment can be molded by both virtuous deeds and beautiful objects. The approach was carried forward and fleshed out by Francis Hutcheson, especially in his *Inquiry into the Original of Our Ideas of Beauty and Virtue* (1726). Following in the footsteps of his predecessor, Hutcheson held that virtue and beauty cannot be based on reason alone, for reason deals only with logical propositions, and neither beauty nor virtue is a proposition. In the absence of logical deduction, the only possible basis for ethics and aesthetics is human sensibility, that is, the "moral sense" manifest in the psychological discrimination between pleasing or "amiable" impressions and painful or disagreeable experiences. In a philosophically erudite manner, moral sense arguments were further developed and deepened by David Hume, especially in his *Treatise of Human Nature* (1740) and later works. In line with earlier empiricists, Hume insisted on the primacy of human sensibility or psychological "feeling" and on the inability of "reason" to determine the meaning of virtue and vice or the quality of aesthetic objects. As for Hutcheson, the guiding criterion for Hume was "moral sentiment," seen as the disposition directing human conduct to what is pleasant or useful.[6]

There can be little doubt about the merit of moral sense arguments: by countering the conceit of deductive rationalists, they appropriately drew attention to the crucial role of human affect and motivation. Yet, this accomplishment came with a price. Quite apart from downplaying the role of obligations, moral sense teachings reinforced and deepened the diremptions of modernity—the bifurcations between inside and outside, passion and reason. As it happened, moral empiricism was not entirely uncontested, even in the confines of English and Scottish philosophy. A vigorous counterargument was launched by, among others, Thomas Reid, a contemporary of Hutcheson and Hume. Reid attacked the feeling-centered approach for sidestepping the concrete reality of the world and, above all, the shared frames of reference undergirding subjective sentiments and beliefs. In light of this stress on shared frames of meaning, his outlook became known as the "common sense" approach, which in time managed to rival the influence of sensationists. To some extent, a similar trajectory was pursued by Edmund Burke in his early aesthetic writings, although his stipulation of common or "objective" standards was still anchored in prevailing psychological dispositions.[7]

Notwithstanding partial anticipations, the decisive struggle against modern diremptions was the hallmark of classical German philosophy and literature. In this respect, several stages of argumentation need to be distinguished: stages leading from the preclassical *Sturm und Drang* period via Kant to the high classical period represented by Fichte, Schiller, and G. W. F. Hegel (and the postclassicism of Friedrich Schelling). During the immediate preclassical period, the voice of Johann Gottfried Herder stood out because of its spirited élan. Deeply affected by the intellectual tendencies of his time, Herder was alarmed both by the arrogance of enlightened rationalism and by the decay of ethical sensibilities, or, rather, by the mutual complicity of rational abstractions and sensual decay. As he wrote in his treatise *Another Philosophy of History for the Education of Humankind* (1774), the ascent of enlightened reason resulted in a deep ambivalence: on the one hand, "light, infinitely elevated and dispersed"; on the other hand, "affective inclination (*Neigung*) and the drive to live incomparably diminished." Everywhere, he noted, the "principles of freedom, honor, and virtue" are publicly extolled, but in reality, people are steadily succumbing to the "heaviest chains of cowardice, disgrace, extravagance, servility, and wretched aimlessness." For Herder, "education of humankind" could not rely on abstract ideas alone, for "ideas only yield ideas." How are they meant to transform human conduct concretely and to "mix within the soul"? The basic task of education, in his view, resided in the reflective cultivation and elevation of human sensibilities—something that cannot be accomplished by depending on either abstract rules or untutored sentiments (in the empiricist vein).[8]

Herder's *Another Philosophy* was imbued with youthful fervor that needed to be further filtered and refined through philosophical reflection. That refinement was basically the work of Kant and Fichte. Philosophically, Kant was reared in the rationalist metaphysics bequeathed by Wolff, but as he himself admitted, he was raised from his "dogmatic [rationalist] slumber" by his encounter with Hume. To be sure, this awakening did not land him in the empiricist camp; instead, it turned him into a rationalist of a special sort—one intent on specifying the precise boundaries of reason. In his first *Critique,* Kant pinpoints the rational conditions a priori of empirical knowledge (beyond which pure reason cannot advance). In his second *Critique,* reason—transcendentally conceived—emerges as supreme moral legislator, as the source of categorical moral imperatives guiding human conduct along the path of duty. In its basic structure, Kantian ethics thus operates in a rationalist, top-down fashion, with reason governing passion or sentiment, albeit with certain restrictions or caveats. Sensitive to Humean complaints, Kant is willing to assign a supportive and facilitating role to human inclinations—making it clear, however, that this role is secondary and passive in comparison to the actively governing role of reason. This top-down arrangement is further relaxed in Kant's aesthetics, and especially in his theory of "aesthetic judgment," which for him is anchored not so much in cognitive reason as in the faculty of "imagination" guiding human "taste." Despite this concession to individual taste, however, care is taken to guard against private or purely subjective whim—a move accomplished through the idea of a "common sense" (borrowed in part from Burke).[9]

Kant's writings had a profound impact on his contemporaries, functioning as a kind of yardstick of philosophical reasoning. Most intellectuals of the time, including Schiller, were subject to its influence, although efforts were soon afoot to modify the more rigid contours of Kantian thought. Leading these efforts in the German context was Fichte, an early follower of Kant and later Schiller's colleague in Jena. What troubled Fichte about Kant's philosophy was the unresolved tension between mind and matter, inside and outside, between the knowledge-constituting role of reason and the external "things-in-themselves." This tension was replicated in the gulf between rational duty and sensual inclination. For Fichte, it was a demand of reason itself not to leave this gulf unattended. Basically, what such attention yielded was insight into the impossibility of one-sided formulas—that is, recognition that the very conception of the self presupposes the nonself, the constitution of the ego presupposes that of the nonego (*Nicht-Ich*). This insight, in turn, led to the conception of the ultimate co-constitution of self and nonself, or the conception of a basic reciprocity (*Wechselwirkung*)—a notion not far removed from Leibnizian relationism and the idea of "dialectics" as developed by classical idealism. In Fichte's view, philosophy could no longer be anchored in cognitive rationality alone but had to invoke another faculty (called "intellectual intuition") that disclosed the dimension of "being" un-dergirding both self and nonself, ego and nonego. With this move, a path was opened to a new understanding of art and aesthetics, but it was a path that Fichte did not pursue.[10]

Schiller's Letters

The preceding sketch of modern intellectual trajectories has led us to the threshold of Schiller's own work. Like a prism, this work reflects all the great intellectual tendencies of his age, while simultaneously transforming and integrating them in a higher, more creative synthe-sis. Literary historians have instructed us about the broad range of influences operating on the poet. As a young college student, he was introduced to Enlightenment rationalism (from Descartes to Wolff), "moral sense" empiricism (from Hutcheson to Hume), and leading texts in contemporary psychology and physiology. In telling fashion, his doctoral thesis (submitted at the end of his medical studies) was devoted to an examination of the "correlation between the animal na-ture and the spiritual nature of human beings." What surfaced was a question that occupied Schiller for the rest of his life: namely, how internal-spiritual freedom is conceivable in the face of humanity's in-sertion in the nexus of natural forces and instinctual drives. By way of a critique of both rationalist metaphysics and British empiricism, the thesis arrived at the conception of a "middle force" or "physiological spirit" (*Nervengeist*) capable of mediating between nature and spirit, *physis* and *logos*. In the words of one expert, Peter-André Alt, the text aimed to establish a compromise between materialism and abstract rationalism, a kind of "balance harmonizing material and intelligible spheres."[11]

After writing his thesis, Schiller quickly emerged as one of the leading literary figures of his age: as a writer of dramatic, quasi-Shakespearean plays; as the author of lyrical poems; and as a histori-ographer of major historical events. These years also provide evidence of his intense involvement with Kantian philosophy, especially the latter's *Critique of Judgment,* first published in 1790. The initial outcome of this involvement was a series of writings composed between 1791 and 1793 dealing with a variety of related topics, such as the "ground of enjoyment," the meaning of "tragic art," and the nature of the "pathetic" and the "sublime." Clearly relying on the Kantian distinction between "noumenal" freedom and "phenomenal" dependence or heteronomy, Schiller located the core of dramatic pathos precisely in the tension and possible collision between freedom and external determinism. The tragic hero in this context was an individual struggling to preserve his autonomy through resistance to external constraints while simultaneously suffering from the consequences of his own failings and limitations. Regarding art and aesthetics, Schiller (together with Kant) opposed their equation with rational cognition while also questioning their reduction to private sensation or pleasure. Going a step beyond Kant, his essays adumbrated the possibility of a reconciliation between freedom and sensibility in the concept of the "beautiful," seen as the sensual manifestation of ethical freedom (*Erscheinung der Freiheit*). This move toward a closer correlation was continued in Schiller's famous 1793 essay on *Anmut und Würde* (Grace and Dignity), where the former was portrayed as the harmony of freedom and nature and the latter as the maintenance of freedom in the face of external adversity. In Alt's words: "*Anmut* reflects the reconciled relation, *Würde* the sustained conflict of reason and nature."[12]

These essays were only preambles to Schiller's most ambitious theoretical work: his "Letters on the Aesthetic Education of Humanity." As previously indicated, these letters were preceded by draft manuscripts sent to the Danish prince of Augustenburg (many of which were destroyed by fire and later partially reconstructed). In these manuscripts, Schiller made the intention of his work abundantly clear: aesthetic education was to remedy the deficit of concrete sensibility evident in Enlightenment rationalism and demonstrated graphically in the brutal aftermath of the French Revolution. What was needed in the modern context was both a tempering of abstract (Jacobin) logic and a refinement of brute sensuality through art.[13] The letters of 1795 are composed of twenty-seven installments that appeared consecutively in a journal edited by the poet. The installments can be grouped in three major segments: the first, discussing the intellectual and historical background (letters 1–9); a second, more philosophical, segment offering a quasi-transcendental analysis of the nature of art and aesthetics (letters 10–16); and a final section exploring the practical-ethical and political implications of the preceding arguments (letters 17–27). Throughout, the letters reveal a continuous engagement with, and transgression of, the Kantian paradigm of aesthetic judgment. They also reflect an adaptation of certain Fichtean initiatives regarding the relation between ego and nonego, self and other—now transposed into the realm of art and aesthetic creativity. Finally, and most prominently, the letters seek to vindicate Schiller's conviction of the importance of the cultivation of aesthetic sensibility as a gateway to genuine freedom and social and political well-being.

The opening segment offers a stark portrayal of the ambivalent character of the modern age, or what has more recently been termed the "dialectic of enlightenment." In his first letter, Schiller invokes the authority of "Kantian principles" that would serve as guideposts in subsequent arguments; however, this authority is immediately qualified by the avowed need to rely on "feelings [or sensibility] no less often than principles." As the letter explains, left to its own devices, philosophical reason tends to demolish sensibility, to "compress sensual appearance into the fetters of rules, to dissect its fair body into concepts, and preserve its living spirit in a mere skeleton of words." Ensuing letters underscore the detrimental effects of modern bifurcations, especially that between reason and desire. On the one hand, Schiller notes, we find "material needs" reigning supreme and bending "a degraded humanity beneath their tyrannical yoke." On the other hand, enlightened reason has led to the advancement of sciences bent on "wresting one province after another from the imagination." In vivid terms, the fifth letter depicts the human and social costs of these developments. The progress of Enlightenment, we read, has laid siege to a natural human condition governed by instincts and has brought into view a different prospect: namely, the possibility of "setting law upon the throne, of honoring humanity at last as an end in itself, and of making true freedom the basis of political association." This prospect, however, has proved to be entirely illusory, giving way instead to "extremes of human depravity." Among ordinary people, Schiller states, we are confronted with "crude, lawless instincts, unleashed with the loosening of the bonds of civil order." Among the educated classes, one finds "the repugnant spectacle of lethargy and of a depravation of character which is all the more offensive as civilization itself is its source." Civilized advancement, in a dramatic reversal, thus is accompanied by a barbaric regression (first noted by Herder and Rousseau): "In the very bosom of the most sophisticated social life, egotism has erected its system, and without ever acquiring a truly sociable heart, we only suffer the contagions and afflictions of a society." Hence, Schiller concludes, the spirit of the age hovers hopelessly "between refined perversity and brutality, between unnaturalness and mere nature, between superstition and moral unbelief."[14]

From this portrayal of modern times, the letters turn to a comparison of ancient and modern culture, conventionally styled as *la querelle des anciens et des modernes*. For Schiller, ancient—especially Greek—culture had much in its favor; above all, it managed to combine in some kind of unity what modernity splits asunder. "The Greeks," he writes, "put us to shame not only by a simplicity alien to our age"; in addition, they succeeded in displaying "fullness of both form and content," sensitivity and energy, the "first youth of imagination," and the "manhood of reason." In ancient Greece, sensibility and intellect did not yet move in opposite directions because no dissension had yet pushed them "into hostile partition." In contrast to the modern division of mind and matter, intellect and passion, ancient reason "always drew matter lovingly with it," and no matter how high it might soar, and however fine a distinction it might make, it did not "proceed to mutilate." How different the situation has become in modernity, with its bent for fragmentation. Whereas antiquity reflected an "all-unifying nature," modern times pay homage to the "all-dividing intellect." In Schiller's view, the change was also manifest in politics and the character of government. Divorced from the lifeblood of an ethical community, modern government develops into a rational artifact, into a "crude and clumsy mechanism" of control. In lieu of the symbiosis of individual and polis, the sixth letter states (anticipating Max Weber) that we witness the rise of "an ingenious clockwork" assembling a vast number of "lifeless," anonymous parts into "a mechanical kind of collectivity." At issue here is that otherwise valuable features—such as reason and civilization—emerge as the sources of a backlash:

> It was civilization itself which inflicted this wound upon modern humanity. Once the increase of empirical knowledge

and more exact modes of analysis made sharper divisions of knowledge inevitable, and once the increasingly complex machinery of the state necessitated a more rigid separation of ranks and occupations, the inner unity of human nature was severed too and a disastrous conflict set its harmonious powers at variance. Intuitive and speculative-rational understanding now withdrew into mutually hostile camps.[15]

Although deploring modern diremptions, Schiller did not view modernity as either avoidable or entirely without merit; the separation of domains also gave a powerful boost to human freedom and the unfolding of individual talents and capabilities. The question for him was how modern divisiveness could be tamed without stifling human freedom or, phrased another way, how freedom could be promoted in such a way as to transcend fragmentation. As he stated the issue: we must find a way "to restore by means of a higher art and culture that very wholeness of our nature which art and civilization have destroyed." But how could this recovery be accomplished? Schiller doubted that modern politics or government offered a suitable means for the purpose. Given their corruption and their reduction to mechanisms of control, modern states—far from being agents of transformation— needed to be transformed themselves. The only hope thus resided in education, and especially in aesthetic education that would cultivate sensibilities and render them congruent with ethical freedom. In accentuating aesthetic education, Schiller was not so much denying modern reason and civilization as attempting to place freedom on a more promising ground. As he wrote in his eighth letter: "Reason has done its work when it has discovered and established the (moral) law; its implementation, however, demands a resolute will and the ardor of feeling." If reason and truth wish to be victorious in the struggle with primitive instincts, they must "become a force (*Kraft*)" and "appoint some drive (*Trieb*) as their champion in the realm of concrete phenomena." In other words, since "the way to the head must be opened through the heart," the cultivation of human sensibilities is "the more urgent need of the age."[16]

As indicated earlier, the middle segment of the letters seeks to provide a philosophical (or quasi-transcendental) grounding of the nature of art and aesthetic education. The influence of Schiller's contemporaries, chiefly Kant and Fichte, is abundantly evident in this segment. From Kant, he derives the bifurcation between "noumenal" and "phenomenal" domains, between absolute freedom and external causality; Fichte, in turn, supplies the notion of reciprocity or reciprocal interaction—a notion deepened by Schiller's own aesthetic concerns. The central aim of the segment is to delineate a "rational" concept of art, such that beauty emerges as a "necessary condition of humanity." To achieve this aim, Schiller affirms, one must pursue a "transcendental path" that, transgressing the "familiar circle of phenomenal existence," will ultimately yield "a firm basis of knowledge." The path immediately discloses a dualism or bifurcation between (what Schiller calls) "person" and external "condition" (*Zustand*); this dualism coincides with that between permanence and change, between "self" and its determining attributes. Exploring the "person," he states, we discover the idea of an "absolute, self-constituted being, that is, freedom"; in contrast, examining the "condition," we encounter the source of "all contingent being and becoming, that is, time." Perception of phenomena in space and time is the work of human senses or sensuality; however, sensuality by itself does not furnish meaning or cognitive validity. In terms of the eleventh letter: "In order not to coincide with 'world,' human beings must give *form* to matter—just as in order not to remain mere form, they must *realize* their inner potential." Two contrary challenges, or "fundamental laws," thus operate in human life: the first insisting on "absolute reality," on the need to "turn everything that is mere form into world"; the second insisting on "absolute formality," the task to "erase everything that is mere world." In a shorthand formula, the dual demand is "to externalize everything inside, and to give form to everything outside."[17]

To enable human beings to comply with this demand, human nature—which is "sensual-rational" in character—has provided them with two different drives or motivations. The first is termed "sensual" or "material drive" (*Sinnentrieb, Stofftrieb*), an impulse rooted in physical existence and sensory experience. The second is called "formal" or "form drive" (*Formtrieb*); rooted in human rationality and absolute subjectivity, its goal is to secure the freedom of personhood or personality. Whereas the first drive operates on the level of particular instances, the second is the source of general or universal norms at all times and places. The two drives are contrary to each other, yet

they do not collide, provided they are properly constituted and operate in their distinct domains. The question is how the drives can be
balanced to prevent derailment. Schiller at this point invokes Fichte's
writings, and especially his notion of reciprocal action or interaction
(*Wechselwirkung*), which is captured in this motto: "without form
no matter, without matter no form." Transposing the notion into a
different idiom, the letters present the balancing act as the province
of culture or civilization. It is the task of culture (*Kultur*), we read,
to "accord equal justice to both drives," rather than sacrificing one
to the other; the goal here is "to preserve sensuality against the en-
croachments of [noumenal] freedom" while also "guarding personality against the impulses of sensation." Culture's function, however, is
not only to safeguard boundaries but also to promote the flourishing
of drives. This balanced flourishing of the two drives constitutes "the
idea of humanity."[18]

Having reached this point, Schiller asks whether the balancing of
drives is entirely fortuitous, or whether nature has perhaps supplied
another support. In answering this question, he advances a new thesis
(which is rightly considered the centerpiece of his letters): namely,
the addition of a balancing impulse that he calls "play drive" (*Spiel-
trieb*). This play drive both affirms and transgresses sensation and reason by taking off their harsh edges. In Schiller's words, the play drive
is destined "to transcend or sublate (*aufheben*) time within time, and
to reconcile becoming with absolute being, change with identity." By
smoothing the rough edges of the two primary drives, playing makes
room for a new and higher form of human freedom—one released
from both the "compulsion of [sensual] nature" and the "compulsion
of [legislating] reason." In terms of the fourteenth letter, the play
drive is able to motivate both physically and morally; "by canceling all
contingency, it cancels all compulsion too and thus inaugurates both
physical and moral freedom." To the extent that sensation aims to
preserve life or survival, and reason aims to provide form or rational
meaning (*Gestalt*), the play drive accomplishes what one might call
"living form" (*lebende Gestalt*), a concept that coincides with "beauty"
(*Schönheit*) in the broadest sense of the term. This notion completes
the "idea of humanity" previously mentioned by establishing a standard of harmony that can serve as yardstick for art and aesthetic education. Judged by this yardstick, Schiller adds, most of the aesthetic

theories prominent during the modern period are faulty or lopsided. What all these theories are missing is the appeal of aesthetics to an ideal of human completion—that is, the intrinsically humanizing quality of art. "To mince words no longer, only when playing are human beings properly and in the full sense human, and only fully human beings are able to play."[19]

In subsequent letters, Schiller elaborates on his basic thesis by adding a number of nuances, such as the distinction between a "relaxing" and a "tensing" (or "energizing") beauty. I do not examine these nuances here because they do not modify the gist of his argument. Instead, I turn to those portions of the letters that concentrate on the humanizing effects of art, as well as its social and political implications. The concluding segment is replete with eloquent passages on these themes. As we read in the twenty-second letter, it is in art and aesthetic beauty that "our humanity is disclosed with a purity and integrity as though it had as yet suffered no impairment from adverse forces." The reason for this purity resides in the fact that art and beauty release us from the compulsions of both instinct and abstract reason—that is, from our domination by nature as well as reason's impulse to dominate nature—and thus reveal a mode of freedom beyond instrumental use. In another passage: "Beauty produces no usable result, neither for the intellect nor for the will; it pursues no particular (intellectual or moral) purpose, does not seek to discover a specific truth or help us perform an individual duty." Above all, art and beauty are not goals to be pursued, panaceas to be executed or implemented; residing in the realm of free play, they are inaccessible to fabrication or social engineering. Unable to willfully fabricate them, humankind cannot properly take credit for beauty and art but must acknowledge them for what they are: gifts bearing the mark of divine grace. The capacity granted to us in the aesthetic dimension, Schiller writes, must be regarded as "the highest of all bounties, as the gift of humanity itself (*Schenkung der Menschheit*)."[20]

Although they are beyond willful manipulation, art and beauty appeal to, and find support in, human sensibility, which must be awakened through aesthetic education. At this point, the pedagogical motive of Schiller's letters assumes center stage. As he writes in a famous passage: "There is no other way of making sensual-instinctual beings rational except by first making them aesthetic" (that is, by fostering their aesthetic sensibility). For Schiller, in order to prosper and not to become destructive, reason and morality require the underpinning of aesthetic sensibility, which alone furnishes a motivation for conduct and a passageway from nature to norm. Therefore, "one of the most important tasks" of culture and education is to prepare through art a seedbed for truth and virtue; the basic point is to teach humans to "desire more nobly" so that they do not instantly have to "will sublimely." In this context, the letters sketch a narrative of civilizational advancement or development that is in many ways indebted to Herder and Rousseau. Basically, for Schiller, there are three stages of human development: the natural-sensual, the aesthetic, and the moral-rational. Whereas the first stage is subject to the impulses of nature, and the last establishes mastery over nature, the second stage operates in the "middle voice" beyond subjection and control. As depicted in the letters, the natural-sensual condition represents a "state of nature." All individuals are basically egotistical, though without having a reflective ego; everything they encounter is either an object of desire or a source of fear. The awakening of reflection triggers a radical change: namely, the unleashing of the "form drive," or the "drive toward the absolute" (*Trieb zum Absoluten*). This unleashing can be destructive unless the drive is channeled through a seasoning of sensibility, which is the work of art and beauty. Such seasoning alone, Schiller affirms, is able to engender the kind of human completeness or harmony that is traditionally called "happiness" or "blessedness" (*Glückseligkeit, eudaimonia*).[21]

By way of conclusion, Schiller reflects on the possible implications of aesthetic education for social and political life. Paralleling his narrative of civilizational development, Schiller distinguishes three types of social-political regimes: natural-dynamic, moral-rational, and aesthetic. In the first type—also termed the "state of natural rights"—human impulses collide like forces of nature, and in the second type, moral duty reigns "with the majesty of law." The aesthetic regime allows individuals to interact playfully as free agents. In Schiller's words, in the midst of "the fearful kingdom of forces" and "the sacred kingdom of laws," the aesthetic faculty guides individuals into a "joyous kingdom of play and semblance in which they are relieved of the shackles of circumstance and released from both physical and moral constraints." Entry into this kingdom is not a haphazard event; nature provides the impulse, and reason provides the norms, but aesthetic sensibility alone sustains society as a mode of sociability: "Although needs drive individuals into society, and reason implants principles of conduct, beauty alone can confer on individuals a sociable character. Taste alone brings harmony into society because it fosters harmony in individuals." In praise of the aesthetic regime, Schiller marshals all the registers of his poetic eloquence. In that condition, he writes, "everything—even the lowliest tool—becomes a free citizen having equal rights with the noblest members, and the intellect—bent on forcing the patient masses under its yoke—must first here obtain their assent." The last letter contains a veritable paean to our complete humanity made possible by this transformation:

> Now weakness becomes sacred and unbridled strength dishonorable. . . . He whom no violence might alarm is disarmed by the tender blush of modesty, and tears stifle a revenge which no blood was able to assuage. Even hatred pays heed to the gentle voice of honor. The sword of the victor spares the disarmed foe, and a friendly hearth sends forth welcoming smoke to greet the stranger on that dreaded shore where earlier only murder was lying in wait.[22]

The Legacy of Beautiful Freedom

In celebrating the taming of brute forces through art, Schiller's letters constitute a manifesto of a gentle and high-minded humanism, extolling the crucial work of humanization through education. In its concrete formulation, to be sure, the manifesto bears the mark of his exceptional and tension-ridden age—an age torn between old regime and revolution, between the classical tradition of the good life and the liberating and disaggregating impulses of modernity. Much of his effort was directed toward bridging the competing attractions and establishing harmony, or at least compatibility, between reason and passion, freedom and particular interests. To this extent, Schiller's text can be seen as the logbook of a precarious journey marked by setbacks and unresolved quandaries. As critics have frequently remarked, the letters pay ample tribute to modern diremptions, sometimes even insisting on the radical incommensurability between competing drives.

At the same time, however, they affirm the possibility of a blending of bifurcations in the higher unity of play and aesthetic beauty. As we read in the eighteenth letter, beauty "unites two conditions which are diametrically opposed and can never become one," but it also "destroys their opposition," such that it "disappears without a trace."[23] For late modern and contemporary readers, full appreciation of the letters may be obstructed by their lingering (though attenuated) attachment to modern "idealism," or what has come to be known as the "metaphysics of subjectivity."

In my view, quandaries of this kind, though not negligible, are ultimately of minor significance and do not affect the central merit of Schiller's work: his attempt to promote morally responsible freedom, and a morally responsible free society, through art and aesthetic sensibility. This central merit tends to be missed by critics who, inspired by political or ideological motives, fasten on simplistic or extraneous objections. One such objection has to do with Schiller's focus on the "play drive" and artistic playfulness, which, some claim, elevates card-players or billiards players to ideal models of humanity. What these critics ignore is that "play" for Schiller is not an occasional pastime or entertainment but rather the synonym for an entirely transformed human life—a life devoted to goodness and beauty beyond utility and calculation.[24] Another objection—equally misguided, in my judgment—attributes to Schiller certain bourgeois or even elitist tendencies at variance with the modern demands of social equality. A closer reading of the letters helps rebut that charge. Schiller at no point substitutes art or playfulness for the material drive (*Stofftrieb*) and the concrete survival needs of people. As he repeatedly insists, creative imagination can play a role only after basic needs are met, but then its role becomes crucial.[25]

Quite aside from such misreadings, Schiller's work has inspired important later debates, often serving as a kind of benchmark for assessing intellectual trends.[26] Well known is the tribute that Hegel (Schiller's junior by a decade) paid to the German poet when he praised him for pointing the way beyond Kantian one-sidedness— more specifically, for having "broken through Kantian subjectivity and abstract reasoning in order to grasp and express through art the truth of unity and reconciliation."[27] Schiller's bold attempt to bridge reason and nature, freedom and sensibility, also connects him with Schelling (even in the absence of any direct mutual influence). Crucial in this regard is the statement in the fourth letter that "the cultured [or educated] person makes a friend of nature and honors her freedom while only curbing her caprice"—a statement not far removed from Schelling's ambition to recuperate nature through sensibility in civilization.[28] To some extent, holistic appreciation persisted during the postclassical period. As many writers have noted, the critique of modern diremptions finds a parallel in Karl Marx's analysis of "alienation" and his aspiration to recover the full range of human capacities in a postindustrial condition. During later decades, however, Schiller's legacy tended to be abandoned; in a way, his letters increasingly fell prey to the very diremptions they critiqued. In this manner, Schiller's legacy succumbed to the Weberian scenario depicted at the beginning of this chapter: the split between "specialists without spirit" and "sensualists without heart."

Fortunately, there are signs of renewed appreciation. Efforts to put the pieces of Schiller's legacy together again surfaced during the twentieth century, especially in the context of Continental philosophy. Prominent European thinkers—from Ernst Cassirer and Karl Jaspers to Martin Heidegger and beyond—have struggled to remedy modern diremptions and to inaugurate a more balanced or holistic mode of individual and social life. Although himself imbued with neo-Kantian leanings, Cassirer acknowledged in Schiller's work a remarkable symbiosis of Shaftesbury and Kant, of moral sense teachings and rational-moral imperatives. In turn, relying on existentialist premises, Jaspers applauded in the letters the linkage of art and freedom, stating that it is only in play that the "freedom of human beings" and their genuine "humanity" become manifest.[29] In a different register, Heidegger attempted to undercut modern diremptions through his depiction of human existence as "being-in-the-world" and his key category of "care" (*Sorge*) located at the cusp between knowing and doing, reasoning and sense experience. At the same time, starting in his middle period, Heidegger increasingly paid tribute to Friedrich Hölderlin, Schiller's near contemporary and Hegel's friend. In several of his hymns and poems, Hölderlin celebrated the liberating quality of art and beauty and, indeed, the constitutive role of poetry in the formation of humanity—a celebration echoed in Heidegger's famous essay " . . . Poetically Man Dwells. . . ."[30]

In my view, it is the correlation of aesthetic education and ethical practice that reveals most clearly Schiller's relevance in our time. Basically, aesthetic education in Schiller's sense does not imply a utopian project or ideological blueprint, but rather the practical initiation into a freer, more ethically responsible and humane way of life. Specifically, his notion of an aesthetic regime—what he sometimes calls an "aesthetic state" (*ästhetischer Staat*)—should not be equated with the modern nation-state (seen as a mechanical artifact); above all, such a regime should not be reduced to a "state for aesthetes" or tailored to private-aesthetic consumption. It it seems to me that one needs to take seriously Schiller's portrayal of aesthetic life as a life of ethical freedom, a freedom that needs to be cultivated and nurtured through the fostering of aesthetic sensibility. In Schiller's own words (from his second letter), to resolve "the problem of politics," we need to take our approach through aesthetics, for "it is only through beauty that we find our way to freedom."[31] Also important here is Schiller's emphasis on the nurturing of sociability through art. To repeat a passage cited before: "Although [nature's] needs drive individuals into society, and reason implants principles of conduct, beauty alone can confer on individuals a sociable character." Thus, far from being an abstract chimera or a recipe for aesthetic retreat, the "aesthetic" regime—the regime of beauty and free play—was for Schiller a synonym for a transformative and humanizing pedagogy that incorporates elements of virtue ethics and character formation and anticipates elements of Hegelian *Sittlichkeit* and (perhaps) Heideggerian "care."[32]

From the contemporary perspective, one of the most impressive and striking features of Schiller's letters is his reconciliation of freedom and ethical virtue or goodness—two categories that tend to be radically split asunder in modernity. Again, it is aesthetic sensibility that accomplishes the mediation by guiding ethical inclination toward freedom from normative constraints and guiding freedom toward sociability with others. Yet, freedom here is a freedom from compulsion operating in the "middle voice" of play—beyond heteronomy and autonomy, beyond being dominated and wishing to dominate. Seen from this angle, Schiller's letters can serve as a classical handbook for civic education or education in civility, especially in our time, when governments are trying to escape, or have already escaped, from the bonds of justice and civic responsibility. Here are some additional passages that might form part of such a handbook. A political regime, Schiller writes, "is still very imperfect if it is able to achieve unity only by suppressing variety or difference." A regime, therefore, should honor not only general rules but also "the particular and unique character of individuals," and in erecting the intelligible realm of morals, it should aim "not to depopulate the sensible realm of appearance." Human life, another passage states, can derail in two major ways: either by becoming "savage," when brute feeling blots out conscience, or by becoming "barbaric," when abstract reason destroys feeling. The remedy for these derailments is the "holistic formation of character," which is possible only through civic engagement in the "realm of freedom."[33]

One other aspect of Schiller's work is crucial in our age marked by globalization and "terror wars": his freedom from ideological fervor, especially from the destructive zeal of nationalism or chauvinism. Together with his Weimar friend and companion Goethe, Schiller was deeply imbued with cosmopolitan leanings, with an openness to the broad range of global humanity. This openness is a hallmark of his plays and poems. Schiller was also the author of the great "Ode to Joy," which Beethoven intoned in the final movement of his Ninth Symphony. The ode contains these captivating lines: "Be embraced, all you millions—this kiss [I give] to the entire world!" In celebrating Schiller's anniversary half a century ago, Thomas Mann focused on this cosmopolitan commitment, citing, among others, these lines of the poet: "It is a poor and petty ideal to write only for a nation; this limit is entirely intolerable for a reflective spirit." Looking at his own period, Mann noted with dismay the gulf separating it from Schiller's legacy. Recent decades, he stated, have witnessed "a regression of humanity, a cultural decay of the most frightening sort, a loss of *Bildung*, decency, civility, and the most elementary kind of reliability." Against this grim background, his "Essay on Schiller" calls readers back to the lofty demands the poet bequeathed to posterity:

> Work in the service of humanity—a humanity which deserves civility, order, justice, and peace in lieu of reciprocal demonization, wild lies and poisonous hatred. This goal is not a flight from reality into lazy aestheticism; rather, it is an engagement in the service of life, guided by the will to heal us from fear and hatred through inner liberation. . . . Cosmopolitanism is

the demand of the hour and of our frightened hearts. The notion of humanity and of the broadest sympathy has long ceased to be the expression of a "weak sentimentalism." Rather, it is precisely this broadest sympathy which is required, urgently required today. For unless humankind as a whole is able to remember its honor and the secret of its dignity, we are all morally and physically lost.[34]

Part II

A Pedagogy for
Our Troubled Times

7. Why the Classics Today?

Lessons from Gadamer and de Bary

We live in a fast-paced age; in fact, the pace of change—at least in the so-called advanced societies—seems to be constantly increasing. Technological innovations that were unheard of just a few decades ago are briskly overturned and rendered obsolete by newer inventions of still more staggering magnitude. Using the parlance of videotapes, some observers have described our age as moving in "fast-forward." The question that remains to be pondered, however, is whether speed is an adequate gauge for the quality of human life. Clearly, no matter how germane it is to certain technical developments, fastness by itself does not adequately capture the peculiar rhythm of a life well lived. Actually, many things in life—perhaps the most important ones—require not speed but slowness and patience, such as the time required to allow understanding to mature, relationships to grow, and good dispositions to take hold. Nature's own rhythm gives us a cue; it is a rhythm that unhurriedly follows the sequence of the seasons and permits trees to grow and flowers to blossom at their own pace. How could human life be radically different, given its embeddedness in the cycle of birth and death, a cycle encompassing the so-called ages of man (infancy, adulthood, old age)?

In the field of education, the sequence of human ages is reflected in the relationship between teacher and student. In past centuries, this relationship was a close and intimate bond of apprenticeship (paradigmatically captured in the Indian formula of *guru-shishya-parampara*) in which the teacher transmitted to the student not only information but also the continuity of a tradition of learning, the fruits of the slow labor of intellectual and moral seasoning (far removed from clever dexterity).[1] A short label for these ripened fruits of learning is the "classics," and in this sense, every major cultural tradition on earth can boast a storehouse of classical texts and insights. What needs to be remembered, however, is that *classics* is not simply a synonym for *oldness* or for *wisdom* construed in the past tense. Treated in this manner, the classics would be a pastime reserved only for teachers and older people, which would vitiate the need for continuity of transmission.

In this chapter, I first clarify the meaning of the *classics*, using as my chief guide the German philosopher Hans-Georg Gadamer (who passed away in 2002). Combating antiquarian leanings or the tendency to reduce the classics to museum pieces, Gadamer eloquently accentuated the continual "timeliness" of classical teachings, that is, their location in *every* time rather than outside of time or in a particular time frame (that of antiquity). He also underscored the critical potential of these teachings: their role as an antidote to the ideological manipulations, or *idola fori* (idols of the market), of a given time and place. The same potential was also the hallmark of the classics in East Asian thought, as has been shown by Confucian expert William Theodore de Bary in several of his writings. I conclude with de Bary's plea to contemporary readers: to allow the classics to guide us toward *wen* (civility) rather than *wu* (warfare).

Gadamer and the Meaning of the Classics

In Gadamer's magisterial work *Truth and Method,* the topic of the classics surfaces in a somewhat unexpected context: namely, in the course of his discussion of hermeneutics and of the effectiveness of historical experience. Here, *hermeneutics* means basically the insertion of human understanding in an interpretive learning process, and *effectiveness* refers to the temporal quality of such understanding, its mediating role between past and future. As can be seen, Gadamer immediately distances the topic from its customary frames of reference—especially from an archaeological study of antiquity, but also from a narrowly historicist treatment that, insisting on rigid periodization, assigns the classics to a specific historical period (that of ancient history). As he notes, such modes of construal have indeed been prominent in modern Western history, especially during the age of Romanticism and the ensuing rise of historical consciousness (epitomized by historicism). As a result of these construals, the notion of the classics, or the classical, was reduced to either a mere stylistic genre or a label for an admired but hopelessly bygone era. Consequently, Gadamer complains, "classical" turned into the name for "a phase of historical development," but a phase devoid of any lasting significance. More sharply put, the "historicization" of the concept amounts to its complete "uprooting" or "deracination" (*Entwurzelung*) and hence to its sidelining, facilitating amnesia.[2]

In Gadamer's presentation, this misconstrual of the concept was not always prevalent in Western history, and it may give way again to a better understanding in our time. Especially during the Baroque age and certain peak moments of German classicism, a different conception held sway. In Gadamer's words: "The concept of classical antiquity and of 'the classical' which dominated pedagogical thought particularly in the days of German 'classicism,' combined both a normative and a temporal-historical dimension." This combination was still clearly present in the writings of Johann Gottfried Herder, who was able to link historical sensitivity with normative-philosophical standards and concerns. Despite a certain tendency to privilege historical development, a similar combination was still operative in G. W. F. Hegel's aesthetic philosophy, as is evident in his definition of the classical as that "which is significant in itself and hence also self-interpretive" (or self-reflective). On a practical, pedagogical level, this normative and prehistoricist view served as a cornerstone in the curriculum of the classical secondary school system in Germany (known as *humanistisches Gymnasium*) and of programs of "liberal" education (or education in the classical "liberal arts") elsewhere. During the first part of the twentieth century, despite formidable obstacles, a slow resurgence of the older conception was noticeable, especially due to scholars such as Werner Jaeger and other representatives of "classical philology." "It was symptomatic of a renewed historical self-criticism," Gadamer remarks, "that, after the First World War, classical philology started to re-examine itself under the banner of a 'new humanism' and hesitantly acknowledged again the combination of normative and historical elements in 'the classical.'" Unavoidably, such a restored humanism shared with the older humanist tradition an awareness of its "direct and exacting commitment to an exemplary model"—a model that, "as something past, is unattainable and yet always present."[3]

For Gadamer, the recovery of the normative or exemplary dimension is crucial for grasping the proper significance of the "classical." Yet, care must be taken not to misconstrue this recovery by lapsing into the opposite tendency. Although sharply critical of historicism and its consignment of the classical example to a limited period, Gadamer is equally reluctant to elevate normativity into a perennial sphere beyond time and space, which would rob it of its concrete "effectiveness." In good Aristotelian (and Hegelian) fashion, he pleads for the combination and mediation of "is" and "ought," of temporal and normative dimensions, in such a manner that the temporal remains impregnated with a qualitative potential. As he writes pointedly: "The classical is a truly historical category precisely by virtue of the fact that it is more than the mere name for an epoch or historical style but at the same time refuses to evaporate into a super- or extra-historical norm." Seen in this manner, the classical does not merely designate some particular historical phenomenon; rather, it signifies "an exemplary mode of being historical or temporal: namely, the historical process of preservation (*Bewahrung*) which, by continuously proving itself anew (*Bewährung*), allows an aspect of truth (*ein Wahres*) to manifest itself." (Note that in this formulation, truth remains linked with a certain temporal effectiveness.) As Gadamer adds, underscoring the preceding point: "The classical is indeed raised above the flux of changing times and changing tastes," but not in such a way as to become unavailable; rather, it is directly accessible at all times. What we discover here is "the awareness of something enduring, of an exemplary significance beyond amnesia and historical contingencies—a kind of timeless present which is contemporaneous with every present."[4]

It had been one of the prejudices of historicism and positivist historiography to assume that the application of critical research methods would finally erase all normative considerations or exemplary qualities. This assumption, in Gadamer's view, was thoroughly misguided; in fact, the use of critical and self-critical methods has, on the contrary, reconfirmed the classics' exemplary normativity. In this sense, one might say that the classical is precisely "what stands up to historical critique by showing that its historical significance—the normative strength of its continuously transmitted and preserving validity—precedes and pervades all historical reflection." With this emphasis on the classics' pervasive and continuing effectiveness, Gadamer's approach concurs with Hegel's previously cited definition (without necessarily endorsing the latter's teleology). Paraphrasing and elaborating on Hegel's statement, *Truth and Method* declares: "Classical is what preserves itself precisely because it is significant in itself and continuously interprets or reflects on itself." Put differently, classical is what speaks in such a way that it does not refer to a distant past but rather "addresses every present generation as if its message was specifically meant for it." Given that it speaks to every generation, classical exemplarity is, in principle, inexhaustible and needs to be continually reappropriated and reinterpreted every time; its resources are such that the possibility of learning never comes to an end—hence the need for continual historical transmission. In Gadamer's words: "The classical, then, is certainly 'timeless,' but this timelessness is a mode of historical being," a timeliness addressing itself to all times.[5]

Since the initial publication of *Truth and Method* (in 1960), Gadamer's approach has been subjected to numerous critical rejoinders focused on different aspects of his work. As a hermeneutical thinker firmly committed to philosophical dialogue, he has responded to a host of critical inquiries, often revising or reformulating his initial observations. His conception of the "classical" has also been the target of critical commentary, but in this case, Gadamer firmly stood his ground. In an afterword written some fifteen years later, he reaffirmed the timeless timeliness of classical teachings. Far from designating a particular genre or a canon of ancient texts, he noted, the "classical" has to be seen as "a basic category of effective history (*Wirkungsgeschichte*)," in the sense that it remains an exemplary challenge for all times. It is true that, in issuing their continuous challenge, classical works transcend their original context; this does not mean, however, that they are blandly transmundane—beyond time and place—or that they testify to a "reassuringly harmonious conception of the 'universally human.'" Rather, classical works have their effect precisely because they address us directly in our present situation—in Gadamer's words, by speaking "as if they were saying something to me in particular." To this extent, it is not quite correct to describe classical teachings as supra- or extrahistorical; their point is to demonstrate, in exemplary fashion, what human temporal experience means or can mean. In this sense, the classics do indeed set a standard, but a concretely lived and potentially transformative standard.[6]

Gadamer as a Teacher of the Classics

Gadamer's comments on the classics are eloquent and insightful. Part of their salience has to do with his own life experience: he was the product of a classical secondary education and later studied classical philology and became a teacher and transmitter of classical teachings. Born in Marburg in 1900, Gadamer spent his youth in the city of Breslau, where he received his secondary education at the Holy Ghost School, a somewhat modified classical school (or *Gymnasium*) with a heavy emphasis on Latin and a slightly lighter emphasis on Greek. This experience laid the foundation for Gadamer's classical competence. After the First World War and his father's transfer to the University of Marburg, Gadamer devoted himself principally to the study of philosophy. Significantly, he chose as his chief mentor during these years the philosopher Paul Natorp, one of the most renowned Plato scholars at the time. It was under Natorp's guidance that, in 1922, he completed his doctoral dissertation: "The Nature of Pleasure according to Plato's Dialogues." When Martin Heidegger joined the Marburg faculty a year later, Gadamer immediately became his postdoctoral student and a close associate, but he did not abandon the study of classical philology. The university boasted a number of eminent scholars in that field, including Paul Friedländer, and it was under Friedländer's expert guidance that Gadamer began an intimate study of Plato and Aristotle. According to his biographer Jean Grondin, it was through Friedländer that Gadamer "learned how to value Plato's dialogical art, and discovered how important it is to know with whom Plato is talking and how philosophical insight accrues to the reader in the process of a dialogue." It is probably not far-fetched to trace a trademark of Gadamerian hermeneutics—its dialogical character—back to his classical studies at Marburg.[7]

In terms of his educational career, Gadamer's studies enabled him to pass the university examination for teachers of classical philology, an examination that covered Greek and Roman classical texts ranging from philosophy to poetry and rhetoric. Impressed by his accomplishments, Heidegger invited Gadamer to write a second dissertation under his tutelage. The theme of this second dissertation, titled "Interpretation of Plato's *Philebus*," was again thoroughly classical. Although a youthful work, the dissertation inaugurated and foreshadowed several of Gadamer's later key ideas and emphases, especially his concentration on questioning and dialogical ethics. What is striking, Grondin notes, is "the choice of the *Philebus* itself, one of the later dialogues but one in which Socrates plays a leading role—which indicates how vital the Socratic motif of questioning after the good remains in Plato's 'dialectical ethics.'" By foregrounding the motif of questioning, the dialogical or hermeneutical element becomes "the key to Plato's philosophy, not just a stylistic ornament"—an aspect that tends to limit the "validity of Aristotle's critique of Plato" (that is, the critique of the latter's conceptual formalism). To be sure, the differences between Plato and Aristotle are not erased by this approach, but neither are the similarities ignored. As Grondin adds: "The *Philebus* and its questions about the 'mixed life' where the humanly good is to be found, show how much common ground Plato and Aristotle in fact share."[8]

Throughout his subsequent academic career—which took him from Marburg and Leipzig to Frankfurt and finally to Heidelberg— the classics remained a stable anchor of Gadamer's teaching and publications. Apart from his writings on Hegel, Heidegger, and other modern and contemporary themes, an impressive body of his work was devoted to preeminently classical authors, especially to Plato's dialogues and Aristotle's ethics (as well as the interrelation between the two Greek philosophers).[9] Similar topics were also a steady focus of his lecture courses and academic seminars throughout his career. Thus, his pedagogical activities in Heidelberg revolved around such themes as "Socrates and Plato," "Platonic Ontology," "Pre-Socratic Philosophy," "Aristotle's *Metaphysics XII*," and "Aristotle's *Nicomachean Ethics*."[10] Of course, as Gadamer always emphasized, the concept of the "classical" cannot be restricted to the period of antiquity or to a privileged set of Greek and Roman authors. If the notion of temporal persistence and exemplarity is taken seriously, it is clear that many modern and even quite recent texts have the quality of timeless timeliness and thus qualify as classical. In Gadamer's own teaching practice, the works of several modern thinkers—from Descartes, Leibniz, and Kant to Hegel and Heidegger—were singled out as exhibiting exemplary, and in that sense classical, qualities. Some readers today may find that Gadamer's own *Truth and Method* has the earmarks of a classical text. The comments of one of his former students, Rüdiger Bubner, are a case in point. In offering a *laudatio,* or homage, to Gadamer, Bubner declared in 1997: "We younger people did not then suppose that Gadamer's book—whatever its richness in individual areas, phenomenological evidence, and acute observations—would develop such vitality that it would last for more than a generation to be translated into many languages of the world and come to be considered as a standard work of present-day philosophy. But it has risen at length to the status of a classic."[11]

To Gadamer, the classics possess an intrinsic worth; hence, studying and teaching classical texts carry their own reward. However, classical teachings also have a social and even political dimension. Basically, these teachings contain a liberating and purifying potential by virtue of their ability to liberate people from the sway of *idola fori,* from the stultifying pressure of reigning ideologies and manufactured public beliefs. In his afterword to *Truth and Method,* Gadamer concludes with a startling confession: "In my work, I brought 'classical' concepts . . . into play not in order to defend classical ideas [or to erect them into public idols] but to transcend the bourgeois conception of the aesthetic as cultural religion" (today, we would say: the unlimited reign of bourgeois consumer culture and the religion of the market). As one can see, the invocation of the classics in Gadamer's writings did not serve the purpose of bolstering an elitist "high culture"; rather, the invocation carried a critical countercultural and counterpolitical connotation, resisting appropriation by the powers that be. In his view, an important precursor of this approach was Herder, who, relying on the classics, boldly confronted some of the *idola fori* of his age. As Gadamer states: "Herder's attack on the Enlightenment's pride in reason had its most effective weapon in the exemplary character of classical antiquity. . . . His *History of Ancient Art* was obviously more than a mere historical account: it was a critique of the present inspired by the exemplary quality of Greek art."[12]

Asian Classics as a Source of Resistance

Obviously, the notion of the "classics" or the "classical" is not restricted to Western culture and philosophy. As stated earlier, all the major civilizations and cultures around the world have their own storehouses of classical teachings and classical wisdom—some of them preserved through oral transmission, and others as written texts. Examples of classical legacies preserved in oral fashion can be found in African cultures and among the Amerindian peoples. Emphasis on canonical texts is a chief feature of the Abrahamic religions, also called the "religions of the book." In the Islamic context, the cultivation and transmission of classical teachings have always been prominent preoccupations, which accounts for the central role of *'adab* ("civility," "civil learning") in traditional Islamic education.[13] In the Indian tradition, the study of the Vedas, Upanishads, and Bhagavad Gita has served as the cornerstone of classical learning through the ages, just as the texts of the Pali canon and the sutras have enjoyed a privileged place in the transmission of Buddhist beliefs and cultural practices. In the present context, I want to turn briefly to Confucianism—a tradition in which classical texts and teachings have enjoyed perhaps the most prestigious and influential role through the centuries.

In the Chinese Confucian tradition, canonical texts are called *ching*, a term that is commonly rendered in English as "classics." Originally meaning an intricately woven fabric, *ching*, when applied to these texts, was meant to convey the idea that they furnish human beings with enduring "threads" or guides for proper behavior and ethical living. During early Confucianism, canonical status was commonly attributed to the so-called Five Classics, which, according to tradition, had been written or at least edited by Confucius himself: the Book of Changes (*I Ching*), the Spring and Autumn Annals, the Book of History (*Shu Ching*), the Book of Rites (*Li Ching*), and the Book of Poetry (*Shih Ching*). During subsequent centuries, these texts were continually interpreted and reinterpreted, and in due course, they became central pillars of Chinese education and were required reading for all people aspiring to civil or ministerial service. Later, especially during the Sung period, the Five Classics were replaced or supplemented by a more accessible collection of Four Books, among which the so-called Great Learning (*Ta-hsüeh*) was most highly valued. As Theodore de Bary, the great China scholar and expert on neo-Confucianism, points out, in troubled times (such as during the Mongol invasions) it became imperative to render the classics more accessible to readers. Thus, people came to appreciate "the ease with which students could master the Four Books," compared with the difficulties presented by the older Five Classics. Despite a certain adjustment or redefinition of the canon, the basic goal of Confucian education—character formation and social responsibility—remained the same. In de Bary's words: "The Neo-Confucian commitment to the 'way' (*tao*) carried with it a sense of deep responsibility for one's obligations in life, a feeling that one's life could not be lived frivolously and thoughtlessly, but should always link self-respect and self-improvement to respect for others and advancement of all in the 'way.'"[14]

As one should note, and as de Bary makes abundantly clear, cultivation of the classics in the Confucian tradition was not merely an instrument of mandarin elitism; it had a critical and politically risky edge: that of restraining the whim of powerful rulers. "The scholar-official," he states, "was obliged to take most seriously the need for government to serve the general welfare (*kung*) rather than private or selfish interests (*ssu*)." For instance, in terms of a minister's role as adviser to the ruler, there was an "obligation to speak out with the utmost candor, upholding the practical validity of the 'way' regardless of the consequences to him personally." According to de Bary and other China experts, the critical role of scholars and ministers was institutionalized during much of Chinese history in the form of the "classics mat" (*ching-yen*), a kind of sanctuary from which the minister was encouraged to speak freely as the ruler's mentor, chiefly by lecturing the ruler on the meaning of classical teachings and their possible conflict with proposed imperial policies. A good example is the attitude of the neo-Confucian sage Ch'eng I (1033–1107) during the early Sung period, when he opposed some brutal policies of the ruler. Ch'eng I is reported to have stated: "When sages and worthies know that the 'way' is being destroyed in the world, can they remain seated, watching the chaos, and refuse to save the world?" Insisting on the basically ethical character of the relation between ruler and scholar-official, Ch'eng I considered it imperative for an official to quit the service of a ruler with whom he was in strong disagreement. In support of this stance, he invoked the testimony of Mencius: "Unless the ruler honors virtue and delights in moral conduct, . . . it is not worthwhile having anything to do with him."[15]

The critical role of Confucian classical teachings is not restricted to the past; it continues into the present. As is well known, Confucianism has experienced a recent resurgence in Asia, but sometimes under autocratic or even totalitarian auspices. In the latter case, Confucian scholars are suspected of being accomplices of the powers that be or hankering for mandarin privileges. But there is another, more hopeful possibility, as de Bary lucidly examines in an essay titled "Why Confucius Now?" There, de Bary frankly concedes the temptation of Confucian scholars to be co-opted by political rulers; he also acknowledges how difficult it is for individual scholars to speak to rulers from the traditional classics mat. The main reason for this difficulty (or near impossibility) is the immense increase in state power—what de Bary calls the rise of the "Leviathan state" in Asia, which exceeds in military and bureaucratic might anything that "could be managed simply by interpersonal ritual relations." As a counterpoise to this imbalance, his essay recommends the strengthening of civil society institutions (what Montesquieu called *corps intermédiaires*), including community schools, to make room for both modern and neo-Confucian classical education. In his words (resonating strongly with Gadamer's views): "Coming to terms with one's own past culture" is "an essential element in arriving at the self-understanding that is a precondition for understanding others." And "the best way to accomplish this is for every curriculum, as part of a shared general education, to have a place for the reading and discussion of classic texts that have stood as landmarks of the developing traditions in each country." He adds (again in full accord with Gadamer) that the meaning of the "classics" has to be expanded:

> In the modern setting something like this—a core curriculum in the humanities—is clearly needed, in each case based on one's own tradition but reaching out to others, that is, in East Asia beyond the Confucian core to include, on a higher level, comparable lessons from other world traditions—moving from a base in one's own culture to a more expansive multicultural education at increasingly higher stages of learning.[16]

More recently, de Bary elaborated on these themes in a book titled *Nobility and Civility,* which can also be read as a study on civil education or civic pedagogy. Relying on classical Confucian teachings, he emphasizes that such pedagogy involves the cultivation of civic virtues in rightful settings (*li*). "Virtue and the rites," he notes, "sum up a moral culture that is conducive to governance based on voluntary compliance—a civility supportive of civilized rule." In this context, he points to the crucial distinction made by Confucius between civil and peaceful culture (*wen*) and the military arts (*wu*), and to Confucius' insistence on the subordination of the latter to the former. De Bary also reminds readers of the teachings of Mencius, especially his distinction between the "ranks of man" and the "ranks of Heaven." In the words of Mencius, "the ranks of duke, minister or high official are the nobility of man," or belong to the "ranks of man," while "humaneness (*ren*), rightness (*li*), loyalty and truthworthiness are the nobility of Heaven," or belong to the "ranks of Heaven." To be sure, making this distinction and privileging the heavenly ranks over human or social rank orders can be risky in times of tyranny or oppression, and Chinese history offers many illustrations of this risk. *Nobility and Civility* refers to a document from the early Qin period in which a prime minister urged the emperor to suppress the classic writings of Confucius whenever they aroused popular dissent: "Anyone referring to the past [the classics] to criticize the present should, together with all members of his family, be put to death."[17]

In the epilogue to his study, de Bary reflects on the meaning of the classics and classical traditions, especially in our time. To make some headway in this field, he urges readers to recognize "two main features" in the evolving tradition and cultural legacies. The first feature (reminiscent of Gadamer's discussion) is that the classics have "commanded attention" within a given culture because "they have taken up central ground and staked out axial positions from which later writers and thinkers get their bearings." The second feature (echoing Hegel) is that these axial positions are "pivotal and multifaceted enough" so that they afford "the grounds for their own internal contestation and self-criticism as well as grounds for responding to the challenge of competing traditions." Once these points are taken into account, the contemporary relevance of the classics is clear. Their role is crucial, de Bary observes,

> at a time when political conflicts and culture wars incline some people to believe in the inevitable clash of civilizations or the basic incompatibility of different cultures. There is enough violence in the twenty-first century to persuade one that the twentieth century's liberal assumptions of "one world" as a natural and rational development are being taken to the ground.

But before we conclude that superior force is the only way to resolve such inherent conflicts we owe it to ourselves to make another, more determined effort to understand how the multivariate and multivalent resources available within these traditions afford the means for a meaningful discourse to take place on each other's terms.[18]

By way of conclusion, de Bary appeals to his readers—to each one of us—to decide where we take our stand: on the side of warfare and military conflicts (*wu*), or on the side of civility and civic virtues (*wen*). This is not an issue that can be left to politicians or so-called leaders. It is an issue in which each one of us has a role to play. "Even the relatively modest contribution of persons whose education bridges two or more cultures," de Bary writes,

could make a difference in gradually advancing civil discourse and a multicultural or intercultural civility. This may represent only a modest advance and perhaps be too slow to overtake the impassioned violence breaking out all over the twenty-first century world; but education genuinely respectful of human dignity, shared in all its manifest diversity, calls for such a patient and determined effort from all of us.[19]

8. Canons or Cannons?
On Mobilizing Global Democracy

"Mobilizing democracy" is a stirring catchphrase, and it was a well-chosen theme for the 2005 meeting of one of the largest social science associations in the United States.[1] In choosing that theme, the organizers obviously wanted to establish a broad agenda, both nationally and globally. In fact, although couched as an ongoing process, the motto can readily be translated into a directive or even an imperative that postulates "mobilize democracy" or "spread democracy everywhere" or simply "democratize the world." The directive is stirring and captivating—but also disorienting, given the serious malaise afflicting contemporary democracy both at home and abroad. How can we heed the agenda to mobilize democracy when democracy is under siege nearly everywhere, being held hostage to huge military-industrial complexes and almost routinely surrendered to "national security" interests? Another troubling or disorienting factor is the basic asymmetry inherent in such general agendas or marching orders; clearly, like every other imperative, the injunction to democratize (or to mobilize democracy) creates a disparity between those issuing the injunction and those subject to it. That is, it establishes an imbalance between those who democratize and those who are being democratized, or between those who command and those who obey. This asymmetry stands in glaring contrast with the democratic ethos, which demands civic equality among all participants.

The discrepancy is probably not troubling for national leaders or policy makers; being solely concerned with power and efficiency criteria, their vision typically stops short of ends. For Western leaders in particular, the agenda to democratize the world is only a variation on a series of similar orders issued during modern and late modern times, such as directives to "modernize," "Westernize," or "develop" the world.[2] What is untroubling to policy makers, however, is of necessity disturbing to political theorists or philosophers who remain faithful to their task of reflecting on what we are doing and trying to make sense of what is happening in the world. For reflective people, the contrast between the imposition and the experience of democracy, between unilateral marching orders and shared standards of life, is unacceptable and in need of reconsideration. Examining the arsenal of options, reflective people are liable to discover a pathway that steers clear of both unilateralism and mutual isolation (or incommensurability): the royal path of teaching and learning, of pedagogy and genuine *Bildung*.[3] A clue along the way is provided by the story of the slave boy in Plato's *Meno*, which indicates that we can learn only what we (implicitly) already know and that teaching is a kind of (mutual) disclosure. In this chapter, I follow that clue, proceeding in three steps. First, I ask whether it is possible to learn across cultures, or to substitute the canons of learning for the cannons of military conquest. Next, I comment on the meaning of canons of learning and on the quality of teaching as a mode of learning. Finally, I draw lessons from these explorations for the enterprise of mobilizing democracy today.

Canons or Cannons?

The notion of cross-cultural learning got off to a bad start in our time. Even before the dawn of the new millennium, the prognosis offered by political experts was grim. In his well-known essay published in 1993 (and subsequently developed into a book), Samuel Huntington painted a somber scenario of global politics in the decades ahead. "The great divisions among humankind and the dominating source of conflict will be cultural," he proclaimed. Hence, "the clash of civilizations will dominate global politics," and "the fault lines between civilizations will be the battle lines of the future." In his view, the globe was already divided between "the West and the Rest," but the most troubling fault line was the one yawning between the West and Islam (or between "the West and several Islamic-Confucian states").[4] The events of September 11, 2001, only extended that fault line, and the rift was deepened by the ensuing "terror wars." The shock waves of these events have enticed even learned intellectuals and philosophers to subscribe to the "culture clash" scenario.[5]

What these intellectuals ignore is that cultures and religions are not monolithic entities endowed with invariant traits. Contrary to the talk about "fault lines" and "civilizational identity," all cultural and religious traditions are inherently multidimensional, composed of many different strands and layers whose relationship is often tensional or obscure—thus triggering the need for continual reassessment and reinterpretation in response to prevailing challenges. In our globalizing era, immense challenges of reassessment are faced by people everywhere, in both Western and non-Western societies. To an unprecedented degree, people around the world are compelled to reinterpret both their own traditions and the traditions of other cultures, to relearn and understand anew both their own canonical texts and the canons of other peoples. And they do so for basic existential reasons: to make sense of their lives, and to give hope to the prospect of living together as equal partners in a global (or globalizing) democracy.

Since Islamic civilization is often treated as beyond the pale of mutual learning and engagement, this issue deserves special attention. Undeniably, Islam has historically clashed with other cultures, including European as well as Indian (or Hindu) culture. But there is another side to the story. In the case of the Indian subcontinent, Islam initially arrived as a conqueror, subjugating much of the region to its rule—a memory that clouded future relations. However, precisely because of these recurring conflicts, the Indian case deserves a closer look. Amartya Sen, the Nobel laureate of Indian descent, recently reexamined the history of his country, paying special attention to the role of Islam in India's overall development. Without neglecting episodes of violence, Sen zeros in on the positive results of traditional antagonisms, such as their contribution to the rich tapestry and multidimensional diversity of Indian civilization—a diversity incapable of being collapsed into a single strand. With regard to Islamic contributions, the laureate's account fondly recalls the legacy of devotional piety and poetry (Sufism); this legacy interacted so closely with forms of devotional Hinduism that the religious identity of some of India's great poet-saints cannot be established with certainty. In the political domain, Sen singles out the "tolerant multiculturalism" of the Moghul ruler Akbar the Great, who codified minority rights for non-Muslims and generally instituted policies of fairness and equity. Although he was only half literate, Akbar managed to fill his court with important intellectuals and artists, and in later years, he set up the earliest known interfaith discussion group, where Muslims, Christians, Jews, Jains, Hindus, and even atheists pondered where and why they differed and how they could live together peacefully.[6]

To students of Western history, of course, Sen's observations are not surprising. Delving into the intellectual origins of medieval Europe, such students quickly discover the crucial role of Islam in the effort to civilize and educationally uplift that still largely "barbarian" continent. It was mostly through Arab philosophers and translators that the treasures of Greek and Roman antiquity—the core of the later classical canon—were transmitted or retransmitted to the medieval heirs of Plato, Aristotle, and Cicero. How can one forget the richly energizing and intellectually enlivening effects of the works of al-Farabi, Ibn Sina, and Ibn Rushd (Arerroes) on the minds of European thinkers at the time? How can one underestimate the importance of the legions of Muslim translators and transcribers involved in cultural transmission? To portray Islam as beyond the pale of dialogue or engagement, from this angle, means to strike at the root of European and Western civilization. To catch a glimpse of medieval cultural symbiosis, one need only visit the Spanish city of Cordoba, where, in different town squares, one can still admire the imposing statues of the Stoic Seneca, the Muslim philosopher Ibn Rushd, and the great Jewish thinker Maimonides.[7] How much mutual learning seems to have happened in such a relatively small space! Of course, all this took place before 1492, that is, before Muslims and Jews were expelled from Catholic Spain, before a concerted effort of ethnic and religious cleansing tried to reduce European civilization to a uniform mold and a single identity.

In the history of Europe, cross-cultural learning was not restricted to the encounter with Islam, of course. On a more limited scale, learning and its transmission also occurred between Europe and the Far East, and the crucial names in this respect are Marco Polo and Matteo Ricci. About two centuries before 1492 and Columbus's voyage to the New World, the Venetian Marco Polo set out to visit far-off China, which at the time was under the dominion of the Mongol ruler Kublai Khan. Encouraged by the khan, Polo and his companions traveled to

China in 1271, following the fabled Silk Road; they returned twenty-five years later. On arrival, Polo immediately embarked on a study of the local languages and soon entered the Mongol public service, where he quickly rose to high administrative positions.[8]

The story of Matteo Ricci was more complicated and punctuated by problems having to do with the fact that he was not a private traveler but a Jesuit missionary tied, however loosely, to instructions from Rome. Like Marco Polo, and perhaps with even greater perseverance, Ricci immersed himself in the study of the Chinese language and culture, emerging as an authority in the field and even earning the respect of leading Chinese literati at the time. Ricci's cultural immersion was guided by the basic conviction that he was in China not only to teach but also to learn. In fact, he believed that Christians and the Chinese could learn much from each other, based on the underlying bond of humanity linking them together. In the words of David Mungello: "Disagreeing with the rigid Spanish and Portuguese treatment of foreign people as pagans whose traditional culture conflicted with Christianity, Ricci and others in the Society of Jesus sought more of a reconciliation of the native culture with Christianity"—a reconciliation that included respect for classical Chinese writings (the Chinese canon), ritual observances, and the practice of ancestor worship.[9]

Quite apart from its encounters with European travelers, Asia has its own rich tradition of cross-cultural and interfaith learning stretching back over two thousand years. Most prominent in this tradition is the encounter between Chinese Confucianism and Taoism, on the one hand, and Indian Buddhism, on the other. As in the European case, the contact was instigated and carried forward by travelers, specifically by Buddhist monks who journeyed from India to China, facing great hardship on their long excursion. One of the principal tasks faced by these itinerant monks was the translation of sacred texts from Sanskrit or Pali into the Chinese idiom, a task that required great skill as well as a good dose of cultural flexibility and mutual learning. As a result of these exegetic labors, Buddhism was infused with prevailing Chinese ideas, especially the teachings of Lao-tzu and Chuang-tzu. Chinese thought, in turn, was amplified and transformed through the integration of Buddhist ontology and metaphysics. In the words of Heinrich Dumoulin, whose study of Buddhism traces the complex interaction between elements of Indian and Chinese culture:

The transplanting of Buddhism from its native soil in India into the culture and life of China may be counted among the most significant events in the history of religions. It meant the introduction of a higher religion—complete with scriptural canon, doctrines, morality, and cult—into a land with an ancient culture of its own. . . . This encounter with the spiritual heritage of ancient China became a fountainhead that was to nourish the various schools of Chinese Buddhism, all of which were intimately related to one another despite doctrinal differences.[10]

From China, Buddhism spread to Japan, Korea, and adjacent lands in the Far East. Again, cultural-religious learning and transmission were mainly the work of traveling monks and scholars disseminating Buddha's message by land and by sea. In the case of Japan, a reverse itinerary was often required; owing to the scarcity of texts and trained teachers, Japanese scholars felt the need to travel to China to obtain genuine instruction. Easily the most impressive of these travelers was the monk Ennin, also known in Japan as Jikaku Daishi. Some four centuries before Marco Polo, Ennin crossed the sea to China and spent about a decade traveling that vast country (then under the T'ang dynasty), keeping a detailed record. Significantly, Ennin's diary was titled "Record of a Pilgrimage to China in Search of the Law" (or *dharma*), which means that Ennin was in search not of riches or political power but of the right way to live (*dharma, tao*). Thus, at least in his case, the canons of learning took clear precedence over, and managed to silence, the cannons of military power and economic gain. The Asia scholar Edwin Reischauer has translated Ennin's diary into English, accompanied by an extensive commentary. In his introduction, Reischauer offers a general observation that deserves mention. "In the present age," he writes, "in which we are experiencing the painful process of amalgamation into one world, a great historical document of this sort, although medieval in time and Far Eastern in place, is part of our common human heritage, with significance beyond these limits of time and space."[11]

Learning from the Slave Boy

In the recited encounters, cross-cultural learning was typically not an effort to foist a doctrine or established canon on alien populations, thereby subjecting them to foreign control. Rather, in almost every instance, great care was taken to find resonance for transmitted ideas in indigenous cultural and religious traditions, that is, to treat the latter as the very resources needed for genuine learning and transformation. In this manner, a measure of interhuman equality was preserved, and the danger of unilateral violence or manipulation was avoided, or at least greatly reduced. This, of course, is the secret of teaching and learning—or of teaching as a mode of learning. As all genuine teachers know, their task is to transmit ideas without manipulating or coercing their students in any way, that is, while fully respecting the students' autonomous capacity for learning and self-discovery. In a lecture presented to teachers in 1962, the German philosopher Martin Heidegger observed that teaching (*lehren*) in its proper sense does not mean to indoctrinate or foist knowledge on others but rather to create a space and opportunity for learning (*lernen lassen*). This kind of teaching, he added, is even more difficult than ordinary learning. In fact, "the genuine teacher is ahead of his students only in the one sense that he/she has to learn much more than they do: namely, how to let learning happen."[12]

With this accent on "letting learn" (*lernen lassen*) or creating a space for learning, Heidegger placed himself clearly in the tradition of the Platonic dialogue titled *Meno*. In that dialogue, Socrates and his interlocutors create an opportunity for the slave boy of the merchant Meno to learn about the basic principles of geometry. The slave boy, we are given to understand, has not received any previous instruction in geometry, nor does he have any acquaintance with Pythagorean theorems. Yet, under the careful prodding and gentle guidance of Socratic questioning, the boy eventually comes to grasp and articulate geometric principles as if he had "known" them from the beginning. By both teaching and not teaching the slave boy, Socrates creates an opportunity for the boy to learn and understand something he "knew" but did not really or clearly know. In this manner, the boy discovers what Socrates always claimed about himself: "he knows that he does not know," which means that he is a learner. If full knowledge were given to us "by nature," without further ado, there would be no need for learning; if knowledge were completely unobtainable or out of reach, there would be no incentive for learning. This is precisely what Socrates says in response to the complaints of an increasingly weary

Meno: "You look on this as a piece of trick-logic, as if a man cannot try to find either what he knows or what he does not know. Of course, he would never try to find what he knows because he already knows it, . . . or what he does not know because he would not know what he is trying to find." But—and here is the Socratic twist—"we must not be guided by this trick-logic, for this would make us idle," whereas "our way makes people active and inquiring."[13]

Unfortunately, in the history of Western education, the advice of Socrates has not always been heeded. Too often, education has been pressed into the antinomy of knowledge or no knowledge; it has been equated with either the rote transmission of fully known and invariant doctrines (leading to top-down indoctrination) or the uncritical rehearsal of current opinions (predicated on the presumed impossibility of finding any true knowledge). In late modern times, the second option has tended to prevail; in particular, it was endorsed by a certain kind of "pragmatism" unconcerned with the search for truth (or equating truth only with desired consequences). Curiously, in this approach, the two sides of the trick-logic chided in *Meno* work in tandem: children are assumed to possess "by nature" all the knowledge they need (rendering learning pointless), and the search for any knowledge beyond opinion is discouraged (producing the kind of lazy idleness denounced by Socrates). Among prominent intellectuals, no one has critiqued the flaws of this program more severely than Hannah Arendt. Detecting a veritable "crisis" in Western education, Arendt puts the blame squarely on the doorstep of pragmatic complacency. The assumptions underlying this program, she notes, though seemingly protecting a "natural" children's world, actually destroy "the necessary conditions for vital human development and growth"—that is, the space in which learning can occur.[14]

There is another drawback in the discussed agenda, and it has to do with the maxim that truth is "what works," or what turns out to be useful in application. A crucial premise of this maxim is the assumption of a finished and preexisting human being occupying the center of the universe and acting as the final judge of what works and what does not, of what is useful or useless to humankind. Heidegger's lecture to teachers (cited earlier) takes aim at this premise. In contrast to the modern craze for utility and technological efficiency, Heidegger maintains that *thinking* actually means something radically different:

"to arouse the sense for the useless." What is useless in this manner has its own quality or dignity; it cannot be appropriated, used, or abused for ulterior purposes. Ultimately, the meaning of *human* cannot be appropriated or used in this manner either. Hence, a new vista opens up, a new space where learning might happen. In Heidegger's words: "Useless in the sense that nothing directly practical can be done with it, is the very meaning of things." His lecture at this point refers to a text by Chuang-tzu, the student of Lao-tzu, in which the Chinese sage celebrates a mighty but crooked tree for which neither loggers nor carpenters have any use.[15]

Moving beyond what is useful in search of the truth or the "meaning of things" is precisely the genuine sense of learning; it is also the proper meaning of the German term *Bildung* (often translated as "formation," "education," or "culture"). In his *Truth and Method*, Hans-Georg Gadamer elaborates on the meaning of *Bildung* in a sensitive and historically nuanced fashion. As he points out, in the High German idiom, the term was never used to designate career training or preparation for a specialized occupation; instead, it denoted the ongoing search for meaning and understanding—above all, the meaning of humanity or of being human. The word *Bildung*, he writes, does not designate the "training of capacities" for the purpose of an extrinsic utilization; rather, educational nurturing carries its goal in itself: "Like nature (in the Greek sense of *physis*), *Bildung* serves no end outside itself." For illustration, Gadamer refers to the famous motto of Johann Gottfried Herder: *Emporbildung zur Humanität*, which means "cultivation in the direction of humanity"—a cultivation that is not undertaken for any ulterior motive. His text also refers to older, traditional conceptions that still resonate in the German term, especially the medieval notion of the *imago Dei* (*Bild* or *Ebenbild Gottes*) imprinted in the human heart and constituting the very sense of humanity.[16]

In an effort to further explicate the meaning of *Bildung*, Gadamer's text turns to the work of G. W. F. Hegel, especially his "Philosophical Propaedeutics" and "Phenomenology of Spirit." In a way, Hegel rescued *Bildung* from the danger of lapsing into a private or individual pastime by elevating it into a task for humanity at large. Like his contemporaries, Hegel insists that *Bildung* obeys no extrinsic motives and carries its telos in itself; more clearly than many others, however, he emphasizes that the goal is not just the cultivation of individuality but a broader interhuman cultivation: the cultivation of self in relation to others, and of cultures in relation to other cultures. Here, a basic leitmotif of Hegel's philosophy comes into view: intersubjective or interhuman recognition, which is possible only through reciprocal engagement and ultimately depends on mutual respect and understanding. To gain such understanding, in Hegel's view, it is necessary for the "self" to transcend or go beyond itself in search of otherness, and initially, this is a search for the unknown (or what is not yet known). Yet for Hegel, moving toward the unknown of otherness is not a leap into a dark abyss but a move in the direction of what we unknowingly search for (and hence somehow "know"): the meaning and truth of humanity. Hence, exodus and alienation are seen not as sheer vagrancy but as the propaedeutic to a possible finding. In Gadamer's words: "To recognize one's own in the alien, to become at home in it, is the basic movement of 'spirit' [in Hegel's sense] whose being consists precisely in returning to itself from otherness. . . . Hence it is clear that the point of *Bildung* is not alienation as such, but a kind of homecoming which, to be sure, presupposes alienation."[17]

Mobilizing Global Democracy

With these Hegelian insights, we are brought back to the issue of mobilizing cross-cultural, or perhaps even global, democracy. It should be clear by now that such mobilization cannot happen through military coercion and force. The use of force violates the axioms of mutual recognition and equal respect, which are the requisites of the ethos of democracy. Despite the obviousness of this point, many policy makers and world leaders (notoriously hesitant to learn) still privilege "cannons" over "canons." According to some of these leaders and their supporters, the policy of an "advanced" nation should be to spread democracy worldwide, by force if necessary. Nowhere has this policy been more clearly stated than in the book *An End to Evil*, written by two intellectuals close to the seat of hegemonic power. As the authors assert, American foreign policy should be committed to a global "war for liberty" and democracy, and this goal can only be achieved "by American armed might and defended by American might," irrespective of the glaring incongruence of means and ends.[18] The same incongruence has surfaced in many other ways. Thus, ingenious politicians have come up with the notion of a "democratic occupation" or an "occupied democracy"—clearly an oxymoron.

Since military cannons do not serve the purpose, the only proper way to mobilize democracy cross-culturally is through reciprocal engagement and recognition, that is, through a process of canonical learning that leads to the cultivation of a sense of equality and mutual respect. I use the term *canonical* here in synecdochic fashion (part standing for whole) to indicate a certain cultural coherence. Learning cross-culturally obviously involves more than the study of canonical texts in a narrow sense; it includes engagement in a broad configuration of lived experiences, or what Wittgenstein called a "language game" seen as a "form of life." What is canonical about these configurations is that they exert a certain claim on members of a language community that cannot willfully be set aside. Moreover, elements of a cultural configuration are not isolated or random features; rather, they hang together in complex clusters, such that translation between cultures must proceed not from concept to concept but from language to language or from tradition to tradition.[19] By virtue of these clustered configurations, cultures maintain their respective differences or otherness, a distinctness that does not amount to a wholly untranslatable incommensurability. It is this difference among cultures (their "unknown" dimension) that renders learning necessary; it is their partial translatability that renders learning possible, or at least not entirely pointless.

Cross-cultural learning, properly pursued, involves a process of peregrination or alienation and hence of transformation—and not in a unilateral fashion. Those who believe that they have something to teach the world need to shoulder this process with particular intensity; they need to learn even more than their students, and in particular, they must master the capacity to "let learn" (*lernen lassen*). Hence, in the encounter, all sides are put to the test. Western advocates of democracy may discover that some of their beliefs have congealed into ideologies or perhaps even dogmas, requiring renewed self-scrutiny. Thus, they may have to reexamine some cherished assumptions, such as the absolute truth of liberal democracy in its association with laissez-faire economics and a preference for "negative" liberties. The outcome of this reexamination may well be a (partial) reaffirmation, but it is likely to be tinged with a sober awareness of limits and a prudent moderation that is uncongenial to a "call to arms." Conversely, societies or cultures that are novices to modern democracy may find that—no longer threatened by Western military domination—they can explore the new terrain without excessive risk or self-abnegation. In the process, they may discover that their own traditions provide resources for the development of their own kind of modernity and their own version of modern democracy.[20] It was in this manner that Mahatma Gandhi discovered in the Indian tradition—or in the complex welter of Indian traditions—the resources for fostering a distinctive kind of Indian self-rule (*swaraj*). And it was in the same manner that Martin Luther King Jr. found in Christianity the resources for combating racial prejudice.

What needs to happen, hence, is not the unilateral exportation of Western democracy to the rest of the world. Instead, a space must be created where learning about democracy can happen and where democracy can take root in a democratic way, without coercion. To some extent, cross-cultural global arenas already exist, but in embryonic or fledgling form. Among the available venues are the United Nations General Assembly, the United Nations Educational, Scientific, and Cultural Organization (UNESCO), and some other specialized agencies, supplemented by a host of regional institutions. The problem with existing venues is that they are dependent on participating state governments, whose policy agendas are typically oriented not toward learning but toward national power and economic self-interest. For this reason, efforts are presently under way to reform and supplement existing global institutions with more people-oriented arenas, such as a People's Assembly in the United Nations and similar transnational (not state-centered) institutions.[21] Irrespective of such efforts (whose outcome is by no means assured), there is plenty of room for innovative experimentation on both the global and regional levels. In particular, the present situation calls for the creation of a World Public Forum (or a series of such venues) to parallel such existing gatherings as the World Economic Forum and the World Social Forum. Anchored in global civil society (rather than state governments), this public forum would serve as the precursor of an emerging global public sphere, where the basic issues of the world could be aired and discussed mainly from an ethical and humanitarian perspective. Such a forum would encourage positive steps for the alleviation of poverty, hunger, and disease worldwide, but it would also act as the voice of conscience and denounce the rampant power politics and greed of national elites, as well as the indiscriminate acts of violence perpetrated by terrorists.

With the establishment and strengthening of global venues of this kind, people around the world will feel that they are no longer at the mercy of political and corporate elites and that they can vent their grievances in an open, nonrepressive, *democratic* way. Viewed in this light, global venues can be seen as spaces that allow learning to happen (*lernen lassen*), especially learning about how to mobilize democracy and its ethos of equal respect. Let me close with a passage from a recent book by Benjamin Barber titled *Fear's Empire*. "Democracy," Barber writes,

grows from inside out and from bottom up rather than from outside in and top down. This is one of the reasons why democratization takes so long. It also suggests that the objective for those seeking a democratic world ought not to be "democracy" in the singular, on the America model or any other, but "democracies" in the plural. . . . Surely the plurality of Western democracy itself argues for an appreciation of variety in considering democratization in transitional societies beyond Europe and North America. As Amartya Sen has insisted, it is critically important to recognize "diversity within different cultures" as well as diversity among cultures. In nations and cultures emerging from nondemocratic regimes, it may be more productive in establishing liberty to draw on indigenous traditions and institutions than to mimic exogenous constitutions and imported political devices.[22]

9. An End to Evil

Conquest or Moral Pedagogy?

Things long ignored or repressed often return with a vengeance. Evil, or the problem of evil, is a case in point. As heirs to the Enlightenment, Western societies in recent centuries have tended to sideline evil as a spook or as the relic of a distant past. In the poignant words of Lance Morrow: "The children of the Enlightenment sometimes have an inadequate understanding of the possibilities of Endarkenment."[1] Two events in more recent times have disrupted this complacency and catapulted evil back into the limelight. The first was the experience of totalitarianism, and especially the atrocities of the Nazi regime summarized under the label "Auschwitz." As Richard Bernstein writes, echoing Hannah Arendt: "What happened in the camps was the most extreme and radical form of evil. 'Auschwitz' became a name that epitomized the entire Shoah, and came to symbolize other evils that have burst forth in the twentieth century."[2] Following the Second World War, the memory of these atrocities was kept alive in some quarters, but it was counteracted by the rising tide of consumerism and the tendency of the culture industry to trivialize evil or turn it into an underground "punk aesthetic." Then came the second major jolt: September 11, 2001, and the ensuing "war on terror" and the offensive against the "axis of evil." To quote Morrow again: "There came a crack in history, September 11, 2001, and [President] George W. Bush's 'Axis of Evil,' and all that followed. The idea of evil regained some of its sinister prestige and seriousness."[3]

In light of the enormous calamities of the past hundred years, it would be entirely vain—as well as foolish and dangerous—to ignore the reality of evil or to underestimate its power. There is simply no passable way back into trivial innocence. Once this is recognized, the central question becomes how to deal with the acknowledged presence of evil in the world—that is, its presence both in ourselves and in others. In a recent book titled *An End to Evil: How to Win the War on Terror,* David Frum and Richard Perle propose a solution to this question: the conquest or forced termination of evil. In their words: "We do not believe that Americans are fighting this evil to minimize it or to manage it. We believe they are fighting to win. . . . There is no middle way for Americans. This book is a manual for victory."[4] Victory over evil is certainly a tall order and an ambitious claim. To assess this claim properly requires an answer to at least two prior questions. First: what is the nature of evil—especially radical evil—such that it can be decisively terminated or vanquished? Second: is it a proper policy objective for the United States—a country dedicated to freedom and democracy—to pursue this goal? In this chapter I explore these and some related questions. I first turn to the meaning of *evil* and briefly discuss how this meaning has been construed by philosophers and theologians through the centuries. I next focus on a famous construal that recognizes both the reality of evil and the importance of human freedom: Friedrich Schelling's treatise, "The Nature of Human Freedom." Following a review of some trenchant readings of this treatise (from Martin Heidegger to Richard Bernstein), I return to the solution proposed by Frum and Perle and offer a counterproposal.

Some Theories of Evil

As philosophers and theologians have always acknowledged, evil is a staggering problem that almost defies comprehension. Some have treated it as utterly recalcitrant—a Sisyphean labor to extract sense from nonsense, meaning from meaninglessness. Still, unwilling to admit defeat, philosophical and theological ingenuity has produced a plethora of formulations designed to shed light on the problem. In the present context, it cannot be my purpose to offer a comprehensive overview of these formulations; some rough typologies must suffice. In her book *The Many Faces of Evil,* Amélie Oksenberg Rorty provides a complex, sixfold typology of metaphysical-theological treatments of evil. In abbreviated form, the six types argue (1) that there is only divine goodness, and evil is an illusion (often called theodicy);

(2) that although some evil exists, it is only a lesser degree of evil, or a "privation" of goodness (a view prominently associated with Saint Augustine); (3) that good and evil are both real and permanently conflicting forces (Manichaeism); (4) that human reason postulates a perfectly rational universe but acknowledges evil as a dilemma (a view ascribed to Kant); (5) that evil is real and the world is a mess (Schopenhauer); and (6) that good and evil are nothing in themselves but only social constructs (Hobbes and possibly Nietzsche).[5] By contrast, Susan Neiman in her book *Evil in Modern Thought* makes do with only two major types: arguments relying on "fire from heaven," and arguments bent on "condemning the architect." Whereas the former are advanced by philosophers celebrating divine or rational "order" despite real-life experience to the contrary, the latter are favored by an assortment of realists, pessimists, and cynics.[6]

From my own perspective, Rorty's typology is a bit cumbersome, and Neiman's account seems overly parsimonious. Without claiming any kind of completeness or greater theoretical adequacy, I find it preferable to distinguish among three major approaches to the understanding of evil. (I might be willing to add a fourth category reserved for skeptics, cynics, and immoralists. However, since they tend to dismiss the distinction between good and evil, their approach would not really constitute an alternative mode of understanding evil.) The three categories that have traditionally dominated discussions of evil are radical monism, radical dualism, and a spectrum ranging from modified monism to modified dualism.[7] Radical monism holds that ultimate reality—being a reflection of the divine or of a benevolent creator—is wholly good and perfect, whereas perceived imperfections are illusions or the result of ignorance. The theory is most famously associated with Leibniz, but it can also be found in versions of Christian and Neoplatonic gnosis, in the work of the great Indian Advaita thinker Shankara, and in esoteric forms of Islamic Sufism. The prototype of radical dualism is Manichaeism, but it can also be found in versions of gnosticism and in extreme Puritan theories of predestination (with their radical opposition between the "elect" and the "damned"). The middle ground between monism and dualism is occupied by Neoplatonic and Christian thinkers who are ready to acknowledge evil but give primacy to divine goodness. Thus, in treating evil as a mere "privation" of goodness, Augustine approximates the monist view; however, by insisting on the "fallenness" of human nature and the distinction between the heavenly and earthly cities, his theory slides toward Manichaean dualism. In a similar way, modern rationalists, such as Descartes and Kant, steer an ambivalent course between rational insight and ignorance. On the one hand, they grant primacy to rational order; on the other hand, their separation of mind from nature (Descartes) or "noumena" from "phenomena" (Kant) carries strong dualist overtones.

Some examples may help illustrate the preceding typology. In Western philosophy, the most famous example of radical monism is Leibniz's *Theodicy* (1710). Seeking to absolve God from any complicity in the evils of the world, Leibniz presents these evils either as illusions or as necessary instruments for the promotion of divine providence. He writes: "God wills order and the good; but it sometimes happens that what appears disorder in some part is actually order in the whole." Regarding the evidence of wicked human acts, the text turns matters around by portraying such acts as evidence of the divine plan of salvation or redemption: "The same wisdom which made God create man innocent, though liable to fall, also makes him re-create or redeem man when he falls; for God's knowledge causes the future to be for him like the present."[8] Outside the confines of the West, examples of monism can be found in several contexts. As indicated earlier, a prominent case is the Indian philosophy of Advaita Vedanta, as articulated chiefly by Shankara (788–820). According to this philosophy, all beings have their true reality in *brahman*, while the assumption of separate existences testifies to ignorance (*avidya*). The goal of believers is to realize the ultimate identity of selfhood, and all its actions, with divine essence (*atman* is *brahman*).[9] Similar formulations can be found in Islam, especially its more mystical or intuitive strands. Rorty refers to the great Persian philosopher and mystic Abu Hamid al-Ghazali (1058–1111), and especially to one of his writings titled (in free translation) "There Is No Evil in Allah's Perfect World."[10] An even more fervent espousal of monism is the hallmark of esoteric Sufism. In a bold text bordering on heterodoxy, the "Great Sheikh" Ibn Arabi (1165–1246) proclaims the ultimate unity of all things with divine reality, without remainder or exception. As he states: "Whosoever knows himself" properly knows himself as integral to divine essence, leading to the conclusion that "*thou art He* without any limitations. And if you know thine existence thus, then thou knowest God; and if not, then not."[11]

Radical dualism is traditionally associated chiefly with Manichaeism, according to which there are two contending and roughly equally matched forces in the world, each guided by a separate ruler or master: God and the "prince of darkness." After originating in ancient Persia, the doctrine was later disseminated throughout the Middle East and came to form the backbone of Hellenistic gnosticism (which does not refer to gnosis, or insight into the ultimate unity of all being, but rather to knowledge of the conflictual division of the world resulting from humankind's partaking of the "tree of knowledge"). Rorty provides passages from writings attributed to Hermes Trismegistus, a Hellenistic devotee of gnosticism obsessed with the interminable warfare between goodness and evil, light and darkness. For example: "I say that there are demons who dwell with us here on earth, and others who dwell above us in the lower air, and others again whose abode is in the purest part of air. . . . And the souls which have transgressed the rule of piety, when they depart from the body, are handed over to these demons, and are swept and hurled to and fro in those strata of the air which teem with fire and hail."[12]

Without fully subscribing to equally matched forces, echoes of these gnostic teachings surface in the works of later Christian authors, especially during the Reformation and post-Reformation period. Thus, in *Paradise Lost*, the Puritan John Milton gives ample room to the voice of "Satan," portrayed as the determined rebel and contender for ultimate control: "But of this be sure, / To do aught good never will be our task, / But ever to do ill our sole delight, / As being contrary to his high will / Whom we resist."[13] In some of his writings, Martin Luther moves even closer to the dualist doctrine. Thus, in commenting on Saint Paul's letters to the Romans and the Galatians, he envisages a quasi-Manichaean combat raging in human life: "These two captains or leaders, the flesh and the spirit, are one against another in your body, so that you cannot do what you would. . . . But we credit Paul's own words, wherein he confesses that he is sold under sin, that he is led captive of sin, that he has a law in his members rebelling against him, and that in the flesh he serveth the law of sin."[14]

The middle ground between monism and dualism is occupied by positions that modify the dominant alternatives, sometimes significantly (though without abandoning their basic premises). Saint Augustine (354–430) is usually credited with introducing an important new dimension into discussions of good and evil: namely, the central role of human will. As he writes in "The Problem of Free Choice": "The mind becomes the slave of passion only through its own will." Hence, "the will is the cause of sin," and the latter cannot be attributed "to anything except to the sinner who wills it." Yet for Augustine, willing the good and willing something evil are not on equal footing (which would have landed him in Manichaeism). Rather, honoring the primacy of divine order, he views only good will (or a will oriented toward goodness) as a proper and efficient exercise of willing, whereas an evil will opts for something characterized only by negativity, privation, or deficiency, and hence for something not truly real: "Vice cannot be in the highest good, and cannot be but in some good. Things solely good, therefore, can in some circumstances exist; things solely evil, never."[15]

Under completely different circumstances—during the period of the European Enlightenment—Immanuel Kant renewed and radicalized Augustine's focus on human will, though extricating this focus from its Christian-theological foil. Without subscribing to a divinely ordered universe, Kant treated "good will"—rooted in "noumenal freedom"— as the essence of human nature and morality. For him, good will meant behavior in accordance with the maxims stipulated by radical human freedom, whereas deviation from these maxims, or the choice of evil, meant nonessence or a basic deficiency or vitiated conception of human nature. Distantly echoing Saint Augustine, Kant writes in *Religion within the Limits of Reason Alone* that the notion that "man is evil" can mean only that "he is conscious of the moral law [postulated by freedom] but has nevertheless adopted into his maxim the (occasional) deviation therefrom." As for the reasons prompting the slide from moral freedom to evil—or the lapse from nature into sin—Kant declares them (with Saint Augustine) to be ultimately "inscrutable."[16]

Schelling on Evil

In my view, the first major advance beyond traditional approaches to good and evil occurred in the immediate post-Enlightenment period, particularly in the work of a thinker whose ideas were formed by the Enlightenment yet pointed resolutely beyond it: Friedrich W. J. Schelling. In this respect, I fully concur with Bernstein when he writes: "I see Schelling not as a transitional figure en route to Hegel, but rather as a transitional figure in *transforming* our (very) understanding of the problem of evil."[17] What is distinctive about Schelling is that he affirms the "reality" of evil without lapsing into Manichaeism, and he affirms the goodness of God without denying God's complicity in the reality of evil. In conformity with Kant, he insists on the centrality of human freedom in all issues having to do with good and evil; departing from Kant and the Enlightenment, he moves beyond anthropocentric "willing" by embedding the choice of good and evil in a larger ontological reality within which good and evil acquire significance in the first place. As Bernstein poignantly writes: "In his 'higher realism' Schelling seeks to avoid two extremes: absolute dualism and an undifferentiated homogeneous monism. . . . He wants to avoid the consequence that there is an absolute duality of good and evil (that is how he understands Manichaeism), as well as those pseudo-solutions that reconcile good and evil by denying the reality of evil." One such pseudosolution is the Augustinian formula of ascribing pure goodness to God while absolving God from any complicity in evil by treating the latter as mere deficiency or privation. For Schelling, such a formula ignores that genuine "freedom is a power for evil."[18]

Schelling's opus is sprawling and stretches over several periods. For present purposes, the most pertinent text is his 1809 study entitled "Philosophical Inquiries into the Nature of Human Freedom" (*Philosophische Untersuchungen über das Wesen der menschlichen Freiheit*). The text is divided into several sections, some of them critical of earlier conceptions; others—the core of the text—offer an alternative conception of both human freedom and its relation to evil. By way of introduction, Schelling clears up some issues that might stand in the way of his inquiry: whether "freedom" can be meaningfully discussed without broader "systematic" considerations; whether "pantheism" (a hotly debated topic at the time) is necessarily hostile to freedom, or only in some cases; and finally, whether and in what sense Spinoza's system could be termed pantheistic or fatalistic. The answers to the first two questions are that freedom does need to be considered in a broader philosophical context and that pantheism is not incompatible with freedom.

The mention of Spinoza opens a longer section of critical observations. For Schelling, Spinoza's work is the epitome of an abstract monism (quite independent of the meaning of his pantheism). In his words: "This system is not fatalism just because it lets things be conceived in God; for, as we have shown, pantheism does not make formal freedom impossible." The error of Spinoza's system is due "not to the fact that he posits *all things in God,* but to the fact that they are mere *things* [or objects]"—that is, "to the abstract conception of the world and its creatures, indeed of the eternal substance itself which is also a thing for him." It was in opposition to the abstract objectivism of Spinoza that later Enlightenment "idealism" constituted a dramatic advance in terms of energizing, revitalizing, and spiritualizing the monistic system. What emerged as the highest idealist principle was free will, or will as "primordial being," as "groundlessness, eternity, independence of time, self-affirmation." Yet, no matter to what height it raised philosophy, idealism necessarily left out its other side: nature and unwilled being. In Schelling's lapidary formulation:

> From this very fact it can be seen in advance that the most profound difficulties which lie in the concept of freedom will be as likely solvable through idealism, taken in itself, as through any other incomplete system. For idealism supplies only the most general conception of freedom, and a merely formal one at that. But the real and vital conception of freedom is that it is the possibility of good and evil.[19]

In discussing idealism, Schelling also reviews correctives introduced by Enlightenment thinkers such as Fichte and Kant. Fichte's decision to construe the highest pinnacle of philosophy as "subjective activity and freedom" seemed to energize monism, but it failed to show how the rest of the world (including nature and the realm of things) was rooted in "subjective activity." In the case of Kant, freedom as "noumenal" capacity was defined as independence from or negation of nature and time, without any effort to move from negativity toward a "positive" notion of freedom (and evil). A similar limitation can be found in theories sublimating evil into goodness and in accounts claiming that "evil is only a lesser degree of freedom," that in the end, "there is nothing at all positive," and that the difference between actions is "a mere plus or minus of perfection." In such accounts, Schelling objects, "no antithesis is established, and all evil disappears entirely." Dissatisfied with this result, thinkers throughout the ages have embraced antithesis and even radical dualism—a "solution" that is equally and perhaps even more objectionable in its consequences. If one assumes (as one should, Schelling writes) that evil is a real force and that freedom is a "positive" power for good and evil, the problem arises how "evil can come from God who is regarded as utter goodness." The conclusion seems to impose itself: if freedom is a power for evil, "it must have a root independent of God." Compelled by this argument, one may be tempted "to throw oneself into the arms of dualism." However, if it is really thought through as the doctrine of "two absolutely different and mutually independent principles," then this dualism "is only a system of self-destruction [or self-diremption, *Selbstzerreissung*] and of the despair of reason."[20]

Against the backdrop of these critical observations, Schelling delineates his own alternative conception, which stresses difference without dualism and unity without monistic sameness. The cornerstone of this conception is the distinction between two dimensions or senses of being: actual or manifest existence (*Existenz*), and the basis or hidden ground (*Grund*) of this existence. With regard to God, these two dimensions are closely linked or even inseparable. "As there is nothing before or outside God," Schelling writes, "he must contain within himself the ground of his existence." This means that "the ground of his existence, though contained in God, is not God viewed as absolute, that is, insofar as he exists"; rather, it is only "the basis of his existence" or "*nature* in God," which is "inseparable but yet distinguishable from him." What emerges here is the notion of a "becoming God" or a becoming "in" God, of a steady self-manifestation or epiphany (provided this process is not viewed in terms of linear temporality).

In things or beings apart from God, a similar process of becoming takes place, but in a different sense. Again, the distinction between "ground" and "existence" prevails. To be separate or distinguished from God, such beings have to undergo their process of becoming in a different manner; yet, since nothing can really be "outside" of God, one must conclude that "beings have their ground in that dimension of God which is not God himself (as existence), but only the ground of his existence." This ground or nature in God, Schelling adds, is "the longing (*Sehnsucht*) which the eternal One feels to give birth to itself"; it is a longing that "seeks to give birth to God in his unfathomable unity, but to this extent has not yet the unity in itself." In a passage that profoundly challenges Enlightenment rationalism, the treatise continues:

> This is the incomprehensible basis of reality in things, the irreducible remainder which cannot be resolved into reason (*Verstand*) by the greatest exertion but always remains in the depths. Out of this which is non-rational (*verstandlos*), reason in the true sense is born. Without this preceding gloom, creation would have no reality; darkness is its necessary heritage. Only God—the existent himself—dwells in pure light; for he alone is self-born . . . [but] human beings are formed in their mother's womb; and only out of the darkness of unreason (out of feeling, out of longing—that sublime mother of understanding) can clear thoughts grow.[21]

Given this grounding in dark nature, how does human growth or maturation occur? For Schelling, this process requires an "inner transmutation or sublimation (*Verklärung*) in light of what was originally the principle of darkness." Considered by itself, and apart from such transmutation, the dark ground can be described as the basic "self-will (*Eigenwille*) of creatures," a self-will reduced to mere "craving or desire." As such, this creaturely will stands opposed to the more universal or "primal" will seeking to be revealed in all creation. In human beings, there is indeed the possibility of such an entrenchment in particularity or a refusal to transform self-will; however, transmutation and "elevation of the most abysmal center into light" are equally possible. For Schelling, the distinctive quality of human beings consists precisely in the relation between darkness and light and in the possible perversion of this relation through self-will. As he writes: "In human beings we find the whole power of darkness and the whole force of light; in them dwell the deepest pit and the highest heaven." Basically, human will can be construed as the latent seed of the eternal longing buried in the ground of God; it is "the divine spark of life, locked in the depths, which God unleashed when he determined to will nature." In comparison with God, human beings are distinguished by the variable character of the relation between "ground" and "existence," by the fact that darkness can vitiate the light. In Schelling's formulation, which pinpoints the gist of his thesis: "If, now, the identity of the two principles were just as indissoluble in humans as it is in God, then there would be no difference—which means that God as existing spirit could not be revealed. Therefore, that unity which is indissoluble in God must be dissoluble in humans—and this constitutes the possibility of good and evil."[22]

The remainder of Schelling's treatise is devoted mainly to the elaboration and clarification of his basic conception. The paths of good and evil, he notes, are indeed based on human choice (which entails ethical responsibility), but the choice itself responds to the structure of possibility (of good and evil). Self-will, we read, can "separate itself from light"; it may "as a particular will seek to be universal or what it can only be in its identity with the universal will." If this happens, there is a division of selfhood from light, or a dissolution of the linkage between ground and existence. By contrast, if human self-will remains embedded in "central will," and if the "spirit of love" is allowed to rule, self-will exists in a divine manner and condition. An important point that is reemphasized in this context is the linkage of freedom with the possibility of real evil—a linkage denied by some (Enlightenment) doctrines that construe freedom as the rational mastery of desires and inclinations, and goodness (or good will) as a synonym of pure reason.

For Schelling, these doctrines completely divorce good and evil from any kind of grounding, ignoring that freedom is not just an empty capacity but a response to the ground-existence nexus. A choice for the good, in particular—far from reflecting arbitrary whim—means a responsiveness to divine existence and self-manifestation; to this extent, it can also be called a "religious" disposition: "Genuine religiosity allows no choice between alternatives, no *aequilibrium arbitrii*, but only the highest commitment to the right, without any choice." A final question raised in the text is whether there is a dimension that antedates or is presupposed by the distinction between ground and existence. Answering affirmatively (and distantly echoing Cusanus), Schelling calls this dimension the "primal ground" (*Urgrund*), "unground" (*Ungrund*), or "absolute indifference"—where *indifference* means not sameness but a difference without duality or monism: "The un-ground divides itself into two equally eternal beginnings only in order that the two . . . should become one through love; that is, it divides itself only so that there may be life and love and personal existence."[23]

Some Interpretations of Schelling

In introducing a recent collection of essays titled *Schelling Now*, the editor presented his book as evidence "that after more than a century and a half of neglect, Schelling's time has arrived" and, in a manner of speaking, Schelling is now "a contemporary Continental philosopher." That statement is only partially correct. Actually, as the editor himself recognizes, such neglect has prevailed mostly in the Anglo-American context, and it is in that context that there is now "a bourgeoning Schelling renaissance."[24] In 1936, Martin Heidegger presented his famous lecture course on Schelling's treatise on human freedom; some twenty years later, Karl Jaspers and Walter Schulz revived interest in Schelling's later philosophy, and Maurice Merleau-Ponty drew attention to Schelling's natural philosophy.[25] In the present context, I cannot present a comprehensive survey of interpretations; so, for the sake of brevity, I concentrate on a limited number of particularly prominent and insightful readings of Schelling's text. As virtually all commentators agree, the most influential and seminal of these readings is Heidegger's lecture course of 1936, which can serve as a useful gateway to subsequent discussions. In this regard, I follow Peter Warnek's judicious advice when he writes: "Anyone who would give thoughtful attention to the historical *timeliness* of Schelling's philosophical work today cannot rightfully neglect the contribution of Heidegger's careful and subtle reading of Schelling's difficult essay of 1809." I also concur with his (somewhat bolder) claim that Schelling's work "reveals itself only through an encounter with Heidegger, only at the limits of a Heideggerian reading."[26]

    In his lecture course, Heidegger makes no secret of the high esteem in which he holds his predecessor. Schelling, he states, "is the truly creative and most far-reaching thinker of this whole age of German philosophy. He is it to *such* an extent that he drives German Idealism from within right past its own fundamental position."[27]

The manner in which Schelling drives idealism beyond its foundations is through a decentering of its premises, particularly his effort
to dislodge (at least partially) the cornerstone of the cogito: human
subjectivity and (more generally) anthropocentrism. In Heidegger's
view, this effort had profound repercussions on the notion of freedom. In modern Western thought, particularly its dominant ideology
of liberalism, freedom tends to be construed as a human property or
faculty, that is, an attribute owned by humans. Following Schelling,
Heidegger's lectures debunk this conception at the outset. This issue
of human freedom, he writes, is usually treated under the rubric of
the "problem of free will," and discussions center on whether human
will is free or unfree and how the one or the other could be demonstrated. Basically, *freedom* here signifies a "property of human beings,"
and one presumes somehow to know what "being human" means.
"With this question of the freedom of the will, a question wrongly
put and not even properly a question," Heidegger counters sharply,
"Schelling's treatise has nothing whatever to do. For in Schelling freedom is not a human property or attribute, but the other way around:
human *Dasein* [existence] figures as a property of freedom." What
this means is that freedom is "the comprehensive and all-pervasive
matrix in and through which human beings become human in the
first place." Stated even more boldly—and this may well be a central
thesis of Heidegger's entire opus: "The essence (*Wesen*) of humans is
grounded in freedom. But freedom itself is the hallmark of authentic
Being as such, a hallmark transcending or transgressing every finite
human existence. Insofar as humans are human, they must needs par-
take in this hallmark of Being."[28]
  Turning to Schelling's conception of freedom as the possibility for good and evil, Heidegger accepts this formulation, but at the
same time, he translates it into his own (ontological) terminology,
perhaps driving Schelling himself beyond his (still idealist) premises.
In Schelling's treatise, he notes, freedom is connected with the variable relation between two modes of being: "ground" and "existence"
(where the former does not coincide with rational presupposition).
In that treatise, the relation is termed "difference" (*Unterscheidung*),
but Heidegger introduces for the same linkage the notion of a "juncture of being" or a joining of modes of being (*Seynsfuge*). Basically,
the juncture reveals a mode of temporal becoming within being it-

self, that is, the unfolding of an embryonic latency into spiritual self-manifestation. In the case of God or the divine, *Seynsfuge* implies a move from the darkness of divine nature to a full spiritual epiphany or self-disclosure (a move not to be confused with emanation). In Heidegger's words:

> Schelling wants to accomplish precisely this: to conceive God's self-development, that is, how God—not as an abstract concept but as living life—unfolds toward himself. A *becoming* God then? Indeed. If God is the most real of all beings, then he must undergo the greatest and most difficult becoming, and this unfolding must exhibit the farthest tension between its "whence" (where-from) and its "wither" (where-to).

The wither, or where-to, is captured in Schelling's language by the term *existence,* construed as the full revealment or epiphany of the divine, while *ground* points to the stage of latent concealment and obscurity—a perspective clearly consonant with Heidegger's notion of *aletheia* as revealment-concealment and his linkage of becoming and being (or "being and time"). As the lecture course elaborates: "Existence (in Schelling) is understood from the outset as a move 'out of oneself,' as an opening-up which, in opening and manifesting itself, precisely involves a coming into one's own (*zu sich selbst Kommen*) and thus the possibility of 'being' oneself (*Seyn*)." With regard to God, this means that, "seen as existence, God is the *absolute* God or simply God himself. Viewed as the ground of his existence, God is not yet actually himself; and yet: God 'is' also his ground."[29]

As previously noted, the variable relation between ground and existence is the source of the capacity for good and evil, which in turn is the emblem of human freedom. For Schelling, divine becoming aims at progressive spiritualization or God's revealment as spirit—a disclosure that requires an otherness or a foil to testify to this process. This foil is humankind or human being as his counterpart, though distinct from God. As creatures, human beings are rooted in "nature" or the latency of divine becoming; at the same time, they are the receptacle of divine light, the locus where God's existence can become most fully apparent. This condition gives rise to conflicting possibilities: either a steady opening to divine existence, or a perversion of the spiritual motif through withdrawal into self-will and ultimate obstinacy. In terms of Heidegger's commentary, *Dasein* can remain faithful to *Seynsfuge* by following the divine spirit, but it can also pervert existence by appropriating it in an act of intellectual conceit; more radically still, *Dasein* can seclude itself entirely in the opacity of its ground or nature. To the extent that both appropriation and seclusion involve self-enclosure, human self-will here rises in an act of rebellion against divine existence and its universal bond. In the words of the lecture course: "Since human self-will is still linked to spirit (as freedom), this will can in the breadth of human endeavor seek to put itself in the place of the universal will; thus, self-will can . . . as particular-separate selfishness pretend to be the ground of the whole. . . . This ability is the capacity for evil." Repeating a point made earlier, what is involved here is not merely a problem of free will but also a kind of ontological perversion. Basically, what happens is "the reversal of *Seynsfuge* into disjuncture or disjointedness (*Ungefüge*) whereby ground aggrandizes itself to absorb the place of existence."[30]

What is crucial in Heidegger's reading, in my view, is his resolute transgression of modern metaphysics centered in subjectivity and subjective will. As a consequence, ethical option (for good or evil) is not simply a freestanding choice but rather a mode of responsiveness to ways of being. For Heidegger, the capacity for good and evil is constitutive of the being of *Dasein,* reflecting its insertion in one form or another into *Seynsfuge.* "Humans alone," he reiterates, "are capable of evil; but this capacity is not a human property or quality; rather, to be capable in this sense constitutes the being of humans." Taken by itself, *Dasein* is neither good nor evil but is capable of both. On the level of sheer possibility, it remains an "undecided being" hovering in "indecision" (*Unentschiedenheit*); however, it is propelled into the arena of decision by the need for self-realization. In Schelling's treatise (as well as in Heidegger's commentary), the transition from capability to living reality is guided neither by arbitrary whim nor by external compulsion but by a kind of inclination or bent (*Hang*) tilting human conduct one way or another. In the case of evil, Schelling traces this bent to a "contraction of the ground" (*Anziehen des Grundes*), that is, to a self-enclosure of particularity that terminates indecision, but in such a way as to provoke divisiveness and disjuncture. In contrast, goodness follows the attraction of spirit or existence, which, in its most genuine form, is the attraction of love (*Liebe*). "Love," Heidegger states, "is the original union of elements of which each might exist separately and yet does not so exist and cannot really be without the other." However, love is not simply unity or identity but rather a unity in difference or a unity that lets otherness be, including the contraction of the ground and the resulting disjuncture. As he adds: "Love must condone the will of the ground, because otherwise love would annihilate itself. Only by letting the ground operate, love has that foil in or against which it can manifest its supremacy."[31]

Among more recent interpretations, Bernstein's reading stands out for its lucidity and its ability to situate Schelling's legacy in broader intellectual networks. What attracts Bernstein to Schelling is primarily his recognition of the reality of evil—a recognition that is crucial after Auschwitz—along with (as indicated earlier) his ability to avoid the temptations of monism and dualism while insisting on the differentiated relationship between good and evil. Schelling, he writes, "seeks to develop a *differentiated* monism in which there is no ultimate divide between nature and spirit"—and, one might add, there is neither an ultimate divide nor an ultimate identity between good and evil. Turning to recent philosophical trends, Bernstein finds an affinity between Schelling's position and contemporary modes of neonaturalism, especially the "enriched nonreductive naturalism" advocated by John McDowell and others. With approval, he cites McDowell's suggestion that "if we can rethink our conception of nature so as to make room for spontaneity . . . we shall by the same token be rethinking our conception of what it takes for a position to deserve to be called 'naturalism.'"[32] In the same context, he portrays as "imaginative and provocative" Slavoj Žižek's proposal, in his book *The Indivisible Remainder*, to establish a linkage between Schelling's philosophy and a nondogmatic and spiritualized kind of "materialism."[33]

Relying on these and related initiatives, Bernstein on the whole concurs with Schelling's complaint about the "common deficiency" of modern European philosophy—its sidelining or disregard of nature—and adds a warning against a widespread "dismissive attitude towards Schelling's project of a philosophy of nature." Among modern philosophers who are neglectful of nature is Immanuel Kant. According to Bernstein, despite Kant's attempt to "bridge the gap," he never managed to establish a "continuity between nature and freedom," between phenomenal and noumenal realms. In Schelling, by contrast, there is "no such gap" because it has given way to "sounder insight." This does not mean that Schelling rejects human freedom or moral responsibility (emphasized by Kant); rather, they are inserted into a broader matrix and never divorced entirely from the dark ground of nature.[34]

In tracing philosophical repercussions and affinities, Bernstein's reading also establishes connections with a number of perspectives that are not normally associated with Schelling's legacy, especially those of Friedrich Nietzsche and Sigmund Freud, seen as the great protagonists of a "moral psychology of evil." By insisting on the "material force" of evil, Schelling "anticipated" these two great protagonists and, in so doing, opened up new (deep psychological) "ways of questioning evil." In the case of Nietzsche, the distinction between good-bad and good-evil contrasts disclosed evil as "closely associated with *ressentiment*." In the case of Freud, the disclosure of unconscious or subconscious drives laid bare the profound "ambivalence" of the human psyche intimated by Schelling. Still more illuminating and intriguing are Bernstein's references to the philosophical-theological writings of Hans Jonas, especially the latter's speculations about a "*becoming* God" (clearly intimated in Schelling's treatise). As Bernstein observes, God for Jonas is a "suffering" and "caring" God, but also (and most of all) a "becoming God." In Jonas's own words: "It is a God emerging in time instead of possessing a completed being that remains identical with itself throughout eternity." In contrast to a certain Hellenic tradition that assigned priority to eternal being over becoming, Jonas privileges the temporal dimension, asserting that the concept of "divine becoming" can be better reconciled with the portrayal of God in the Hebrew Bible, where God is affected and indeed altered by what human beings do (to one another and to the world). This view of God's dependence on humans—or a reciprocal dependence—implies a revision of the conception of God as all-powerful or omnipotent (in the sense of worldly power). To quote Jonas again: "But if God is to be intelligible in some manner and to some extent (and to this we must hold), then his goodness must be compatible with the existence of evil, and this it is only if he is not all-powerful. Only then can we uphold that he is intelligible and good, and there is yet evil in the world."[35]

Politics and Evil

The topic of evil is not confined to philosophy but looms large in both personal and political life. The notion of the "reality" of evil—stressed in the preceding discussion—points precisely to this ominous presence. The twentieth century and the beginning of the twenty-first amply testify to the destructive potency of evil in the world, and the end is by no means in sight. Steady advances in weapons technology herald breakthroughs to previously unfathomed levels of devastation. In the words of Morrow: "The globalization, democratization, and miniaturization of the instruments of [mass] destruction (nuclear weapons or their diabolical chemical-biological step brothers) mean a quantum leap in the delivery systems of evil." When virtually anyone—states as well as nonstate actors—can acquire doomsday machines, destructiveness is both localized and globalized. Microevil and macroevil, Morrow adds, achieve "an ominous reunion in any bid for the apocalyptic gesture. That is the real evil that is going around." Simpleminded naïveté surely is not the appropriate stance to adopt at this point. In fact, given the danger of global destruction, it may be "catastrophic not to think clearly about evil, not to be aware of what it is capable of doing."[36]

The question remains, however, what does it mean to "think clearly" about evil, both philosophically and politically? More specifically, what are the implications when "evil" is used as a political category? Recent history provides a pointer. As we all know, and as Morrow reminds us, soon after September 11, President Bush spoke of an "axis of evil" in reference to several Islamic countries (plus North Korea). This designation was promptly reciprocated by talk about the "Satanic" West. In light of the above philosophical discussions, one may ask here, which of the various theories of evil has the closest fit with this rhetoric? It seems to me that Manichaeism stands at the top of the list. As Morrow remarks pointedly, the president and his advisers "use the word 'evil' in ways that suggest both sides are fighting the last war" (that is, Armageddon). The Manichaean streak is particularly pronounced when Western leaders employ the word "in an aggressively in-your-face born-again manner" that takes its resonance "from a long Judeo-Christian tradition of radical evil embodied in heroically diabolical figures." Perhaps the closest parallel exists with some forms of radical Puritanism during the post-Reformation period. For Morrow, evil here has "the perverse prestige of John Milton's defiant Luci-fer," where "evil emanates, implicitly, from a devilish intelligence with horns and a tail, an absolutely malevolent personality, God's rival in the cosmos, condemned to lose the fight (eventually), but nonetheless powerful in the world." Given the Manichaean imagery at work here, it is clear that there can be no truce or compromise in the ongoing struggle seen as the "last war."[37]

Besides this struggle between good and evil forces, Manichaeism also implies the ultimate victory of one side and the utter destruction of the other. This brings us back to the issue raised at the beginning of this chapter: the conquest of evil by political force, as advocated by Frum and Perle in their book *An End to Evil*. As previously indicated, their book proposes a "winning" strategy: all-out warfare against evil, with the ultimate goal of victory. Americans, they write, are "fighting to win," and although achievement of that goal may still be in the fu-ture, the "end to evil" will be "brought into being by American armed might and defended by American might."[38] In terms of theories or conceptions of evil, this proposal clearly has a Manichaean cast, with some borrowings from theodicy—legacies that render it profoundly questionable if not pernicious. As an account of the role of evil in the world, Manichaeism has been emphatically denounced by philoso-phers and religious leaders at least since the time of Saint Augustine; even moderate forms of metaphysical dualism have suffered a similar fate. Borrowings from theodicy do not help at all. At least since Ausch-witz, theodicy-like arguments have lost most of their luster and ap-peal, and American-style theodicy is no exception. In the blunt words of Bernstein: "After Auschwitz, it is obscene to continue to speak of evil and suffering as something to be justified by, or reconciled with, a benevolent cosmological scheme" that permits apparent evil to hap-pen.[39]

The proposal of a political or military end to evil becomes even more dubious when placed in the context of Schelling's nuanced con-ception of evil. As indicated earlier, the notions of good and evil in Schelling's thought are intimately linked with human freedom; in fact, freedom signifies precisely the possibility for good and evil. In light of these premises, extermination of evil by political or military force also means the termination of human freedom, including political free-dom. This result—the conflation of an end to evil and an end to freedom—is a curious upshot of a strategy ostensibly aiming at the victory of freedom (especially "enduring" freedom) over nonfreedom in the rest of the world. However, the defect of the proposal resides not only in its danger to freedom but also in its contamination of goodness with willful particularity—in this case, the particularity of one country's military might. Recall that, in Schelling's account, evil consists chiefly in self-glorification and the usurpation of universal goodness by particular self-will. Seen in this light, the triumph *over* evil through military might shades over into the triumph *of* evil. On this point, Žižek's commentary on Schelling offers some telling insights:

> "Evil" in its most elementary form is such a "short circuit" between the particular and the universal, such a presumption to believe that my words and deeds are directly words and deeds of the big Other (nation, culture, state, God), a presumption which "inverts" the proper relationship between the particular and the universal: when I proclaim myself the immediate "functionary of humanity" (or nation or culture), I thereby effectively accomplish the exact opposite of what I claim to be doing—that is, I degrade the universal dimension to which I refer (humanity, nation, state) to my own particularity. . . . The more I refer to the universal in order to legitimate my acts, the more effectively I abase it to a means of my own self-assertion.[40]

In *Radical Evil*, Bernstein echoes Žižek's comments, writing: "Evil turns out to be not particularity as such but its erroneous, 'perverted' unity with the universal: not 'egotism' as such, but egotism in the guise of its opposite."[41] With these words, Bernstein does not mean to endorse evil nor to deny that evil needs to be countered and combated wherever possible. The question is, how should this be done? How might we contemplate an end to evil?

My argument here has been that this cannot be done along Manichaean lines through military might, that is, by arrogating to oneself all the goodness and assigning all the evil to one's opponents. If Manichaeism (together with theodicy) is put aside, the struggle against evil can only be a *common* struggle, a pedagogical struggle in which all particularities combine in the search for goodness. A first step along this road has to be an admission by all parties of their failings and imperfections, shunning self-glorification of any kind. The next step has to be a sincere willingness, among all parties, to set aside conceit in favor of ethical learning or the search for a shared good life. For religious people—Christians and non-Christians alike—this search can proceed only with divine assistance. Yet much room is left for human effort and engagement, especially the fostering of goodwill through education and personal example. In terms of the notion of a "becoming God" formulated by Jonas (but traceable to Schelling), God must assist humans in becoming properly human, while humans need to assist God to be properly God. Jonas quotes from the diaries of Etty Hillesum, a young Jewish woman from the Netherlands who perished in Auschwitz in 1943: "I will always endeavor to help God as well as I can. . . . With every heartbeat it becomes clearer to me that you cannot help us, but that we must help you and defend up to the last your dwelling within us."[42]

10. Transnational Citizenship
Paths beyond the Nation-State

At the dawn of Western civilization (so called), we find two conceptions of citizenship: one Greek, arising in Athens, and the other Christian, inspired by Jerusalem. The first conception of citizenship, usually associated with Aristotle, is that of membership in a polis, or city-state (with Aristotle holding that such membership is "natural" for, or constitutive of, human beings). The second conception, most prominently formulated by Saint Augustine, assumes a duality of membership: that is, membership in the earthly city (*civitas terrena*) and the heavenly city (*civitas Dei*). The two conceptions clearly do not coincide. In fact, as has often been claimed, the entire history of Western civilization unfolds as an antagonism between Athens and Jerusalem. A closer look, however, reveals that the difference is less pronounced than is usually claimed. A certain tension or duality can also be found in Aristotle, who clearly distinguishes between membership in a corrupt, unjust, or tyrannical community and membership in a just city devoted to a good and virtuous civic life. In this respect, Aristotle is largely following the lead of Plato, who, in the *Republic,* distinguishes between a community governed by sheer survival needs—what he calls a "city for pigs"—and a city imbued with justice and other civic virtues. For his part, Saint Augustine does not allow duality to result in a radical rupture that would place the "heavenly city" beyond all civic bonds. Resisting the temptation of private withdrawal, the *civitas Dei* is differentiated from other cities by its special divine calling or its quality as a "pilgrim city."

As is evident from these "founding" conceptions, citizenship is not merely a matter of formal, legal status (although it may be that as well). Reverberating through the centuries and down to our own time, the formulations of Aristotle and Saint Augustine point to deeper, recessed dimensions of citizenship—its linkage with conceptions of what it means to be human and how we should live together with others in this world. In the context of Western modernity, the legacies of Athens and Jerusalem are often treated as irrelevant, but at a steep cost. Under the impact of modern liberal individualism, citizenship is often portrayed as entirely optional or voluntary—as the contractual adherence to formal rules and procedures, without any need for social bonding. As it happens, however, the exiled civic bond—which Aristotle declared to be constitutive of human beings—returns sheepishly through the backdoor in the form of the backlash of nationalism or ethnic "identity." It is precisely this combination of formal legal rules and an untutored, particularistic identity that forms the nature of the modern nation-state (where *state* means "rule of law" and *nation* is an ascriptive marker).

In this chapter, I join ongoing discussions—sometimes called "citizenship debates"—in an effort both to clarify the meaning of modern citizenship and to explore possible paths beyond the nation-state formula.[1] After tracing the emergence of the modern conception of citizenship, I examine some of the theoretical quandaries and antinomies implicit in this conception. By way of conclusion, I discuss a number of "transnational" options, recollecting at this point both the Aristotelian notion of a just community and the Augustinian reflections on the pilgrim city.

The Emergence of Modern Citizenship

The notion of "citizenship" in the West has a long pedigree, tracing its origins back to classical and biblical conceptions of life in a city. A primary concept, at least for political thinkers, has always been the Greek idea of the *polites*, as articulated by Aristotle and his successors. In a well-known and remarkable essay on the topic, John Pocock traces the evolution of citizenship "since classical times," that is, since the time of the Greek *polis*. As he notes, political thinkers in the West have always treated citizenship as a "classical ideal," as "one of the fundamental values that we claim is inherent in our 'civilization' and its 'tradition.'" In Pocock's account, the Greek polis was not grounded in kinship or any purely ascriptive ties; rather, it was a community of citizens in which "speech took the place of blood, and acts of [public] decision the place of acts of vengeance." In Aristotle's formulation, in particular, citizenship carried an eminently practical and praxis-centered connotation, pointing to the ability of "free men" to participate in the public place by simultaneously ruling and being ruled (a definition that obviously excluded a majority of the inhabitants of a polis). Where this kind of practice prevailed, Pocock comments, citizens were able to collaborate in making decisions "where each decider respects the authority of the others, and all join in obeying the decisions they have made." To be sure, public or political practice was not just a random activity for Aristotle, for it exhibited an intrinsic telos: the promotion of a good and flourishing human life (*eu zen*) and of a virtuous happiness (*eudaimonia*).[2]

The idea of participatory citizenship was not limited to the Greek polis but extended into the early Roman Republic, where the Greek notion of *polites* was translated into the Latin *civis*. With the passage of time, however, profound changes took place in this domain and ultimately overwhelmed the older, classical conception. With the rise of the Roman Empire and the expansion of imperial rule, the status of "citizen" was increasingly transformed into that of "subject"; that is, the individual was no longer actively engaged in ruling and being ruled but rather was controlled by and subjected to laws and edicts issued by a distant imperial authority. Intellectually and politically, the transition was fostered and endorsed by some Stoic thinkers, and especially by a distinguished series of imperial jurists (such as Gaius and Ulpian). In Pocock's words: "The advent of imperial jurisprudence moved the concept of the 'citizen' from the [Aristotelian] *zoon politikon* toward the *homo legalis,* and [later] from the *civis* and *polites* toward the *bourgeois* or *burger.*" In contrast to the older focus on public engagement, the citizen conceived as subject was mainly a law-governed human being, an identity constructed chiefly for legal and judicial purposes: "Over many centuries, the *homo legalis* will come to denote who can sue and be sued in certain courts," with court actions obviously depending on the existence of an imperial legal structure firmly in place. Reflecting on the difference between the classical citizen and the imperial subject, Pocock comments: "The former ruled and was ruled, which meant among other things that he was a participant in determining the laws by which he was to be bound." By contrast, the imperial subject could at best "appeal to Caesar," that is, "go into court and invoke a law that granted him rights, immunities, privileges, and even authority," but he usually had "no hand whatever in making that law or in determining what it was to be."[3]

The change to the citizen-subject was full of ominous portents whose ramifications emerged clearly only in much later contexts. Pocock draws attention to one such portent: the growing focus on property relations. Once public engagement receded into the background, citizen-subjects began to orient themselves not toward the common good or public happiness but toward tangible things or objects and toward one another as proprietors of such objects. Under the aegis of imperial jurisprudence, Pocock comments, people were encouraged to act "upon things," and most of the actions of citizen-subjects were directed at "taking and maintaining possession" of things; it was through the medium of possessions—not the medium of shared ethical aspirations—that individuals "encountered each other and entered into relationships which might require regulations," that is, the protective umbrella of a shared but abstract rule of law. For Pocock, the most important feature of imperial citizenship was the accent on governance over people and things. "A 'citizen,'" he states, "came to mean someone free to act by law, free to ask and expect the law's protection"; hence, citizenship turned basically into a "legal status, carrying with it rights to certain things—perhaps possessions, perhaps immunities, perhaps expectations—available in many kinds and degrees." The departure from the classical Aristotelian notion of *politics* was palpable, providing a seedbed for important future developments: "From being *kata phusin zoon politikon,* the human individual came to be by nature a proprietor or possessor of things; hence, it is in jurisprudence, long before the rise and supremacy of the market, that we should locate the origins of possessive individualism."[4]

The reference to the rise of the market is, of course, somewhat hasty and elliptical; it jumps briskly over at least a thousand years of history and, above all, over the so-called European Middle Ages. To get a grip on medieval and postmedieval developments, one has to turn from Pocock to other social thinkers, particularly to Max Weber and his followers.[5] As is well known, Weber pinpointed the basic political structure of the European Middle Ages by focusing on the antagonism and complementarity of the principles of "patrimonialism" and "feudalism." In his usage, the term *patrimonialism* refers basically to the management of the royal household and the royal domains by an array of appointed servants. Central to the patrimonial system was the secular and religious authority of the king, who, as patriarchal master of his household, exercised absolute power over his subjects—although, in principle, such power was assumed to entail a responsibility to protect the people. In a way, patrimonialism emulated the model of imperial jurisprudence, but without the accent on general governance. The term *feudalism*, in Weber's sense, refers to rulers' efforts to maintain or extend their control through complex fealty relationships with aristocratic notables of independent means, relationships predicated on reciprocal responsibilities (involving protection and support, respectively). Under neither system was there room for citizenship in either the participatory or the imperial sense, because of the complexity or confusion of social structures. In Weber's famous formulation:

> The individual carried his *professio juris* with him wherever he went. Law was not a *lex terrae*, as the English law of the King's court became soon after the Norman Conquest, but rather the privilege of the person as member of a particular group. . . . The result was the co-existence of numerous "law communities," the autonomous jurisdictions of which overlapped, the compulsory political association being only one such autonomous jurisdiction insofar as it existed at all.[6]

Weber's insights have been further developed and refined by numerous social scientists. In his book *Nation-Building and Citizenship,* Reinhard Bendix both elaborates on Weber's analysis and carries it forward into modern times. Regarding the complex, multidimensional structure of medieval society, Bendix notes that the contentious relationship between the patrimonial and the feudal principle resulted in a "system of divided and overlapping jurisdictions," with each jurisdiction providing a set of public rights that "entitled particularly privileged persons and corporate groups to exercise a specific authority and to levy fees or tolls for that exercise." In a general sense, the medieval political community consisted of an "aggregate" of diverse jurisdictions held together "firmly or precariously," depending on "the momentum of past events, external circumstances, the personal capacity of participants, and the vicissitudes of the political struggle." In this setting, citizenship in both its Greek and its imperial modalities was either completely defunct or highly marginalized. Although not entirely devoid of rights or entitlements, Bendix adds, the medieval individual enjoyed rights and performed duties "by virtue of his status," which in turn was "defined by heredity or by membership in an organization possessing certain immunities or liberties." Except for a handful of powerful nobles and their retainers, individual status involved "a mediated relation in the sense that the vast majority of persons did *not* stand in a direct legal or political relationship to the supreme authority of the king" or the power of feudal barons.[7]

The situation changed radically during the age of absolutism and the ensuing revolutionary upheavals. During the seventeenth and eighteenth centuries, the older medieval pattern was progressively replaced by a system of "absolutist rule," in which the king exercised nationwide powers through his appointed officials, despite the persistence in various places of hereditary estates and older "constituted bodies." The rise of absolute royal power occurred first and most prominently in England, largely as a result of the Norman Conquest. Curiously, however, the sway of royal sovereignty was steadily tempered in England by the strength of countervailing powers, especially Parliament and the common law. Developments took a different course on the Continent. There, Bendix writes, political regimes either were bent on "a greater destruction of independent estates and hence a greater administrative effectiveness of central power, as in France," or witnessed the ascendancy of "many principalities with some internal balance between king and estates but at the expense of overall political unity, as in Germany." It was the French Revolution and its Napoleonic aftermath that finally wiped away the legacy of hereditary privileges and oligarchic estates and ushered in the era of the modern nation-state. Reflecting its composite character, the nation-state paradigm is marked by two crucial but conflicting features. First of all, in opposition to feudal distinctions, the paradigm is (or is intended to be) a legal or rule-of-law state granting civic equality—distantly patterned on the model of Roman imperial jurisprudence. At the same time, the paradigm is perceived and utilized as the bulwark of national identity and self-determination. In Bendix's words, the Old Regime and the French Revolution in tandem destroyed medieval hierarchies "by creating among all citizens a condition of abstract equality"—most importantly, equality before the law. Because citizens in an abstractly legal state are left to their own private devices, in the words of Alexis de Tocqueville, they are left "at once independent and powerless," and the desire arises to find a unifying bond in national power. Hence, in the new paradigm, traditional royal paternalism is transformed into an "ideology of national government" or national glory.[8]

With regard to the actual development of citizenship in the nation-state, Bendix relies on a celebrated study: T. H. Marshall's *Citizenship and Social Class* (subsequently incorporated into *Class, Citizenship and Social Development*). In this study, Marshall distinguishes among three types of rights: civil or legal rights, political or voting rights, and social-economic rights. Consequently, three different sets of public institutions were designed to protect and enhance these rights: courts or judicial institutions, assemblies or representative bodies, and social welfare services and schools. Among the successive generations of rights, legal equality or equality before the law signaled the first rupture with medieval heritage. "Legal equality," Bendix writes, "advances at the expense of legal protection of inherited privileges," because citizens are now construed as "free to conclude valid contracts, to acquire and dispose of property." Over a period of time, this legal construction helped "eliminate hereditary servitude, equalize the status of husband and wife, circumscribe the extent of parental power, facilitate divorce, and legalize civil marriage." The advancement of political rights occurred more slowly, involving a series of protracted confrontations. Basically, the extension of such rights to all adult citizens faced a battery of obstacles, including property and literacy requirements, restrictions based on household responsibilities, and gender and residence criteria. Most bitterly contested—and never fully accomplished—was the institutionalization of social and economic rights as corollaries of citizenship; in this domain, the rights to unionize, to demonstrate, and to strike were crucial markers of public recognition. In Bendix's view (following Weber), the acceptance of such rights involved a process "through which, at the level of the national community, the reciprocity of rights and duties was gradually extended and redefined."[9]

Modern Citizenship: Some Debates

As the title of his study indicates, citizenship for Bendix is basically tied to nation building and thus to the fortunes of the modern nation-state. In this respect, his work is not unique but follows the approach of a number of social theorists for whom modernization and nation building are intimately linked if not synonymous.[10] As has become clear, however, that approach rests on premises that have been challenged by many factors, including the process of globalization. Quite apart from the more recent challenges of globalization, the very idea of the modern nation-state was troubled from the outset by a profound tension whose constituent elements pointed in opposite directions: the tension between the state (as law-state, or *Rechtsstaat*) and the nation (as a marker of identity). Seen as an institution embodying the rule of a general, neutrally disengaged law, the modern state carries a potentially universal or cosmopolitan significance; the corollary notion of equality before the law potentially extends equal treatment to people everywhere, regardless of nationality, creed, or gender. Conversely, the connection of state with nation inevitably injects into political regimes an aura of particularism that is recalcitrant to neutral indifference. Whereas the first feature harks back in many respects to Roman imperial jurisprudence, the second feature preserves aspects of medieval localism. In his study of citizenship "since classical times," Pocock (as indicated) boldly projects the imperial legacy into the future when he writes that "the Gaian formula became the formula for liberal politics and a liberal ideal of citizenship during the early modern and modern historical periods."[11]

Nowhere have the dilemmas of the modern nation-state been more vividly and trenchantly exposed than in Alasdair MacIntyre's well-known essay "Is Patriotism a Virtue?" In MacIntyre's usage, *patriotism* does not denote simply an untutored chauvinism but rather a disposition of loyalty or fidelity displaying its own mode of virtue. Patriotism, he writes, is defined in terms of "a loyalty to a particular nation which only those possessing that particular nationality can exhibit." Far from evincing a "mindless" attachment, the patriot's loyalty involves regard not just for one's nation but also for that nation's merits and achievements (resulting in ethical approval). The main point, however, is that "the particularity of the relationship is essential and ineliminable." From this angle, the patriot's attachment departs radically from the view of morality that has become dominant in the West since the Enlightenment: the morality of universal principles. From the latter perspective, MacIntyre notes, to act morally means "to act in accordance with impersonal judgments" or rules, and to be able to act in such a way, the agent has to "abstract himself or herself from all social particularity or partiality." Placed side by side, the two types of outlook—the moral and the patriotic—turn out to be "systematically incompatible." Moreover, as MacIntyre reminds us, one should not be misled here by terminology: the patriotic outlook is no less "moral" than the moral outlook. The difference resides in the meaning of morality. Whereas for the Enlightenment or modern liberal view, the question "*where* and *from whom* I learn the principles and precepts of morality" is basically irrelevant; for the patriot, the same question turns out to be "crucial for both the content and the nature of moral commitment."[12]

Being systematically at odds, the two standpoints—moral universalism and particularistic attachment—level accusations against each other that cannot be fully rebutted by either side. The basic ambition of the modern, or modern liberal, stance is to liberate individuals from "the bondage of the social, political, and economic *status quo.*" From this angle, rational abstraction and detachment from social ties are viewed as "a necessary condition of moral freedom." In MacIntyre's words: "It is of the essence of the morality of liberalism that no limitations are or can be set upon the criticism of the social *status quo,*" in the sense that no institution, practice, or loyalty is exempt from challenge. It is precisely this challenge that patriotism cannot accept. Although willing to critique specific policies, patriotism requires that loyalty to the nation as such or "as a project" be unconditional—something that is deeply suspect and even pernicious to liberals. In return, patriots consider unsound and morally dangerous the liberal stress on "impartiality and impersonality" because of the corrosive effects on social bonds. MacIntyre asks, "suppose the bonds of patriotism [were] to be dissolved: would liberal morality be able to provide anything adequately substantial in its place?" This question must be answered negatively, given the glaring deficit of motivation in the morality of principles. Hence, countering the liberal charge of deficient rational critique, the patriot finds that liberal morality tends toward the "dissolution" of the fabric of social life as such. The upshot for MacIntyre is (once again) that the "morality of liberal impersonality" and the "morality of patriotism" are "deeply incompatible." This conclusion, however, jeopardizes the very notion of the modern nation-state, to the extent that *state* signifies an impersonal rule system and *nation* a patriotic attachment: "We inhabit a kind of polity whose moral order requires systematic incoherence in the form of public allegiance to mutually inconsistent sets of principles."[13]

The merit of MacIntyre's essay is that it pinpoints the stark fissure troubling modern Western politics, as well as the difficulty of reconciling the conflicting elements in a viable synthesis. Aware of this difficulty, most recent and contemporary theorists of citizenship prefer to focus on one or the other of the two components, thus accentuating either the abstract "law-state" or modes of local attachment. To this extent, recent citizenship debates shade over into the familiar dispute between liberalism and communitarianism (which need not be rehearsed at this point). Among defenders of particularistic loyalties, mention must be made of Roger Scruton's "In Defense of the Nation," where *nation* is defined largely in terms of cultural-historical identity. For Scruton, citizenship as a political concept is entirely parasitic on nationhood as a social and cultural concept, with the corollary effect that minority groups desiring to share in citizenship must be assimilated first into the "national idea."[14] Such an argument is anathema to liberal defenders of the neutral law-state, for whom national or local attachments either are irrelevant or play a strictly subordinate role. Let us look at a prominent example: If, in constructing a system of "just" rules, John Rawls insists on placing prospective citizens initially under a "veil of ignorance," this is done to ensure the abstract neutrality of such rules, uncontaminated by particularistic loyalties. As a sensible liberal, of course, Rawls does not deny the existence of such loyalties, noting that particular "convictions and attachments help to organize and give shape to a person's life." From the perspective of justice, however, such convictions function as a private or "non-public identity," strictly subordinated to the "public identity" of citizens as subjects of common laws.[15] A similar arrangement can be found in Jürgen Habermas's notion of "constitutional patriotism," where national attachment remains entirely ancillary to constitutional law.[16]

Reviewing and pondering different contemporary conceptions of citizenship, Ronald Beiner basically concurs with MacIntyre's verdict of conceptual incoherence. Liberalism as a political philosophy, he writes, is concerned with upholding "the dignity and inherent rights of individuals, understood as instantiations of a *universal* humanity"; hence it is unclear "why this philosophy would accord any special moral status to the claims of citizenship. Why concern ourselves with the quality of civic life within *our own* national boundaries?" For Beiner, these questions have troubling consequences for the modern nation-state, whose constituent components "render the meaning of citizenship deeply problematic." What afflicts modern citizenship, in his view, is the near schizophrenia inhabiting the nation-state. On the one hand, there are "the various kinds of universalism that exalt the invisible moral worth of individuals, seen as human beings *as such*"; on the other hand, we have "the forces of exclusivity and particularism that celebrate and affirm just those forms of group identity that distinguish sets of individuals from one another." This dilemma exemplifies the kind of universalism-particularism conundrum for which there is no ready solution: "To opt wholeheartedly for universalism implies deracination-rootlessness. To opt wholeheartedly for particularism implies parochialism, exclusivity, and narrow-minded closure of horizons." The challenge is to find a third possibility that would escape these respective deficits. But as Beiner adds despairingly: "I lack any confidence that I can come up with a third account that will satisfy readers or satisfy myself."[17]

Moving Past the Nation-State

The dilemmas highlighted by Beiner and MacIntyre are staggering, but perhaps not entirely unmanageable. As it happens, a long line of philosophical reflection—in both Western and Eastern thought— wrestles in multiple ways with this universalism-particularism conundrum. Under such rubrics as "participation" (*methexis*), "nondualism," and "dialectical mediation," major thinkers through the ages have sought to disclose the linkage between general principles and particular contexts. Without delving into recondite arguments, the cogency of these endeavors seems warranted by common sense. Clearly, to be viable and meaningful, general principles always need to be instantiated in concrete contexts and situations—a point that inevitably bends the abstractness of universalism in the direction of particular engagements and modes of participation. Conversely, in asserting its concrete situatedness, particularity cannot remain narrowly self-contained and thus necessarily points beyond itself toward a broader framework that silhouettes its role as "particular." This kind of self-transcendence, one can argue, was the hallmark of Aristotelian ethics as well as Hegelian *Sittlichheit*—a realization that casts doubt on a self-enclosed "patriotism" or patriotic "virtue." Contrary to MacIntyre and a host of other interpreters, Aristotelian virtue cannot (or should not) be domesticated in a circumscribed particularism or narrative identity—an aspect illustrated by Aristotle's treatment of genuine friendship as an act of self-transcendence toward the friend's goodness. It is precisely this retrieval of the open-ended, nonparochial quality of Aristotelian ethics that points the way toward the recovery of genuine citizenship in our time, adumbrated in Beiner's groping for a "third possibility."[18]

These considerations have a practical, political import as well as a theoretical one. What renders the Aristotelian "mediation" particularly significant in our time is the process of globalization, coupled with the upsurge of multiculturalism and the decline (though not demise) of the traditional nation-state. A prominent illustration of ethical mediation is the spreading phenomenon of "multicultural" or "differentiated" citizenship. Obviously, the objective of such citizenship is to call into question the universalism-particularism conundrum, along with the public-private divide marking modern Western politics. One of the most eloquent defenders of this new phenomenon is Iris Marion Young, well known for her elaboration of a "politics of difference." In an essay entitled "Polity and Group Difference: A Critique of the Ideal of Universal Citizenship," Young zeros in on the shortcomings of an abstract, state-centered citizenship. As she observes, ever since the Enlightenment, an "ideal of universal citizenship" has fueled the "emancipatory momentum of modern political life." In terms of that ideal, citizenship was considered a right belonging to "everyone qua citizen," in such a way that citizenship status would transcend "particularity and difference." The problem with this conception was, first of all, that abstract universality stopped at the borders of the nation-state; more important, even within the nation-state, the conception forced underprivileged and minority groups to assimilate to a dominant cultural model, neglectful of their situated needs and aspirations. In large measure, the distinction between abstract universality and concrete situatedness coincided with the public-private bifurcation endemic to the modern law-state. In Young's words, inequality of treatment—behind the legal facade—resulted from the "dichotomy between public and private that defined the public as a realm of generality [and rationality] in which particularities are left behind, and defined the private as the particular, the realm of affectivity, affiliation, need, and the body."[19]

In an effort to overcome modern bifurcations, Young resorts to a mediated perspective that would reconcile citizenship with legitimate (that is, ethically relevant) group and gender differences. A properly designed political life, she insists, should not require "the creation of a unified public realm in which citizens leave behind their particular group affiliations, histories, and needs to discuss the general interest or common good." Instead of the abstractly universal citizenship extolled (though never achieved) by the modern nation-state, "we need a group differentiated citizenship and a heterogeneous public" where "relevant differences are publicly recognized and acknowledged as irreducible." It is important to note that "differentiated citizenship" in Young's treatment does not equal a retreat into myopic parochialism or self-enclosed ghettos. Inspired by moral teachings (perhaps more Kantian than Aristotelian in origin), group differentiation for her does not cancel out a concern for the "common good" or, more specifically, a commitment to "the need and desire to decide together the society's policies" via "communication across differences." Thus, in Young's formulation, subnational groups or communities—whether based on race, creed, gender, or economic status—should not be seen simply as empirical entities advancing self-centered and nonnegotiable claims against society at large (a practice associated with some forms of "identity politics"). Rather, the accent is on empowerment or enablement in an ethical sense. Basically, the point of "differentiated citizenship" is to make sure that the "common good" of a society is not dictated "from on high" by ruling elites but articulated "from the ground up" by all participants in society, including underprivileged and marginalized groups. This is what Young stresses when she writes: "A democratic public, however constituted, should provide mechanisms for the effective representation and recognition of the distinct voices and perspectives of those of its constituent groups that are oppressed or disadvantaged within it."[20]

Young is not the only proponent of a path leading beyond the modern nation-state. With varying degrees of emphasis, her mediating approach is seconded by a host of writers and political thinkers, including Bhikhu Parekh and Charles Taylor. As Parekh forcefully argued at one point, citizenship in our time needs to be seen as "a much more differentiated and far less homogeneous concept than has been presupposed by political theorists," especially theorists of the modern nation-state.[21] The most probing and comprehensive presentation of the approach, however, has been offered by Taylor, especially in his discussion of the "politics of recognition." What distinguishes Taylor from many other writers in this genre is his thorough grounding in the traditions of Aristotelian *phronesis* and Hegelian *Sittlichheit*, a grounding that lends to his arguments a strongly practical-ethical flavor. His discussion of "recognition" pays special tribute to Hegel, who gave the topic "its most influential early treatment." In the same context, Taylor distinguishes between two modes of recognition in modernity: one aiming at universality, the other at particular distinctness. Whereas the first approach favors nondiscrimination in the sense of "difference-blindness," the second approach seeks to open our eyes to relevant individual and group differences. Although critical of a blandly homogenizing universalism, Taylor is by no means a devotee of parochial segregation, which he rejects in favor of a mutual dialogical engagement presented as "the crucial feature of human life."[22]

Differentiated or multicultural citizenship, as articulated by Young, Taylor, and others, is an important step in overcoming the problems of the modern nation-state. To some extent, however, the focus remains on subnational groups contained within existing state structures. A more radical way of tackling modern conundrums results from the ongoing globalization and weakening of the Westphalian system, a process that gives multiculturalism a global cast. In light of the growing interdependence and interpenetration of cultures in the world, the notion of "multiple citizenships" has been advanced, an arrangement whereby citizens maintain loyalties to several nation-states while simultaneously transcending confining nationalist strategies or ambitions. The notion is favored especially by proponents of "cosmopolitan democracy"—an agenda that usually stops short of endorsing a global superstate and is predicated instead on "transnational networks" operating at the level of global "civil society." In some treatments, multiple citizenship shades over into the concept of a global or cosmopolitan citizenship, but without altering the civil society focus. The guiding principle of multiple or cosmopolitan citizenship is the desire for ethical restraints imposed on both national power schemes and the ambitions of hegemonic global elites. In the words of Christian van den Anker: "A new model of global citizenship would not require the existence of a global state but of a global community that provides protection against the overwhelming power of the nation-state to its citizens and the power of multinational corporations over people's lives." To this extent, he adds, "global citizenship should mean that people show their sense of justice and responsibility to care for all other human beings anywhere in the world."[23]

To be sure, in the present world situation, the chances of achieving global justice and responsibility are exceedingly slim, given the prevalence of brute power politics pursued by both national and global hegemonic elites. This is where a different and more recessed conception of citizenship comes into play, one in which the status of citizenship is not so much a legal actuality but more of a promise and a possibility. What I have in mind is the notion of a bifurcated citizenship first introduced by Saint Augustine and mentioned at the beginning of this chapter. In this perspective, citizenship (or being properly human) involves a profound *periagogé* or *metanoia:* a turning away from power politics and brute self-aggrandizement. For Saint Augustine, membership in the earthly and heavenly cities was based on different affective loyalties or modes of love: in the one case, love of power, selfish gain, and worldly possessions; in the other case, love for the unconditional, the transmundane, the "other," or the divine. As we read in a famous passage from *The City of God:* "Two societies have issued from two kinds of love: worldly society has flowered from a selfish love which dared to despise even God, whereas the communion of saints is rooted in a love of God that is ready to trample on the self." Whereas the former city "seeks the praise of men," the other city delights "to hear God in the witness of conscience." What is important to remember in this context is that, for Augustine, the two cities were not radically separated but mutually implicated and interpenetrating, in the sense that the one city harbored a promise for the other: "So long, then, as the heavenly city is wayfaring on earth, she invites citizens from all nations and tongues, and unites them into a single pilgrim band. She takes no issue with that diversity of customs, laws, and traditions whereby human peace is sought and maintained."[24]

Although sidelined by modern Enlightenment, glimpses of the Augustinian vision have reached modern and contemporary thought in multiple ways. Confining myself initially to some French thinkers, I briefly cite three exemplars: Paul Ricoeur, Pierre Hadot, and Jacques Derrida. When writing about the role of Christians in modern politics, Ricoeur exhorts them to be the "salt of the earth" (Matthew 5:13); he clearly wishes them to be neither worldly conformists nor ascetic exiles but rather "pilgrims" and agents of transformation in Augustine's sense. In a slightly different idiom, Hadot—inspired by both classical Greek and biblical teachings—cites with approval a passage penned by Philo Judaeus stating that seekers of wisdom and salvation may "remain on earth" but "give wings to their souls," so that they may "truly become citizens of the world." They have received "their civic rights from virtue which has been entrusted with presiding over the universal commonwealth."[25] Adding a more contemporary political slant, Derrida preserves Augustinian echoes in his text "On Cosmopolitanism." There, relying on both Kantian and biblical instructions, Derrida adumbrates a recessed mode of city life: life in "cities of refuge" buttressed by an "ethics of hospitality" and even a "new cosmopolitics of cities of refuge." In the same context, he cites Paul's letter to the Ephesians, which alludes to a new world co-citizenship where believers would "no longer be foreigners nor metics in an alien land, but fellow-citizens with God's people, members of God's household" (Ephesians 2:19).[26]

By way of conclusion, I take my bearings from Richard Falk, a renowned expert on contemporary international politics. In an essay titled "An Emergent Matrix of Citizenship," Falk ponders the multiple dimensions and shifting meanings of contemporary citizenship. Impressed by the staggering political perversions in our present world—evident in ceaseless warfare, violent power plays, and economic exploitation—his text draws attention to a recessed form of public counteragency and resistance that, in a distantly Augustinian vein, he describes as networks of "citizen pilgrims." Such networks, Falk insists, cannot lamely be tied to present actuality but must be open to, and serve as precursors of, a potentiality; they must be "rooted in the future, the not-yet," rather than unconvincingly affirming as "real" the prevailing status quo. As he elaborates: "I have used the metaphor of 'citizen pilgrim' to describe the spirit of a sojourner, committed to transformation that is spiritual as well as material, that is premised on the wholeness and equality of the human family." Going somewhat beyond the Augustinian model, Falk is willing to draw on both religious and secular resources, convinced that "a sustainable world community can only result from a combination of secular and spiritual energies." In his words: "The citizen pilgrim will have prefigured a community of believers in the collective destiny of the human species." To perform this task, the pilgrim's outlook has to be anchored in "an ethos of non-violence, sustainability, compassion and solidarity," an ethos that constitutes "the clay out of which the citizen pilgrim is beginning to mould the political sculptures of a benevolent human future."[27]

11. Religious Freedom
Preserving the Salt of the Earth

The history of the Jewish people is, in large measure, a history of exile, captivity, and diaspora, but it is also a story of redemption. The book of Exodus reports the tribulations endured by the Jews during their exile in Egypt, before they were led into the wilderness by Moses, but it also speaks of a promised land and of the "steadfast love" with which God guides the people to his "holy abode" (Exodus 15:13). The tribulations did not end with the Jews' arrival in their new home; their troubles returned with even greater intensity after the fall of the two kingdoms, Israel and Judah. The books of Jeremiah and Lamentations tell us about the assaults of the Assyrians and Babylonians, the destruction of Jerusalem, and the ensuing Babylonian captivity of the Jewish people. Lamentations is particularly eloquent, bitterly mourning the loss of "the city that was full of people" but has become "like a widow" and a "vassal." Yet both texts also speak in a different voice. Jeremiah exhorts Israel "not to be dismayed," for the Lord "will save you from afar, and your offspring from the land of their captivity" (Jeremiah 30:10). And Lamentations holds out the prospect that the Lord "will not cast off people for ever, but, though he cause grief, will have compassion according to the abundance of his steadfast love" (Lamentations 3:31–32). This combination of, or alternation between, grief and promise has continued throughout the long period of the diaspora and up to the climactic events of the Holocaust and a return to the biblical land.

This entire history is replete with lessons and guideposts. One such lesson—too often or too readily sidelined—concerns the role of suffering in what is called "salvation history," the role of transformative seasoning as a prerequisite for any kind of redemption. Another lesson has to do with the difference between—or the difficult mutual implication of—land and promised land, of any given city and the holy city seen as that Lord's "holy abode." The problem is that the latter cannot be just any empirical location; in that case, it would be meaningless to speak of its special holiness. Nor can it be completely extraterritorial, for in that case, it could not be called a city. But the psalmist explicitly states: *"Jerusalem aedificata sicut civitas"* (Jerusalem built like a city; Psalms 122:3). Thus, the holy city, seen as the lodestar of religious faith, exhibits a peculiar ambivalence, finding itself at the cusp of territory and extraterritoriality, of place and no place (or utopia). Christian scripture recognizes this ambivalence, or this location beyond location, when it exhorts faithful people to be "the salt of the earth" (Matthew 5:13). If the salt remained outside or aloof from the earth, it could not exert its seasoning or transformative role; at the same time, if it fused or coincided with the earth, its "saltiness" would be lost. This ambivalence was well captured by Paul Ricoeur when he wrote, in a somewhat hopeful vein: "After several centuries during which Christians have been preoccupied with the inner life of personal salvation, we are discovering afresh what is meant by 'the salt of the earth.' We are discovering that the salt is meant for salting, the light for illuminating, and that the church exists for the sake of those outside itself."[1]

Ricoeur's reference to the "inner life of personal salvation" points to a momentous development in modern religion, and especially in post-Reformation Christianity: the growing withdrawal of religious faith from worldly institutions and its retreat into a realm of inwardness. This development, sometimes labeled the "privatization of faith," is surely one of the major achievements of Western modernity, but it is also one of its most dubious and problematic legacies. On the one side, the turn to inwardness involved a decisive process of liberation, that is, the exodus of religious faith from the stranglehold of secular powers and potentates; under the rubric of "religious liberty" or "free exercise of religion," most modern democratic societies pay tribute to this achievement of individual liberation. On the other side, by allowing itself to be "privatized," religious faith paved the way to its own social obsolescence in the face of the surging tide of materialism and consumerism. In response to the latter danger, efforts have been afoot to rescue religion from its exile, to "de-privatize" or "re-publicize" religious faith by permitting it to reenter the public sphere or the previously "naked public square" (to use an expression of Richard Neuhaus).[2] The problem at this point is to define what is meant by this reentry or—differently phrased—to figure out how the "saltiness" of faith can be restored without conjuring up the danger of dubious political entanglements or a new kind of "Babylonian captivity."

In this chapter, I explore this problem with reference to contemporary contexts. After discussing the general issues involved in the privatization and de-privatization of faith, I turn to the recent reconnection of religion and political power in the United States (what has been called the Americanization of Christian faith). By way of conclusion, I delineate a pedagogy of religious freedom that would safeguard the integrity of religious faith while also preserving its role as "prophetic witness," or as the salt of the earth.

Private and Public Faith

During long stretches of human history, the public character of religion was obvious and taken for granted. In most societies, public power was exercised by religious leaders either directly or in tandem with kings or military-aristocratic elites. According to a widely shared view, worldly society was supposed to be governed by kings and priests—or perhaps by priestly kings—in the same way that the universe as a whole is governed by God's will and spirit. In other words, society was seen as a "cosmion" reflecting the order and power structure of the "cosmos."[3] In the Western context, this kind of analogical arrangement prevailed throughout the Middle Ages and even into early modernity (the French Revolution constituting a kind of watershed). Progressively, however, the individualizing tendencies of the Reformation and Enlightenment gained the upper hand; increasingly, the turn inward, coupled with the demand for individual liberty, eroded the traditional power structure—what Charles Taylor calls the structure of "Christendom," with its amalgamation of religion and power. Despite religious wars and episodes of religious persecution, modernity steadily made room for a new form of religiosity, a mode of uncoerced religious freedom. This kind of freedom, Taylor comments, "we have only when nobody (that is, no particular outlook) is running the show. So a vote of thanks to Voltaire and others for (not necessarily wittingly) showing us this and for allowing us to live the gospel in a purer way, free of that continual and often bloody forcing of conscience which was the sin and blight of all those 'Christian' centuries."[4]

There can be no question that the upsurge of religious freedom was a crucial historical event, a kind of exodus of faith from worldly captivity (and also from a quasi-pagan cosmology). Taylor, for instance, praises the modern breakthrough for inaugurating "the freedom to come to God on one's own or, otherwise put, moved only by the Holy Spirit, whose barely audible voice will often be heard better when the loudspeakers of armed authority are silent."[5] Though applauding this modern development, Taylor also perceives its dark underside: the tendency to foster a self-enclosed humanism or anthropocentrism that is no longer open to (what he calls) "transcendence." One way to better understand this underside is to place religious freedom in its historical context: the emergence of modern liberalism. As is well known, modern liberalism—as inaugurated by Thomas Hobbes and John Locke—erected its theoretical edifice on the basis of so-called natural rights, or endowments possessed by individuals in an original "state of nature" existing prior to the formation of a civic community. "Natural" individuals, or people in the state of nature, were conceived to be basically self-interested or self-seeking to varying degrees—in Hobbes's case, quite nastily self-seeking; in Locke's case, somewhat less so. Among the natural endowments enjoyed by individuals in the original condition were individual freedom and equality, with freedom gradually proliferating over time to encompass not only the freedom to own external possessions but also freedom of assembly, freedom of conscience and personal faith, and even freedom to own and control one's own body and soul. The latter aspect seems to be the preeminent feature of what Taylor calls an "exclusive humanism," that is, an anthropocentric outlook "based exclusively on a notion of human flourishing, which recognizes no valid aim beyond this."[6]

Again, it would be pointless to deny some of the merits of liberal modernity, especially the fostering of creative talents and individual moral responsibility. Above all, liberalism's doctrine of natural rights served (or was meant to serve) as a bulwark against the caprice of rulers and against absolutism of any kind. The basic drawback of modern liberalism as originally formulated, however, was its addiction to a static essentialism—its assignment of essential qualities to human beings quite apart from any effort to cultivate or nurture them. Human beings in the original state were assumed to be "free and equal" or to have "inalienable rights" endowed "by nature" or by the fiat of "nature's God." Thus, modern liberalism assigned to individuals a "human nature" instead of conceiving of them as a bundle of possibilities, as creatures endowed with multiple potentialities for good or ill that require exercise or cultivation, again for good or ill. Taylor comes close to this point when he detects in liberal modernity an inability or unwillingness to encourage self-transformation or a "change of identity." Typically, modern liberal and Enlightenment philosophy starts from the premise of a shared rationality—the Cartesian *ego cogito*—a rationality that serves as a permanent yardstick and is possessed by "natural" individuals, without further ado. Pointing to both Christian and Buddhist religious traditions, Taylor finds traces of a very different outlook: namely, an emphasis on a "radical decentering of the self," involving possibly painful transformations. Being human in these traditions, he notes, implies not so much possessing a "stable identity" as being open to a continuous search. Acknowledging (what he calls) the "transcendent" means "aiming beyond [a given empirical mode of] life or opening yourself to a change in identity."[7]

To be sure, liberal essentialism was not universally endorsed, even during the heyday of the Enlightenment. In the very heartland of enlightened thought—prerevolutionary France—voices were heard exposing the ambivalence or underside of enlightened reason. Probably the most eloquent of these voices was that of Jean-Jacques Rousseau. In his *Discourse on the Origin of Inequality,* Rousseau challenges and chastises the most praised achievement of the age: triumphant and self-confident reason. "It is reason," we read,

> that engenders self-love [or self-centeredness] and it is rational reflection that strengthens it. It is reason that makes "man" shrink into himself; and it is reason that makes him keep aloof from everything that can trouble or afflict him. It is [modern] philosophy that destroys his connections with other men; and it is in consequence of her dictates that he mutters to himself at the sight of another in distress: You may perish for aught I care; I am safe.

The same work also challenges Hobbes's postulate of "ferocious self-love" as the primary human impulse. This challenge is mounted in the name of a different, more outgoing disposition: an "innate abhorrence to see beings suffer that resemble him," or the disposition of pity or compassion, which is "suitable to creatures weak as we are and liable to so many evils." Still more important as an antidote to liberal essentialism is another human trait mentioned in the *Discourse:* the "faculty of improvement" (or perfectibility),·which, given appropriate contexts, "successively unfolds all the other faculties and resides among us not only in the species, but in the individuals that compose it."[8]

To some extent, Rousseau's remonstrations found an echo across the Rhine, among some of the great literary figures of *Sturm und Drang* and the ensuing classical period. In terms of spirited élan, the French thinker's arguments were matched and deepened by Johann Gottfried Herder, especially in the latter's marvelously zestful *Another Philosophy of History for the Education [Bildung] of Humankind,* as well as his later *Letters toward the Advancement [Beförderung] of Humanity.* What troubled Herder most about the so-called Age of Reason was its addiction to abstract generalities and its disdain for concretely lived experience and transformative pedagogical possibilities. In the opinion of many of his contemporaries, civilization had finally reached its zenith, a point where all human learning and wisdom of the past had been assembled in a vast "encyclopedia of all human knowledge." To this "highest pinnacle" of civilization Herder opposed a "heavier," more difficult kind of approach, one concentrating on "slow maturation, profound penetration, and postponed judgment"— that is, on the labor involved in the formation and transformation of habits and character and the persistent opening of new horizons. In actuality, what modern Enlightenment had yielded was a stabilization and self-confinement of the (Cartesian) *ego cogito* and the reduction of genuine inquiry to "abstracted spirit, a philosophy out of two maxims."[9] As one should recall, Herder was not only a writer and philosopher but also a Christian minister with pastoral duties; thus, he wished to keep open not only the horizons of literature and erudition but also the windows of faith and spirituality.

To some extent, this concern with literary and spiritual horizons was shared by Herder's younger contemporary, the poet Friedrich

Schiller, as is evident especially in his pedagogical writings. Partly under the influence of modern liberal teachings, Schiller saw education or civilization (*Bildung*) as an arduous process leading from a primitive "natural" condition to the higher level of art and ethical responsibility. In his view, emergence from this primitive condition was so difficult that people were often tempted to take shortcuts, claiming access to the higher realm while still being thoroughly mired in primitive selfishness. Instead of undergoing any seasoning or self-transformation, individuals in this case merely magnified their selfishness by subjecting even ethics and religion to the demands of possessive individualism. In Schiller's poignant phrase (contained in his letters on aesthetic education): "In the very midst of his animal condition, the drive toward the 'absolute' catches the individual unawares." And because, in this state, all efforts are directed toward material-temporal things, the impulse arises to extend self-interest indefinitely, without any effort toward self-transgression. Thus, the same impulse that is meant to lead to "truth and ethics" produces nothing but "infinite instinctual need." As he adds, the fruits of this shortcut are "all your systems of unqualified eudemonism whether concerned with the present day or our whole life."[10]

The issue Schiller addresses here has plagued religion and moral righteousness through the ages: the danger that they can be (and often are) used, appropriated, or instrumentalized for worldly or selfish interests. His letters on aesthetics are eloquent and forthright on this point. "Even what is most sacred in human affairs, the moral law," he writes, "when it first makes its appearance in sensual-instinctual life, cannot escape this perversion" or abuse. The reason for this perversion is that human beings are not stuck in a fixed nature or identity; they can become human, or be "humanized," only through transformative experiences. Because in ordinary life sensuality precedes moral conscience and ethical sensibility, the temptation is great for human beings to reduce the latter to positive empirical objects amenable to appropriation and possession. For Schiller, the effects of this appropriation are corrupting both for human pedagogy and for the very meaning of ethics and the divine. In his words, from the angle of this corruption, we are dealing "no longer with a holy Being but only with a mighty or powerful Being." At this point, the spirit in which human beings worship God is "the spirit of fear (*Furcht*) which degrades them, rather than reverence (*Ehrfurcht*) which would uplift them in their own estimation."[11]

The Americanization of Faith

In our time, complaints about the use and abuse of religion are leveled mainly against non-Western forms of fundamentalism, especially against societies where religion and politics have traditionally been fused or mingled. Given the long-standing separation between faith and politics, or between church and state, Western democracies are usually exempt from such complaints. A closer look, however, reveals that this exemption is unfounded. American democracy is a case in point. Despite the vaunted "wall of separation" enshrined in the Bill of Rights, religion and politics in the United States are entwined and contaminated in many ways, and usually at the expense of religious faith. Although religious symbols are, in principle, banished from public places, public symbols—chiefly the national flag—are displayed prominently in all the churches of the country, usually in tandem with religious icons. Wherever this arrangement prevails, the "wall of separation" is basically sidelined in favor of the appropriation or colonization of faith by politics. Using different terminology, one can speak here of the "de-privatization" of religious faith, with perilous and possibly abusive connotations. Basically, what is involved is the nationalization or, more specifically, the Americanization of faith.

Concern about the co-optation of faith by American politics is not of recent origin. Like a shadow, this concern has accompanied the unfolding of liberal Protestantism in America—a Protestantism bent on accommodating itself to modern liberal culture. Some seventy years ago, Richard Niebuhr, a professor at the Yale Divinity School, denounced what he saw as a new kind of "Babylonian captivity" of Christian faith: the captivity of the church at the hands of American popular culture. Sounding a wake-up call, his book *The Church against the World* appealed to Christian believers to shake off their complacency and embark on a new exodus from the "fleshpots of Egypt." Although faith and society, or church and world, were meant to be in fruitful tension, in Niebuhr's view, American religion was fast losing its "salt" by amalgamating itself too cozily with the surrounding civilization. When the church enters into an alliance "with converted emperors and governors, philosophers and artists, merchants and entrepreneurs, and begins to live at peace in the culture," he writes, "faith loses its force . . . , repentance grows formal, corruption enters with idolatry, and the church, tied to the culture which it sponsored, suffers corruption with it." For Niebuhr, the task for American religion, and especially for Protestant Christians, was momentous; it was nothing less than "the liberation of the church from its bondage to a corrupt civilization," and hence the recovery of its transformative élan, enabling it to preach the "good news" to the world.[12]

Although quickly swept aside by the tides of cultural accommodation, Niebuhr's remonstrations were never completely silenced, and some of its echoes still reverberate in our time. Some sixty years after Niebuhr's study, Laurence Moore—in a book titled *Selling God*—chastised American Christians for their lethargy and for cultivating a self-image promoted by popular culture and resting on nothing but "fast, friendly, and guiltless consumption." Given this self-image, Moore concludes, American religion has indeed lost its "transformative power."[13] A few years later, a group of evangelical Christians issued a declaration that basically endorsed this indictment. "Evangelical churches today," the declaration states, "are increasingly dominated by the spirit of this age rather than by the spirit of Christ." This domination is evident in their teaching: instead of preaching good news to the world, the emphasis is now on teaching a "self-esteem gospel" or a "health and wealth gospel" favoring the privileged few.[14]

Still more recently, in a book titled *American Jesus,* Stephen Prothero attempts to trace the story of the progressive Americanization of Christian faith—or, in terms of its subtitle, the story of "how the son of God became a national icon." "How did the United States," Prothero asks, "become a Jesus nation," and how was it possible to transform the crucified Lord into "a personality, a celebrity, and finally an icon"? His answer: "Jesus became a major personality in the United States because of the ability of religious insiders to make him culturally inescapable. He became a national icon because outsiders have felt free" to appropriate him and "to interpret him in their own fashion."[15] Prothero's book harks back to Niebuhr's critical observations and his emphasis on a necessary tension—in fact, an "optimal tension"—between religion and politics or between faith and worldly culture. Whenever this tension is suspended or lacking, religious faith is in danger of being co-opted or leveled into dominant cultural paradigms. As Prothero writes, echoing Niebuhr: "Jesus has no doubt transformed the nation, but the nation has also transformed him. At least in the United States, he has been buffeted about by the skepticism of the Enlightenment, the enthusiasm of revivalism, and the therapeutic culture of consumer capitalism"—with the culture increasingly winning out (yielding the predominance of the so-called religion of the market).[16]

Love in Two Cities

The preceding discussion of nationalized religion was meant as a cautious reminder. Although designed to rescue faith from the exile of pure inwardness, a rigorous de-privatization of faith conjures up an equally great danger: captivity and enslavement at the hands of worldly powers and *idola fori* (idols of the market). This leads me back to a point stressed earlier: the differential relation and entwinement of world and faith, of place and no place, city and holy abode. The relation between land and promised land is one of neither coincidence nor segregation. The two "domains" (to use the term loosely) are neither identical nor extraterritorial to each other, for both cases would destroy the "saltiness" of faith. Although differentiated in their character and aim, the two realms are connected by a hidden passageway. In distinguishing between genuine and corrupt forms of religious belief, the Iranian philosopher Abdulkarim Soroush ascribes the contrast to the different guiding "passions" of believers—that is, to their selfish or self-transcending passion, respectively.[17] Another word for *passion* here is *love*, which leads to the distinction between a selfish or self-aggrandizing love and a self-transforming or purifying love.

In the Christian tradition, the classic text discussing this distinction is Saint Augustine's *City of God,* and especially the section (Book 14) that deals with the different motivations or orientations guiding the earthly city and the heavenly (or saintly) city, respectively. Deviating from merely a worldly geography, Augustine acknowledges only "two kinds of society" that can rightly be called the "two cities." One kind, the earthly city, is the place where people "live according to the flesh," or their selfish desires; the other kind, called the heavenly city, is where people "live according to the spirit," or divine guidance.

What matters most to Augustine at this point is not institutional structure but inner direction. In his words, the two cities have basically "issued from two kinds of love." Whereas the worldly (or earthly) city is anchored in "a selfish love which dares to despise even God," the heavenly (or saintly) city is "rooted in a love of God that is ready to trample on or transcend the self." Strongly opposing religious cooptation or any nationalization of faith, Augustine adds the following passage designed to preserve the "saltiness" of faith. In the worldly city, he writes, "both the rulers themselves and the people they rule are dominated by the lust for domination"; by contrast, in the heavenly city, or the city of God, "all citizens serve one another in charity." Whereas the former city loves and exalts its leaders "as symbols of its own worldly power," the latter city "says to its God: I love thee, O Lord, source of my strength."[18]

Several lessons can be gleaned from Augustine's account. One has to do with the entwinement of the two cities. Although differentiated, both cities are linked by a recessed passageway, which is none other than love. This means that, properly guided or channeled, love has a transformative or self-transcending quality that can lead us from the prison of a self-seeking humanism toward the wider horizons of unconditional self-giving. Seen in this light, love provides a ladder of ascent, sustaining a kind of "pilgrim's progress" or transformative-spiritual pedagogy. This pedagogy is recognized by Augustine when he writes that both loves often "coexist" in the same person: "This co-existence is good for human beings in that they can, by increasing in themselves the love for what is right, decrease their love of what is wrong until their whole life has been transformed to good and thus brought to perfection."[19] In his epilogue to *A Catholic Modernity?* Taylor follows both Plato and Augustine in stressing the role of moral pedagogy and pilgrim's progress. "For Plato," he writes, "the very definition of justice requires that we identify a higher and a lower [domain] and distinguish our love of one from our love of the other." In turn, Christian faith has adopted this model of transformative ascent while giving it additional spiritual connotations; thus Augustine spoke explicitly of "two loves"—a terminology followed by later Christian thinkers from Saint Bonaventure and Pascal to Kierkegaard and beyond.[20]

Another lesson, closely connected with the ladder of ascent, concerns the status and meaning of religious freedom. As previously indicated, modern liberalism—in its founding formulations—tended to assign human beings a fixed identity or "nature" that was immune to transformative change. In this conception, human beings were defined by a series of basic endowments or "natural rights," including freedom of conscience and religious freedom. Once the accent is shifted to moral ascent and the pedagogy of love, however, the plausibility of this liberal conception crumbles. Clearly, there cannot be a natural right to loving or being loved, just as there cannot be a right or entitlement to redemptive healing. Rather, loving and being loved are unearned gifts exempt from managerial planning and control. Seen in this light, religious freedom is not a human property but rather an enabling potency making room for open horizons and possibilities. By the same token, the "target" of religious faith—God or the divine—cannot possibly be appropriated, domesticated, or nationalized, for any such effort would "objectify" God, reducing him to a thing among other things. (This, in my view, is the deeper sense of monotheism as affirmed in the Jewish prohibition against images and the Islamic idea of *tawhid*. The point here is not to substitute one preferred thing for myriad things in the world; rather, it is to abandon the entire impulse to cling to any and all things amenable to appropriation, in favor of a released openness to redemptive grace and unearned love.)

Viewed in terms of release, religious freedom is not the monopoly of monotheistic (or, loosely, Western) religions; the same kind of detachment from worldly bondage can be found in pluralist and even nontheistic modes of faith. Taylor gives the example of Mahayana Buddhist teachings, with their emphasis on self-overcoming in favor of "no-self" or the present-absence of selfhood. In Buddhism, he notes, the transformative change of identity is "quite radical," for the famous "eightfold path" of liberation leads "from self to 'no self' (*anatta*)," that is, from identity to the emptiness or self-emptying of selfhood.[21] A similar message of release and freedom is presented in the Bhagavad Gita, the sacred book of Hinduism. In that text, God—in the person of Krishna—instructs human beings about the path (*yoga*) to be followed in pursuit of spiritual ascent and transformation. Speaking specifically about the path of action (*karma yoga*), Krishna alerts us to the possibility of being actively involved in the world while being free from bondage or confining attachments. "Set thy heart upon thy work," we read, "but never on its reward. . . . Perform work in the peace of *yoga* and, free from self-centered desires, be not moved in either success or failure." As shown here, action performed without selfish clinging has a liberating and transformative quality; in fact, it constitutes a kind of worship exhibiting "sacramental" or consecrating features.[22]

It should be noted that religious freedom as release does not equal a simple retreat, granting one an alibi from worldly cares and obligations. In terms of the "saltiness" of faith, the basic question is not *whether* but *how* to be involved in the world. Augustine celebrates the immense freedom of believers, their release from corruption and false attachments, but he also insists on their engagement in the world through acts of love and charity.[23] With this engagement, faith is subtly de-privatized (though without allowing itself to be co-opted); in a way, faith becomes embodied or incarnated in the world, thus recovering its role in an unfolding redemptive story. This emphasis on religious embodiment or incarnation is especially important in contemporary times as an antidote to a radical transcendentalism that, proclaiming the divine to be "wholly other," offers the temptation of escapism. The importance of this emphasis is recognized by Taylor when he writes that "redemption happens through incarnation, the weaving of God's life into human lives" that are not blandly homogenized but "different, plural, irreducible to each other." In even stronger and more forthright language, the corrective is underscored by the Italian philosopher Gianni Vattimo, who urges us to be "suspicious of an excessive emphasis on the transcendence of God, as mystery, radical alterity, and paradox." Seen in the light of the "good news," he states, "God descends from the heaven of transcendence, . . . thus fulfilling the transition announced by the gospels, after which we shall no longer be called servants or children, but friends."[24]

As an expression of "incarnate" faith, love cannot be neatly segmented or limited to narrowly circumscribed sectarian or confessional groupings. In Christ's biblical exhortation, loving others is not restricted to Catholics or Protestants or even to Christians; it extends to all fellow beings. Especially in our globalizing age, incarnate love necessarily acquires an ecumenical or cosmopolitan cast. Yet, although this love is, in principle, addressed *urbi et orbi* (to humanity at large), religious faith urges us to pay special attention to the needy, the marginalized, the persecuted. With its stress on the practice of justice and equity—"justice, and only justice, you shall follow" (Deuteronomy 16:20)—biblical faith (and in fact, every genuine faith) places itself on the side of the victims rather than the victimizers, the oppressed rather than the oppressors. In recent times, this has come to be known as the "preferential option for the poor." In a speech given in 1980 shortly before his assassination, Archbishop Oscar Romero of El Salvador explicitly endorsed this option. "In a world which has no human face," he stated, "we have made the effort not to pass by, not to walk around the injured person on the road, but to go up to him as a good Samaritan. . . . We are dealing with a true 'option for the poor.' This means that the church incarnates herself in the world of the poor, proclaims a good news, gives hope, inspires liberating praxis, defends the cause of the poor and participates in their destiny."[25]

Being released from, but also engaged in, the world, religious people necessarily have the character of sojourners or friendly strangers—that is, of people who, though not alien to structures of injustice, befriend fellow beings everywhere, bringing good news and good wishes. As Augustine writes: "So long as the heavenly city is sojourning on earth, she invites citizens from all nations and all tongues, and gathers them into a harmonious pilgrim band. She takes no issue with the diversity of customs, laws, and traditions whereby human peace is sought and maintained."[26] Thus, in Augustine's view, sojourning on earth is an ecumenical enterprise, and this aspect must be even more strongly underscored in our age. Diversity of customs, traditions, and beliefs can and should be welcomed and encouraged, provided that all the "pilgrims" set their sights on justice and the "holy abode," while relinquishing their attachment to worldly power. In a recent book entitled *The God Who May Be*, Richard Kearney elaborates on the Augustinian metaphor by emphasizing that the coming kingdom, or "holy abode," can be neither accomplished and controlled nor abandoned by human beings. "The kingdom," he writes, "is precisely that which can never be fully possessed in the here and now, but always directs us toward an advent still to come." Indeed, "we can only ever find the kingdom by losing it, by renouncing the illusion that we possess it here and now." However, release from mastery does not cancel human obligation to participate in the world and to act in such a way as "to bring the coming kingdom closer, making it more possible, as it were, by each of our actions."[27] Thus, without pretending to be in charge, all our words and deeds should point quietly yet insistently in one direction. They should all carry a silent subscript that says, "Come." Yes indeed, may it come.

12. Love and Justice
A Memorial Tribute to Paul Ricoeur

On May 20, 2005, the French philosopher Paul Ricoeur died in Paris at age ninety-two. This chapter is dedicated to his memory. In my view, Ricoeur's writings and his persona were in complete harmony—something that is not often the case among distinguished intellectuals. I had the good fortune to encounter him at various conferences both in the United States and in Europe and thus was able to discern the human being animating his texts. In 1999 I participated in a meeting held in his honor when he bade farewell to the University of Chicago, where he had taught periodically for many years.[1] In my recollection, the traits that were particularly striking were Ricoeur's genuine modesty and reticence, his passion for inquiry and dialogical learning, and his warm friendliness toward both old and young, philosophers and nonphilosophers. His broad public acclaim never dented his simple humanity.

Ricoeur's writings are voluminous and multifaceted. In their ability to integrate major strands of both Continental and Anglo-American thought, they constitute a kind of summa of twentieth-century Western philosophy. It would be audacious and even reckless to try to present an overview of this far-flung opus in such a brief tribute. Instead, I focus here on a moderately sized text—but one that, in its basic orientation, can claim a certain representative quality. As in a prism, the argument of the text assembles the different facets of Ricoeur's work into a nodal or central point: the relation between love and justice. The text dates from 1989, the year the University of Tübingen bestowed on the French thinker the Leopold Lucas Prize. It was on that occasion that the recipient delivered a lecture titled *Amour et Justice*.[2]

It seems appropriate to comment briefly on the background of this event. The prize given to Ricoeur had been established in 1972 to commemorate the centenary of the birth of Leopold Lucas. After studying Oriental languages and Jewish history in Berlin and Tübingen, Lucas became one of the leading Jewish scholars and intellectuals in pre-Weimar Germany. In 1902 he cofounded the Society for the Promotion of Jewish Sciences; much later, in 1941, at the age of nearly seventy, he heeded the call of Leo Baeck to join the Institute for the Wissenschaft des Judentums in Berlin. The following year, he and his wife were deported to the concentration camp of Theresienstadt, where he perished in the fall of 1943; his wife died a year later at Auschwitz.

In introducing Ricoeur in 1989, Oswald Bayer (professor of philosophy at Tübingen) underscored the appropriateness of awarding the Lucas Prize to the French philosopher. As he observed in his *laudatio*, the prize was given to Ricoeur "in recognition of his border-crossings mediating between peoples" and in view of his tireless efforts to reconnect "philosophy, psychology, literary theory, and theology" by relying on "phenomenological and hermeneutical traditions." In the same speech, Bayer also pointed to some concrete border crossings in the philosopher's own life. Born into an old Huguenot family, Ricoeur grew up in a country torn between agnosticism and the Catholic faith. Captured by the Germans at the beginning of World War II, he spent his years in a prisoner-of-war camp studying German philosophy and translating the first volume of Husserl's *Ideas for a Pure Phenomenology and Phenomenological Philosophy* (a steppingstone to his later publications on Husserl).[3] In 1947 he became the coeditor of *Esprit,* a progressive Christian journal seeking to mediate between the Enlightenment and religious faith. During the same period, having accepted an appointment as philosopher in Strasbourg, he encouraged and supported repeated meetings between German and French professors and students. In 1956 he moved to the Sorbonne in Paris, and a decade later he transferred to the University of Nanterre. While still holding the latter position, he entered into a teaching arrangement with the University of Chicago, which for many years involved repeated border crossings between Europe and America.

One crucial feature of Ricoeur's outlook underscored by Bayer was his mediating position between polar opposites or stark antitheses. Ricoeur, he remarked, was neither a local chauvinist nor a shallow universalist dedicated to a global melting pot of cultures. "It is a distinguishing quality of the life-work of Paul Ricoeur," the *laudatio* states, "that it lent just as little support to narrowly self-centered identity claims as to premature, overly simplified ecumenical syntheses—syntheses bent on removing the plurality of languages and modes of reasoning as mere obstacles to universalization." Although fully aware of the ongoing process of globalization and even committed to a global kind of social justice, Ricoeur did not acknowledge a "universal canon" but only "separate and mutually contesting theories" or perspectives, between which mediation or reconciliation must be sought.[4] In his 1989 lecture, the task was to find a mediation—neither synthesis nor stark opposition—between *amour et justice* (love and justice). In the following, I discuss the two topics separately before exploring the possibility as well as the significance of their mediation.

Love

With regard to the first theme of his title, Ricoeur moves cautiously and soberly. As he concedes at the beginning, it is difficult to talk and write properly about love. For many, there is a tendency to derail into hyperbole or emotional platitudes. Others, especially "analytical" philosophers, prefer an abstract conceptualism bent on reducing thematic content to formal principles or propositions, in which case the experiential richness of the theme of love vanishes. His lecture is on guard against both dangers. Derailment into platitudes is countered by the coupling of love with justice. The temptation of abstract formalism is obviated at the outset through recourse to one great philosopher who, in his thinking, made room for the *raison du coeur*: Blaise Pascal. Ricoeur cites a passage from Pascal's *Pensées* that can be read as a kind of passkey to the entire lecture: "All the bodies in the world and all the intellects with all their achievements do not match the smallest stirring of the love for God. The latter belongs to an infinitely higher order" (*un ordre infiniment plus élevé*). With these words, the theme of love is immediately located on a plane that is far removed from both banality and formalism.[5]

In an effort to chart a philosophically fruitful path to his theme, Ricoeur concentrates on three distinguishing traits of the "discourse of love." He calls these traits "oddities" and does not hesitate to speak of "the strangeness or bizarre character of the love-discourse" (*l'étrangeté ou la bizarrerie du discours de l'amour*). The first distinguishing trait is the intimate connection between love and praise or eulogy (*louange*). In his words: "The discourse of love is first of all a discourse of encomium or praise." Praising or eulogizing someone or something combines several dispositions—lifting up, revering, finding delight. To discover something considered the "highest" is captivating, enticing, and joyful. To illustrate the meaning of this trait, Ricoeur's lecture offers examples from scripture and poetry. At the top of that list is the hymn of praise, or paean to love, that Saint Paul penned in his first letter to the Corinthians: "If I speak in the tongues of men and of angels, but have not love, I am a noisy gong or a clanging cymbal" (1 Corinthians 13:1). Love and praise coalesce in this passage because it is love that is being eulogized. Also cited are the great hymns of praise contained in many of the psalms (in Hebrew, *tehillim*). Praise in these texts is often linked with blessing or benediction. Thus, we read: "Praise to the man (or blessed is the man) who walks not in the counsel of the wicked. . . . He is like a tree planted by streams of water, that yields fruit in its season" (Psalms 1:1, 3), or, "O Lord of hosts, blessed (praised) is the man who trusts in thee" (Psalms 84:12).[6]

Similar to these hymns of praise are the biblical blessings, the most famous of which can be found in the Sermon on the Mount: "Blessed are the poor in spirit, for theirs is the kingdom of heaven. Blessed are those who mourn, for they shall be comforted" (Matthew 5:3–4). As Ricoeur comments: "Hymns of praise, benedictions, and laudations form a whole bundle of literary devices which can be assembled under the rubric of praise." He refers in this context to the wealth of literary expressions examined by Robert Alter in his book *The Art of Biblical Poetry*. To be sure, the topic cannot be restricted to biblical poetry, because it has ramifications in "secular" poetry and literature as well. The field is too vast to permit an overview in this context, so it must suffice here to turn to the famous "Sonnets to Orpheus" by Rainer Maria Rilke. In the seventh sonnet, we read:

Praising's what matters! Summoned for praise
He issued forth like the ore from a stone's
silence. His heart: a mortal vineyard

for humans of deathless wine. . . .
Neither decay in royal sepulchers
nor any shadow falling from the gods
can detract from his glorious praising.
For he is one of the permanent heralds,
holding far into the tombs of the dead
bowls of ripe, praise-worthy fruit.

And then there are these lines from the eighth sonnet:

Only in the realm of praising should Lament
proceed, the nymph of tears' fountain,
watching over our dejected complaint,
so that it be limpid on the very rock
that bears the palaces and the altars.[7]

The second distinguishing trait of the discourse of love is the connection between love and demand or obligation. What is the relation between love and ethical standards, especially the kind of moral
imperatives stipulated by Kant? "Is love," Ricoeur queries, "ethically comparable to moral principles, that is, to propositional standards from which practical maxims can be derived or deduced?"
To underscore this query, his lecture points to some (initially) con-
fusing biblical passages linking love and command: for example, in
Deuteronomy 6:5 and Leviticus 19:18 (repeated in Matthew 22:37,
39): "You shall love the Lord your God with all your heart, and with
all your soul, and with all your might. . . . And you shall love your
neighbor as yourself." How can love be expressed in the language of
"shall"? How can love be demanded and even commanded? To shed
light on this difficult topic, Ricoeur turns to an unexpected source:
Franz Rosenzweig's *The Star of Redemption*. Rosenzweig's work is
divided into three major parts, each of which is subdivided into several books. The first part deals with basic "elements" and the permanent "proto-cosmos" (*Vorwelt*), the second part pursues the "path"
of history and the "ever-renewed world," and the last part refers to
the coming "kingdom" and the "eternal hyper-cosmos" (*Überwelt*).
Ricoeur's comments focus on the second part—discussing the three
stages of creation, revelation, and redemption—and particularly on

the transition from creation to revelation. At the beginning of the section devoted to revelation—and thus at the juncture where divine creation still overshadows the Mosaic law—Rosenzweig alerts readers to the dictate of love that (for Ricoeur) clearly reveals "the primacy of the original language of creation over inter-human (moral) communication."[8]

The second book of the historical part of Rosenzweig's work bears the title "Revelation, or the Ever-Renewed Birth of the Soul." The ever-renewed birth of the human soul occurs as a result of divine love, which absolutely precedes revealed biblical laws (as recorded especially in Leviticus and Deuteronomy). In Rosenzweig's own words: "The capstone (*Schlusstein*) of the somber arch of creation becomes the cornerstone (*Grundstein*) of the bright house of revelation. For the soul, revelation means the experience of a present which, although resting on the existence of a past, yet does not dwell in it but rather walks in the light of the divine countenance." At the beginning of the section on revelation, Rosenzweig invokes a biblical passage that is taken from neither Leviticus nor Deuteronomy but from the Song of Solomon or Song of Songs. The opening lines read: "O that you would kiss me with the kisses of your mouth! For your love is better than wine." Later, the song makes another comparison: "Set me as a seal upon your heart, as a seal upon your arm; for love is strong as death" (Song of Solomon 8:6). It is this phrase—"love is strong as death"—that forms the opening line of Rosenzweig's book on revelation. Yet, for the Jewish thinker, love is stronger than death. In his presentation, death is the capstone of the story of creation (discussed in the preceding book); now, under the new dispensation, God reveals himself first of all as love, or rather as "lover." "Death as the capstone of creation," Rosenzweig writes, "first stamps every created thing with the ineradicable mark of creatureliness, with the label 'has been' (*Gewesen*). This mark of death is challenged by love which solely knows the present, thrives on the present, pines for the present."[9]

In his discussion of revelation, and specifically in the section titled "Love," Rosenzweig distinguishes between two phases of the self-revealing or self-manifestation of the divine: the original creation, in which God himself remains concealed, and the revelation of love, when God completely surrenders or gives of himself. "Precisely for the sake of its revelational character," he writes, "the first revelation in creation demands the eruption of a 'second' revelation which is nothing other than self-revelation. . . . It is love which meets all the demands made on the concept of self-revealing: the love of the lover (not the beloved). Only the love of the lover is such a continuously renewed self-surrender (*Sebsthingabe*); only the lover gives himself away in love."[10] Returning to Ricoeur: what is essential for him in Rosenzweig's reflections is the status of love as a preamble to and precondition of every divine legislation or revealed law. This also explains the peculiarity of the demand or command to love. What Rosenzweig's text shows in a "truly sublime way," Ricoeur writes, is how the demand to love emerges out of the prior bond of love between God and human beings: "The demand which precedes every law or legislation is the request which the lover addresses to the beloved: love me!" Thus, it is important here to identify the demand or command with love itself, with a love that "commands itself." Differently put: "We are dealing here with a command which contains the condition of its observance in the very gentleness of its request: love me!" To avoid any possibility of misunderstanding, he adds that, in the command to love, we encounter something like a "poetic mode of imperative," a mode that is clearly distinguished from the moral (or moralizing) mode of the Kantian imperative.[11]

The third distinguishing mark of the discourse of love is its connection with feelings or sentiments, with the entire gamut of expressions and dispositions testifying to the "power of metaphor." The lover's request addressed to the beloved—"Love me"—gives love a dynamic power that enables it to evoke a broad spectrum of feelings and even to balance conflicting sentiments: "pleasure and pain, fulfillment and disappointment, joy and sorrow, happiness and misery." According to the lecture, one can find here a "play of analogy" between feelings —that may be very different or even antithetical yet are still animated by love. In this context, Ricoeur points to Max Scheler's book *On the Phenomenology and Theory of Sympathy and on Love and Hatred*, a text later republished under the title *Nature and Forms of Sympathy* (*Wesen und Formen der Sympathie*). What attracts him to this work is Scheler's broad scale of sentiments and his portrayal of a certain dynamic movement of ascent and descent. Just as in the case of praise, love seen as feeling has the tendency to elevate the target of love—a tendency that can be countermanded by an opposite move of vilification. In Ricoeur's account, love as presented by Scheler is basically "a positive movement"—a movement that (in Scheler's words) "leads from a lower to a higher estimation of a thing or person and which allows the higher esteem to burst forth in a sudden epiphany." By contrast, hatred is a negative movement lowering or demeaning its target. Viewed in this light, Ricoeur comments, love is not merely a passive reaction but involves "an increase or elevation": "Love creates anew, while hatred destroys."[12]

It is this dynamic movement of human feelings or sentiments that makes it difficult, if not impossible, to impose external criteria or limitations on the spectrum of love. Ricoeur's lecture at this point takes a critical stand against the radical distinction between *eros* and *agape*—a distinction that is popular among some theologians and philosophers of religion. As he points out (or, rather, insists), erotic love is entirely capable of "signifying *more* than itself," and this capability derives from the "play of analogy" and the "power of metaphor." A good example here is the Song of Songs, whose language oscillates almost playfully between sensual-erotic and Platonic-spiritual love. For Ricoeur, it is important to realize "that the opposition between *eros* and *agape* lacks a biblical-exegetical basis." In lieu of this opposition, the lecture speaks of a "substantive tropology" of love, where *tropology* means more than a decorative interplay of tropes; it signifies the ability "simultaneously to capture the real analogy of sentiments and the power of *eros* to signify and express *agape*."[13]

Justice

In Ricoeur's lecture, the theme of justice is less extensively discussed. Basically, the lecture distinguishes between two dimensions: the dimension of legal practice manifest in a society's judicial system and in the principle of the "rule of law" (*Rechtsstaat*), and the philosophical or theoretical dimension that revolves around issues of fair distribution. The field of legal practice exhibits a plethora of relevant phenomena: precedents, legal procedures, judicial competences, and court decisions. The entire field can be analyzed as a mode of social communication. "We find ourselves in the field of legal practice," Ricoeur states, "when a judicial forum is called upon in order to rule on the claims of competing interest groups or conflicting parties." In this case, as in other legal practices, the emphasis is on interhuman interests or claims that require argumentative negotiation and judicial settlement. Legal negotiations involve rhetoric, persuasion, and argumentation—that is, modes of communicative reasoning (though mainly of a strategic sort). In contrast to purely academic modes of argumentation, however, legal negotiations are ultimately oriented toward settlement. Whereas arguments per se are infinite, by virtue of the constant generation of counterarguments, legal practice operates in the realm of finitude, in the sense that litigation is meant to ultimately result in a decision that is "fair" to the contending parties. By operating under finite constraints, judicial decision making involves not a purely logical deduction but also (in varying degrees) an exercise of political power and authority in society.[14]

As can be seen, legal practice displays a feature that distinguishes it sharply from the discourse of love: namely, the "formality" of law and jurisprudence, which ultimately derives from the fact that law and ethics never coincide or harmonize completely. This formality also emerges in the philosophical discourse of justice. In this domain, a general continuity of legal reflection can be detected from the Greeks to the present, from the works of Aristotle to the writings of John Rawls. Throughout, there is a tendency to equate justice with a mode of distribution, particularly with conceptions of arithmetical and proportional distribution. Whereas arithmetical distribution insists on complete equality among individuals (for example, the principle of "equality before the law"), proportional distribution demands that each party receive the portion that is his or her due in relation to others (*suum cuique tribuere*). From the perspective of proportional distribution, Ricoeur observes, the entire society "appears as a network distributing or allocating roles, rights and duties, advantages and disadvantages, benefits and obligations" among its members. Justice from this angle is predicated on an organic social holism, which in turn depends on the interests and claims of participating individuals: "In a distributive conception, society cannot exist without individuals to whom portions are allocated and who hence participate proportionally in the totality; but the individuals would lose their social status in the absence of the rules of distribution allocating to them their place in society."[15]

As indicated earlier, the conception of justice as a mode of distribution still persists in the case of Rawls. His *Theory of Justice* stipulates two basic principles of justice: the principle of strict equality or "equal liberty," and the "difference principle," according to which unequal treatment must proportionally benefit the disadvantaged. In Ricoeur's account, the theory is a new interpretation of Aristotle and his two modes of justice under the aegis of modern liberalism (with its accent on individual rights). As he adds, with particular reference to proportional justice, Rawls's "difference principle" seeks to salvage the idea of justice under conditions of unequal distribution by requiring that "the greater benefits enjoyed by the privileged must be compensated in such a way that the disadvantaged or less privileged suffer fewer or smaller costs." The "maximin" rule in Rawls's theory means precisely this: to upgrade the lesser part in compensation for inequality. The general idea operating in this conception, however, is much older: "to upgrade the lesser part is simply the modern version of the Aristotelian notion of proportional justice." What is new (to the extent that novelty is an issue) is the higher degree of abstraction characterizing modern liberal thought—that is, the greater distance between general principles and ethical conduct. This distance is evident, for example, in the key Rawlsian categories of the "original position" and the "veil of ignorance."[16]

The point that matters most to Ricoeur in this context is the formal character of conceptions of justice, especially in their modern formulations. Seen as a general scheme of distribution, justice is not so much an ethical virtue guiding human conduct as an organizing principle superimposed on a society whose members are basically assumed to be motivated by private self-interest and to face off against other members in multiple conflicts of interests. For Ricoeur, this formal conception is far removed from mutual ethical engagement and genuine social solidarity. As he writes: "The highest point to which this [formal] conception can reach is that of a society in which the sentiment of mutuality or mutual dependence . . . remains subordinated to that of mutual disinterest" or aloofness. To be sure, Rawlsian theory—like other modern liberal theories—pays lip service to social solidarity, but only in attenuated form or as an aside. The primacy assigned to private interests and their relentless conflict make it impossible, in Ricoeur's view, for "the idea of justice" to "be located on the plane of a real recognition and solidarity where participants would or could regard each other as reciprocal debtors (*Schuldner*)" in a shared enterprise.[17]

Love and Justice: An Attempt at Mediation

In the concluding part of his lecture, Ricoeur attempts to build a bridge between the two antagonists of his theme—between the "poetry of love" and the "prose of justice." As he states at the beginning, his goal is neither the fusion of the antagonists nor the confirmation of their antithesis. Above and beyond both fusion and antithesis, he notes, there is "a third, difficult path" that allows the antagonists to remain in a state of "tension" but, precisely because of this tension, encourages a mutual learning and rapprochement. In charting this mediating path, the lecture turns once again to a biblical text: the Sermon on the Mount, as recorded in the fifth chapter of Matthew, supplemented by the so-called Sermon on the Plain, recorded in the sixth chapter of Luke. Both gospel passages juxtapose two basic commands: the command to "love one's enemies," and the Golden Rule as a synonym for the principle of justice. In a way, the entire theme of Ricoeur's lecture is put to the final test here.

The passage in Luke is particularly eloquent and revealing. Following a series of blessings addressed to a large crowd, Jesus says sharply: "But I say to you who hear me: love your enemies, do good to those who hate you, bless those who curse you, pray for those who abuse you. To him who strikes you on the cheek, offer the other also; and from him who takes away your coat, do not withhold even your shirt" (Luke 6:27–29). Almost abruptly and without preparation, this "new" command to love one's enemies is followed by the statement (which is a variation of the traditional Golden Rule): "And as you wish that people would do to you, do so also to them" (6:31). Then, this traditional statement gives way to a further elaboration on the new love command, stated with stirring intensity:

> If you love those who love you, what credit is that to you? For even sinners love those who love them. And if you do good to those who do good to you, what credit is that to you? For even sinners do the same. And if you lend to those from whom you hope to receive, what merit is that on your part? Even sinners

lend to sinners, to receive as much back again. But love your
enemies, and do good and lend, expecting nothing in return.
(6:32–35)

What is happening here? Ricoeur asks. Does this paean to the new
love command not "imply a harsh disapproval of the Golden Rule?"
And if the Golden Rule is put aside, does this not imply a disapproval
of the idea of justice itself? The cited passage in the Gospel of Luke,
Ricoeur notes, must "inevitably puzzle" readers, especially to the extent that the Golden Rule is viewed as equivalent to, or a stand-in for,
the "demand of justice." His lecture at this point clearly moves into
difficult philosophical and theological terrain, requiring both caution
and courage at every step. Ricoeur's dexterity in navigating this terrain
immediately becomes evident when he characterizes the new command to love one's enemies as a "supra-ethical" demand operating
under the auspices of a higher "economy of the gift" (*économie du
don*) and a "logic of super-abundance." The new command is "supra-
ethical," he observes, because it exceeds the usual norms of reciprocity and manifests an outlook "approximating a domain transcending
ethics as such: namely, the economy of the gift." Turning again to the
work of Rosenzweig, Ricoeur finds the economy of the gift operative
both in the primal phase of creation and in the eschatological promise
of redemption and God's kingdom. On both ends of the spectrum, he
notes, we find an economy of the gift where "the God of creation and
the God of promise are one and the same." In this economy, Mosaic
law and revelation function, in a way, like the hyphen "linking creation and eschatology." Opposed to this economy and to the "logic of
super-abundance" stands the "logic of equivalence," that is, the logic
of the Golden Rule, which ultimately is predicated on mutuality and
reciprocity and thus on exchange and substitutability.[18]
    What comes into view here is an ethical chasm because, as Ricoeur
states, it is "nearly impossible" to reconcile the logic of equivalence
with the entirely different logic of superabundance. Undaunted, his
lecture proceeds into this chasm, fully aware (it seems) of the intense
philosophical-theological disputes surrounding it. It seems appropriate at this point to recall some of the discussions triggered by the rise
of the "new transcendentalism" in recent European, and especially
French, philosophy. In a provocative and nearly confrontational man-

ner, representatives of this movement have tended to extol and prioritize the economy of the gift, sometimes at the expense of justice viewed as a mode of distribution. Prominent spokesmen in this regard are Emmanuel Levinas and Jacques Derrida (especially the latter's *The Gift of Death*), as well as some of their students and followers.[19] What supporters of this view find defective in the traditional notion of justice is the aspect of reciprocity and mutuality, the principle of equality or symmetry governing the transaction of giving and taking. Pushed to their logical consequence—and not all supporters are willing to go that far—both justice and the Golden Rule are ethically devalued and equated with a mode of instrumental rationality, with a calculation of costs and benefits that is ultimately reducible to the formula *do ut des* (where giving occurs solely for the sake of receiving). By contrast, the gift (*le don*) is presented as an expression of pure altruism, as a sign of asymmetrical renunciation and even self-sacrifice or self-surrender (to the "other"). Viewed in this manner, the opposition between the two "logics" appears irremediable: between pure self-love and self-surrender, no common ground can be found.[20]

Ricoeur is fully aware of this dilemma and of the obstacle it places on his "third path." Through one-sided celebrations of the logic of superabundance, he notes, "the Golden Rule has become suspect" and even an object of scorn, and the same suspicion extends to principles of social justice and corollary social practices. He even shares this suspicion, *provided* justice is seen as a mere calculus of interests; in this case, "would one not have to agree that it functions simply as a disguised version of utilitarianism?" For Ricoeur, however, the situation is not quite so hopeless, because justice and utility are *not* simple synonyms. In terms of his lecture, it is possible to interpret justice and the Golden Rule in two different ways: either in the sense of utilitarianism, or in the sense of a social ethics that, though respecting reciprocity, also makes room for superabundance. This second interpretation explains how, in both the Sermon on the Mount and the Sermon on the Plain, the two demands—the Golden Rule *and* the new command to love one's enemies—are joined together. According to this second reading, Ricoeur states, "the new love command does not cancel the Golden Rule, but rather construes the latter in the direction of generosity." In this manner, he adds, room is made in social relations for a commandment that, due to its supraethical status, can penetrate into social ethics "only at the price of paradox and seemingly extreme modes of conduct: precisely those modes of conduct recommended by the new love command 'Love your enemies, do good to those who hate you.'" In the same manner, a certain balance between demands is achieved: the Golden Rule is saved from sliding into utilitarianism, and the logic of superabundance is protected against otherworldly aloofness and a socially detached (and possibly irresponsible) "ethics of intention."[21]

As one can see, Ricoeur is mainly concerned about imbalance or the tendency to sacrifice one logic in favor of another. Basically, he is quite ready to embrace the economy or theology of the gift, provided it does not require him to abandon the demands of social justice and social responsibility. His lecture testifies in many ways to his fondness for gift giving and superabundance; thus, one passage cites a series of exemplary individuals devoted to superabundance: Francis of Assisi, Mahatma Gandhi, and Martin Luther King Jr. (none of whom was inclined to negate social responsibility). What he does not embrace is a certain moral rigorism or extremism willing to expunge social justice per se. As he observes: "What kind of penal code or what legal order (*règle de justice*) could possibly be derived from a maxim of conduct which erects non-equivalence into a general principle? What distribution of functions, roles, advantages and disadvantages reflecting distributive justice could be implemented if the axiom of lending or giving without return would become the general norm?" Without abandoning the new (and higher) love command, the lecture aims precisely at its reconciliation with social reciprocity and mutual respect: "If it is not to degenerate into immorality, the hyper-morality [of superabundance] must accord with the kind of morality which is announced in the Golden Rule" and formalized in the idea of justice.[22]

Paraphrasing—and perhaps sharpening—Ricoeur's point, one might ask: How can the nonrule of nonequivalence be transformed into a general rule? How can a command predicated on asymmetry or inequality (such as the command to love one's enemies) be established as a rule that is equally valid for all? Perhaps some concrete examples will help illustrate the problem. In the case of the concentration camps in Hitler's Germany or the more recent ethnic cleansing in the former Yugoslavia, can one really stipulate as an ethical norm the survivors' obligation to love or at least forgive their enemies? Is this not an excessive demand and an extreme hypermorality? According to a Jewish proverb, only the victim can forgive the victimizer. What this indicates is that love and forgiveness are singular modes of conduct whose very dignity resides in their inability to be reduced to general rules or principles. Being singular (and superethical), these dispositions do not collide or compete with the generality of justice and the Golden Rule. And yet, there is more than just noncollision or noncoincidence; there is a kind of mutual challenge and contestation.

In Ricoeur's view, the rules of justice should remain open and vulnerable to the logic of superabundance, in the sense that justice should be interpreted in the light of "generosity." Again, some concrete examples may clarify this argument. In recent decades, considerable experience has been accumulated regarding the relation of justice and generosity, generated by the so-called Truth and Justice or Truth and Reconciliation Commissions established in South Africa and parts of Central and Latin America in the aftermath of apartheid and dictatorship. The commissions' first task was to establish a record of the criminal acts committed by officials who were guilty under both national and international rules of justice, and then to take some tentative steps beyond the sordid past in the direction of ethical renewal. The two steps could not be collapsed, nor were they strictly antithetical. Without the effort to establish a record and to call the guilty parties to account, ethical life in society would remain smothered under mountains of falsehoods and allegations; without the determination of criminal guilt, there would be no possibility of repentance and no chance for reconciliation. Thus, we find here supporting evidence for Ricoeur's point about the noncoincidence but also the mutual tension of love and justice. In these commissions, justice and the Golden Rule were not ignored or abolished; rather, they were supplemented and corrected in the direction of superabundance and reconciliation—and rightly so, because only in this way can society escape the curse of revenge. Here are some pertinent words penned by Bishop Desmond Tutu in the spirit of Christian faith and hope:

> I saw the power of the gospel when I was serving as chairperson of the Truth and Reconciliation Commission in South Africa. . . . The Commission gave perpetrators of political crimes

the opportunity to appeal for amnesty by telling the truth of their actions and an opportunity to ask for forgiveness, an opportunity that some took and others did not. The Commission also gave victims of political crimes an opportunity to unburden themselves from the pain and suffering they had experienced. As we listened to accounts of truly monstrous deeds of torture and cruelty, it would have been easy to dismiss the perpetrators as monsters because their deeds were truly monstrous. But we are reminded that God's love is not cut off from anyone.[23]

Whatever the limitations of these commissions may be, their contributions to societal healing cannot be overestimated. Maybe the time has come for humanity to contemplate the establishment of a global Truth and Reconciliation Commission, where the misdeeds and injustices committed by global power holders can be recorded and exposed, thus paving the way, beyond retribution, for global reconciliation and peace. Yet, the possibility of such an institution appears quite remote—an event perhaps looming on the horizon. In the meantime, the tension between justice and generosity requires continuous attention and negotiation. In the concluding section of his lecture, Ricoeur points to some devices for managing this relation and preventing a harmful rupture. One such device is the Rawlsian notion of "reflective equilibrium," which rescues the idea of justice from its reduction to an instrumental calculus. Behind this notion stands the venerable tradition of Aristotelian "prudence" (*phronesis*) and situational judgment—a judgment that is able to balance competing claims and allocate to each one its due (including the claims of love and justice). Unfortunately, in the history of Western thought, Aristotelian prudence has too often been equated with calculating cleverness or "enlightened" self-interest, at the expense of the demands of ethical generosity. In an attempt to obviate this danger, Ricoeur (without abandoning Aristotelian prudence) prefers to emphasize the dimension of superabundance and the gift, stating: "I would say that the effort to introduce step-wise, but persistently additional degrees of compassion and generosity into all our legal codes—from penal to welfare codes—constitutes an entirely reasonable task, though one that is difficult and interminable."[24]

Appendix A

Multiculturalism and the Good Life

Comments on Bhikhu Parekh

There was a time, not too long ago, when multiculturalism was largely a matter of taste or aesthetic sensibility. Despite occasional skirmishes, the issue was generally one of personal preference for either the comforts of one's familiar culture or the benefits of cultural variety—the proverbial "spice of life." With his talent for the felicitous turn of phrase, Stanley Fish aptly described the latter option as "boutique multiculturalism," or a delight in folkloric entertainment and exotic knickknacks.[1] In many schools and colleges throughout the United States (including my own), it is customary to celebrate Cultural Diversity Week, a period highlighted by the display of stunning traditional costumes and the consumption of Asian food. Today, under the impact of globalizing pressures, many such practices appear quaint. Samuel Huntington's prognosis of a looming "clash of civilizations" has injected harsh conflictual accents into multicultural debates, underscored by the grim events of September 11 and its aftermath. In light of the dark shadows over the global scenario, multiculturalism acquires new ethical and existential connotations, beyond the range of private whim. These connotations have to do with war and peace, that is, with the possibility or impossibility of the peaceful survival of humankind.

To discuss the topic under contemporary circumstances requires a combination of talents that is rare among academic intellectuals: broad erudition, sharp theoretical acumen, and practical real-life experience (especially exposure to both the joys and the agonies of cross-cultural interactions). Bhikhu Parekh belongs to a small group of writers equipped to undertake the task. Renowned as one of the leading political thinkers of our time, Parekh has devoted much of his life to the exploration of the history of Western political thought, while simultaneously gaining a solid reputation as an expert on Gandhi, colonialism, and postcolonialism. Broad erudition of this kind is undergirded by his own cross-cultural background. A native of India, he has charted his professional career both on the subcontinent (where he served for a time as vice-chancellor of the University of Baroda) and in England (first at the University of Hull and later at the London School of Economics and the University of Westminster). Academic learning has always been accompanied by practical, real-life involvement in the day-to-day problems of interethnic and cross-cultural relations in contemporary society. Among other positions, Parekh has served as acting chair of the Commission for Racial Equality in the United Kingdom and as chair of the Commission on the Future of Multi-Ethnic Britain, as well as being a member of the House of Lords. Such concrete experience gives added weight and substance to his theoretical reflections, lending them a quality of seasoned judgment that is uncommon among academics. It is principally this quality of reflective judgment—the intimate correlation of theory and praxis—that makes his book *Rethinking Multiculturalism: Cultural Diversity and Political Theory* a genuine milestone in this field.[2]

Heeding Fish's admonition, Parekh's book does not deal with matters of private taste or personal idiosyncrasies; nor does he dwell on individual lifestyles or partisan preferences. As he observes (2–4), social diversity comes in many shapes and forms, not all of which should be termed "multicultural." Thus, whereas "subcultural" differences revolve around unconventional practices within an overarching cultural framework, and "perspectival" differences reflect partisan viewpoints ignored by that framework, "multicultural" diversity is anchored in a plurality of distinct cultural communities and hence is more "robust and tenacious" than other types. In Parekh's treatment, multiculturalism is not about any and all kinds of differences, but only about those "that are embedded in and sustained by culture," by "a body of beliefs and practices in terms of which a group of people understand themselves and the world and organize their individual

and collective lives." Unlike individual tastes or preferences, culturally derived differences "carry a measure of authority" growing out
of a "shared and historically inherited system of meaning and significance." Given their communal or collective structure, cultural differences often have political implications that are not usually associated
with personal preferences. Basically, they carry the ominous potential
of culture clashes while underscoring the difficult labor of peaceful
negotiation. Parekh in this connection makes an important distinction
between two different meanings of *multicultural*: empirical and normative (6). On an empirical level, *multicultural* simply refers "to the
fact of cultural diversity"; on a different level, the same term (or the
modified expression *multiculturalist*) points to "a normative response
to that fact," that is, to the acceptance or rejection, the repression or
celebration, of cultural plurality. Without ignoring empirical descriptions, Parekh focuses on normative evaluation; to this extent, his book
is a treatise on political ethics, on a multicultural conception of the
good life.[3]

In developing his perspective, Parekh immediately draws attention to the gravity of contemporary circumstances. Without ignoring
instances of cultural plurality in the past, he finds present-day multiculturalism besieged by four distinguishing features (7–8). First, in
premodern societies, minority communities usually accepted their
subordinate or ghettoized status; today, such acceptance can no
longer be assumed, as evidenced by intensified struggles for recognition. Second, the experiences of colonial oppression and totalitarian domination have deepened social awareness of the "sources and
subtle forms of violence," leading to the insight that "just as groups
of people can be oppressed economically and politically, they can
also be oppressed and humiliated culturally." Hence, the concern for
social justice needs to include not just economic but "also cultural
rights and well-being." Third, contemporary multiculturalism is intimately bound with "the immensely complex process of economic and
cultural globalization," with the increasingly rapid transfer of goods,
ideas, and technological gadgets across boundaries. Hence, questions
regarding the prospect of global homogenization and the preservation
of cultural integrity impose themselves "inexorably" on societies everywhere. Fourth, major strands of present-day multiculturalism have
emerged from, and are intelligible only against, the background of

several centuries of the "culturally homogenizing nation-state," that is, the imposition of political unity on premodern life-forms by the territorially administered state. The confrontation between the modern state and multiculturalism is inescapable, pointing (once again) to the intricate linkage between politics and culture—to the pervasive impact of politics on culture, and vice versa.

In light of these dramatic accents, the opening chapters of the book are somewhat disappointing. Parekh sees his text as falling roughly into three parts—"the historical, the theoretical, and the practical" (11)—among which the last two are clearly more interesting. Given this sequence, I reverse the usual practice of reviewers, offering some of my critical reservations first, before highlighting what I consider to be some of the book's outstanding accomplishments. In an effort to differentiate the approach chosen, the book starts with two chapters titled "Moral Monism" and "Forms of Pluralism," headings meant to capture two dominant traditions of Western thought from antiquity to the recent past. Whereas monism seeks to reduce all forms of diversity or plurality to a higher unity or unitary principle, traditional pluralism relinquishes moral coherence and lapses into an amorphous relativism devoid of criteria of significance. Although the aim of the opening chapters is plausible—to profile multiculturalism against competing formulas—the execution is unconvincing, lacking the nuanced discernment one has come to expect from Parekh. When diverse thinkers from Plato and Aristotle to Saint Augustine, Aquinas, and beyond are all neatly tucked away as "moral monists," one gets the impression of a summary "deconstruction" along postmodern lines. Likewise, when the "pluralist" label is attached to thinkers such as Vico, Montesquieu, and Herder, the impression is one of cardboard figures with little or no relevance to posterity.[4] The most worthwhile and intriguing aspect of these chapters is the discussion of modern liberalism as a form of moral monism—something that seems counterintuitive at first blush, given liberals' ostensible hospitality to diversity. As Parekh shows with considerable persuasiveness (33–49), however, modern liberals from Locke forward have always preferred to occupy a superior "rational" stance, while relegating cultural differences to private idiosyncrasies (or else to the immaturity of "backward" peoples).

The opening chapters give rise to an additional reservation. Basically, the discussion is restricted to prominent figures in Western political thought, which seems odd, given the global reach of multiculturalism. This point is connected with a broader issue involving the book as a whole: the question of the perspective from which its entire argument is presented. On this issue, Parekh sometimes waivers between a superior liberal standpoint above culture (a "view from nowhere") and a more situated dialogical or hermeneutical perspective in the interstices of diverse cultures, although his preference is clearly in the latter direction. As he writes, distancing himself from cultural self-enclosure (13): "By definition multicultural society consists of several cultural communities with their own distinct systems of meaning and significance and views of man and the world. It cannot therefore be adequately theorized from within the conceptual framework of any particular political doctrine" or any "particular cultural perspective." This statement is followed by a passage indicative of both oscillation and its final overcoming (14–15): "We need to rise to a higher level of philosophical abstraction," Parekh notes (seemingly endorsing the view from nowhere). "And since we cannot transcend and locate ourselves in a realm beyond liberal and nonliberal cultures, such a basis is to be found in an institutionalized dialogue between them." Invoking the legacy of Hans-Georg Gadamer and others, he concludes by characterizing his own approach as "dialogically constituted" and by stressing "the centrality of a dialogue between cultures and ethical norms, principles, and institutional structures." Hence, although containing some "strong liberal" features, his approach departs from canonical liberalism by shunning the pretense of a superior neutrality.

As the remainder of the book demonstrates, the chosen perspective is well suited to its topic and prone to reap ample benefits. Having performed my role as critic, I now want to cite some of the genuine merits of the study, focusing briefly on three areas: the issue of "human nature" or the "human condition," the political dimensions of multiculturalism, and the modes of deliberation and practical judgment suitable for cross-cultural encounters. Following a chapter exposing the monist remnants in recent liberal thought (John Rawls, Joseph Raz, and Will Kymlicka), Parekh turns to the problem of appropriate ontological or anthropological premises of multiculturalism. This is a notoriously difficult problem that philosophers have wrestled with through the ages. Congruent with his hermeneutical and dialogical preferences, Parekh nimbly steers a course through the nature-nurture conundrum, seeking to avoid the pitfalls of both reductive "naturalism" and "culturalism." Proceeding in this manner, he challenges the assumptions of both a rigid determinism and an infinite indeterminacy, where the former reduces human existence to physiology or to a few a priori categories, and the latter champions protean variety. As he writes sensibly (117), human beings are not simply exiled from nature but share certain common features that may be termed "natural," such as "to have a potency for action, a tendency to behave in a certain way, and to be subject to certain constitutional limitations." What guards against monistic temptations is attentiveness to historical, social, and cultural contexts and to processes of "individuation" not subsumable under general categories. For Parekh, the proper way to arrive at a comprehensive view of the human is neither to adopt a top-down universal formula nor to succumb to relativist despair, but to pursue universalism in and through cross-cultural encounters (127): "It would seem that a dialectical and pluralist form of universalism offers the most coherent response to moral and cultural diversity."

The last comment has a direct bearing on the relation between culture and politics, particularly on the nexus between cultural diversity and the political structure of the state. In a remarkably trenchant chapter, *Rethinking Multiculturalism* lays bare the dominant features of the modern state as differentiated from earlier political regimes. In most earlier polities, Parekh observes (181–184), people had multiple identities—ethnic, religious, social, and other; in contrast, the modern state is "unique in privileging territorial identity" to such an extent that the latter becomes "overarching, dominant" and exclusive. Unlike premodern political systems, which were "embedded in and composed of such communities as castes, clans, tribes, and ethnic groups," the modern state is basically defined as "an association of individuals," a definition that "abstracts away their class, ethnicity, religion, social status, and so forth," while uniting them "in terms of their subscription to a common system of authority which is similarly abstracted from the wider structure of social relations." Akin to liberal-monist preferences, the modern state elevates itself to a superior position (a "view from nowhere") vis-à-vis cultural and other differences, professing to treat the latter with neutral indifference. This does not mean, of course, that the state is entirely non- or

transcultural. On the contrary: precisely by either assimilating or ex-
purgating existing differences, the liberal state fosters its own political
solidarity, called "national identity," which explains the intimate linkage of "state" and "nation-state." In Parekh's words: "Since the state
presupposes and seeks to secure homogeneity [among its members],
it has a tendency to become a nation," which is not an aberration but
a supplement to its "neutrality." Given the state's overarching structure, membership has the character of uniform "citizenship," a status
involving "a unitary, unmediated and homogeneous relation between
the individual and that state."[5]

Contemporary multiculturalism clearly presents a major challenge
to the modern state. A central merit of Parekh's book is its circumspect
treatment of this challenge. Bypassing fashionable modernist-post-
modernist debates, Parekh is unwilling either to discard the modern
state or to celebrate uncritically its blessings. His preferred path is
to "reconceptualize the nature and role" of the state, which means
"loosening the traditionally close ties between territory, sovereignty,
and [national] culture" and "liberating political imagination from the
spell of the dominant theory" (194–195). A major task of political
imagination today, in his view, is to "rethink" the relation between
cultural diversity and the polis in such a way that the former is neither
simply assimilated or homogenized by the state nor expelled into the
netherworld of alien disturbances or private idiosyncrasies. What this
means is that justice or fairness in a multicultural society cannot be
legislated from the top down in monistic style nor be left to societal
power plays; it needs to be interactively cultivated on a broad basis. In
this context, Parekh distinguishes three models of "political integration" (199–206)—the proceduralist, the civic assimilationist (or civic
republican), and the "millet" models—none of which is satisfactory.
While, as a premodern arrangement, the millet system ignores the
modern state, the proceduralist model erects the state into a transcultural and neutral shibboleth that, claiming to be "equally hospitable
to all cultures," is "logically impossible." Although civic republicanism
acknowledges a "public" political culture (of a nationalist kind), it rel-
egates all other differences to private whims, thus reifying the public-
private divide. The failing of all three models is their unwillingness
to take cultural differences seriously and to make them the basis of a
shared or continuously renegotiated public space. In Parekh's words

(219): "A multicultural society needs a broadly shared culture to sustain it. Since it involves several cultures, the shared culture can only grow out of their interactions and should both respect and nurture their diversity and unite them around a common way of life."[6]

The notion of a shared culture and its interactive negotiation is closely related to the issue of what mode of deliberation and evaluative judgment is appropriate in a multicultural setting. A crucial feature of Parekh's book is his proposal for the creation of a "public forum" where pending issues could be discussed and negotiated by different groups. Given the fact that neither parliaments (divided along party lines) nor courts are suitable for the purpose, he argues (306–309) that new institutional platforms must be invented, "where representatives of different communities can meet regularly to explore contentious issues [and] acquire a better understanding of each other's ways of thinking and living." The proposal clearly has some similarity with recent theories of the "public sphere" and "deliberative democracy" (associated with such thinkers as John Rawls, Jürgen Habermas, and Joshua Cohen). However, in keeping with his antimonist and contextualist stance, Parekh distances himself from the one-sidedly "rationalist" and argumentative overtones of these theories. "*Contra* Rawls [and Habermas]," he writes, rationality is not an a priori premise but rather a "product of political debate" and is "constantly reconstituted and pluralized by it."[7] In a multicultural society, moreover, political deliberation cannot be merely cognitive or epistemic; it has multidimensional functions, including "deepening mutual understanding between different groups, sensitizing each to the concerns and anxieties of others," and performing "a vital community-building role." Political deliberation cannot simply revolve around an "exchange of arguments" or validity claims, "with victory going to those advancing the most compelling ones." What is neglected in this view is the role of practical judgment and persuasion, which—without shunning reason—also appeal to "emotions, self-understanding, moral values, and sense of identity." As Parekh adds, in an Aristotelian vein: "Persuasion relates to an area of life lying between personal taste and logical demonstration. In the former, persuasion is impossible, in the latter unnecessary. . . . Persuasion is possible and necessary when an activity is based on interpersonally sharable reasons and leaves room for judgment."[8]

The virtue of reflective judgment (or *phronesis*) is abundantly displayed in the "practical" portions of Parekh's book devoted to a discussion of concrete problems besetting contemporary multiculturalism. Readers from diverse backgrounds are bound to be struck by the sensitivity, fair-mindedness, and critical acumen evident in the treatment of contentious issues such as polygamy, female circumcision, arranged marriages, the wearing of head scarfs by Muslim schoolgirls, and the refusal of Sikhs to wear helmets in lieu of traditional turbans when driving motorcycles or working on building sites. In the discussion of all these cases, reflective judgment involves the weighing of particular cultural traditions against the values of the larger multicultural society, that is, the balancing of diverse forms of "thick" and "thin" considerations. Because of its special virulence, a chapter titled "Politics, Religion and Free Speech" gives broad room to the aftermath of Salman Rushdie's *Satanic Verses,* with Parekh suggesting (304) that much of the acrimony could have been avoided if the parties had had access to a public forum where perceptions and emotions could have been aired and mutually tested.

His conclusion eloquently stresses the contribution of multiculturalism to the "good life" and to the cultivating of a "good society" attentive to present-day needs. "The common good and the collective will that are vital to any political society," he states (341), "are generated not by transcending cultural and other particularities, but through their interplay in the cut and thrust of a dialogue." Constituted and sustained in this manner, multicultural society has "a strong notion of common good," consisting in "respect for a consensually grounded civil authority and basic rights, maintenance of justice, institutional and moral conditions of deliberative democracy, a vibrant and plural composite culture, and an expansive sense of community."[9] All one can hope, after reading *Rethinking Multiculturalism,* is that Parekh's vision of ethical pluralism will be given a chance. The odds, one has to admit, are not very good. With the resurgence of a cold war mentality and "clashes of civilizations" breaking out around the globe, Parekh's vision urgently requires practical commitment, probably along the Gandhian lines Parekh has championed so persuasively before.

Appendix B

Modalities of Intercultural Dialogue

UNESCO at Sixty

No better topic could have been chosen to celebrate the sixtieth anniversary of the founding of the United Nations Educational, Scientific, and Cultural Organization (UNESCO) than the theme "Cultural Diversity and Transversal Values." Our world today is being pulled apart by two conflicting tendencies: global uniformity and local fragmentation. The first trend is propelled by the forces of globalization, to the extent that globalization is identified with economic, scientific, and technological unification. The second trend is manifest in the continually erupting fissures and conflicts between cultures and traditions—what is known as the looming "clash of civilizations" (which would be better termed the clash of militant creeds). The theme of this symposium stands in opposition to both trends by recognizing the worth and legitimacy of cultural diversity and the importance of fostering standards, values, or beliefs that are shared "transversally" (rather than uniformly or universally). This dual recognition has been the task of UNESCO since its founding, when it was charged to promote the educational, scientific, and cultural endeavors of humankind and to do so not by imposing a uniform pattern but by stimulating cross-cultural interaction and dialogue on a global scale.

My intent here is to discuss the idea of cross-cultural or intercultural dialogue by pointing out different types of dialogical interactions. To be sure, not all relations between societies and cultures are dialogical or communicative. At a minimum, dialogue implies a mutual exchange of views. One can place intercultural relations along a spectrum ranging from complete monologue to genuine dialogue, from radical unilateralism to full-fledged multilateralism (and perhaps cosmopolitanism). In one of my writings, titled *Beyond Orientalism: Essays on Cross-Cultural Encounter*, I discuss this spectrum, paying particular attention to the monological end, where one can find such prominent examples of nonmutuality as military conquest, forced conversion, and ideological indoctrination. In *Beyond Orientalism* I use the Spanish conquest of the Americas as the model exemplifying the convergence of conquest, conversion, and indoctrination, but the model has continued to reverberate in later episodes of Western imperialism and colonialism. In the same study, I also refer to more limited types of unilateralism, such as cultural borrowing, partial assimilation, and the like. The entire overview of the spectrum leads to the high point of genuine mutuality: intercultural dialogue. In that category, I take my bearings from Tzvetan Todorov, who, in his *Conquest of America*, writes of a relationship "in which no one has the last word" and where "no voice is reduced to the status of a simple object" or mere victim.[1]

Today, I want to concentrate on the communicative side of interactions. At that end of the spectrum, I distinguish three (or maybe three and a half) different possibilities. I draw initially from an essay by Jürgen Habermas titled "On the Pragmatic, the Ethical, and the Moral Employments of Practical Reason" (the opening chapter in his book *Justification and Application*). In that essay, Habermas differentiates among three distinct uses of "practical reason," or a reason geared toward practical interaction: the pragmatic, the ethical, and the moral. The first type derives from utilitarianism and finds expression in the confrontation between, and the possible accumulation of, individual interests. The second (ethical) type draws its inspiration from Aristotelian ethics, as filtered through Hegel's dialectical philosophy. It was Hegel, Habermas notes, who "tried to achieve a synthesis of the classical communal and modern individualistic conceptions of freedom with his theory of objective spirit and his 'sublation' (*Aufhebung*) of morality into ethical life (*Sittlichkeit*)." Those thinkers who emphasis the ethical use appropriate "the Hegelian legacy in the form of an Aristotelian ethics of the good," while abandoning "the universalism of rational natural law." The third (moral) type operates "in a Kantian spirit" and accentuates "the unavoidable presuppositions" of argumentation and the "impartiality" required of anyone judging from "a moral point of view." For Habermas, adopting a rationalist stance, the third type is "grounded in the communicative structure of rational discourse as such." His own moral theory, called discourse ethics, "forces itself intuitively on anyone who is at all open to this reflective form of communicative action." In this manner, discourse ethics "situates itself squarely in the Kantian tradition."[2]

Here, I want to dwell a bit longer on the distinctive features of Habermas's three categories of practical reason; subsequently, I indicate how and why I diverge from the Habermasian scheme in favor of my own version of the different modalities of intercultural dialogue. For Habermas, the pragmatic use of practical reason revolves around a utility calculus in which each party, in communicative negotiation with other parties, seeks to maximize gains and minimize costs. The "rational thing" to do in this situation, he writes, "is determined in part by what one wants: it is a matter of making a rational choice of means in the light of fixed purposes or of the rational assessment of goals in the light of existing preferences." Given the emphasis on the means-ends nexus, practical reason here proceeds within the confines of "purposive" or "instrumental" rationality, guided by the aim to discover "appropriate techniques, strategies, or programs." A dominant form of this pragmatic outlook is the "theory of rational choice," which today is migrating (or has already migrated) from economics to other social sciences. In terms of normative criteria, the outlook permits at best "conditional imperatives" or a "relative ought," where the "ought" is entirely dependent on chosen preferences.[3]

As indicated earlier, the "ethical" use of practical reason in Habermas's essay can be traced back to Aristotelian virtue ethics, complemented by, or filtered through, Hegelian *Sittlichkeit*. Practical reason is said to be governed by "strong preferences" guiding one's life in concrete social and historical circumstances and in the context of "a particular self-understanding." Normative standards are not merely anchored in utilitarian preferences, yet they are situational and hence "not absolute." "What you 'should' or 'must' do," Habermas states, "has here the sense that it is 'good' for you to act in this way in the long run, all things considered. Aristotle speaks in this connection of paths to the good and happy life." To be sure, more is involved here, he concedes, than just individual preferences and the "good" of an individual life. Remembering Aristotle's concern with the polis and Hegel's reflections on the state, the text extends the meaning of ethics to public or community life: "To that extent the life that is good for me also concerns the forms of life that are common to us. Thus, Aristotle viewed the *ethos* of the individual as embedded in the polis comprising the citizen body."[4]

Finally, the moral use of practical reason has its roots in Kantian philosophy, as this philosophy has been continued by neo-Kantians, John Rawls, and Habermas himself. As the latter writes: "As soon as my actions affect the interests of others and lead to conflicts which should be regulated in an impartial manner," we employ practical reason "from a moral point of view." The emphasis here is on universal and impartial rules—what Kant called "categorical imperatives"—by which actions are judged to be rational or irrational, just or unjust, not merely contextually but in and of themselves. At this point, practical reason is oriented toward not a situated but a "universally valid form of life," toward an absolute rule structure whose maxims are just insofar as they can be endorsed by all. Paraphrasing Kant, Habermas states: "*Everyone* must be able to will that the maxims of our actions should become a universal law." In contrast to the pragmatic use, the governing standard here is not a "relative ought" but a "categorical or unconditional" principle claiming universal validity.[5]

In what follows, I partially appropriate but also significantly modify Habermas's tripartite scheme for my own purposes: the exploration of different modalities of intercultural dialogue. My main departure from Habermas has to do with his portrayal of the ethical use of reason. It seems to me that his portrayal involves a radical misconstrual of both Aristotle and Hegel, a misconstrual that operates on two levels. For one thing, ethics in the Aristotelian and Hegelian sense is reduced to a purely descriptive-empirical fabric of prevailing customs or situated practices (against which absolute standards are then silhouetted). When this is done, one loses sight completely of the inherent "ought" quality of Aristotle's notion of virtue and of the Hegelian striving for *Sittlichkeit*. (Differently stated, the Kantian "is-ought" or "fact-value" dichotomy is simply foisted onto an entirely different, substantive mode of ethics.) The second problem has to do with a misreading deriving from Cartesian blinders. For both Aristotle and Hegel, Habermas writes, "ethical questions by no means call for a complete break with the egocentric perspective; in each instance they take their orientation from the telos of one's own life" and hence focus on "my identity, my life, and my interests." To impute a modern-style egocentrism on a classical Greek thinker seems more than far-fetched, and Hegel's struggle with Cartesianism is well known. Moreover, the imputation collides with the acknowledgment (mentioned earlier) of the concern with virtuous community life.[6]

Adapting as well as modifying the Habermasian scheme, I distinguish three basic modalities of intercultural dialogue: pragmatic-strategic communication, moral-universal discourse, and ethical-hermeneutical dialogue. To these one could add a fourth type, but I prefer to treat it as a subcategory under the third type: agonal dialogue or contestation.

In pragmatic-strategic communication, each partner seeks to advance his or her own interests in negotiation with other parties (here I follow Habermas's account completely). To the extent one can describe such communication as "dialogue," it takes the form mainly of mutual bargaining, sometimes involving manipulation and even deception. This kind of communicative exchange is well known in international or intersocietal relations and constitutes the central focus of the so-called realist and neorealist schools of international politics. Prominent examples of such communication are trade or commercial negotiations, negotiations about global warming and ecological standards, disarmament negotiations, settlement of border disputes, peace negotiations, and the like. Much of traditional diplomacy is in fact carried on in this vein.

In moral-universal discourse, partners seek consensus on basic rules or norms of behavior that are binding on all partners, potentially on a global level. Here, the legacies of modern natural law and Kantian moral philosophy retain their importance. Basic rules of (potentially) universal significance include the rules of modern international law; the international norms regarding warfare, war crimes, and crimes against humanity; the Geneva Conventions; and the Universal Declaration of Human Rights. One does not need to be a Kantian in a strict sense to recognize the importance and even the "categorically" binding character of these norms (which have been accepted by the great majority of governments and endorsed by the vast majority of humankind). Surely, this is not the time to disparage or tamper with the mandatory quality of international norms. Thus, the rules of the Geneva Conventions are mandatory, no matter what nomenclature individual governments choose to adopt. Likewise, launching an unprovoked war is a crime against humanity, whether particular leaders choose to acknowledge it or not. So is the wanton killing of civilian populations. Here, the collective conscience of humanity has reached a certain level below which we dare not regress.

In ethical-hermeneutical dialogue, partners seek to understand and appreciate each other's life stories and cultural backgrounds, including religious (or spiritual) traditions, literary and artistic expressions, and existential agonies and aspirations. It is in this mode that important cross-cultural learning takes place. It is also on this level that one encounters the salience of Aristotle's teaching about virtues and of the Hegelian practice of *Sittlichkeit*. Ethics here is oriented toward the "good life"—not in the sense of an abstract "ought," but as the pursuit of an aspiration implicit in all life-forms yet able to take on different expressions in different cultures. Since ethics on this level speaks to deeper human motivations, this is the dimension that is most likely to mold human conduct in the direction of mutual ethical recognition and peace. Hence, there is an urgent need in our time to emphasize and cultivate this kind of ethical pedagogy.[7] On a limited scale, cross-cultural dialogue is already practiced today; examples include interfaith dialogues, the Parliament of the World's Religions, the World Public Forum, the World Social Forum, various centers for "dialogue among civilizations," exchange programs of scholars and students, and the like.

To the three main modalities mentioned so far, one may add the category of agonal dialogue or contestation, but I prefer to treat it as a subcategory of ethical dialogue. In the agonal situation, partners seek not only to understand and appreciate each other's life-forms but also to convey their experiences of exploitation and persecution, that is, grievances having to do with past or persisting injustice and suffering. Along with better understanding, agonal dialogue adds the dimension of possible retribution and rectification of grievances. Yet retribution does not necessarily involve the desire to "get even," take revenge, and possibly repay injustice with injustice by turning the previous victimizers into victims. When the latter happens, the element of understanding—constitutive of genuine dialogue—is crushed in favor of sheer antagonism and possibly violent conflict. At that point, we reenter the domain of the "clash" of cultures and societies that is at the margins of intercultural dialogue.

This is why I prefer to list the agonal case as a subcategory within ethical-hermeneutical dialogue. In this context, confrontation and contestation are not ends in themselves but are placed in the service of ethical reconciliation and healing. There are prominent examples of such an agonal hermeneutics in our time: the Truth and Justice or Truth and Reconciliation Commissions established in various parts of the world to investigate crimes committed during ethnic conflicts or by dictatorships. The point of these commissions was both to establish a record of past criminal actions and injustices and to promote a process of social healing that would prevent the recurrence of victimization. In light of the horrendous forms of oppression and injustice prevailing in the world today, one can only hope that humankind will someday have the wisdom and courage to establish a global Truth and Reconciliation Commission charged with exposing and rectifying existing abuses and laying the groundwork for a more just and livable global future.[8]

Not all the modalities discussed are examples of "intercultural dialogue" in a strong sense. Pragmatic communication basically involves an exchange and negotiation of selfish interests, which are often predominantly material and economic in character. If this is the case, cultural concerns recede into the background, making room for a considerable sameness of demands. Yet, interests are sometimes advanced in terms of cultural traditions, which justifies the inclusion of the pragmatic mode in the chosen typology. In moral discourse, participants are expected to put aside their cultural and historical particularities (to the extent possible) and reach a general consensus on valid norms from a standpoint of impartiality. To this extent, moral discourse is more supracultural and universal in character than intercultural and transversal. Still, cultural particularity can rarely if ever be fully expunged. The most full-bodied intercultural modality is ethical-hermeneutical dialogue. Here, particular cultural experiences can enter the dialogue in a genuine way, while still preserving the requisite openness to the "other." Hence, universal and particular dimensions intermingle or are held in balance, which justifies the designation of such dialogue as transversal.

UNESCO is uniquely situated to cultivate the modality of ethical dialogue in our world. From the time of its establishment, UNESCO has been attentive to cultural diversity, while simultaneously fostering the prospect of dialogical harmony and peaceful mutuality in the midst of that diversity. Today more than ever, the work of UNESCO is needed to ensure a peaceful global future. Through conferences and symposia like this one, along with its other educational initiatives, UNESCO contributes to better intercultural understanding and appreciation. At the same time, by putting a searchlight on possible threats to intercultural dialogue—dangers arising from oppression, exploitation, and other forms of injustice—UNESCO can pave the way to a redress of grievances and possible global healing through truth and reconciliation.

Appendix C
In a Different Voice
Some Afterthoughts on Violence

It is a privilege to participate in this conference dealing with religion, violence, and women in South Asia (held at the Kroc Institute for International Peace Studies at the University of Notre Dame in March 2004). And it is an honor to be asked to offer my comments at its conclusion. Having listened to papers for almost two days, I find my task challenging and nearly impossible. The presentations were professionally accomplished, extremely rich in detail, and also highly diverse, ranging from micropolitical modes of resistance in Sri Lanka to alternative forms of agency in Burma to multiple strands of violence in Bangladesh, Pakistan, and India. The presenters were well-trained academics in a number of disciplines, including anthropology, political science, and history.

Given the enormous wealth of information and its breadth of scope, I forgo the endeavor of offering an overview of the conference, which would force me to ascend to a high level of abstraction or adopt a detached bird's-eye view. Such abstraction is always dubious; it is especially so in the case of a conference whose main topic is "the effects of violence on women in South Asia." What were and are these effects? All the papers in some way addressed this question. But I was particularly struck by one that dealt with the effects of violence perpetrated on women in the so-called liberation war of 1971 in Bangladesh. Since, in my view, violence is not simply an empirical occurrence nor an abstract category, but a traumatic happening that befalls or "violates" concrete victims and is experienced by them as such, I want to dwell on this particular paper, which for me, sums up the basic issues of the conference.

The title of the paper is "Overcoming the Silent Archive in Bangladesh: Women Bear Witness to the Violence in the 1971 Liberation War." The presenter, Yasmin Saikia, is a historian who hails from northeastern India, just north of Bangladesh. In her paper, Yasmin reports on horrendous acts of violence, including rape and mutilation, committed against women in 1971 by militants from both (or all) sides of the conflict—crimes that were subsequently suppressed in the interest of national unity and security. To overcome this repression, or what she calls the "silent archive" of violence, Yasmin interviewed a large number of women who had been victimized in 1971. Many of the women she approached were willing to cooperate and thus, at long last, to "bear witness to the violence" they had suffered. The paper is replete with detailed stories of acts of violence against women: killings, rapes, humiliations. In the middle of this historical narration, however, something happened that was not part of the story and was not written down in the paper: the presenter's voice suddenly faltered, as if seized by an inner trembling; she could not go on and had to stop and collect herself. A well-prepared and professionally crafted text suddenly was invaded by a subtext that had not been prepared or planned. Thus, perhaps unintentionally, in reporting on female victims in Bangladesh, Yasmin herself "bore witness" to the meaning of violence as violation and inflicted suffering.

This moment in the presentation—this invasion from elsewhere—reminded me of another occurrence not long ago that also involved a woman presenting an account of violence against women. A few months ago, I attended a conference in Shillong in northeastern India (the very region of Yasmin's original home). The conference dealt with "identity construction" in general and focused particularly on South Asia, which today is the scene of many forms of violence. Some of the most horrible acts in recent times were committed in Gujarat, the home state of Mahatma Gandhi. During the past two decades, I have been a frequent visitor to India, and a large portion of my time was spent in Gujarat, and especially in the city of Baroda (which became a home away from home). At the Shillong conference, a female colleague from Gujarat, Gita Viswanath, presented a paper titled "Constructing Communal Identities: A Case Study of the Gujarat Carnage." Gita teaches English literature at the University of Baroda, where I had come to know her during my repeated visits.

Since the events discussed in her paper were still fresh in everyone's memory, her panel attracted a large audience that followed the presentation in rapt attention.

As a native and resident of Gujarat, Gita had lived through the events of February and March 2002, and her demeanor still showed the imprint of that shock. The basic question of her paper was: what can identities "do" to individual and communal life? The issue was not merely how individuals construct communal identities but also how individual identities are constructed by communities. "What have the riots done," she asked, "to the experience of bearing a Muslim identity?" And "what have they done to the Hindu identity?" In Gita Viswanath's opinion, the Gujarat events form a "watershed" in the history of Indian constitutionalism by exposing and problematizing "the very origins of the Indian nation-state." In her words:

> The violence unleashed on several thousands of Muslims, purportedly as a revenge for the burning of one of the coaches of the Sabarmati Express, calls for a rethinking of all that goes into the making of India. The pluralism of the Indian nation, the secularism written into the foundational text of the nation, the so-called reverence for women—were all subverted during the riots. The polarization of communities on religious lines reached its apogee. . . . The state which is supposed to protect its citizens, connived with the communal groups instead [by fomenting hatred and revenge].

As in so many other instances, women—here, Muslim women—were the victims of the most outrageous acts of abuse: they were "raped, burnt, rendered homeless, and yet coerced into *not* registering complaints with the police." Thus, just as in the 1971 war in Bangladesh, violence committed against women was turned into a "silent archive" (to use Yasmin's phrase). However, Gita interviewed the victims and induced them to "bear witness" to the carnage in Gujarat. What she discovered in her research was a gruesome kind of "biopolitics," a form of "bodily" politics in which power was directly inscribed on women's bodies. As in most wars and other forms of aggression, she notes, "the Muslim female body became a synecdoche of the communal body in the Gujarat carnage." She recounts in detail some of the horrors visited upon women during the riots: "The sheer savagery and bestiality of acts like ripping open pregnant women's bellies and wrenching out the fetus was horrifying enough. What accompanied these acts invariably were the words 'We need to kill it before it is born.'" Thus, the fetus growing in a Muslim woman's belly was "no longer the product of an act of love emerging into the world 'trailing clouds of glory' to use a Wordsworthian phrase"; instead, it was imagined as "a threat to the Hindu Rashtra which has been in the making for some decades now." Other incidents occurred in Kheda district in Gujarat, where rioters shaved the heads of Muslim women and etched the *Om* symbol on their scalps with knives, in a "macabre ritual of reconversion."

It was at this point, in the midst of this account of horror, that the unplanned happened here too: the presenter's voice faltered and trembled, as if gripped by an inner revulsion and overcome by a deep and unpremeditated compassion for the victims of violence. The entire audience gasped, finding themselves suddenly turned from listeners or spectators into participants in human agony. At that moment, my relation to the presenter also changed. I had known her as a colleague: professional, competent, unemotional. Suddenly, I saw her as a woman, a fellow human being, a friend. I talked with her later that same day, and she recounted several other incidents that had occurred during the riots. But she also said that the events had changed her, had been a seasoning experience for her. Gita is a Hindu, raised in the Vaishnava tradition, but she told me that she has made a commitment to learn more about the Muslim faith; to associate more with Muslims, especially with Muslim women; and to make her home a refuge for them in the event of any future communal disturbances. Looking at her, I realized that these were not just words; her learning experience would translate into action.

That same day, I talked to another Indian woman, the wife of a senior professor of English at the university in Baroda. She told me the story of a strange happening—an event that startled her and left her wondering and amazed: She was traveling with her son by train from Delhi to Shillong, a journey of some twenty hours. In her compartment was a young man, a soldier in the Indian army. Given the long train ride, a conversation developed between them, starting at first haltingly and almost absentmindedly and then turning more serious. The woman had been raised in the Vaishnava tradition and had never devoted much thought to Muslim beliefs and practices. During the conversation, it emerged that the young man was a Muslim—a deeply religious and knowledgeable Muslim. Prodded by her questions, the young man began to talk about the Islamic faith, the long history of Islam, and the deeper meaning of Qur'anic passages. It was as if he illuminated from within a building that had always seemed to her dark and uninviting. As she confessed to me, she was profoundly moved by this sincere (and nonproselytizing) disclosure of faith, and something happened to her on that train ride that she had not planned or anticipated. Somehow—and she was still not quite sure how—the encounter had transformed her, had opened her heart to new possibilities and a new dimension of human relations. As in Gita's case, the change was both inner and outer, manifest on the levels of both understanding and practice. Together with the mayhem of early 2002, that encounter led her to a new commitment to reach beyond the bounds of hatred and to make her home a place of welcome and refuge for people in distress, irrespective of their communal background.

This excursion to Gujarat and Shillong leads me back to the Notre Dame conference, and especially to Yasmin Saikia's paper. It seems to me that violence is not really violence as long as it merely recounted, described, or analyzed. This does not mean that reportage is unimportant—for after all, there is a continuing need to expose the "silent archive" of violence to public knowledge. However, reportage alone misses the target. This is particularly true in our time of media bombardment, when people around the world are turned into passive voyeurs of unspeakable acts of violence, genocide, and warfare reported to them ceaselessly by the media, as if for purposes of macabre entertainment.

Here I want to address Yasmin Saikia directly. Thank you, Yasmin, for the brief disruption of your presentation. Thank you for allowing your professional discourse to be disturbed and unsettled by another discourse, for permitting the historian's narrative to be invaded and contested by another story that addresses us on a different level, in a different voice. Unprompted and unrehearsed, that different voice announces another trajectory, another possibility of human living— something we might call a "promise." Countering mere reportage, the voice insists that the violence must end and give way to a reign of justice and peace—a reign where no carnage and slaughter can ever penetrate. Perhaps we might call it an Easter promise or a "promised land." (Please forgive the religious language here; these lines were written during Easter week. Of course, one could also call the land *ramarajya*, or "pure land," or the reign of the "Mahdi").

Thus, hidden or sheltered amidst the horrors of our time, something else lies in wait—waiting quietly for the chance to be heard, the chance to bear witness to a healing or redemptive message. In the spirit of Passover and Easter, one may recall the words of the psalmist (126:5): "Those who sow in tears shall reap in joy." However, in light of the theme of this conference, and in light of my own preceding excursion, I prefer to conclude in an Indian voice. Permit me to cite a few verses of the great sixteenth-century woman poet Mirabai, renowned for her deeply devotional poetry:

Let us go to a realm beyond going,
Where death is afraid to go,
Where the high-flying birds alight and play,
Afloat in the full lake of love.
There they gather—the good, the true—
To strengthen an inner regimen,
To focus on the hidden form of the Lord
And refine their minds like fire. . . .
There where the love of God comes first
And everything else is last.

Appendix D

Building Peace—How?

> When one is well grounded in non-violence, there is
> cessation of violence in one's presence.
>
> —Patanjali, *Yoga Sutra*

I want to thank the organizers for inviting me to participate in the concluding section of this conference on "Building Peace through Interreligious Encounters." I have read most of the papers presented yesterday, and I have listened attentively to the papers presented this morning. All the papers, in my view, are rich in content and highly informative. I will not attempt to summarize or critique the papers, something that has been done competently by others.

I have just one preliminary remark on all the presentations: I think they all showed very clearly that violent conflicts are rarely motivated chiefly by religion or religious faith. Frequently, the root cause of conflict is economic, social, ethnic, or political, even though it may be dressed up in religious garb. Still, despite this widely accepted fact, religion is not entirely blameless. Quite often, religion has been used (and continues to be used) as a tool of radical mobilization for the sake of basically worldly and nonreligious goals. As John Esposito notes, religion often serves as a marker of collective "identity"—not as a marker of human beings' relation to God but as an emblem of collective social enterprises oriented toward worldly ends, sometimes through violent means.

Unfortunately, this use or abuse of religion is widespread, and it is widespread because it is so convenient and easy. When I say that the abuse is easy, I mean that it does not require any serious involvement in religious faith or any serious transformative experience. It seems to me that religiously motivated violence is a sign of small faith. It is practiced by people who merely dabble in faith or are novices in faith and thus do not hesitate to abuse religion for their own ends. For people with deep faith, this is no longer possible, for such people are grabbed and transformed from on high; thereafter, they are in the service of the divine and cannot use God in their own service. Such people can be peace builders.

I want to reflect briefly on peace builders, on what kind of people peace building requires. I do not deny the role of institutions, networks, and procedures, but I believe that they are secondary to human qualities. So my question is: what qualities or dispositions are required for peace building? I suggest that there are mainly two such qualities: gentleness and toughness. Although these two qualities seem to be in conflict, they are actually complementary. By *gentleness,* I mean something like meekness, a peaceful or peaceable disposition. To put this more strongly: in order to be peace builders, we need to be peaceful in the sense of exemplifying in our lives the peace we seek to bring—or, more pointedly, we need to "be" the peace we wish to build. How is this possible? I do not know any shortcut that bypasses such practices as prayer, meditation, or contemplation. By *toughness,* I do not mean an aggressive or macho disposition but rather the courage or determination to stand up to injustice, resist domination or exploitation, and "speak truth to power."

Recently, I had the opportunity to meet (again) the great Iranian philosopher Abdulkarim Soroush. He was spending an academic year at the Wissenschaftskolleg in Berlin (which is similar to the Center for Advanced Studies at Princeton). Soroush is a man of deep faith, not a novice in religious matters; he exudes an aura of quiet gentleness and serenity that affects anyone who meets him. Precisely because he is a man of deep faith, he is strongly devoted to tolerance and opposed to violence of any kind. Not long ago, in late 2004, he was awarded the Erasmus Prize in Amsterdam, a prize given in memory of the great Dutch religious humanist who was himself a peacemaker. On the occasion of this award, Soroush delivered a talk titled "Treatise on Tolerance," which is an exemplary expression of gentleness and peacefulness.

In all his writings, Soroush is fond of citing the great mystical Sufi poets and especially the Persian poets Hafiz and Rumi. "Treatise on

Tolerance" is no exception. There he quotes these lines from Hafiz: "In these two expressions lies peace / in this world and the next: / With friends magnanimity; / With enemies tolerance." Entering into the spirit of Hafiz, Soroush draws these lessons from the quoted verses: "Truth and religiosity must never be used as weapons. For they are of the nature of language, not of claws. Rather than encouraging arrogance and imperiousness, they should foster humility and forbearance. Someone who is closer to the truth is more humble and more tolerant toward others than someone who is self-righteous in the delusion of possessing the truth. . . . This is a kind of mild and moderate Erasmian form of doubt which . . . bears within it a call to tolerance."[1]

Turning to the great Maulana, Jalal ad-Din Rumi, Soroush finds the same lesson: that genuine religion is transformative, not vindictive; a gift, not a possession. In his words: "Prophets and religions have come to human beings mainly to cultivate their spirits and to heal their souls; not to fill their minds with empty knowledge, but to fill their hearts with the love of God and love for one another, and to cleanse them of sickness and hatred." Paraphrasing Rumi, he adds that religion is "like a cane in the hand of the blind, not a weapon in the hands of antagonists." If religion is turned into such a weapon, it inflicts violence not only on others but also on religion itself, which becomes corrupted in its core. As Rumi himself states: "When the cane becomes an instrument for clamor and war, / smash it into a thousand pieces, O blind one!" Soroush interprets this to mean: "When something is misapplied and used for the opposite purpose from the one for which it was intended, it must be discarded, even if it is the cane of reason and religion. If religions and ideologies turn into instruments of animosity and if, instead of filling hearts with love and magnanimity and inclining them toward their creator, sow hatred, vindictiveness and arrogance, they must be abandoned."[2]

For good measure, Soroush turns to Rumi's contemporary, the Sufi mystic and "Great Sheikh" Ibn Arabi, who wrote these lines: "I am a disciple of the religion of love; / Wherever the convoy of love goes, / my religion and faith follow." The emphasis on a "religion of love" is again the precise antipode to a religion of arrogance and conceit that breeds violence. Soroush's treatise contains this marvelous comment: "One of the reasons why humility has been considered the greatest virtue and arrogance the greatest vice is that arrogance breeds violence and humility tolerance. Our Sufis held love in high esteem precisely because love makes the lover humble. They, therefore, considered conceit to be the slayer of love."[3] Ibn Arabi's verses and Soroush's comment remind me of an old antiphon that Christian churches use during Easter week, specifically on Maundy Thursday. The antiphon says: *Ubi caritas et amor, Deus ibi est,* which means, "Where there is charity and love, there God is present." Note that God's presence is found not in ornate clerical robes or in magnificent buildings or in hierarchies or patriarchies, but wherever there is love and charity.

This leads me to some reflections on Christian faith. Unfortunately, Christian faith is too often used or abused in the service of power, greed, war, domination, and even empire—an abuse that makes Christ's suffering on Calvary a mockery. But there is also a deeper, more genuine kind of faith that, mindful of Christ's teachings and example, abjures power lust and greed and puts itself in the service of divine healing. This brings to the fore the second human quality I mentioned earlier as being required for peace building: toughness, or the willingness to stand up to injustice and oppression. It just so happens that a few days ago, another conference was held here at the University of Notre Dame. That conference commemorated the assassination of Archbishop Oscar Romero, the champion of the poor and oppressed in El Salvador. In March 1980, while performing his priestly functions, Romero was gunned down by paramilitary forces (trained and supported by the North). As a person, Romero was gentle and peaceful, a follower of the one who is called the Prince of Peace, but he was also tough and resolute in opposing the oppression of the poor by the rich and powerful. In this regard, he was similar to Mahatma Gandhi, who likewise was of a gentle, peaceable disposition but resolute in his struggle against British imperialism.[4]

Let me quote here from a speech given by Archbishop Romero about a month before he was killed. He begins with a grim portrayal of conditions in our world, especially conditions in so-called third-world countries, pointing to the challenge these conditions pose to Christian faith. "In a world," he states,

> which has no human face, which is a real sacrament of the suffering servant of Yahweh, my archdiocese has managed to

incarnate itself. . . . We have made the effort not to pass by, not to walk around the injured person on the road, but to go up to him as a good Samaritan. This encounter with the poor has enabled us to recover the central truth of the gospel: that the word of God urges us to a conversion. The church has "good news" to announce to the poor. Those who have heard the bad news in a secular context and have lived even worse realities, are now listening again to the word of Jesus: "The reign of God is near."

Romero at this point endorses a crucial teaching of so-called liberation theology as inaugurated by Gustavo Gutierrez and Juan Luis Segundo: namely, that the church cannot remain neutral in the face of the yawning gulf between rich and poor, oppressors and oppressed; it must take a stance in accordance with the gospels—the so-called preferential option for the poor. "We are dealing," he said pointedly, "with a true 'option for the poor.' This means that the church incarnates herself in the world of the poor, proclaims a good news, gives hope, inspires liberating praxis, defends the cause of the poor and participates in their destiny. . . . It cannot be any other way if, like Jesus, the church is to go out to the poor" (and to the widows and orphans).[5]

Romero's address continues with a passage that, though penned in 1980, seems to be written for our time and our agonies. Going beyond its specific context, the passage illustrates what is meant by giving "prophetic witness," a witnessing that harks back to ancient prophecies but at the same time is replete with prophetic anticipations of the future. "Thus, it is not mere routine," Romero affirms,

that, once again, we denounce the existence of a structure of sin in our country [and in the world]. It is sinful because it produces the fruits of sin: the death of Salvadorans [and people in other third-world countries[6]]—the rapid death of execution and the slow, but no less real death of structural oppression. For that reason, we have denounced the idolatry that exists in our country. Wealth is made a God, private property is absolutized by the economic system, while national security is elevated to the highest good by the political powers who institutionalize the insecurity of individuals [and of the common people].

Intensifying this commitment to prophetic witnessing, Romero concludes his address with these words: "The faith in the God of life is what explains the depth of the Christian mystery. To give life to the poor, one must give from one's own life, indeed even give one's own life."[7] One month later, he did precisely that.

This is a grim and sobering tale: Romero assassinated; Gandhi assassinated; Martin Luther King Jr. (who in many ways followed Gandhi) assassinated. It is a sobering tale for all peace builders who must be mindful of the intimate connection between peace and justice, as expressed in Isaiah's words that "peace is the fruit of justice" (Isaiah 32:17). Neither Romero nor Gandhi nor King were seeking martyrdom. They were devoted to the "God of life" and wanted to foster and promote the "good life," especially for the downtrodden. But when martyrdom befell them, they accepted it, thereby setting an example for all peace builders and reminding them of the necessary human qualities that are always in short supply. Christians call it *memoria crucis*. With Easter just around the corner, this may be a good time for peace builders to ponder the hazards and perils lying in wait along the road to their chosen destination: the promised "city of peace."

Notes

Introduction

1. Walter Lippmann, *The Good Society* (1936; New York: Grosset and Dunlap, 1943), 3. The book did not exempt Western powers from the general indictment: "Virtually all that now passes for progressivism in countries like England and the United States calls for the increasing ascendancy of the state: always the cry is for more officials with more power over more and more of the activities of men" (5).

2. Ibid., 378.

3. Aristotle, *Nicomachean Ethics,* trans. Terence Irwin (Indianapolis: Hackett, 1985), 1095a18–19 (bk. 1, chap. 4), 1140a28 (bk. 6, chap. 5). Lippmann refers intermittently to Aristotle, though not in a philosophically sustained way. He criticizes Aristotle where the latter is most vulnerable, such as with regard to the issue of slavery. See *The Good Society*, 384–386.

4. Lippmann, *The Good Society*, 233, 246.

5. Ibid., 339–342.

6. Ibid., 37–40, 313.

7. Ibid., 92–93, 159–160, 303.

8. Ibid., 184–186.

9. Ibid., 186, 190–192. As Lippmann adds: "Were there any question about the thesis that capitalism developed in a context of historic law and not in the free realm of Nowhere, the conclusive evidence would be found in the fact that the substance of law has been continually modified. What is it that courts and legislatures have been doing these hundred and fifty years if not defining, redefining, amending, and supplementing the laws of property, contract, and corporations, and of human relations? . . . The whole of it, all property, and everything which we include in the general name of private enterprise, is the product of a legal development and can exist only by virtue of the law" (190, 273).

10. Ibid., 194, 237, 355. Although the book does not cite Hegel in this context, it is not difficult to find affinities between Lippmann and Hegel's *Philosophy of Right,* especially those passages that argue that modern *Sittlichkeit* (ethical life) cannot recapture the unity of the ancient polis because of the modern growth of individual freedom. See *Hegel's Philosophy of*

Right, trans. T. M. Knox (Oxford: Oxford University Press, 1967), 42–43 (par. 46), 123–124 (par. 185), 280 (add. 154). See also my *Hegel: Modernity and Politics,* rev. ed. (Lanham, Md.: Rowman and Littlefield, 2004), 100–101, 123–124.

11. Lippmann, *The Good Society,* 322, 346–347, 363. Lippmann also calls the common law maintained by shared virtues an "unwritten higher law." However, he makes it clear that law is not simply higher because it may be old; rather, as a living fabric, law has to be continually adjusted to prevent injustice and possible injury to the weak and disadvantaged: "Only by adhering to this unwritten higher law can [people] make actual law effective or have criteria by which to reform it. . . . This law which is the spirit of law is the opposite of an accumulation of old precedents and new fiats. By this higher law, that men must not be arbitrary, the old law is continuously tested and the new law reviewed" (347). On "virtue," see also chap. 11 in Walter Lippmann, *A Preface to Morals* (New York: Macmillan, 1929), where we read: "To transcend the ordinary impulses is . . . the common element in all virtue. . . . There are, to be sure, certain residual and obsolete virtues which no longer correspond to anything in our own experience. . . . But the cardinal virtues correspond to an experience so long and so nearly universal among men of our civilization that, when they are understood, they are seen to contain a deposited wisdom of humanity" (222, 226).

12. Walter Lippmann, *The Public Philosophy* (Boston: Little, Brown, 1955), 144. The quotation is from Baron de Montesquieu, *The Spirit of Laws,* ed. David W. Carrithers (Berkeley: University of California Press, 1977), 200 (bk. 11, chap. 3). To Montesquieu's notion of an ethical freedom, Lippmann (143) opposes Hobbes's doctrine of "negative" freedom, where the latter means simply "the absence of opposition," and also the Lockean formula of "positive" freedom, that is, "the power a man has to do or forebear doing any particular action." See Thomas Hobbes, *Leviathan* (Oxford: Clarendon Press, 1943), pt. 2, chap. 21; and John Locke, *An Essay Concerning Human Understanding,* ed. A. C. Fraser (Oxford: Clarendon Press, 1894), vol. 1, bk. 2, chap. 21, sec. 15. See also Isaiah Berlin, *Four Essays on Liberty* (New York: Oxford University Press, 1969).

13. Prominent texts exemplifying the recent upsurge of virtue ethics are Alasdair MacIntyre, *After Virtue: A Study in Moral Theory,* 2nd ed. (Notre Dame, Ind.: University of Notre Dame Press, 1984); Michael Slote, *From Morality to Virtue* (New York: Oxford University Press, 1992); Roger Crisp and Michael Slote, eds., *Virtue Ethics* (New York: Oxford University Press, 1997); Nancy Sherman, *Making a Necessity of Virtue: Aristotle and Kant on Virtue* (Cambridge: Cambridge University Press, 1997); and Rosalind Hursthouse, *On Virtue Ethics* (New York: Oxford University Press, 1999). Partly under the influence of this philosophical upsurge, some "liberal" political thinkers have also turned their attention to virtue ethics. See, for example,

Stephen Macedo, *Liberal Virtues* (New York: Oxford University Press, 1990); William A. Galston, *Liberal Purposes: Goods, Virtues, and Diversity in the Liberal State* (New York: Cambridge University Press, 1991); and Mark Blitz, *Duty Bound: Responsibility and American Public Life* (Lanham, Md.: Rowman and Littlefield, 2005).

14. Regarding communitarianism, see, for example, David Rasmussen, ed., *Universalism vs. Communitarianism: Contemporary Debates in Ethics* (Cambridge, Mass.: MIT Press, 1990); Shlomo Avineri and Avner de-Shalit, eds., *Communitarianism and Individualism* (New York: Oxford University Press, 1992); and Stephen Mulhall and Adam Swift, eds., *Liberals and Communitarians* (Oxford: Blackwell, 1992). For one of the most eloquent (and forward-looking) defenses, see Amitai Etzioni, *The Spirit of Community: Rights, Responsibilities, and the Communitarian Agenda* (New York: Crown, 1993); *Rights and the Common Good: The Communitarian Perspective* (New York: St. Martin's Press, 1995); *The New Golden Rule: Community and Morality in a Democratic Society* (New York: Basic Books, 1996); and *Next: The Road to the Good Society* (New York: Basic Books, 2001).

15. Michael J. Sandel, *Public Philosophy: Essays on Morality in Politics* (Cambridge, Mass.: Harvard University Press, 2005), 9, 11, 27, 33.

16. Ibid., 10, 27. Somewhat confusingly, Sandel uses the term *liberals* when his target is clearly a certain kind of liberal (mainly laissez-faire and procedural liberals). On the relation between democratic freedom and shared traditions, see also Jeffrey Stout, *Democracy and Tradition* (Princeton, N.J.: Princeton University Press, 2004), and *Ethics after Babel* (Princeton, N.J.: Princeton University Press, 2001).

17. Sandel, *Public Philosophy*, 10, 28, 45. The notion of the "naked public square" refers implicitly to Richard John Neuhaus, *The Naked Public Square: Religion and Democracy in America* (Grand Rapids, Mich.: Eerdmans, 1984).

18. Sandel, *Public Philosophy*, 23–24, 44. As he notes, the issue tends to be bypassed by social conservatives who are otherwise attached to community values. Sandel points in this context to the "civic conservatism" of Ronald Reagan, which extolled the values of family, religion, and patriotism but completely sidestepped the problems posed by "unfettered capitalism" (22–23).

19. Ibid., 24–25. In contrast, when public leaders instantiate corruption and power lust (as is more commonly the case today), society decays. To be sure, for good leaders to emerge in a democracy, the people must have sufficiently good judgment to support them. This means that there has to be a mutual learning process.

20. Ibid., 25–26. His argument in this respect finds ample support in the writings of contemporary political thinkers; above all, Charles Taylor eloquently states the need for mutual recognition and dialogical engage-

ment. See Charles Taylor, "The Politics of Recognition," in *Multiculturalism: Examining the Politics of Recognition,* ed. Amy Guttman (Princeton, N.J.: Princeton University Press, 1994), 25–73. For additional recent literature on political and ethical pluralism, see William A. Galston, *Liberal Pluralism: The Implications of Value Pluralism for Political Theory and Practice* (New York: Cambridge University Press, 2002); Seyla Benhabib, *The Claims of Culture: Equality and Diversity in the Global Era* (Princeton, N.J.: Princeton University Press, 2002); and William E. Connolly, *Pluralism* (Durham, N.C.: Duke University Press, 2005).

21. Sandel, *Public Philosophy,* 196–197. Sandel refers particularly to David Hartman, *A Living Covenant: The Innovative Spirit in Traditional Judaism* (New York: Free Press, 1985), and *A Heart of Many Rooms: Celebrating the Many Voices within Judaism* (Woodstock, Vt.: Jewish Lights Publishing, 1999). For a similar position, see Jonathan Sacks, *The Dignity of Difference: How to Avoid the Clash of Civilizations* (London: Continuum, 2002), and "A Dignity of Difference: A Salute to Jonathan Sacks," in my book *Small Wonder: Global Power and Its Discontents* (Lanham, Md.: Rowman and Littlefield, 2005), 209–217. For a religiously grounded pluralism, see Rabbi Michael Lerner, *Jewish Renewal: A Path to Healing and Transformation* (New York: Putnam's Sons, 1994), and Charles Taylor, *A Catholic Modernity?* ed. James L. Heft (New York: Oxford University Press, 1999).

22. Sandel, *Public Philosophy,* 30–33. See also Pheng Cheah and Bruce Robbins, eds., *Cosmopolitics: Thinking and Feeling beyond the Nation* (Minneapolis: University of Minnesota Press, 1998).

23. Sandel, *Public Philosophy,* 33–34. See also Seyla Benhabib, *Situating the Self* (New York: Routledge, 1992), and my *Twilight of Subjectivity: Contributions to a Post-Individualist Theory of Politics* (Amherst: University of Massachusetts Press, 1981).

24. Elise Boulding, *Building a Global Civic Culture: Education for an Interdependent World* (Syracuse, N.Y.: Syracuse University Press, 1990), xix–xxi.

25. Ibid., xxi–xxiii, 164. The references are to John Dewey, *Human Nature and Conduct* (New York: Henry Holt, 1922), 217; Paulo Freire, *Pedagogy of the Oppressed* (New York: Continuum, 1979) and *Pedagogy of the Heart* (New York: Continuum, 1997). See also Martha Nussbaum, *Cultivating Humanity: A Classical Defense of Reform in Liberal Education* (Cambridge, Mass.: Harvard University Press, 1997), and Nel Noddings, ed., *Educating Citizens for Global Awareness* (New York: Teachers College Press, 2005).

26. Boulding, *Building a Global Civic Culture,* 140–141, 145, 148, 156. Regarding "cities of refuge," see Daniel Payot, *Des ville-refuges: Témoignage et espacement* (Paris: Editions de l'Aube, 1992), and Jacques Derrida, *On Cosmopolitanism and Forgiveness,* trans. Mark Dooley and Michael Hughes (London: Routledge, 2001), 17–23.

27. Lippmann, *The Good Society*, 375–377. The versions of the Golden Rule are taken from Joyce O. Hertzler, *The Social Thought of the Ancient Civilizations* (New York: McGraw-Hill, 1936), 227, 335, and, more specifically, from the Indian epic *Mahabharata* and the Confucian *Doctrine of the Mean.*

28. William Theodore de Bary, *Neo-Confucian Orthodoxy and the Learning of the Mind-and-Heart* (New York: Columbia University Press, 1981), 69, 85; see also Roger T. Ames, *The Art of Rulership: A Study of Ancient Chinese Political Thought* (Albany: State University of New York Press, 1994). An (inadequate) excuse for the above omissions is that I have commented on the mentioned figures elsewhere, albeit in a limited way. Regarding al-Farabi, see chap. 9 in my book *Peace Talks—Who Will Listen?* (Notre Dame, Ind.: University of Notre Dame Press, 2004); regarding the Confucian tradition, see chap. 5 in my *Alternative Visions: Paths in the Global Village* (Lanham, Md.: Rowman and Littlefield, 1998) and chap. 8 in *Peace Talks;* regarding Erasmus, see chaps. 1, 2, and 9 in *Peace Talks;* and regarding Herder, see chap. 1 in *Alternative Visions.* See also the discussion of Ibn Rushd and the Persian poet Hafiz in chaps. 7 and 8 in my *Dialogue among Civilizations: Some Exemplary Voices* (New York: Palgrave/Macmillan, 2002). For additional literature, see *Alfarabi: The Political Writings,* trans. Charles E. Butterworth (Ithaca, N.Y.: Cornell University Press, 2001); al-Farabi, *Fusul al-Madani* (Aphorisms of the Statesman), ed. D. M. Dunlap (Cambridge: Cambridge University Press, 1961); Tu Weiming, *Confucian Thought: Selfhood as Creative Transformation* (Albany: State University of New York Press, 1985) and *Humanity and Self-Cultivation: Essays in Confucian Thought* (Berkeley, Calif.: Asian Humanities Press, 1979); *The Works of Mencius,* trans. and ed. James Legge (New York: Dover, 1970); Chu Hsi, *Learning to Be a Sage,* trans. and ed. Daniel K. Gardner (Berkeley: University of California Press, 1990); *The Essential Erasmus,* ed. and trans. John P. Dolan (New York: Mentor Books, 1964); *The Erasmus Reader,* ed. and trans. Erika Rummel (Toronto: University of Toronto Press, 1996); Robert T. Clark Jr., *Herder: His Life and Thought* (Berkeley: University of California Press, 1955); and Isaiah Berlin, *Vico and Herder: Two Studies in the History of Ideas* (New York: Viking Press, 1976).

29. De Bary, *Neo-Confucian Orthodoxy,* 85. In other contexts, I have discussed Mahatma Gandhi and the significance of his example. See, for example, chap. 2 in my *Margins of Political Discourse* (Albany: State University of New York Press, 1989); chap. 4 in *Alternative Visions;* chap. 12 in *Dialogue among Civilizations;* and chap. 7 in *Peace Talks.*

1. A Pedagogy of the Heart

1. As Ewert Cousins writes: "It was in 1205 that Francis heard the crucifix in the church of San Damiano speak to him and direct him on a path that

was to lead to his founding a new religious order. Within four years Francis had obtained the approval of Pope Innocent III for his rule of life based on the gospel. The young Franciscan Order grew with surprising rapidity, attracting followers from all walks of life and spreading geographically over central Europe, soon extending to Spain, England, and to foreign missions in Africa and the Middle East." See his introduction to *Bonaventure: The Soul's Journey into God, The Tree of Life, The Life of St. Francis,* trans. Ewert Cousins (New York: Paulist Press, 1978), 2–3.

2. See, for example, Michael Novak, *The Catholic Ethic and the Spirit of Capitalism* (New York: Free Press, 1993), and *Toward a Theology of the Corporation* (Washington, D.C.: American Enterprise Institute, 1981); see also David Loy, "The Religion of the Market," *Journal of the American Academy of Religion* 65 (1997): 275–290.

3. Regarding the designation as "second founder," see Liam Brophy, "Saint Bonaventure—Answer to the Modern Dilemma," in Saint Bonaventure, *The Mind's Journey to God,* trans. Lawrence S. Cunningham (Chicago: Franciscan Herald Press, 1979), 101.

4. Etienne Gilson, *History of Christian Philosophy in the Middle Ages* (New York: Random House, 1955), 340. As Lawrence Cunningham adds: "Francis, of course, was not a philosopher, nor was he interested in the pursuit of philosophical questions. Bonaventure's great contribution was in the reconstruction of the Christocentric mysticism of Saint Francis into a coherent whole." See his introduction to *The Mind's Journey to God,* 8.

5. In the prologue to his "Life of Saint Francis," Bonaventure speaks of a boyhood illness that was cured by the spiritual intervention of the *poverello,* but the circumstances of the cure are unclear. For some comments, see Cousins, introduction to *Bonaventure,* 3–4.

6. Bonaventure, "The Life of St. Francis," in *Bonaventure,* 182–183 (prologue).

7. Cousins, introduction to *Bonaventure,* 42–43. The three headings are divided into three subthemes: the first into austerity, humility, and love of poverty; the second into piety, charity, and zeal for prayer; and the third into scriptural understanding, efficacy of preaching, and union with God (manifest in the stigmata).

8. Bonaventure, "The Life of St. Francis," 185–196.

9. Ibid., 199–212.

10. Ibid., 228–241.

11. Ibid., 250–273. I bypass in silence (and embarrassment) Francis's missionary activities, especially with regard to Muslims or so-called infidels. Although common in the age of the crusades, this kind of mission does not quite meet the standard of love and charity demanded of Christians.

12. Ibid., 280, 291, 297, 305–309.

13. Ibid., 315–318, 325–327.

14. Cousins, introduction to *Bonaventure*, 2.

15. Cunningham, introduction to *The Mind's Journey to God*, 11–12.

16. Cousins, introduction to *Bonaventure*, 19–20, 24–25. In an effort to avoid mentalist or Cartesian connotations, Cousins translates the Latin *mens* as "soul"—for a reason: "I have chosen 'soul' in preference to 'mind' or 'spirit.' However, 'soul' must not be taken here in its Aristotelian sense of the animating principle of the body, but rather as the image of God in the depth of the person, the most profound dimension of man's spiritual being" (21).

17. Cunningham, introduction to *The Mind's Journey to God*, 12–13.

18. Bonaventure, *The Mind's Journey to God* (trans. Cunningham), 31–48; *Bonaventure* (trans. Cousins), 61–75. Here and in the following citations, I alternate between the translations of Cunningham and Cousins, sometimes synthesizing the two.

19. *The Mind's Journey to God*, 53–68; *Bonaventure*, 79–90.

20. *The Mind's Journey to God*, 71–83; *Bonaventure*, 94–107.

21. *The Mind's Journey to God*, 84–87; *Bonaventure*, 109–114.

22. *The Mind's Journey to God*, 23–24; *Bonaventure*, 53–54, 179–180.

23. Cousins, introduction to *Bonaventure*, 7.

24. Cunningham, introduction to *The Mind's Journey to God*, 4. According to a contemporary chronicle: "Greeks and Latins, clergy and laity followed his bier with bitter tears, grieving over the lamentable loss of so great a person." See Cousins, introduction to *Bonaventure*, 8.

25. Cousins, introduction to *Bonaventure*, 7.

26. *Epistola de tribus quaestionibus*, 13, quoted in Cousins, introduction to *Bonaventure*, 6.

27. Bull of Canonization, cited in Cousins, introduction to *Bonaventure*, 5.

28. *Bonaventure*, 303.

29. See José Cabezón, *H. H. the Dalai Lama, the Bodhgaya Interviews* (Ithaca, N.Y.: Snow Lion, 1988), 62. There is a certain parallel between Bonaventure's six-step journey and the famous eightfold path of the Buddhist ascent toward nirvana.

30. *Bonaventure*, 67. In his introduction (27–29), Cousins differentiates Francis's simplicity from Bonaventure's more speculative or intellectual approach to nature, but the distinction appears somewhat overdrawn.

31. Raimon Panikkar, "Colligite Fragmenta: For an Integration of Reality," in *From Alienation to At-Oneness*, ed. F. A. Eigo (Villanova, Pa.: Villanova University Press, 1977), 74. See also Raimon Panikkar, *The Cosmotheandric Experience: Emerging Religious Consciousness*, ed. Scott Eastham (Maryknoll, N.Y.: Orbis Books, 1993), and my "Rethinking Secularism—with Raimon Panikkar," in *Dialogue among Civilizations: Some Exemplary Voices* (New York: Palgrave/Macmillan, 2002), 185–200.

32. Enrique Dussel, "The Eco-Technological Issue: Toward a Liberating Production Theology," in *The Intercultural Challenge of Raimon Panik-*

kar, ed. Joseph Prabhu (Maryknoll, N.Y.: Orbis Books, 1996), 194. See also Raimon Panikkar, *Ecosofia: La nuova saggeza—Per una spiritualitá della terra* (Assisi, Italy: Citadella Editrice, 1993).

33. Cousins, introduction to *Bonaventure,* 46.

34. Paulo Freire, *Pedagogy of the Heart,* trans. Donald Macedo and Alexandre Oliveira (New York: Continuum, 1997), 105.

2. Walking Humbly with Your God

1. James F. Edwards, *Dnyaneshwar: The Out-Caste Brahmin* (Poona, India: Aryabhushan Press, 1941), 60. Edwards gives a useful overview of various accounts of Jñanadev's life (52–86). For another account, see B. P. Bahirat, *The Philosophy of Jñanadeva: As Gleaned from the Amritanubhava* (Delhi: Motilal Banarsidass, 1984), 8–15. Bahirat gives the name of Vithalpant's wife as Rukmini, and he claims that the guru's name in Banaras was Ramashrama (not Ramananda). He also reports that Rukmini committed suicide a year after her husband.

2. This point is reminiscent of Martin Buber's Hasidic outlook, expressed in this statement: "God carries his absoluteness into his relationship with man. Hence the man who turns toward him need not turn his back on any other I-Thou relationship: quite legitimately he brings them all to God and allows them to become transfigured 'in the countenance of God.'" See Buber, *I and Thou* (New York: Scribners, 1970), 182.

3. Still, the story is not entirely black and white. Although Vithalpant is seriously tempted by and attracted to *sannyasa,* there is also the wise guru and "renouncer," Ramananda, who is able to see the legitimacy of different redemptive paths. To this extent, the story is not one of class (or caste) war.

4. For some of the details of the story, see Philip C. Engblom, introduction to D. B. Mokashi, *Palkhi: An Indian Pilgrimage,* trans. P. C. Engblom (Albany: State University of New York Press, 1987), 12–14. In Engblom's words: Pundalik "not only brought Vitthal [Vithoba] to stay at the temple and thereby established the sacred complex surrounding him; he also provided, by his example, the archetype of devotion for all the subsequent long lineage of *Warkari* saints and established the basis for the *Warkari* devotion to the saints" (13).

5. I have told the story as it was reported secondhand by Edwards in *Dryaneshwar,* 38, 61–62.

6. We also read in Ezekiel (37:4): "Prophesy to these dry bones, and say to them: O dry bones, hear the word of the Lord."

7. The Changdev story is taken from Edwards, *Dryaneshwar,* 39–42, 62 (I omitted the episode of the burning hut from which the three brothers and their sister are miraculously saved). The translation of the passage from *Jñaneshwari* is taken from Bahirat, *The Philosophy of Jñanadeva,* 3.

8. See Edwards, *Dnyaneshwar,* 62–67; Bahirat, *The Philosophy of*

Jñanadeva, 14–15. Namadev outlived his friend by more than fifty years and devoted a famous series of poems, or *abhangas*, to his memory. I am aware that some writers have raised doubts about the dates of Jñanadev's life and about his relationship with Namadev. However, my concern is not so much with historiography as with symbolic significance.

9. At one point of his *Amritanubhava* (III, 17) he even says: "It is not because Shiva or Shri Krishna has spoken thus, that we are making our statement. It would have been the same if they had not spoken." For the English rendering of this passage, see Bahirat, *The Philosophy of Jñanadeva*, 38, 171.

10. Bahirat, *The Philosophy of Jñanadeva*, 31, 33. The assimilation of Jñanadev to Shankara has been propounded by such authors as S. V. Dandekar, S. D. Pendse, L. R. Pangarkar, and R. D. Ranade (especially in Ranade's *Mysticism in India: The Poet-Saints of Maharashtra* [Albany: State University of New York Press, 1983]). The linkage with Ramanuja has been defended by Pandurang Sharma and others.

11. *Amritanubhava*, VI, 94, 96; see Bahirat, *The Philosophy of Jñanadeva*, 36–39, 196–197. Despite his critique of scripture worship, Jñanadev was by no means disrespectful of classical scriptures, as is evident in his commentary on the Bhagavad Gita and in his poems devoted to the remembrance of the classical "name" of God (the so-called *Haripatha*).

12. *Amritanubhava*, IV, 40; V, 1, 10–13, 19, 21; see Bahirat, *The Philosophy of Jñanadeva*, 39–40, 178–181.

13. *Amritanubhava*, IV, 25–28. Bahirat is one of those ascribing a "nihilistic" outlook to Madhyamika Buddhism. As he writes: "Nagarjun was the propounder of nihilism and his philosophy is neither idealism nor realism nor absolutism but blank phenomenalism which only accepts the phenomenal world as it is but without any kind of essence, ground or reality behind it." Curiously, despite his perceptive reading of Jñanadev's comments on *sat-chit-ananda*, Bahirat persists in using these terms as essential descriptors, saying: "Reality is pure existence, pure knowledge, and pure bliss. This is the positive description of reality." See *The Philosophy of Jñanadeva*, 41, 43.

14. *Amritanubhava*, I, 1–4, 9–10, 19; see Bahirat, *The Philosophy of Jñanadeva*, 152–154.

15. *Amritanubhava*, VII, 281. The "refutation of *ajñanavada*" in chapter VII is followed in chapter VIII by a "refutation of (epistemic) knowledge." Bahirat is perceptive in pinpointing the distinctness of Jñanadev's "metaphysics," although he tends to link Shankara (perhaps too quickly) with essentialism. As he writes: "Jñanadev's view of God and Goddess, as expressed in his *Amritanubhava*, is quite distinct from the Samkhya view of *purusha* and *prakriti* or the Vedantic doctrine of *brahman* and *maya*. . . . Samkhya has the drawback of assuming two eternal principles, and of regarding matter as evolving out of itself. . . . The Vedantic view is also marred by the as-

sumption of *avidya* which seems to overpower even *brahman,* the ultimate reality." Regarding Vedanta, he adds that Jñanadev "refuted the doctrine of *ajñana(vada)* which is identical with *maya* of Shankara; he has clearly declared that the entity which is called *maya* by Vedantins is nothing but ignorance." At a later point in his book, Bahirat discusses in detail the differences between Jñanadev and Shankara (some of which seem more plausible than others). Still, he admits that "Jñanadev had great reverence for Shankara. In his *Jñaneshwari* he says that he is merely following the footsteps of the great *bashyakar* (i.e. commentator)." See *The Philosophy of Jñanadeva,* 46–47, 54, 108–110.

16. *Amritanubhava,* IX, 29; see Bahirat, *The Philosophy of Jñanadeva,* 235, and his comments on *sphurtivada* and *childivas* on 17–18, 74–75, 103, 129. Borrowing a suggestion from Heidegger, one might say that the divine (Shiva-Shakti) *is* the world and its myriad things—not in a static-metaphysical sense, but in a transitive-ontological one. (The difference between Jñanadev and Ramanuja seems to reside chiefly in the fact that, for Ramanuja, the relation between God and the world is akin to that between spirit and body—in a modified version of Samkhyanism. For Jñanadev, the mind-body nexus cannot even serve as a distant analogy to the bond of parents and offspring and their loving care.)

17. *Amritanubhava,* IX, 30, 34; X, 31; see Bahirat, *The Philosophy of Jñanadeva,* 235, 243. For some intriguing comparisons between Jñanadev and the views of Henri Bergson and Rudolf Otto, see 94–95.

18. Eleanor Zelliot, "A Historical Introduction to the *Warkari* Movement," in Mokashi, *Palkhi,* 39–40, 42–43. Although egalitarian and anticaste, one probably should not equate the Warkaris with a radical movement for social change, which would be at variance with the intrinsic gentleness and nonviolent outlook of the Warkari ethos. Hence, the statement by Jayant Lele that Jñanadev's legacy "advocates a revolutionary and critical productive activity within social practice" needs to be taken with a grain of salt. See his "Community, Discourse and Critique in Jñanesvar," in *Tradition and Modernity in Bhakti Movements,* ed. Jayant Lele (Leiden: Brill, 1981), 111. Unsurprisingly, the gentleness and quasi-Gandhian quality of the Warkaris have been chided by radical revolutionaries and "extremist" nationalists, including Bal Gangadhar Tilak. See in this context Bhalchandra Nemade, "The Revolt of the Underprivileged: Style in the Expression of the *Warkari* Movement in Maharashtra," ibid., 113–123.

19. Zelliot, "A Historical Introduction," 42–43.

20. Charlotte Vaudeville, "The Shaiva-Vaishnava Synthesis in Maharashtrian Santism," in *The Sants: Studies in a Devotional Tradition in India,* ed. Karine Schomer and W. H. McLeod (Berkeley, Calif.: Religious Studies Series, 1987), 217. On this point, see also Wendy O'Flaherty, "The Interaction of *Saguna* and *Nirguna* Images of Deity," ibid., 47–52. See also Zelliot, "A

Historical Introduction," 35–37. The combination of *saguna* and *nirguna* aspects can be traced to Jñanadev and Namadev. Although they were devotees of Vithoba, they both preferred the invocation of the "name" (*namasmarana*) to the worship of visible images (as can be seen in Jñanadev's *Haripatha* and *Namana*). Regarding nonsectarianism, note this passage in the *Jñaneshwari* (XVII, 222): "Let a single name, be it Shiva or Vishnu, dwell on your tongue—such is the penance of speech." Also note this passage in the *Amritanubhava* (IX, 62): "Hari and Hara (Shiva and Vishnu) are really the same; the difference of their names and forms is blended." On the connection between Jñanadev's thought and Kashmir Shaivism, see Bahirat, *The Philosophy of Jñanadeva*, 104–105.

21. Engblom, introduction to Mokashi, *Palkhi*, 23, 27; Gabriel Marcel, *Homo Viator*, trans. Emma Craufurd (New York: Harper Torchbooks, 1962). See also E. Alan Morinis, *Pilgrimage in the Hindu Tradition: A Case Study of West Bengal* (Delhi: Oxford University Press, 1984); Irawati Karve, "On the Road: A Maharashtrian Pilgrimage," *Journal of Asian Studies* 22 (1962): 13–29. From the vantage of a certain postmodern "nonfoundationalism," journeying has been captured in this motto: "We secularists, it seems, know where we are going. We're on the road to nowhere. . . . No illusions about eternal life." See William E. Connolly, *Identity/Difference: Democratic Negotiations of Political Paradox* (Ithaca, N.Y.: Cornell University Press, 1991), 16.

22. See Engblom, introduction to Mokashi, *Palkhi*, 22, 25, for Dandekar's statement.

23. *Jñaneshwari*, XVIII, 1793–1794. The translation is taken (with a few minor alterations) from Edwards, *Dnyaneshwar*, 70. Some English renditions of the *Jñaneshwari* do not include this closing prayer. Thus, it is not contained in Swami Kripananda, *Jñaneshwari's Gita: A Rendering of the Jñaneshwari* (Albany: State University of New York Press, 1989).

Chapter 3. Wise Ignorance

1. Ernst Cassirer, *The Individual and the Cosmos in Renaissance Philosophy*, trans. Mario Domandi (New York: Harper and Row, 1964), 10, 13.

2. The phrase "being-in-the-world" is, of course, a key feature of Martin Heidegger's philosophy. For a discussion of the philosophical significance of lived experience in Heidegger's thought, see Charles Taylor, "Engaged Agency and Background in Heidegger," in *The Cambridge Companion to Heidegger*, ed. Charles Guignon (New York: Cambridge University Press, 1993), 317–336.

3. John Patrick Dolan, ed., *Unity and Reform: Selected Writings of Nicholas de Cusa* (Notre Dame, Ind.: University of Notre Dame Press, 1962), 101–102 (translation slightly altered).

4. Nicolai de Cusa, *Idiota de Sapientia—Der Laie über die Weisheit*, ed. Renate Steiger (Hamburg: Felix Meiner, 1988), xii–xiv, xvi. Steiger also

draws parallels between Cusanus's text and Heinrich Seuse's *Horologium sapientiae,* as well as Johannes Tauler's life history styled as a "dialogue between a doctor and a layman" (xx–xxi). In addition, she finds inspiration for Cusanus's text in Saint Bonaventure's *Itinerarium mentis in Deum* (xxiii).

5. Cassirer, *The Individual and the Cosmos,* 48–50. The reference is to Pierre Duhem, *Etudes sur Léonard de Vinci,* 2nd ser. (Paris: A. Hermann, 1909). Contemporary readers may recognize in Leonardo's distinction the bifurcation between (what is called) the "logic of discovery" and the "logic of verification"—a bifurcation that is often invoked today by neo-Kantian and analytical philosophers, with the aim of disparaging discovery in favor of discursive validation.

6. "These men," Cassirer writes, "were not concerned with giving scientific determination and definition to fundamentally religious issues. Nor did they demand a return to the great tradition of antiquity, to seek the regeneration of mankind. Instead, they dealt with concrete, technical and artistic problems for which they sought a 'theory.'" See *The Individual and the Cosmos,* 48.

7. Dolan, *Unity and Reform,* 106 (translation slightly altered).

8. Ibid., 106–107.

9. Ibid., 107–108 (translation slightly altered). In a nearly Heideggerian vein, Cusanus continues (108): "Every spirit seeks after 'being' (*omnis intellectus appetit esse*), and being means to live, and living means to understand, and understanding means being nurtured on wisdom and truth." In the introduction to *The Layman on Wisdom,* Renate Steiger points to biblical passages speaking of "manna" (Exodus 16:4) or "milk and honey" (Exodus 3:8), and also to Psalms 34:8: *Gustate et videte, quoniam suavis est Dominus.* See her edition of Nicolai de Cusa, *Idiota de Sapientia,* xxxi.

10. Dolan, *Unity and Reform,* 112.

11. Cassirer, *The Individual and the Cosmos,* 44–45. For the reference, see Nicolai de Cusa, *Idiota de Mente—Der Laie über den Geist,* ed. Renate Steiger (Hamburg: Felix Meiner, 1995), 34–35. (Cassirer's translation of the Latin text is quite free.)

12. Maurice Merleau-Ponty, *The Visible and the Invisible, Followed by Working Notes,* ed. Claude Lefort, trans. Alphonso Lingis (Evanston, Ill.: Northwestern University Press, 1968), 3, 31–32. He continues by saying: "Reflection recuperates everything except itself as an effort of recuperation; it clarifies everything except its own role" (33).

13. See Nicolai de Cusa, *De Beryllo—Über den Beryll,* ed. and trans. Karl Bormann (Hamburg: Felix Meiner, 1987), 7.

14. Karl Jaspers, *Nikolaus Cusanus* (Munich: Piper, 1964), 48–49. The reference is to Nicolai de Cusa, *De coniecturis—Mutmassungen,* ed. and trans. Josef Koch and Winfried Happ (Hamburg: Felix Meiner, 2002), 189 (pt. 2, chap. 16).

15. Nicolai de Cusa, *De coniecturis—Mutmassungen,* 184–187 (pt. 2, chap. 16). In this text, Cusanus sometimes departs from his usual terminology by subordinating intellect to reason (*ratio*).

16. Nicolai de Cusa, *De docta ignorantia—Die belehrte Unwissenheit,* vol. 1, trans. Paul Wilpert, ed. Hans Gerhard Senger (Hamburg: Felix Meiner, 1994), 6–9 (bk. 1, chap. 1). For an English translation (that I have slightly altered), see Jasper Hopkins, *Nicholas of Cusa on Learned Ignorance* (Minneapolis: Arthur J. Banning Press, 1981), 50. See also Peter Casarella, ed., *Cusanus: The Legacy of Learned Ignorance* (Washington, D.C.: Catholic University of America Press, 2006).

17. Nicolai de Cusa, *De docta ignorantia—Die belehrte Unwissenheit,* 8–15 (bk. 1, chaps. 1–3); Hopkins, *Nicholas of Cusa on Learned Ignorance,* 50–53.

18. On this point, see also the passage in Nicolai de Cusa, *Tu quis es (De principio)—Über den Ursprung,* trans. and ed. Karl Bormann (Hamburg: Felix Meiner, 2001), 26–27, 30–31: "We do not call God the 'one' as something fully known, but because prior to any knowledge our yearning/desire is directed toward the one. . . . And although (ultimate being) cannot be cognitively grasped, we are yet not in complete ignorance, because we 'know' what we desire (*scit ipsum esse quod desiderat*). Our intellect which knows that ultimate being exists as incomprehensible, is all the more perfect the more it realizes this incomprehensibility. For the access to the incomprehensible lies in learned ignorance (*scientia ignorantiae*)." Regarding the notion of truth or ultimate being "calling on" human understanding, see Martin Heidegger, *Was heisst Denken?* 3rd ed. (Tübingen: Niemeyer, 1971); translated as *What Is Called Thinking?* by J. Glenn Gray (New York: Harper and Row, 1968). Regarding the notion of "truth" (beyond rational correspondence), see Heidegger's discussion in *Zeit und Sein,* 11th ed. (Tübingen: Niemeyer, 1967), 212–230, par. 44; translated as *Being and Time* by Joan Stambaugh (Albany: State University of New York Press, 1996), 196–211.

19. Nicolai de Cusa, *De venatione sapientiae—Die Jagd nach Weisheit,* ed. Paul Wilpert and Karl Bormann (Hamburg: Felix Meiner, 2003), 44–51 (chap. 12). As Cusanus adds, most past philosophers, with the possible exception of Plato (as interpreted by Proclus), have missed or fallen short of this standard. Thus, those "philosophical hunters" who tried to "hunt down the essence of things" and to transform the telos of all inquiry into "an object of knowledge" have "labored in vain, remaining outside the field of learned ignorance."

20. Ibid., 50–55 (chap. 13). See also his longer treatment of this argument in *De possest—Dreiergespräch über das Können-Ist,* ed. Renate Steiger (Hamburg: Felix Meiner, 1973).

21. See, for example, Emmanuel Levinas, *Totality and Infinity,* trans. Alphonso Lingis (Pittsburgh: Duquesne University Press, 1969) and *Of God*

Who Comes to Mind, trans. Bettina Bergo (Stanford, Calif.: Stanford University Press, 1989); Jean-Luc Marion, *God without Being,* trans. Thomas A. Carlson (Chicago: University of Chicago Press, 1991); and Dominique Janicaud, "The Theological Turn of French Phenomenology," in Janicaud et al., *Phenomenology and the "Theological Turn"* (New York: Fordham University Press, 2000), 3–103.

22. Nicolai de Cusa, *De venatione sapientiae—Die Jagd nach Weisheit,* 56–61. As Cusanus adds in a remarkable passage: "God does not stand in opposition to any determination since He precedes the difference of opposites. It would be a less appropriate way of speaking if one described God as a living being in contrast to non-living things, or as an immortal being in contrast to mortal beings. Better to describe Him as the Not-Other who stands in opposition neither to anything other nor to nothingness, since He precedes even nothingness" (60–61). For a fuller discussion of "not-other," see his *De li non aliud—Vom Nichtanderen,* ed. Paul Wilpert (Hamburg: Felix Meiner, 1987); for an English version, see Jasper Hopkins, *Nicholas of Cusa on God as Not-Other* (Minneapolis: University of Minnesota Press, 1979).

23. Norbert Winkler, *Nikolaus von Kues zur Einführung* (Hamburg: Junius Verlag, 2001), 104–106. See also my "Conversation across Boundaries: E Pluribus Unum," in *Dialogue among Civilizations: Some Exemplary Voices* (New York: Palgrave/Macmillan, 2002), 31–47.

24. Gerd Heinz-Mohr and Willehad Paul Eckert, *Das Werk des Nicolaus Cusanus* (Cologne: Wienand Verlag, 1963), 41–42. For a complete English translation, see Nicholas of Cusa, *The Catholic Concordance,* trans. Paul E. Sigmund (New York: Cambridge University Press, 1991).

25. Among others, Jaspers reaches the harsh verdict that, rising to prominence in the turbulent conditions of his time, Cusanus was ultimately "impotent in the implementation of truth and goodness"; thereby, he became an "unwitting accomplice" in the course of events. Jaspers also refuses to consider Cusanus a precursor of either the Reformation or the Enlightenment. See his *Nikolaus Cusanus,* 216–221. Pointing to the cardinal's attitude toward the Hussites, Winkler reaches a similar conclusion: that Cusanus was "not a reformer before the Reformation"; see *Nikolaus von Kues zur Einführung,* 176.

26. Nicholas of Cusa, *On Interreligious Harmony* (Text, Concordance, and Translation of *De Paci Fidei*), ed. James E. Biechler and H. Lawrence Bond (Lewiston, N.Y.: Edwin Mellen Press, 1990), 3–7.

27. Ibid., xxvii, xlv; the reference is to chapter 19 of the text (61–62). They continue: "University and particularity, necessity and contingency, interiority and externality are enfolded as one in God's mind, are unfolded as distinct in the finite world and coincide as one and plural in God's plan for religious peace" (xlv). See also Cary Nederman, "Natio and the 'Variety of Rites': Foundations of Religious Toleration in Nicholas of Cusa," in *Religious*

Toleration: The "Variety of Rites" from Cyrus to Defoe, ed. John Christian Laursen (New York: St. Martin's Press, 1999), 59–74.

28. The interfaith deliberations took place at the Council of Ferrara-Florence (in 1439) and produced a short-lived success. In a later autobiographical statement, Cusanus recalls: "When he was 37 years old, Pope Eugenius IV sent him to Constantinople, and he conducted the Greek Emperor, the Patriarch and 28 archbishops of the Eastern Church back with him. They then at the Council of Florence accepted the faith of the Roman Church." Cited in Biechler and Bond, introduction to *On Interreligious Harmony,* xi. It was during his return voyage from Constantinople that Cusanus was inspired by the idea of "learned ignorance"—an idea that, in his dedicatory letter attached to *De Docta Ignorantia,* he calls "a heavenly gift from the Father of lights, from whom every excellent gift comes." See Hopkins, *Nicholas of Cusa on Learned Ignorance,* 158.

29. Nicolai de Cusa, *Cibratio Alkorani—Sichtung des Korans,* ed. Ludwig Hagemann and Reinhold Glei (Hamburg: Felix Meiner, 1989), 13 (bk. 1).

30. Jasper Hopkins, "The Role of *Pia Interpretatio* in Nicholas of Cusa's Hermeneutical Approach to the Koran," in his *A Miscellany of Nicholas of Cusa* (Minneapolis: Arthur J. Banning Press, 1994), 50–51. The *Miscellany* also contains chapters on fervently anti-Muslim writers such as Ricoldo of Montecroe and John of Torquemada (a contemporary of Cusanus and a fellow cardinal). The reference is to *Cibratio Alkorani,* 54–55 (bk. 1, chap. 7).

31. On this point, see Biechler and Bond, introduction to *On Interreligious Harmony,* xxx.

32. See K. Venkata Ramanan, *Nagarjuna's Philosophy* (Delhi: Motilal Banarsidass, 1975), 141; see also David J. Kalupahana, *Nagarjuna: The Philosophy of the Middle Way* (Albany: State University of New York Press, 1986). For the Buddhist tradition, see also Nishida Kitaro, "Coincidentia Oppositorum and Love," trans. Michiko Yusa, in *Cusanus-Rezeption in der Philosophie des 20. Jahrhunderts,* ed. Klaus Reinhard and Harald Schwaetzer (Regensburg, Germany: S. Roderer Verlag, 2005), 221–225, and Michiko Yusa, "Nishida Kitaro and 'Coincidentia Oppositorum'—An Introduction," ibid., 211–219. Regarding Indian philosophy, and especially Advaita and Vishisht-Advaita Vedanta, see Eliot Deutsch, *Advaita Vedanta: A Philosophical Reconstruction* (Honolulu: University of Hawaii Press, 1968); S. R. Bhatt, *Studies in Ramanuja Vedanta* (New Delhi: Heritage Publishers, 1975); and John B. Carman, *Theology of Ramanuja* (New Haven, Conn.: Yale University Press, 1974).

33. Nicolai de Cusa, *De venatione sapientiae—Die Jagd nach Weisheit,* 98–99 (chap. 22). The reference to Saint Paul is found in *Tu quis es (De principio)—Über den Ursprung,* trans. and ed. Karl Bormann (Hamburg: Felix Meiner, 2001), 42–43.

34. See "De Visione Dei," in Dolan, *Unity and Reform,* 149, 161.

4. The Natural Theology of the Chinese

This chapter is dedicated to Henry Rosemont Jr.

1. Daniel J. Cook and Henry Rosemont Jr., *Gottfried Wilhelm Leibniz: Writings on China* (Chicago: Open Court, 1994), 10.

2. Ibid., 1.

3. Hans Heinz Holz, *Leibniz* (Stuttgart: Kohlhammer Verlag, 1958), 21–22. See also Nicholas Malebranche, *Dialogue between a Christian Philosopher and a Chinese Philosopher on the Existence and Nature of God*, trans. A. Dominick Iorio (Washington, D.C.: University Press of America, 1980).

4. Cook and Rosemont, *Leibniz: Writings on China*, 2.

5. Holz, *Leibniz*, 49–50. Regarding the interrelation of Leibnizian monads, consider the statement by Franklin Perkins: "*Li* [principle] is one, but its manifestations are many; the single moon has countless reflections in the water. The image is strikingly similar to Leibniz's conception of monads as diverse expressions of God." See his *Leibniz and China: Commerce of Light* (Cambridge: Cambridge University Press, 2004), 21.

6. Henry Rosemont Jr., *A Chinese Mirror: Moral Reflections on Political Economy and Society* (Chicago: Open Court, 1991), 7. Compare in this context Roxanne L. Euben, *Enemy in the Mirror* (Princeton, N.J.: Princeton University Press, 1999).

7. Henry Rosemont Jr., *Rationality and Religious Experience: The Continuing Relevance of the World's Spiritual Traditions* (Chicago: Open Court, 2001), 78.

8. Cook and Rosemont, *Leibniz: Writings on China*, 3.

9. Ibid., 4.

10. Ibid., 46–48. As Perkins sensitively comments: "The Preface is a wonderful document, with its call for cultural exchange, the need to learn from China, and its discussion of the complementary strengths of East and West." See *Leibniz and China*, 114. See also Donald F. Lach, ed., *The Preface to Leibniz's Novissima Sinica* (Honolulu: University of Hawaii Press, 1957).

11. Cook and Rosemont, *Leibniz: Writings on China*, 48–50.

12. Ibid., 51.

13. Ibid., 70–71.

14. Ibid., 7–8.

15. Ibid., 78–81.

16. Ibid., 105.

17. Rosemont, *Rationality and Religious Experience*, 55, 101, n. 33.

18. Ibid., 80–81. Regarding the immanence-transcendence problem, see "Small Wonder: Finitude and Its Horizons" in my *Small Wonder: Global Power and Its Discontents* (Lanham, Md.: Rowman and Littlefield, 2005), 13–32.

19. On the Spanish conquest of the Americas, see Tzvetan Todorov, *The Conquest of America: The Question of the Other*, trans. Richard Howard

(New York: Harper and Row, 1984). Regarding the ambivalence involved in Napoleon's spreading of revolutionary ideas through French armies, see Immanuel Wallerstein, *Geopolitics and Geoculture: Essays on the Changing World System* (Cambridge: Cambridge University Press, 1992), 216–217.

20. Rosemont, *Rationality and Religious Experience*, 3, 10.

21. Cook and Rosemont, *Leibniz: Writings on China*, 5. See also David Mungello, *Leibniz and Confucianism: The Search for Accord* (Honolulu: University of Hawaii Press, 1977), 339.

22. Rosemont, *Rationality and Religious Experience*, 61, 89. See also Herbert Fingarette, *Confucius—The Secular as Sacred* (New York: Harper and Row, 1972).

23. Rosemont, *Rationality and Religious Experience*, 34.

24. See Jean Grondin, *Hans-Georg Gadamer: A Biography*, trans. Joel Weinsheimer (New Haven, Conn.: Yale University Press, 2003), 250.

25. Cook and Rosemont, *Leibniz: Writings on China*, 51.

5. *Montesquieu's* Persian Letters

This chapter is based on a paper presented at a conference held in Toronto in September 2005 in commemoration of the 250th anniversary of Montesquieu's death. The general theme of the conference was "Modernity in Question: Montesquieu and His Legacy."

1. I follow here the writings of Charles Taylor on alternative or multiple modernities. See his *Sources of the Self: The Making of Modern Identity* (Cambridge, Mass.: Harvard University Press, 1989), 509–513; *A Catholic Modernity?* ed. James L. Heft (New York: Oxford University Press, 1999), 16–19; and "Two Theories of Modernity," *Public Culture* 11 (1999): 153–173. See also Scott Lash, *Another Modernity, a Different Rationality* (Oxford: Blackwell, 1999), and Dilip P. Gaonkar, ed., *Alternative Modernities* (Durham, N.C.: Duke University Press, 2001).

2. See Hannah Arendt, *The Human Condition* (Chicago: University of Chicago Press, 1958), 6, and *Between Past and Future: Six Exercises in Political Thought* (Cleveland: Meridian Books, 1963), 14.

3. Voltaire's comment is taken from Kingsley Martin, *The Rise of French Liberal Thought*, ed. J. P. Mayer (New York: New York University Press, 1954), 153. Montesquieu reciprocated by stating: "As for Voltaire, he has too much wit to understand me. He reads no books but those he writes, and he then approves or censures his own progeny as the wind takes him" (150, n. 2).

4. See Montesquieu, *The Persian Letters,* trans. with an introduction by George R. Healy (Indianapolis: Hackett, 1964), xv–xviii. For a similar verdict, see Werner Stark, *Montesquieu: Pioneer of the Sociology of Knowledge* (Toronto: University of Toronto Press, 1960). In the introduction to his translation of *The Spirit of Laws,* David W. Carrithers presents Montesquieu as

navigating uneasily between the poles of "rationalism" and "relativism." See *The Spirit of Laws by Montesquieu,* ed. with an introduction by David W. Carrithers (Berkeley: University of California Press, 1977), 34–44.

5. Hans-Georg Gadamer, "On the Possibility of a Philosophical Ethics," in *Hermeneutics, Religion, and Ethics,* trans. Joel Weinsheimer (New Haven, Conn.: Yale University Press, 1999), 28–29.

6. Martin, *The Rise of French Liberal Thought,* 153.

7. *The Spirit of Laws of Montesquieu,* 98 (bk. 1, chap. 1). Although accepting the notion that humans are "naturally" sociable, Montesquieu recognizes that in this case, nature has to be supplemented by culture—that is, through government and civil laws (101). The conception of law as relational resonates with Confucian ethics as well as with the classical Indian notion of dharma. See Chaihark Hahm and Daniel A. Bell, eds., *The Politics of Affective Relations: East Asia and Beyond* (Lanham, Md.: Lexington Books, 2004).

8. In our time, the need for this underpinning has been clearly recognized by Charles Taylor in his insistence that rules and principles make sense only in a broader "horizon of significance." See Taylor, *The Ethics of Authenticity* (Cambridge, Mass.: Harvard University Press, 1992), 35–37, 66. See also *The Spirit of Laws by Montesquieu,* 289 (bk. 19, chap. 4). The passage from *Considerations on the Causes of the Greatness of the Romans and Their Decline* (1734) is taken from Carrithers's introduction, 25.

9. See *The Spirit of Laws of Montesquieu,* 107 (bk. 2, chap. 1), 117–124 (bk. 3, chaps. 3–9), 130, 132–133 (bk. 4, chap. 5, and bk. 5, chaps. 2 and 3).

10. Ibid., 200 (bk. 11, chap. 3).

11. Norman L. Torrey, ed., *Les Philosophes: The Philosophers of the Enlightenment and Modern Democracy* (New York: Capricorn Books, 1960), 90–91.

12. See *Hegel's Philosophy of Right,* trans. T. M. Knox (Oxford: Oxford University Press, 1967), 16 (introduction, par. 3), 161 (par. 261), 177–178 (par. 273). Hegel's appreciation of Montesquieu's work was not complete, however. A main point of disagreement concerned the "separation of powers" and "checks and balances." As Hegel states sharply (282, par. 300, add. 178): "The idea of the so-called 'independence of powers' contains a fundamental error of supposing that the powers, though independent, are to check one another. This independence, however, destroys the unity of the state." Hegel fully shared Montesquieu's concern about the proper functioning of "intermediary bodies," however, especially on the local and regional levels; this concern is traceable to the baron's early service as counselor of the Parlement of Bordeaux and later as *président* of the Parlement of Guyenne. On this point, see Carl J. Friedrich, *The Philosophy of Hegel* (New York: Random House/Modern Library, 1954), xxiii.

13. Montesquieu, *Persian Letters,* xi–xii.

14. Ibid., 22–30 (letters 11—14). In a cross-cultural perspective, Montesquieu's preference for ethical practice over formal laws resonates to some extent with Confucian teachings and definitely with the words of Lao tzu: "When people lost sight of the way to live (*tao*), came codes of love and honesty; learning came, charity came, hypocrisy took charge." See *The Way of Life According to Laotzu,* trans. Witter Bynner (New York: Perigee Books, 1972), 46.

15. See *The Spirit of Laws of Montesquieu,* 99 (bk. 1, chap. 1); and *Persian Letters,* 205–206 (letter 122).

16. *Persian Letters,* 139–141 (letter 83). Although the reference is elusive, one can probably link the fideist target with certain extreme forms of Augustinianism and Jansenism prevalent during the Reformation period.

17. *Persian Letters,* 156–158. See also my "The Law of Peoples: Civilizing Humanity," in *Peace Talks—Who Will Listen?* (Notre Dame, Ind.: University of Notre Dame Press, 2004), 42–63.

18. *Persian Letters,* 202–205 (letter 121). For similar sentiments expressed half a century later by Johann Gottfried Herder, see my "Truth and Difference: Some Lessons from Herder," in *Alternative Visions: Paths in the Global Village* (Lanham, Md.: Rowman and Littlefield, 1998), 36–38. See also Sankar Muthu, *Enlightenment against Empire* (Princeton, N.J.: Princeton University Press, 2003).

19. *Persian Letters,* 142–144 (letter 85). Quite plausibly, Healy perceives in the example of Shah Suleiman a veiled reference to the revocation of the Edict of Nantes in 1685 by Louis XIV, which ended the toleration of Protestants in France (142, n. 2).

20. Ibid., 60 (letter 35), 191 (letter 114), 196 (letter 117). Another letter to his Persian friend in Venice criticizes Muslims' otherworldly orientation, manifest by an eagerness to reach paradise that shortchanges one's tasks and obligations in this world: "Hard and useful work, concern about an assured fortune for our children, all projects which carry beyond a short and fleeting life, seem somehow absurd to us. Tranquil in the present, free from worry about the future, we cannot be bothered to repair the public buildings, to reclaim wasteland, or cultivate land which is ready for our care. We live in a kind of general insensitivity, and leave everything to providence" (200, letter 119).

21. Ibid., 61 (letter 35), 75 (letter 46), 101–102 (letter 60). The comments on the future of faith are not wistful ruminations but are backed up by scripture—especially by the words of Jesus to the woman at Jacob's well: "The hour is coming, and now is, when the true worshippers will worship [God] in spirit and truth" (John 4:23). At one point (102, letter 60), Usbek expresses the hope that the divisions within Islam might also be healed and that "peace were established once and for all between Ali and Abu Bakr," that is, between Shiites and Sunni Muslims. I am aware that *The Spirit of Laws*

often reveals a less ecumenical outlook and even an occasional prejudice against Islam; see, for example, *The Spirit of Laws of Montesquieu*, 122–123 (bk. 24, chap. 3).

22. See Montesquieu, *Pensées* (Paris: Belles Lettres, 1925), cited in Torrey, *Les Philosophes*, 84.

23. *Persian Letters*, 204 (letter 121). Regarding the recent reemergence of empire, see Michael Hardt and Antonio Negri, *Empire* (Cambridge, Mass.: Harvard University Press, 2000), and Benjamin R. Barber, *Fear's Empire: War, Terrorism and Democracy* (New York: Norton, 2003).

24. Martin, *The Rise of French Liberal Thought*, 156; *Persian Letters*, 223 (letter 131).

25. *The Spirit of Laws of Montesquieu*, 118–119 (bk. 3, chap. 3).

26. *Persian Letters*, 17 (letter 8), 237 (letter 140).

27. Ibid., 261 (letter 146).

6. Beautiful Freedom

1. Max Weber, "Die Protestantische Ethik und der Geist des Kapitalismus," in *Gesammelte Aufsätze zur Religionssoziologie*, vol. 1 (Tübingen: Mohr, 1988), 204. Compare Weber's "Science as a Vocation," in *From Max Weber: Essays in Sociology*, trans. and ed. H. H. Gerth and C. Wright Mills (New York: Galaxy Book, 1958), where he states: "The fate of our times is characterized by rationalization and intellectualization and, above all, by the 'disenchantment of the world.' Precisely the ultimate and most sublime values have retreated from public life either into the transcendental realm of mystic life or into the brotherliness of direct and intimate human relations" (155). Alasdair MacIntyre, *After Virtue: A Study in Moral Theory*, 2nd ed. (Notre Dame, Ind.: University of Notre Dame Press, 1984), 11–12, 23–24, 34–35. MacIntyre adds a third stock character—the "therapist," who manages or manipulates other people's lives.

2. Letter to the Danish Prince of Augustenburg, July 13, 1793, in *Schillers Werke: Nationalausgabe*, vol. 26, ed. Norbert Oellers (Weimar: Hermann Böhlaus, 2002), 263.

3. Thomas Mann, *Versuch über Schiller* (Berlin: Fischer Verlag, 1955), 102.

4. Hans-Georg Gadamer, "On the Possibility of a Philosophical Ethics" (1963), in *Hermeneutics, Religion, and Ethics*, trans. Joel Weinsheimer (New Haven, Conn.: Yale University Press, 1999), 18, 28–29.

5. See, for example, Christian Wolff, *Vernünftige Gedanken von Gott, der Welt und der Seele der Menschen* (1720; New York: Olms, 1983), and *Vernünftige Gedanken von der Menschen Tun und Lassen* (1751; New York: Olms, 1976).

6. See Anthony Ashley Cooper, Earl of Shaftesbury, *An Inquiry Concerning Virtue* (1699; Manchester: Manchester University Press, 1977);

Francis Hutcheson, *An Inquiry into the Original of Our Ideas of Beauty and Virtue* (1726; New York: Garland, 1971); David Hume, *A Treatise of Human Nature* (1740; Oxford: Oxford University Press, 2000).

7. See especially Edmund Burke, *A Philosophical Enquiry into the Origin of Our Ideas of the Sublime and Beautiful* (1757), ed. J. T. Boulton (London: Routledge and Kegan Paul, 1958). In his editor's introduction (xxviii, xxxv), Boulton observes: "In the Newtonian tradition Burke looks for—and finds—immutable laws governing taste. . . . Sense experience is, for Burke, the obvious starting point; provided they are organically sound, all men are alike in their perceptions of external objects." Regarding Reid, see his *An Inquiry into the Human Mind, on the Principles of Common Sense* (1769; London: Cadell, 1785).

8. Johann Gottfried Herder, *Another Philosophy of History, and Selected Political Writings*, trans. Ioannis D. Evrigenis and Daniel Pellerin (Indianapolis: Hackett, 2004), 52–53. Today, he adds, everything is staked on knowledge and refined intelligence, "as if any of this could change or mold inclinations." We have "textbooks of education" and "codes of rules" ad nauseam, "and the world remains as it is." In Gadamer's nuanced assessment, Herder sought to correct not only the Enlightenment but also the counter-Enlightenment (Rousseau), not only "the intellectualism of 'abstract schemata'" but also the "rebellion of mere sentiment." Behind Herder's symbiosis of reason and sensibility, of nature and history, "an ontological outlook is operative which transcends the Cartesian dualism of *res extensa* and *res cogitans*" and which "stands in the tradition of the great Leibniz." See his "Nachwort" in Herder, *Auch eine Philosophie der Geschichte zur Bildung der Menschheit* (Frankfurt: Suhrkamp, 1967), 157, 165.

9. See Immanuel Kant, *Kritik der Urteilskraft*, ed. Karl Vorländer (Hamburg: F. Meiner, 1967), 20–68, and *Critique of Judgment*, trans. Werner S. Pluhar (Indianapolis: Hackett, 1987). For a sensitive discussion of Kant's notion of aesthetic judgment, see Cathleen Muehleck-Müller, *Schönheit und Freiheit: Die Vollendung der Moderne in der Kunst, Schiller-Kant* (Würzburg: Königshausen und Neumann, 1989), 25–53.

10. See Johann Gottlieb Fichte, *Über den Begriff der Wissenschaftslehre* (1794), ed. Edmund Braun (Stuttgart: Reclam, 1972); the relation between Fichte and Schiller is accentuated by Hans-Georg Pott in *Die schöne Freiheit: Eine Interpretation zu Schillers Schrift "Über die ästhetische Erziehung des Menschen in einer Reihe von Briefen"* (Munich: Fink Verlag, 1980). According to Pott (16), Schiller's proximity to Fichte has been "vastly underestimated." See also Dieter Henrich, *Fichtes ursprüngliche Einsicht* (Frankfurt: Suhrkamp, 1967).

11. Peter-André Alt, *Friedrich Schiller* (Munich: C. H. Beck, 2004), 20–23.

12. Ibid., 70–71. On the writings of 1791–1793, including the so-called

Kallias Letters addressed to Gottfried Koerner, see Muehleck-Müller, *Schönheit und Freiheit*, 15–24, 66–123. As she writes (116): "Starting from the consideration that the individual in the totality of his/her faculties is meant to become ethical and that this is possible only through the cultivation of ethical praxis, Schiller raises the question how sensibility can participate in moral praxis and in which way ideas of practical reason . . . can help to awaken concrete sensibility for purposes of ethical cultivation."

13. There is extensive literature dealing with the relation between the manuscripts sent to the Danish prince and the letters of 1795. For some of this literature, see Hans Lutz, *Schillers Anschauungen von Kultur und Natur*, new ed. (Nendeln, Liechtenstein: Kraus Reprint, 1967); Wolfgang Düring, *Friedrich Schiller: "Über die Ästhetische Erziehung des Menschen"* (Munich: C. Hanser, 1981); and Muehleck-Müller, *Schönheit und Freiheit*, 125–140.

14. See Friedrich Schiller, *On the Aesthetic Education of Man, in a Series of Letters* (English and German facing), ed. and trans. Elizabeth M. Wilkinson and L. A. Willoughby (Oxford: Clarendon Press, 1967), 2–7, 24–29 (translation slightly altered). In a variation of a passage contained in the earlier Augustenburg manuscripts (cited above), the fifth letter states: "Enlightenment of reason of which our refined classes not altogether groundlessly boast, has had on the whole so little an ennobling effect on feeling and character that it has rather bolstered depravity by supplying it with maxims" (26–27).

15. Ibid., 30–35.

16. Ibid., 42–53. By invoking the notion of sensible-ethical "force" (*Kraft*), Schiller places himself explicitly in the tradition of Leibniz and Herder. Schiller does not believe that the artist or the educator (in the field of aesthetics) should assume the role of a dictator or legislator, but only the role of a guide or motivating agent. In terms of the ninth letter: "Impart to the world you would influence a *direction* toward the good, and the quiet rhythm of time will bring it to fruition. You will have given it this direction if, by your teaching, you have elevated its thoughts to the necessary and eternal; if, by your actions and your creations, you have transformed the necessary and the eternal into an object of the heart's desire" (58–59).

17. Ibid., 68–77.

18. Ibid., 78–95. The reference to Fichte is found in an extensive footnote in the thirteenth letter. Another footnote there refers to a certain "transcendental philosophy" that subordinates sensation rigidly to reason or the "form drive," stating: "Such conception, it is true, is entirely alien to the *spirit* of the Kantian system, but it may very well be found in the *letter* of it." In the same letter, Schiller mentions some radical derailments of the sense-form relationship—derailments in which either sensation cancels reason or reason cancels sensation. Given that humans are "sensual-rational" creatures, such cancellation reduces them to "non-entities" (*Null*).

19. Ibid., 96–107. The last passage is crucial enough to be cited in the original (106–107): "*Der Mensch soll mit der Schönheit nur spielen, und er soll nur mit der Schönheit spielen. Denn, um es endlich auf einmal herauszusagen, der Mensch spielt nur, wo er in voller Bedeutung des Worts Mensch ist, und er ist nur da ganz Mensch, wo er spielt.*"

20. Ibid., 146–151.

21. Ibid., 160–175. As Schiller adds (186–187), aesthetic beauty also reconciles subject and object, thought and action: "Beauty is indeed an object for us, because reflection is the condition of our having sensation of it; but it is at the same time a state of the perceiving subject, because feeling is a condition of our having any perception of it. Thus, beauty is indeed 'form,' because we contemplate it; but it is at the same time 'life,' because we feel it. In a word: it is at once a state of our being and an activity we perform."

22. Ibid., 212–219. In this realm, he adds (216–219), "even the mightiest genius must divest himself of his highness and stoop in humility to the mind of a child. Strength must allow itself to be bound by the divine Graces and the ferocious lion to be bridled by Cupid."

23. Ibid., 122–125.

24. Schiller explicitly comments on the difference between art as "play" and the various games played by people on different occasions; see ibid., 104–107, 208–209 with note. As he writes in the fifteenth letter (106–107): "With the ideal of beauty set up by reason an ideal play-drive is established for human beings enjoining them to follow it in all their doings. . . . With beauty humans shall *only play,* and it is *only with beauty* that they shall play."

25. In his next-to-last letter, Schiller writes explicitly: "To the extent that real need and attachment to reality are consequences of some lack, indifference to reality and interest in art constitute a genuine broadening of humanity and a decisive step toward culture. . . . For, as long as necessity dictates and need compels, imagination remains tied to external reality with powerful bonds; only when wants are stilled does imagination unfold its unlimited potential" (ibid., 192–193). For some criticisms of Schiller's supposedly "bourgeois" leanings, see Georg Lukács, "Zur Ästhetik Schillers," in *Beiträge zur Geschichte der Ästhetik* (Berlin: Aufbau Verlag, 1954), 11–96; Peter Bürger, *Theorie der Avantgarde* (Frankfurt-Main: Suhrkamp, 1974). A different appreciation can be found among members of the early Frankfurt School. Herbert Marcuse, for example, strongly rebutted charges of elitism and irresponsible "aestheticism"; see his *Eros and Civilization: A Philosophical Inquiry into Freud* (New York: Vintage Books, 1962), 164–175.

26. For a detailed overview of Schiller's effective history (*Wirkungsgeschichte*), see Lesley Sharpe, *Schiller's Aesthetic Essays: Two Centuries of Criticism* (Columbia, S.C.: Camden House, 1955); Gert Schröder, *Schillers Theorie ästhetischer Bildung: Zwischen neukantianischer Vereinnahmung*

und ideologiekritischer Verurteilung (Frankfurt-Main: Peter Lang, 1998). Schröder presents Schiller's aesthetic legacy in large measure as wedged between neo-Kantianism and neo-Marxism.

27. Georg W. F. Hegel, *Vorlesungen über die Ästhetik,* in *Werke,* vol. 13 (Frankfurt-Main: Suhrkamp, 1970), 89.

28. Schiller, *On the Aesthetic Education,* 20–21. For a discussion of both the similarities and differences between Schiller and Schelling, see Pott, *Die schöne Freiheit,* 111–119.

29. Karl Jaspers, *Von der Wahrheit* (Munich: Piper, 1947), 352–353; see also Ernst Cassirer, *Idee und Gestalt: Goethe-Schiller-Hölderlin-Kleist* (Berlin: Bruno Cassirer, 1921) and *Freiheit und Form: Studien zur deutschen Geistesgeschichte* (1916; reprint, Darmstadt: Wissenschaftliche Buchgesellschaft, 1961); and Dieter Henrich, "Beauty and Freedom: Schiller's Struggle with Kant's Aesthetics," in *Essays in Kant's Aesthetics,* ed. Ted Cohen and Paul Guyer (Chicago: University of Chicago Press, 1982), 236–257.

30. Martin Heidegger, ". . . Poetically Man Dwells . . . ," in *Poetry, Language, Thought,* trans. Albert Hofstadter (New York: Harper and Row, 1971), 211–229. According to Charles Taylor: "For Schiller, the enjoyment of beauty gives us a unity as wholeness beyond the divisions that arise in us from the struggle between morality and desire." See his *The Ethics of Authenticity* (Cambridge, Mass.: Harvard University Press, 1992), 65.

31. Schiller, *On the Aesthetic Education,* 8–9.

32. The last paragraph of the letters stresses the transformative and challenging character of aesthetic pedagogy. "But does such a regime of aesthetic semblance really exist, and if so, where can it be found?" Schiller asks. He responds: "As a need, it exists in every finely tuned soul. As a reality we are prone to find it, like the pure church and the pure republic, only in a few chosen circles . . . where humans make their way, with bold simplicity and quiet innocence, and have no need either to infringe the freedom of others to assert their own, or to discard their own dignity in order to manifest pleasant grace." See *On the Aesthetic Education,* 218–219. Although few in number, the "chosen circles" mentioned in the passage can serve as examples for the rest of society.

33. Ibid., 18–19, 22–23.

34. Mann, *Versuch über Schiller,* 100–102.

7. Why the Classics Today?

1. For a recent discussion of the role of master teachers in the transmission of cultural learning, see George Steiner, *Lessons of the Masters* (Cambridge, Mass.: Harvard University Press, 2003).

2. See "The Example of the Classical," in Hans-Georg Gadamer, *Truth and Method,* 2nd rev. ed., trans. Joel Weinsheimer and Donald G. Marshall (New York: Crossroad, 1989), 287, 289.

3. Ibid., 286–287, 289 (translation slightly altered); Georg W. F. Hegel, *Aesthetics: Lectures on Fine Art,* vol. 2, trans. T. M. Knox (Oxford: Clarendon Press, 1975), 3. See also Werner Jaeger, ed., *Das Problem des Klassischen und die Antike,* Proceedings of the Naumburg Symposium on the Classics of 1930 (Leipzig: Felix Meiner, 1931).

4. Gadamer, *Truth and Method,* 287–288 (translation slightly altered).

5. Ibid., 287–290.

6. Ibid., 577–578.

7. Jean Grondin, *Hans-Georg Gadamer: A Biography,* trans. Joel Weinsheimer (New Haven, Conn.: Yale University Press, 2003), 121, 123.

8. Ibid., 126–127, 134–135. Completed in 1928, the second dissertation was published in revised form as *Plato's Dialectical Ethics* (Leipzig: Felix Meiner, 1931).

9. See especially Hans-Georg Gadamer, *The Idea of the Good in Platonic-Aristotelian Philosophy,* trans. P. Christopher Smith (New Haven, Conn.: Yale University Press, 1986); *Dialogue and Dialectic: Eight Hermeneutical Studies on Plato* (New Haven, Conn.: Yale University Press, 1980); *Hegel's Dialectic: Five Hermeneutical Studies* (New Haven, Conn.: Yale University Press, 1976); *Idee und Zahl: Studien zur platonischen Philosophie* (Heidelberg: Winter, 1968); *Um die Begriffswelt der Vorsokratiker* (Darmstadt: Wissenschaftliche Buchgesellschaft, 1968).

10. For a list of Gadamer's announced classes and lectures at German universities from 1929 to 1985, see Grondin, *Hans-Georg Gadamer,* 366–380.

11. Rüdiger Bubner, "Laudatio auf Hans-Georg Gadamer," *Sinn und Form* 49 (1997): 8, cited in Grondin, *Hans-Georg Gadamer,* 302.

12. Gadamer, *Truth and Method,* 200, 579.

13. In this context, see Asma Afsaruddin, *Excellence and Precedence: Medieval Islamic Discourse on Legitimate Leadership* (Leiden: Brill, 2002).

14. William Theodore de Bary, *Neo-Confucian Orthodoxy and the Learning of the Mind-and-Heart* (New York: Columbia University Press, 1981), 14, 57.

15. Ibid., 15, 24, 28–29. For the statements of Ch'eng I, de Bary refers to the latter's texts *I-chuan* and *Chin-ssu.*

16. William Theodore de Bary, "Why Confucius Now?" in *Confucianism for the Modern World,* ed. Daniel A. Bell and Hahm Chaibong (Cambridge: Cambridge University Press, 2003), 365, 368, 370. On the contemporary relevance of Chinese and Western classics, see G. E. R. Lloyd, *Ancient Worlds, Modern Reflections* (Oxford: Oxford University Press, 2004); and Zhang Longxi, "The Relevance of Antiquity," *Ex/Change* 10 (July 2004): 12–17.

17. William Theodore de Bary, *Nobility and Civility: Asian Ideals of Leadership and the Common Good* (Cambridge, Mass.: Harvard University Press, 2004), 3–4, 6, 12. See also his *Chinese Classics in Global Education* (Hong Kong: Chinese University Press, 2006).

18. De Bary, *Nobility and Civility,* 227.

19. Ibid., 233. In a similar vein, Joseph S. Nye Jr. notes that cultivating global civility is likely to take "years of patient, unspectacular work, including close civilian cooperation with other countries." See his *The Paradox of American Power: Why the World's Only Superpower Can't Go It Alone* (New York: Oxford University Press, 2002), xv.

8. Canons or Cannons?

1. "Mobilizing Democracy" was the general theme for the annual meeting of the American Political Science Association (APSA) held in Washington, D.C., September 1–4, 2005.

2. The different marching orders are conveniently bunched together under the summary label *mission civilisatrice,* a designation favored by French imperialists but matched by the notion of the "white man's burden" in the case of British imperialism. On the continued relevance of *mission civilisatrice,* see the comments of Richard Rorty in Rorty and Gianni Vattimo, *The Future of Religion,* ed. Santiago Zabala (New York: Columbia University Press, 2005), 72.

3. The connection between "mobilizing democracy" and the issue of education or pedagogy was actually drawn by the chair of the section "Political Thought and Philosophy" at the 2005 annual meeting of the APSA when she wrote: "Have we reached the point when others are no longer willing to learn from the 'canon' of political theory, and hence has this canon exhausted itself just as it is called upon to play a truly global role? . . . In today's world, what, if anything, does the West have to teach the rest?" See APSA Annual Meeting Program 2004, "Call for Papers—2005 APSA Annual Meeting," 248.

4. Samuel Huntington, "The Clash of Civilizations?" *Foreign Affairs* 72, no. 3 (Summer 1993): 22, 39, 48.

5. Thus, Richard Rorty asserted at one point that "the idea of a dialogue with Islam is pointless." See *The Future of Religion,* 72–73.

6. See Amartya Sen, *The Argumentative Indian* (London: Allen Lane, 2005). See also Emmy Wellesz, *Akbar's Religious Thought* (London: Allen and Unwin, 1952).

7. On Ibn Rushd and his intellectual heritage, see my "Reason, Faith, and Politics: A Journey to Muslim Andalusia," in *Dialogue among Civilizations: Some Exemplary Voices* (New York: Palgrave/Macmillan, 2002), 121–146. See also Robert Hammond, *The Philosophy of Alfarabi and Its Influence on Medieval Thought* (New York: Hobson, 1947); A. M. Goichon, *La philosophie d'Avicenne et son influence en Europe médiévale* (Paris: Adrien-Maisonneuve, 1951); and Mark D. Meyerson and Edward D. English, eds., *Christians, Muslims, and Jews in Medieval and Early Modern Spain* (Notre Dame, Ind.: University of Notre Dame Press, 2005).

8. For a fuller discussion, see "Partial Assimilation: Cultural Borrowing" in my book *Beyond Orientalism: Essays on Cross-Cultural Encounter* (Albany: State University of New York Press, 1996), 18–24. See also Henry H. Hart, *Marco Polo: Venetian Adventurer* (Norman: University of Oklahoma Press, 1967).

9. David E. Mungello, *Leibniz and Confucianism: The Search for Accord* (Honolulu: University Press of Hawaii, 1977), 19. See Gottfried Wilhelm Leibniz, *Writings on China*, trans. Daniel J. Cook and Henry Rosemont Jr. (Chicago: Open Court, 1994), and chapter 4 of this book.

10. Heinrich Dumoulin, *Zen Buddhism: A History*, vol. 1, *India and China*, trans. James W. Heisig and Paul Knitter (New York: Macmillan, 1988), 64–65, 68. See also Kenneth Ch'en, *Buddism in China: A Historical Survey* (Princeton, N.J.: Princeton University Press, 1964). The two most celebrated itinerant monks from India were Kumarajiva, a historically well-attested scholar of the later fourth century, and Bodhidharma, a somewhat more legendary figure of the early sixth century. Kumarajiva is credited with establishing a large translation institute in Ch'ang-an (later Xian) that published hundreds of translated texts. Bodhidharma is revered as the founder and patriarch of Ch'an or Zen Buddhism.

11. Edwin O. Reischauer, *Ennin's Travels in T'ang China* (New York: Ronald Press, 1955), vii–viii. See also *Ennin's Diary: The Record of a Pilgrimage to China in Search of the Law*, trans. Edwin O. Reischauer (New York: Ronald Press, 1955). Another remarkable cross-cultural journey was that of the Muslim Ibn Battuta, who, between 1325 and 1349, traveled from Tangier to Mecca and through the Near East to India and China; see Ross E. Dunn, *The Adventures of Ibn Battuta: A Muslim Traveler of the 14th Century* (Berkeley: University of California Press, 1986). See also Roxanne Euben, *Journeys to the Other Shore: Muslim and Western Travelers in Search of Knowledge* (Princeton, N.J.: Princeton University Press, 2006).

12. Martin Heidegger, *Überlieferte Sprache und technische Sprache*, ed. Hermann Heidegger (St. Gallen, Switzerland: Erker Verlag, 1989), 5.

13. See *Meno* in *Great Dialogues of Plato*, trans. W. H. D. Rouse (New York: Mentor Book, 1956), 41–42 (79C–80B). At a later point in the dialogue (85C), Socrates adds this comment: "I should not like to take an oath on my whole story (or argument); but one thing I am ready to fight for as long as I can, in word and in deed: that is, that we shall be better, braver and less idle people if we believe it right to look for what we do not (yet) know, than if we believe that there is no point in looking because what we don't know we can never discover."

14. Hannah Arendt, "The Crisis in Education," in *Between Past and Future: Six Exercises in Political Thought* (Cleveland: Meridian Books, 1963), 180–183, 187.

15. Heidegger, *Überlieferte Sprache und technische Sprache*, 6–8. The

reference is to Chuang-tzu, *Das wahre Buch vom südlichen Blütenland*, trans. Richard Wilhelm (Jena, Germany: Eugen Diederichs, 1923), 7.

16. Hans-Georg Gadamer, *Truth and Method*, 2nd rev. ed., trans. Joel Weinsheimer and Donald G. Marshall (New York: Crossroad, 1989), 9–11.

17. Ibid., 14. Although endorsing Hegel's dialectic of self and other (or known-unknown), Gadamer—following Heidegger—does not accept Hegel's notion of an ultimate synthesis in which "knowledge" would finally be complete. As he states: "We can acknowledge that *Bildung* is an element of 'spirit' without tying ourselves to Hegel's philosophy of 'absolute spirit' " (15).

18. David Frum and Richard Perle, *An End to Evil: How to Win the War on Terror* (New York: Random House, 2003). See also Natan Sharanksy, *The Case for Democracy: The Power of Freedom to Overcome Tyranny and Terror* (New York: Public Affairs, 2004), and, in a critical vein, Richard N. Haas, "Freedom Is Not a Doctrine: Promoting Democracy Is the Wrong Priority for Foreign Policy," *Washington Post,* January 24, 2005, A15. In this context, note the comment by Johann Gottlieb Fichte, referring mainly to Napoleon: "he wants to topple potentates—but only in order to assume their place, albeit in the name of freedom." See *Werke,* vol. 2, ed. I. H. Fichte (Neudruck and Berlin: W. de Gruyter, 1971), 711.

19. In adopting the notion of "clusters" of meaning, I am following the lead of Henry Rosemont Jr. in his discussion of human rights. See his "Why Take Rights Seriously? A Confucian Critique," in *Human Rights and the World's Religions,* ed. Leroy S. Rouner (Notre Dame, Ind.: University of Notre Dame Press, 1988), 167–182; see also my " 'Asian Values' and Global Human Rights," in *Achieving Our World: Toward a Global and Plural Democracy* (Lanham, Md.: Rowman and Littlefield, 2001), 51–69.

20. I am inspired here primarily by the writings of Charles Taylor on alternative modernities. See especially his *A Catholic Modernity?* ed. James L. Heft (New York: Oxford University Press, 1999), and "Two Theories of Modernity," *Public Culture* 11 (1999): 153–173. See also Scott Lash, *Another Modernity, a Different Rationality* (Oxford: Blackwell, 1999), and Dilip P. Gaonkar, ed., *Alternative Modernities* (Durham, N.C.: Duke University Press, 2001).

21. Some of the ongoing efforts to reform the United Nations are discussed by Richard Falk in "Reforming the United Nations: Global Civil Society Perspectives and Initatives," in *Global Civil Society Yearbook, 2005/2006* (London: Sage, 2006), 150–186.

22. Benjamin R. Barber, *Fear's Empire: War, Terrorism, and Democracy* (New York: Norton, 2003), 176, 178. The reference is to Amartya Sen, *Development as Freedom* (New York: Alfred A. Knopf, 1999), 247.

9. An End to Evil

1. Lance Morrow, *Evil: An Investigation* (New York: Basic Books, 2003), 16.

2. Richard J. Bernstein, *Radical Evil: A Philosophical Interrogation* (Cambridge: Polity Press, 2002), 1.

3. Morrow, *Evil*, 12. Regarding the trivialization of evil and its reduction to a "punk aesthetic," Morrow refers to Andrew Delbanco, *The Death of Satan: How Americans Lost the Sense of Evil* (New York: Farrar, Straus and Giroux, 1995).

4. David Frum and Richard Perle, *An End to Evil: How to Win the War on Terror* (New York: Random House, 2003), 9.

5. Amélie Oksenberg Rorty, ed., *The Many Faces of Evil: Historical Perspectives* (London: Routledge, 2001), xiv–xv. I have slightly changed the numbering.

6. Susan Neiman, *Evil in Modern Thought: An Alternative History of Philosophy* (Princeton, N.J.: Princeton University Press, 2004), 11. Neiman includes in the first category thinkers such as Leibniz, Pope, Rousseau, Kant, and Hegel, and in the second category thinkers such as Pierre Bayle, Hume, Voltaire, and Schopenhauer. Because of their greater psychological nuances, she makes separate room for Nietzsche and Freud.

7. Readers familiar with Indian philosophy will detect the main forms of Vedanta philosophy: Advaita Vedanta, Dvaita Vedanta, and Vishishtadvaita Vedanta. On this tradition, see Sarvepalli Radhakrishnan, *Vedanta According to Shankara and Ramanuja* (London: Allen and Unwin, 1928); H. N. Raghavendracharya, *The Dvaita Philosophy and Its Place in the Vedanta* (Mysore, India: University of Mysore, 1941).

8. G. W. von Leibniz, *Theodicy: Essays on the Goodness of God, the Freedom of Man and the Origin of Evil*, trans. E. M. Huggard (La Salle, Ill.: Open Court, 1985), cited in Rorty, *The Many Faces of Evil*, 159–162. As Leibniz adds: "The permission of evil comes from a kind of moral necessity: God is constrained to this by his wisdom and his goodness; *this necessity is happy*" (164).

9. See, for example, Paul Deussen, *Outline of the Vedanta System of Philosophy According to Shankara*, trans. J. H. Woods and C. B. Runkel (New York: Grafton Press, 1906); Troy Wilson Organ, *The Hindu Quest for the Perfection of Man* (Athens: Ohio University Press, 1980), 181–193.

10. Rorty, *The Many Faces of Evil*, 54–55.

11. See Ibn Arabi, "Whoso Knoweth Himself . . . ," trans. T. H. Weir (Gloucestershire, U.K.: Beshara Press, 1976), 4–5. For a fuller discussion, see my "A Global Spiritual Resurgence? Some Christian and Islamic Legacies," in *Peace Talks—Who Will Listen?* (Notre Dame, Ind.: University of Notre Dame Press, 2004), 80–82.

12. Hermes Trismegistus, *Hermetica*, cited in Rorty, *The Many Faces of Evil*, 25. On gnosticism, see Hans Jonas, *The Gnostic Religion* (Boston: Beacon Press, 1963) and *Gnosis und spätantiker Geist*, 2 vols. (Göttingen: Vanderhoek und Ruprecht, 1934–1935); and Elaine Pagels, *The Origin of Satan* (New York: Random House, 1995) and *The Gnostic Gospels* (New York: Random House, 1979).

13. John Milton, *Paradise Lost*, quoted in Rorty, *The Many Faces of Evil*, 124.

14. Martin Luther, *Selections from His Writings* (Garden City, N.Y.: Doubleday, 1961), cited in Rorty, *The Many Faces of Evil*, 111–112.

15. Saint Augustine, *The City of God* and "The Problem of Free Choice," cited in Rorty, *The Many Faces of Evil*, 49, 52–53. In *The City of God*, the account of evil differs significantly from Luther's incipient dualism: "We must not attribute to the flesh all the vices of a wicked life, in case we thereby clear the devil of all those vices, for he has no flesh" (51). During the Reformation, John Calvin closely followed Saint Augustine's teachings about evil as privation and also his opposition to Manichaeism. See *The Many Faces of Evil*, 121–122.

16. See Immanuel Kant, *Religion within the Limits of Reason Alone*, trans. T. M. Greene and H. H. Hudson (New York: Harper Torchbooks, 1960), 27, 33, 46, 56. For an excellent discussion of Kant's approach, see Bernstein, "Radical Evil: Kant at War with Himself," in *Radical Evil*, 11–45. For Saint Augustine's refusal to inquire into the exercise of will, note this statement: "If there were a cause of the will . . . what could precede the will and be its cause? Either it is the will itself, and nothing else than the will is the root; or it is not the will which is not sinful. Either the will itself is the original cause of sin, or no sin is the original cause of sin. . . . I do not know why you would wish to look for anything further." See Rorty, *The Many Faces of Evil*, 53.

17. Bernstein, "Schelling: The Metaphysics of Evil," in *Radical Evil*, 80.

18. Ibid., 80, 85; *Schelling: Of Human Freedom*, trans. James Gutman (Chicago: Open Court, 1936), 27. In the following, I use Gutman's translation, but I also consult and constantly compare this translation with the German original, as found in *Philosophische Untersuchungen über das Wesen der menschlichen Freiheit und die damit zusammenhängenden Gegenstände*, ed. T. Buchheim (Hamburg: Meiner Verlag, 1997).

19. *Schelling: Of Human Freedom*, 22–24, 26. A little later, Schelling adds this passage that, in effect, "deconstructs" idealism and points way beyond it: "The whole of modern European philosophy since its inception (with Descartes) has this common deficiency that nature does not exist for it and that it lacks a living basis. On this account Spinoza's realism [objectivism] is as abstract as the idealism of Leibniz. Idealism is the soul of philosophy; realism is its body; only the two together constitute a living whole. Realism can never furnish the first principles but must be the basis and the instrument by which idealism realizes itself and takes on flesh and blood" (30). For a fuller discussion of Leibniz, see 45–46.

20. Ibid., 24–25, 27–28.

21. Ibid., 31–35 (translation slightly altered).

22. Ibid., 38–39 (translation slightly altered).

23. Ibid., 40–41, 47, 71, 87, 89 (translation slightly altered).

24. Jason M. Wirth, "Introduction: Schelling Now," in *Schelling Now:*

Contemporary Readings, ed. Jason M. Wirth (Bloomington: Indiana University Press, 2005), 9.

25. Martin Heidegger, *Schellings Abhandlung über das Wesen der menschlichen Freiheit (1809)* (Tübingen: Max Niemeyer, 1971), translated by Joan Stambaugh as *Schelling's Treatise on the Essence of Human Freedom* (Athens: Ohio University Press, 1985). See also Karl Jaspers, *Schelling: Grösse und Verhängnis* (Munich: Piper, 1955); Walter Schulz, *Die Vollendung des deutschen Idealismus in der Spätphilosophie Schellings* (Pfullingen: Neske, 1955, 1975); Maurice Merleau-Ponty, *La Nature: Notes de Cours du Collège de France,* ed. Dominique Séglard (1956–1960; Paris: Editions du Seuil, 1995).

26. Peter Warnek, "Reading Schelling after Heidegger," in Wirth, *Schelling Now,* 168–169.

27. Heidegger, *Schelling's Treatise,* 4.

28. Ibid., 9 (translation slightly altered, especially to correct for gender bias). To underscore his point, Heidegger adds a memory aid (*Merksatz*): "Freedom not the attribute of humans, but humans the possession of freedom." In light of this key sentence, it is altogether unintelligible how Benjamin S. Pryor can write that "Heidegger will gradually turn away from freedom as a preoccupation." See his "Giving Way to . . . Freedom: A Note after Nancy and Schelling," in Wirth, *Schelling Now,* 231. Regarding freedom, see also Heidegger, "On the Essence of Truth," in *Martin Heidegger: Basic Writings,* ed. David F. Krell (New York: Harper and Row, 1977), 117–141.

29. Heidegger, *Schelling's Treatise,* 109 (translation slightly altered). For Schelling and Heidegger, "becoming" does not involve a linear temporality and thus is far removed from historicism. In Heidegger's words: "One forgets to notice that in this 'becoming' that which becomes is already in the ground as ground. . . . God's becoming cannot be serialized into phases in the succession of ordinary 'time'; rather, in this becoming everything 'is' simultaneously. . . . This simultaneity of authentic temporality, this *kairos,* 'is' the essence of eternity—not the merely arrested presence or *nunc stans*" (113). In view of Heidegger's extensive comments on God and the divine, it is perplexing how Joseph P. Lawrence can detect in his work a "new paganism" or a return to "the blind forces of pagan religiosity." See his "Philosophical Religion and the Quest for Authenticity," in Wirth, *Schelling Now,* 16–17.

30. Heidegger, *Schelling's Treatise,* 141–143 (translation slightly altered). It is important to realize that for Heidegger (as for Schelling), evil, or the capacity for evil, is not simply a mode of privation or deficiency but rather is endowed with its own ontological potency. As he adds: "Reversal and rebellion are nothing merely negative or nugatory, but rather involve the mobilization or nay-saying and nihilation into the dominant force" (143). In a strange departure from both Schelling and Heidegger, Jacques Derrida privileges disjuncture over juncture (*Seynsfuge*) and even identifies justice

with disjuncture; see his *Rogues: Two Essays on Reason,* trans. Pascale-Anne Brault and Michael Naas (Stanford, Calif.: Stanford University Press, 2005), 88–89.

31. Heidegger, *Schelling's Treatise,* 147–149, 151. Toward the end of his commentary, Heidegger adds these lines, containing a kind of postmetaphysical theodicy: "God allows the oppositional will of the ground to operate in order to foster what love unifies and subordinates to itself for the glorification of the absolute. The will of love stands above the will of the ground and this predominance, this eternal decidedness—this love for itself as the essence of being—this decidedness is the innermost core of absolute freedom" (160). In view of this and similar passages, Jean-Luc Nancy accuses Heidegger's account of harboring a new "ontodicy in which is preserved the possibility of a 'safeguard' or 'shelter' of being." See his *The Experience of Freedom,* trans. Bridget McDonald (Stanford, Calif.: Stanford University Press, 1998), 133. However, Nancy's own account seems to endorse an empty decisionism in which evil is no longer a perversion, and good and evil are equally free choices. See also Pryor, "Giving Way to . . . Freedom," 226–233.

32. John McDowell, *Mind and World* (Cambridge, Mass.: Harvard University Press, 1994), 77.

33. Slavoj Žižek, *The Indivisible Remainder: An Essay on Schelling and Related Matters* (London: Verso, 1996).

34. Bernstein, "Schelling: The Metaphysics of Evil," 82–83, 90, 92, 249, n. 8. Given that Heidegger (following Schelling) likewise seeks to overcome the rift between nature and spirit or between being and morality (or "is" and "ought"), it is strange that, at another point, Bernstein agrees with Levinas and others that "there is no place for ethics in Heidegger's philosophy" (187). However, in the absence of a neat gulf between "is" and "ought," ethics clearly can no longer occupy a separate "place" from ontology. Heidegger's critique of the reduction of freedom to the "problem of free will" points in the same direction.

35. Ibid., 6, 95, 97, 196, 198. The citations are from Hans Jonas, "The Concept of God after Auschwitz: A Jewish Voice," in *Mortality and Morality: A Search for God after Auschwitz,* ed. Lawrence Vogel (Evanston, Ill.: Northwestern University Press, 1996), 137, 140. Note that Jonas privileges becoming over being, whereas Heidegger's reading reconciles becoming and being (or "being and time").

36. Morrow, *Evil,* 5, 17.

37. Ibid., 15–16.

38. Frum and Perle, *An End to Evil,* 9, 279. The concluding chapter in their book is titled "A War for Liberty," that is, liberty in the world at large.

39. Bernstein, *Radical Evil,* 229.

40. Žižek, *The Indivisible Remainder,* 64–65.

41. Bernstein, *Radical Evil,* 91. As he adds: "Schelling's conception of

evil as a 'spiritualized' assertion of a perverted self-will that glorifies itself, has delusion of omnipotence, and takes itself to be the expression of universal will is especially relevant for an understanding of twentieth-century totalitarianism and terrorism. Even in a post-totalitarian world, we witness the temptation of those who think that they can impose their particular self-will on others by claiming universality for it" (96).

42. Etty Hillesum, *An Interrupted Life: The Diaries of Etty Hillesum, 1941–43* (New York: Pantheon Books, 1989), quoted in Jonas, *Mortality and Morality,* 192, and in Bernstein, *Radical Evil,* 199.

10. Transnational Citizenship

1. See, for example, Gershon Shafir, ed., *The Citizenship Debates: A Reader* (Minneapolis: University of Minnesota Press, 1998). In my sketch of "modern" citizenship, I concentrate on the perspective of modern liberalism, which arguably has occupied a hegemonic position in Western history. Thus, I bypass the tradition of "civic republicanism"—associated with Machiavelli, Rousseau, Hannah Arendt, and others—which deliberately attempted to preserve the classical idea of a civic bond.

2. John G. A. Pocock, "The Ideal of Citizenship since Classical Times," in *Theorizing Citizenship,* ed. Ronald Beiner (Albany: State University of New York Press, 1995), 29–33. See also Philip Brook Manville, *The Origins of Citizenship in Ancient Athens* (Princeton, N.J.: Princeton University Press, 1997).

3. Pocock, "The Ideal of Citizenship," 36–39.

4. Ibid., 35–36. The implicit reference is to C. B. Macpherson, *The Political Theory of Possessive Individualism: Hobbes to Locke* (Oxford: Clarendon Press, 1962).

5. In Pocock's somewhat summary view, the entire history of the West can be seen as a contest between Aristotle and the imperial jurists: "We can simplify the history of the concept of citizenship in Western political thought by representing it as an unfinished dialogue between the Aristotelian and the Gaian formulae, between the ideal and the real, between persons interacting with persons and persons interacting through things." See "The Ideal of Citizenship," 42.

6. Max Weber, *Law in Economy and Society* (Cambridge, Mass.: Harvard University Press, 1954), 143.

7. Reinhard Bendix, *Nation-Building and Citizenship: Studies of Our Changing Social Order* (New York: John Wiley and Sons, 1964), 38, 42.

8. Ibid., 39–40, 47–49; Alexis de Tocqueville, *Democracy in America,* vol. 2 (New York: Vintage Books, 1945), 311.

9. Bendix, *Nation-Building and Citizenship,* 73–77, 93–95. The main references in this account are to T. H. Marshall, *Class, Citizenship and Social Development* (Garden City, N.Y.: Doubleday, 1964), 71–94; Franz Wieacker,

Privatrechtsgeschichte der Neuzeit (Göttingen: Vandenhoeck und Ruprecht, 1952); and Joseph Tussman, *Obligation and the Body Politic* (New York: Oxford University Press, 1960).

10. See Karl W. Deutsch and William J. Foltz, eds., *Nation-Building* (New York: Atherton Press, 1963); Karl W. Deutsch, *Nationalism and Social Communication: An Inquiry into the Foundations of Nationality* (Cambridge, Mass.: MIT Press, 1953); Rupert Emerson, *From Empire to Nation* (Cambridge, Mass.: Harvard University Press, 1960); M. F. Millikan and D. L. Blackmer, *The Emerging Nations: Their Growth and United States Policy* (Boston: Little, Brown, 1961); Lucian W. Pye, *Politics, Personality and Nation-Building* (New Haven, Conn.: Yale University Press, 1962).

11. Pocock, "The Ideal of Citizenship," 43.

12. Alasdair MacIntyre, "Is Patriotism a Virtue?" in Beiner, *Theorizing Citizenship*, 210–212, 215. As MacIntyre elaborates: "*Qua* member of this or that particular community I can appreciate the justification for what morality requires of me from within the social roles that I live out in my community. By contrast . . . , liberal morality requires of me to assume an abstract and artificial—perhaps even an impossible—stance, that of a rational being as such, responding to the requirements of morality not *qua* parent or farmer or quarterback, but *qua* rational agent who has abstracted himself or herself from all social particularity" (219).

13. Ibid., 220–224, 226–228.

14. See Roger Scruton, "In Defense of the Nation," in *The Philosopher on Dover Beach* (Manchester, U.K.: Carcanet, 1990), 299–337.

15. John Rawls, "Justice as Fairness in the Liberal Polity," in *The Citizenship Debates: A Reader,* ed. Gershon Shafir (Minneapolis: University of Minnesota Press, 1998), 63–64. See also John Rawls, *A Theory of Justice* (Cambridge, Mass.: Harvard University Press, 1971), 48–51, 120–126.

16. As Habermas observes at one point: Modern law is "a medium which allows for a much more abstract notion of the citizen's autonomy" than was conceivable in earlier times; hence citizenship today can be enacted through "compliance with the [purely] procedural rationality of political will-formation." See Habermas, "Citizenship and National Identity: Some Reflections on the Future of Europe," in Beiner, *Theorizing Citizenship*, 269. See also his "Historical Consciousness and Post-Traditional Identity," in Habermas, *The New Conservatism,* ed. Shierry Weber Nicholson (Cambridge, Mass.: MIT Press, 1989), 249–267; and "Struggles for Recognition in the Democratic Constitutional State," in *Multiculturalism: Examining the Politics of Recognition,* ed. Amy Gutman (Princeton, N.J.: Princeton University Press, 1994), 107–148.

17. Beiner, "Introduction: Why Citizenship Constitutes a Theoretical Problem in the Last Decade of the Twentieth Century," in *Theorizing Citizenship,* 2, 12, 16. Intermittently, Beiner points in the direction of a "third

possibility," but without elaborating its concrete character: "We are left deprived of a suitable vision of political community unless we can come up with a third possibility that is neither liberal nor nationalist, and that somehow escapes the liberal's arguments against nationalism and the nationalist's arguments against liberalism. . . . This elusive synthesis of liberal cosmopolitanism and illiberal particularism, to the extent that it is attainable, is what I want to call 'citizenship'" (13, 16).

18. The above reading of Aristotelian ethics is indebted to Hans-Georg Gadamer, especially his essays "On the Possibility of Philosophical Ethics" and "Friendship and Self-Knowledge" in his *Hermeneutics, Religion, and Ethics,* trans. Joel Weinsheimer (New Haven, Conn.: Yale University Press, 1999), 18–36, 128–141. See also Christopher P. Long, *The Ethics of Ontology: Rethinking an Aristotelian Legacy* (Albany: State University of New York Press, 2004). Long distinguishes between two main readings of Aristotle: one emphasizing a totalizing ontology in which particulars are purely derivative from universals; the other stressing a practical dynamics in which particulars enjoy autonomy, rendering necessary a continuous search for commonality. Together with Long, Gadamer, and Heidegger, I favor the second reading.

19. Iris Marion Young, "Polity and Group Difference: A Critique of the Ideal of Universal Citizenship," in Beiner, *Theorizing Citizenship*, 175–176, 181. As she adds: "The bourgeois world instituted a moral division of labor between reason and sentiment, identifying masculinity with reason and femininity with sentiment, desire, and the needs of the body" (179).

20. Ibid., 184, 188–189. See also Iris Marion Young, *Justice and the Politics of Difference* (Princeton, N.J.: Princeton University Press, 1990), and her "Impartiality and the Civic Public: Some Implications of Feminist Critiques of Moral and Political Theory," in *Feminism as Critique,* ed. Seyla Benhabib and Drucilla Cornell (Oxford: Polity Press, 1987), 56–76.

21. Bhikhu Parekh, "The Rushdie Affair: Research Agenda for Political Philosophy," *Political Studies* 38 (1990): 702. See also Parekh, *Rethinking Multiculturalism: Cultural Diversity and Political Theory* (London: Macmillan, 2000), especially this passage: "The common good and the collective will that are vital to any political society are generated not by transcending cultural and other particularities, but through their interplay in the cut and thrust of a dialogue" (341). In this genre, see also Joseph H. Carens, *Culture, Citizenship, and Community* (Oxford: Oxford University Press, 2000) and "Aliens and Citizens: The Case for Open Borders," *Review of Politics* 49 (1987): 251–273; and Will Kymlicka, *Multicultural Citizenship: A Liberal Theory of Minority Rights* (Oxford: Clarendon Press, 1995), especially this comment: "Citizenship is an inherently group-differentiated notion. Unless one is willing to accept a single world government or completely open borders between states . . . then distributing rights and benefits on the basis of citizenship is to treat people differentially on the basis of their group mem-

bership" (124). See also Will Kymlicka and Wayne Norman, "Return of the Citizen: A Survey of Recent Work on Citizenship Theory," in Beiner, *Theorizing Citizenship*, 283–315.

22. Charles Taylor, "The Politics of Recognition," in Gutman, *Multiculturalism*, 32, 38–39. A similar approach can be found in Taylor's *The Ethics of Authenticity* (Cambridge, Mass.: Harvard University Press, 1992), which emphasizes the "need for recognition" (43–53) and bemoans a certain postmodern "slide into subjectivism" (55–69).

23. Christian van den Anker, "Global Justice, Global Institutions and Global Citizenship," in *Global Citizenship: A Critical Introduction*, ed. Nigel Dower and John Williams (New York: Routledge, 2002), 167–168. See also David Held, "The Transformation of Political Community: Rethinking Democracy in the Context of Globalization," ibid., 99–100 (where Held strongly supports "the recovery of an intensive and more participatory democracy at local levels as a complement to the public assemblies of the wider global order"). See also Ronald Axtmann, "What's Wrong with Cosmopolitan Democracy," ibid., 101–113 (where Axtmann stresses the need for a mediation between local and global commitments); Andrew Linklater, *The Transformation of Political Community: Ethical Foundations of the Post-Westphalian Era* (Cambridge: Polity Press, 1998); and Gerard Delanty, *Citizenship in a Global Age: Society, Culture, Politics* (Buckingham, U.K.: Open University Press, 2000).

24. Saint Augustine, *The City of God*, ed. Vernon J. Bourke (Garden City, N.Y.: Image Books, 1958), 321 (bk. 14, chap. 28), 465 (bk. 19, chap. 17). The last passage continues as follows: "Instead of nullifying or tearing down, she [heavenly city] pressures and appropriates whatever in the diversity of nations is aimed at one and the same objective of human peace, provided only that they do not stand in the way of the faith and worship of the one supreme and true God." On the "inalienable freedom" in the heavenly city, see 541–542 (bk. 22, chap. 30).

25. Paul Ricoeur, "Ye Are the Salt of the Earth," in *Political and Social Essays*, ed. David Stewart and Joseph Bien (Athens: Ohio University Press, 1974), 105–124; Pierre Hadot, *Philosophy as a Way of Life*, ed. Arnold I. Davidson, trans. Michael Chase (Oxford: Blackwell, 1995), 264. On Ricoeur, see chapters 11 and 12 in this volume.

26. Jacques Derrida, "On Cosmopolitanism," in his *On Cosmopolitanism and Forgiveness* (London: Routledge, 2001), 5, 17–19, 23. Regarding cities of refuge, Derrida relies specifically on Emmanuel Levinas, *L'Au-delà du Verset* (Paris: Minuit, 1982), and Daniel Payot, *Des villes-refuges* (Paris: Editions de l'Aube, 1992).

27. Richard Falk, "An Emergent Matrix of Citizenship: Complex, Uneven, and Fluid," in Dower and Williams, *Global Citizenship*, 27–28. For Falk, cross-cultural dialogue is a much needed steppingstone toward the

envisaged future: "The many initiatives associated with inter-civilizational dialogue can be seen as a crucial part of this world cultural preparation for the next stage in world order centered on human solidarity, sustainable development, global civil society, and multi-level arrangements of global governance" (27). In an interesting aside (26), the text comments on the so-called neomedieval thesis—the alleged analogy between contemporary networks and medieval social arrangements—finding the analogy flawed because of the medieval deficit of a strong sense of (Aristotelian) citizenship.

11. Religious Freedom

1. Paul Ricoeur, "Ye Are the Salt of the Earth," in *Political and Social Essays*, ed. David Stewart and Joseph Bien (Athens: Ohio University Press), 105.

2. Richard John Neuhaus, *The Naked Public Square* (Grand Rapids, Mich.: Eerdmans, 1984).

3. See Eric Voegelin, *The New Science of Politics: An Introduction* (Chicago: University of Chicago Press, 1952), 54–55.

4. Charles Taylor, "A Catholic Modernity?" in *A Catholic Modernity? Charles Taylor's Marianist Award Lecture*, ed. James L. Heft (New York: Oxford University Press, 1999), 17–18.

5. Ibid., 19.

6. See C. B. Macpherson, *The Political Theory of Possessive Individualism: Hobbes to Locke* (Oxford: Clarendon Press, 1962), 3; Taylor, "A Catholic Modernity?" 19.

7. Taylor, "A Catholic Modernity?" 21.

8. Jean-Jacques Rousseau, *The Social Contract and Discourse on the Origin of Inequality*, ed. Lester G. Crocker (New York: Pocket Books, 1967), 187, 201, 203. Rousseau's idea of education or pedagogy (perhaps under the influence of Hutcheson and Hume) placed great stress on "sentiments" as a corollary of and corrective to reason. "Let moralists say what they will," the *Discourse* states (188), "human understanding is greatly indebted to the passions which, on their side, are likewise universally allowed to be greatly indebted to human understanding. It is by the activity of our passions that our reason improves." See also *La Nouvelle Héloïse* (University Park: Pennsylvania State University Press, 1968), and *Emile* (London: Dent and Sons, 1933). I do not endorse the gender biases evident in these writings.

9. Johann Gottfried Herder, *Another Philosophy of History, and Selected Political Writings*, trans. Ioannis D. Evrigenis and Daniel Pellerin (Indianapolis: Hackett, 2004), 42, 45, 50–51.

10. Friedrich Schiller, *On the Aesthetic Education of Man, in a Series of Letters* (English and German facing), ed. and trans. Elizabeth M. Wilkinson and L. A. Willoughby (Oxford: Clarendon Press, 1967), 170–177. For a discussion of Schiller's letters, see chapter 6 of this volume.

11. Schiller, *Aesthetic Education of Man,* 178–179.

12. H. Richard Niebuhr, Wilhelm Pauck, and Francis Miller, *The Church against the World* (New York: Willet, Clark, 1935), 123–124, 128. Niebuhr modified and nuanced his position somewhat in his later study *Christ and Culture* (New York: Harper, 1951).

13. R. Laurence Moore, *Selling God: American Religion in the Marketplace of Culture* (New York: Oxford University Press, 1994), 276, 275.

14. "The Cambridge Declaration of the Alliance of Confessing Evangelicals," http://www.alliancenet.orga/intro/CamDec.html.

15. Stephen Prothero, *American Jesus: How the Son of God Became a National Icon* (New York: Farrar, Straus and Giroux, 2003), 12–16. See also Henry J. Cadbury, *The Peril of Modernizing Jesus* (New York: Macmillan, 1937).

16. Prothero, *American Jesus,* 297, 300. See also John M. Giggic and Diane Winston, eds., *Faith in the Market: Religion and the Rise of Urban Commercial Culture* (New Brunswick, N.J.: Rutgers University Press, 2002).

17. Abdulkarim Soroush, *Treatise on Tolerance, Praemium Erasmianum Essay 2004* (Amsterdam: Foundation Horizon, 2004), 17–18.

18. Saint Augustine, *City of God,* trans. Gerald G. Walsh et al., introduction by Etienne Gilson (Garden City, N.Y.: Image Books, 1958), 295, 321–322 (bk. 14, chaps. 1 and 28).

19. Ibid., 238 (bk. 11, chap. 28).

20. Charles Taylor, "Concluding Reflections and Comments," in Heft, *A Catholic Modernity?* 120–121. "For Plato," he adds, "the issue was, What do you love (*philein*)?" (125, n. 5). See also Saint Bonaventure, *The Enkindling of Love,* ed. William I. Joffe (Paterson, N.J.: St. Anthony Guild Press, 1956); Blaise Pascal, *Discours sur les passions de l'amour* (Paris: Mille et une nuits, 1995); Søren Kierkegaard, *Works of Love,* ed. Howard V. Hong and Edna H. Hong (Princeton, N.J.: Princeton University Press, 1995); Hans Urs von Balthasar, *Love Alone: The Way of Revelation* (London: Sheed and Ward, 1968); and Julia Kristeva, *Tales of Love,* trans. Leon S. Roudiez (New York: Columbia University Press, 1987).

21. Taylor, "A Catholic Modernity?" 21. For a philosophical discussion of the Buddhist notion of "emptiness" (*sunyata*), see Keiji Nishitani, *Religion and Nothingness,* trans. Jan Van Bragt (Berkeley: University of California Press, 1982); and my "Heidegger and Zen Buddhism: A Salute to Keiji Nishitani," in *The Other Heidegger* (Ithaca, N.Y.: Cornell University Press, 1993), 200–226, and "*Sunyata* East and West," in *Beyond Orientalism: Essays on Cross-Cultural Encounter* (Albany: State University of New York Press, 1996), 175–199. In an insightful manner, the Buddhist thinker Masao Abe compared *sunyata* with the Pauline notion of the *kenosis* (self-emptying) of Christ; see Abe, *Zen and Western Thought,* ed. William R. LaFleur (Honolulu: University of Hawaii Press, 1985), and John B. Cobb Jr. and Christopher

Ives, eds., *The Emptying God: A Buddhist-Jewish-Christian Conversation* (Maryknoll, N.Y.: Orbis Books, 1990). Regarding *kenosis,* see also Gianni Vattimo's (Heideggerian) comment on the so-called death of God: "If it is the mode in which the weakening of Being realizes itself as the *kenosis* of God, which is the kernel of the history of salvation, then secularization shall no longer be conceived of as abandonment of religion but as the paradoxical realization of Being's religious vocation." See "The God Who Is Dead," in Vattimo's *After Christianity,* trans. Luca D'Isanto (New York: Columbia University Press, 2002), 24.

22. Bhagavad Gita, trans. with an introduction by Juan Mascaró (New York: Penguin Books, 1962), 52, 56–57 (bk. 2:47–48, bk. 3:7, 9, 30–31). These passages have a clear parallel in Taoist teachings, especially in these lines from *Tao Te Ching:* "Being *(tao)* is a sanctuary. . . . Clever performances come dear or cheap. But goodness renders free." See *The Way of Life According to Laotzu,* trans. Witter Bynner (New York: Perigee Books, 1972), 90 (chap. 62).

23. Augustine, *City of God,* 191, 541 (bk. 10, chap. 3; bk. 22, chap. 30). Augustine speaks of an "inalienable freedom" of believers, "emancipating us from every evil and filling us with every good" (542).

24. Taylor, "A Catholic Modernity?" 14; Vattimo, *After Christianity,* 38–39.

25. Oscar Romero, "The Political Dimension of Faith," trans. Dick Krafnich, reprinted in *Catholic Peace Voice* (March–April 2005), 7.

26. Augustine, *City of God,* 465 (bk. 21, chap. 17).

27. Richard Kearney, *The God Who May Be: A Hermeneutics of Religion* (Bloomington: Indiana University Press, 2001), 108, 110.

12. Love and Justice

1. Papers presented at that meeting were edited and published by John Wall, William Schweiker, and W. David Hall under the title *Paul Ricoeur and Contemporary Moral Thought* (New York: Routledge, 2002).

2. Paul Ricoeur, *Liebe und Gerechtigkeit/Amour et Justice,* ed. Oswald Bayer (Tübingen: Mohr, 1990).

3. Oswald Bayer, "Laudatio auf Paul Ricoeur," in Ricoeur, *Liebe and Gerechtigkeit,* 85–86. Compare Ricoeur, *Husserl: An Analysis of His Phenomenology,* trans. Edward G. Ballard and Lester E. Embree (Evanston, Ill.: Northwestern University Press, 1967), and Edmund Husserl, *Idées directrices pour une phénoménologie pure,* trans. Paul Ricoeur (Paris: Gallimard, 1950).

4. Bayer, "Laudatio auf Paul Ricoeur," 87–88.

5. Ricoeur, *Liebe und Gerechtigkeit,* 6–11. The reference is to *Les Pensées de Pascal,* ed. Francis Kaplan (Paris: Les Editions du Cerf, 1982), 540.

6. Ricoeur, *Liebe und Gerechtigkeit,* 10–13.

7. Robert Alter, *The Art of Biblical Poetry* (New York: Basic Books,

1985); *The Selected Poetry of Rainer Maria Rilke,* ed. and trans. Stephen Mitchell (New York: Vintage International, 1989), 234–237 (translation slightly altered). See also Ricoeur, *Liebe und Gerechtigkeit,* 12–15.

8. Ricoeur, *Liebe und Gerechtigkeit,* 14–19.

9. Franz Rosenzweig, *The Star of Redemption,* trans. William W. Hallo (Boston: Beacon Press, 1972), 156–166 (translation slightly altered). See also Ricoeur, *Liebe und Gerechtigkeit,* 18–19.

10. Rosenzweig, *The Star of Redemption,* 161–162 (translation slightly altered).

11. Ricoeur, *Liebe und Gerechtigkeit,* 18–21.

12. Ibid., 24–25, 74–76, n. 6.3; Max Scheler, *Wesen und Formen der Sympathie* (6th rev. ed. of *Zur Phänomenologie und Theorie der Sympathiegefühle und von Liebe und Hass*), in *Gesammelte Werke,* vol. 7 (Bern: Francke, 1973), 155–156.

13. Ricoeur, *Liebe und Gerechtigkeit,* 24–25, 76–77, n. 7. Among writers defending the separation between eros and agape, Ricoeur mentions especially Andres Nygren, *Agape and Eros,* trans. Philip S. Watson (New York: Harper and Row, 1969).

14. Ricoeur, *Liebe und Gerechtigkeit,* 26–31. Without mentioning any names, the discussion seems to refer implicitly to Jürgen Habermas, *The Theory of Communicative Action,* 2 vols., trans. Thomas McCarthy (Boston: Beacon Press, 1984). For a fuller treatment of "justice" and its implications, see Ricoeur, *The Just,* trans. David Pellauer (Chicago: University of Chicago Press, 2000).

15. Ricoeur, *Liebe und Gerechtigkeit,* 30–35.

16. John Rawls, *A Theory of Justice* (Cambridge, Mass.: Harvard University Press, 1971); Ricoeur, *Liebe und Gerechtigkeit,* 34–37. Ricoeur's lecture does not specifically elaborate on the concepts of the "original position" and the "veil of ignorance."

17. Ricoeur, *Liebe und Gerechtigkeit,* 38–39.

18. Ibid., 42–49. As he notes, what is involved in the logic of equivalence is "the interplay between what one person does and what is done to another, and thus between acting and undergoing and between actors and patients who, although irreplaceable, are nonetheless regarded as exchangeable" (50–51).

19. See, for example, Emmanuel Levinas, *Of God Who Comes to Mind,* trans. Bettina Bergo (Stanford, Calif.: Stanford University Press, 1998); Jacques Derrida, *The Gift of Death,* trans. David Wills (Chicago: University of Chicago Press, 1995); Jean-Luc Marion, *Réduction et donation* (Paris: Presses Universitaires de France, 1989); Dominique Janicaud, "The Theological Turn of French Phenomenology," trans. Bernard G. Prusak, in Janicaud et al., *Phenomenology and the "Theological Turn"* (New York: Fordham University Press, 2000), 16–103.

20. Ricoeur, *Liebe und Gerechtigkeit*, 50–53.

21. Ibid., 52–55. The phrase "ethics of intention" is an awkward translation of Max Weber's notion of *Gesinnungsethik*, which he opposes to an "ethics of responsibility" (*Verantwortungsethik*). For the opposition of the two terms, see "Politics as Vocation," in *From Max Weber: Essays in Sociology*, ed. and trans. H. H. Gerth and C. Wright Mills (New York: Galaxy Book, 1958), 120.

22. Ricoeur, *Liebe und Gerechtigkeit*, 56–61.

23. Desmond Tutu (with Douglas Abrams), *God Has a Dream: A Vision of Hope for Our Time* (New York: Doubleday, 2004), 10. See also Tutu's *No Future without Forgiveness* (New York: Doubleday, 1999); Mark R. Amstutz, *The Healing of Nations: The Promise and Limits of Political Forgiveness* (Lanham, Md.: Rowman and Littlefield, 2005); Teresa Godwin Phelps, *Shattered Voices: Language, Violence, and the Work of Truth Commissions* (Philadelphia: University of Pennsylvania Press, 2004); Guido Klumpp, *Vergangenheitsbewältigung durch Wahrheitskommissionen* (Berlin: Arno Spitz, 2000).

24. Ricoeur, *Liebe und Gerechtigkeit*, 62–67. For the effort to reconcile Aristotle with Levinasian superabundance, see also his "little ethics" in Ricoeur, *Oneself as Another*, trans. Kathleen Blamey (Chicago: University of Chicago Press, 1992), 169–296. See also my "Ethics and Public Life: A Critical Tribute to Paul Ricoeur," in Wall, Schweiker, and Hall, *Paul Ricoeur and Contemporary Moral Thought*, 213–232.

Appendix A. Multiculturalism and the Good Life

1. Stanley Fish, "Boutique Multiculturalism, or Why Liberals Are Incapable of Thinking about Hate Speech," *Critical Inquiry* 23 (Winter 1997): 378–396.

2. Bhikhu Parekh, *Rethinking Multiculturalism: Cultural Diversity and Political Theory* (London: Macmillan, 2000). Subsequent page numbers in parentheses refer to this edition.

3. Parekh's distinction between *multicultural* and *multiculturalist* corresponds to the difference between factual *plurality* and ethical *pluralism*, as outlined by Kenneth L. Schmitz in "The Unity of Human Nature and the Diversity of Cultures," in *Relations between Cultures*, ed. George F. McLean and John Kromkowski (Washington, D.C.: Council for Research in Values and Philosophy, 1991), 305–322.

4. To give an example, here are some statements about Herder: "Like Vico, Montesquieu, Burke and many other writers on the subject, [Herder] makes the all too familiar mistake of seeing culture as a tightly knit and tensionless whole informed and held together by a single overreaching principle or spirit. . . . Despite his intentions to the contrary, Herder's theory teeters over the edge of cultural relativism" (73, 75).

5. As Parekh elaborates perceptively, since citizenship "involves abstracting away cultural, ethnic and other identities and seeing oneself solely as a member of the state, all citizens are directly and identically related to the state, not differentially and through their membership in intermediate communities." To this extent, the modern state "represents the triumph of human will [and artifact] over natural and social circumstances" (183). On this issue, see chapter 10 in this volume.

6. Growing out of complex interactions, the shared culture cannot aspire to the "thickness" of one of the traditional cultures; nor can it be satisfied with the "thinness" of proceduralism (or with the unitary "publicness" of civic republicanism). Instead, multiculturalism requires a dialectical balance between thinness and thickness, as well as between public and private domains. As Parekh adds: "The spirit of multiculturality flows freely through all areas of life. . . . In such a society unity and diversity are not confined to public and private realms respectively, but interpenetrate and permeate all areas of life. Its unity therefore is not formal and abstract but embedded in and nurtured by its diversity; and the latter, being grounded in and regulated by the shared interactive framework, does not lead to fragmentation and ghettoization." National identity in such a society "cannot and should not be culturally neutral as it then satisfies nobody and lacks the power to evoke deep historical memories, nor biased towards a particular community as it then delegitimizes and alienates others, nor culturally so eclectic as to lack coherence and focus" (224, 235).

7. Although he is aware of some of the differences between Rawls and Habermas, Parekh finds important parallels: "All arguments are articulated and conducted in a particular language which, *contra* Habermas and Rawls, cannot be 'purified' or purged of its deep cultural and evocative associations either. . . . Rawls's theory of public reason does not seem to appreciate these basic features of it. It has a rationalist bias, homogenizes and takes a one-dimensional view of public reason, assimilates political to judicial reason, and unwittingly universalizes the American practice, and that too in its highly idealized version. In spite of all its strength, even Habermas's discourse ethics is vulnerable on all three counts" (310, 312).

8. In its Aristotelian mode, Parekh adds, persuasion is "neither like Plato's dialectic with its concern for truth, nor like his rhetoric with its manipulative thrust, but belongs to a wholly different genre" (309).

9. In light of the book's subtitle, "Cultural Diversity and Political Theory," the conclusion also has an important lesson for political theorists. Lacking an "Archimedean standpoint or a God's-eye view," Parekh notes, the theorist has "several coigns of vantage in the form of other cultures. He can set up a dialogue between them, use each to illuminate the insights and expose the limitations of others, and create for himself a vital in-between space, a kind of immanent transcendentalism, from which to arrive at a less

culture-bound vision of human life and a radically critical perspective on his society" (339).

Appendix B. Modalities of Intercultural Dialogue

This text is based on a talk presented at a UNESCO conference held in Paris in November 2005.

1. Fred Dallmayr, *Beyond Orientalism: Essays on Cross-Cultural Encounter* (Albany: State University of New York Press, 1996), 1–37; Tzvetan Todorov, *The Conquest of America: The Question of the Other,* trans. Richard Howard (New York: Harper and Row, 1984), 247–251. See also my "Against Monologue: For a Comparative Political Theory," *Perspectives on Politics* 2 (2004): 249–257.

2. Jürgen Habermas, *Justification and Application: Remarks on Discourse Ethics,* trans. Ciaran P. Cronin (Cambridge, Mass.: MIT Press, 1995), 1. See also Seyla Banhabib and Fred Dallmayr, eds., *The Communicative Ethics Controversy* (Cambridge, Mass.: MIT Press 1990).

3. Habermas, *Justification and Application,* 2–3.

4. Ibid., 4–6.

5. Ibid., 5, 7–8.

6. Ibid., 6.

7. Much of my own recent work is focused on this domain. See the chapters "Dialogue among Civilizations: A Hermeneutical Perspective" and "Conversations across Boundaries" in my *Dialogue among Civilizations: Some Exemplary Voices* (New York: Palgrave/Macmillan, 2002), 17–30, 31–47; and the chapters "Gandhi and Islam: A Heart-and-Mind Unity" and "Confucianism and the Public Sphere" in my *Peace Talks—Who Will Listen?* (Notre Dame, Ind.: University of Notre Dame Press, 2004), 132–151, 152–171. See also Michael Oakeshott, "The Voice of Poetry in the Conversation of Mankind," in *Rationalism in Politics, and Other Essays* (New York: Basic Books, 1962), 197–245.

8. Regarding truth commissions, see Bishop Desmond Tutu (with Douglas Abrams), *God Has a Dream: A Vision of Hope for Our Time* (New York: Doubleday, 2004); Mark R. Amstutz, *The Healing of Nations: The Promise and Limits of Political Forgiveness* (Lanham, Md.: Rowman and Littlefield, 2005); and Teresa G. Phelps, *Shattered Voices: Language, Violence, and the Work of Truth Commissions* (Philadelphia: University of Pennsylvania Press, 2004).

Appendix D. Building Peace—How?

This text is based on a paper presented at a conference held at the Kroc Institute for International Peace Studies at the University of Notre Dame in March 2005.

1. Abdulkarim Soroush, *Treatise on Tolerance: Praemium Erasmia-*

num Essay 2004 (Amsterdam: Foundation Horizon, November 2004), 10, 13.

2. Ibid., 17. As Soroush adds: "The people who turn religiosity into a factor that feeds selfishness and a sense of superiority—and are arrogant and self-righteous because they claim to be pious and obedient to religious law—truly commit the greatest injustice against celestial creeds. Erasmus was a committed Christian and, at the same time, a humble and tolerant humanist" (20).

3. Ibid., 18, 20.

4. I should add that one can find the same combination of gentleness and toughness in Soroush. This passage from his treatise bears a close resemblance to the outlook of Gandhi and Romero: "Islamic Sufism, despite its shortcomings, was the bearer and teacher of values that we are in great need of today if we are to bolster the element of tolerance. In denigrating power and wealth, Sufis used to teach people to view these two things with the utmost suspicion and to be extremely wary of the afflictions they could give rise to, and to know what mortifications their emergence, growth and unchecked existence could bring. We can even use the denigration of power and wealth to strengthen—from a moral perspective—the fair distribution of power and wealth which is among the pillars of liberal democracy and social democracy" (19).

5. Oscar Romero, "The Political Dimension of Faith," trans. Dick Krafnich, reprinted in *Catholic Peace Voice* (March–April 2005), 7. The address was given in Louvain, Belgium, on February 2, 1980.

6. The "Building Peace" conference was held on the weekend before Easter. The concluding session took place on March 18, 2005—the second anniversary of the American invasion of Iraq. According to various reports, between 50,000 and 100,000 Iraqi civilians have been killed as a result of this invasion.

7. Romero, "The Political Dimension of Faith," 7–8.

Index